*Frontispiece: George Chinnery's portrait of William and Mary Prinsep. Oils. (See page 160 and Plate 96)*
Hongkong and Shanghai Banking Corporation

# George Chinnery

## 1774-1852

### ARTIST OF INDIA AND THE CHINA COAST

## PATRICK CONNER

*Antique Collectors' Club*

*For Harry*

© 1993 Patrick Conner
World copyright reserved
First published 1993

ISBN 1 85149 160 0

British Library Cataloguing in Publication Data:
A catalogue record for this book is available from the British Library

Printed on Consort Royal Satin
from Donside Mills, Aberdeen

The publisher acknowledges the generous assistance of the following in underwriting the costs of colour separations in this book:
Anthony J. Hardy
Mr. and Mrs. P.J. Thompson
Mr. and Mrs. R.J.F. Brothers
Anonymous sponsor, London

Printed in England by the Antique Collectors' Club Ltd., Woodbridge, Suffolk

# Contents

| | |
|---|---|
| List of Colour Plates | 6 |
| Foreword | 7 |
| Acknowledgements | 8 |
| Introduction | 10 |

**PART I: ENGLAND AND IRELAND**

| | |
|---|---|
| 1. Scribes and Embezzlers: the Chinnery Family | 15 |
| 2. 'A new style of painting': London and the Royal Academy Schools | 24 |
| 3. Ireland | 31 |

**PART II: INDIA — FROM MADRAS TO DACCA**

| | |
|---|---|
| 4. Madras | 50 |
| 5. The Russell Commission | 84 |
| 6. Dacca and the D'Oylys | 89 |

**PART III: CALCUTTA**

| | |
|---|---|
| 7. Calcutta Portraits | 102 |
| 8. Freemasonry and the Theatre | 130 |
| 9. Village Life in Bengal | 135 |
| 10. Sons and Rivals | 148 |
| 11. Escape from Debt | 155 |

**PART IV: THE CHINA COAST**

| | |
|---|---|
| 12. Canton and the Chinese | 164 |
| 13. Macau | 182 |
| 14. China Traders | 212 |
| 15. Images of the Artist | 238 |
| 16. The Opium War, and After | 246 |
| 17. Chinnery and Lamqua | 263 |

**APPENDICES**

| | |
|---|---|
| i. Technique and Theory: the Treatise | 271 |
| ii. Chinnery's Shorthand | 275 |
| iii. Chinnery's Studio, as described in *Tom Raw, the Griffin* | 276 |
| iv. Artists and Amateurs associated with Chinnery | 280 |

| | |
|---|---|
| Notes and References | 291 |
| Bibliography | 305 |
| Chinnery Family Tree | 311 |
| Glossary | 312 |
| Photographic Acknowledgements | 313 |
| Index | 314 |

# Colour Plates

Frontispiece: William and Mary Prinsep
Colour Plate 1: Charles James Fox, 27
Colour Plate 2: Portrait of a gentleman, 27
Colour Plate 3: Marianne Chinnery, 31
Colour Plate 4: Boy with a drum, 31
Colour Plate 5: Two girls by an urn, 65
Colour Plate 6: Study for a portrait group, 65
Colour Plate 7: 'Col. Armstrong', 68
Colour Plate 8: Lt.-Col. William Ormsby, 68
Colour Plate 9: Mrs. Lucy Lord, 69
Colour Plate 10: Ruined mosque, Madras, 72
Colour Plate 11: Temples, Mahabalipuram, 72
Colour Plate 12: The Kirkpatrick children, 73
Colour Plate 13: Palanquin bearers, 76
Colour Plate 14: Bungalow at Ennore, 77
Colour Plate 15: Crow's Tope, Madras, 77
Colour Plate 16: Durbar of Azim-ud-Daula, 80
Colour Plate 17: Lt. Thomas Watson, 98
Colour Plate 18: Sir Charles and Lady D'Oyly, 98
Colour Plate 19: 'Tom Raw's introduction...', 99
Colour Plate 20: Portrait of a gentleman, 102
Colour Plate 21: Member of the Pery family, 103
Colour Plate 22: George Siddons, 106, 107
Colour Plate 23: William Locker, 110
Colour Plate 24: Patrick Savage, 111
Colour Plate 25: Marquess of Hastings, 113
Colour Plate 26: Mrs. Da Silva, 116
Colour Plate 27: Woman in black, 116
Colour Plate 28: Mrs. Jane Pearson, 117
Colour Plate 29: Margaret Erskine, 117
Colour Plate 30: Woman in black, 117
Colour Plate 31: Woman in dark blue, 117
Colour Plate 32: Vase in a landscape, 120
Colour Plate 33: John and Mary Larkins, 124
Colour Plate 34: Children of Captain Comyn, 125
Colour Plate 35: Lady Paget and children, 128
Colour Plate 36: Trevor Plowden, 130
Colour Plate 37: Design for a 'transparency', 131
Colour Plate 38: Chowkidar, 135
Colour Plate 39: Bengal village scene, 138
Colour Plate 40: Bengal village scene, 139
Colour Plate 41: Bullock cart by tomb, 139
Colour Plate 42: Tombs and lean-to dwellings, 142
Colour Plate 43: Overgrown tomb, 142
Colour Plate 44: Bengal landscape, 143
Colour Plate 45: Goats in a landscape, 143
Colour Plate 46: Bengal river scene, 143
Colour Plate 47: Joshua Marshman, 161
Colour Plate 48: Western factories, Canton, 164
Colour Plate 49: Western factories, Canton, 165
Colour Plate 50: Junks and sampans, 168
Colour Plate 51: Junk at sunset, 168
Colour Plate 52: Junks and sampans, 169
Colour Plate 53: Howqua, 172
Colour Plate 54: Mowqua, 173
Colour Plate 55: Mowqua, 173
Colour Plate 56: Mowqua, 176
Colour Plate 57: Mah Chih Ping, 176
Colour Plate 58: Seated watchman, 176
Colour Plate 59: Chinese woman, 178
Colour Plate 60: Chinese porter, 179
Colour Plate 61: Praya Grande, 182
Colour Plate 62: Praya Grande, 182
Colour Plate 63: Praya Grande from the east, 183
Colour Plate 64: São Domingos Church, 186
Colour Plate 65: Grotto of Camões, Macau, 186
Colour Plate 66: Casa Gardens, Macau, 187
Colour Plate 67: A-Ma Temple, Macau, 190
Colour Plate 68: A-Ma Temple, Macau, 191
Colour Plate 69: Harriet Low, 193
Colour Plate 70: Tanka boatwoman, 197
Colour Plate 71: Tanka boatwoman, 200
Colour Plate 72: Tanka boat dwellings, 200
Colour Plate 73: Tanka boat dwellings, 200
Colour Plate 74: Fisherman, 201
Colour Plate 75: Street traders, Macau, 204
Colour Plate 76: Street scene, Macau, 204
Colour Plate 77: Street market, Macau, 205
Colour Plate 78: Blacksmiths, Macau, 205
Colour Plate 79: Blacksmiths, Macau, 205
Colour Plate 80: Farmers in a landscape, 208
Colour Plate 81: São Lourenço Church, 208
Colour Plate 82: Macau from the north-east, 210
Colour Plate 83: Macau from the north-east, 210
Colour Plate 84: Macau from the south-west, 211
Colour Plate 85: Beach at evening, Macau, 211
Colour Plate 86: William Jardine, standing, 214
Colour Plate 87: William Jardine, seated, 215
Colour Plate 88: Henry Wright, 218
Colour Plate 89: Captain Clifton, 218
Colour Plate 90: Sir Jamsetjee Jeejeebhoy, 219
Colour Plate 91: Woman at a piano, 222
Colour Plate 92: Harriet Mary Daniell, 223
Colour Plate 93: Family group, 225
Colour Plate 94: Family group, 228
Colour Plate 95: Dr. and Mrs. Colledge, 229
Colour Plate 96: Dr. Colledge in his surgery, 232
Colour Plate 97: Benjamin Chew Wilcocks, 233
Colour Plate 98: Eliza Morrison, 236
Colour Plate 99: Robert Morrison, 237
Colour Plate 100: Self-portrait, 240
Colour Plate 101: Self-portrait, 240
Colour Plate 102: Self-portrait, 242
Colour Plate 103: J.A. Durran, 246
Colour Plate 104: Murray Barracks and Old
  Church, Hong Kong, 246
Colour Plate 105: Canal and bridge, Honam, 247
Colour Plate 106: 'Grande Odalisque', Lamqua
  after Ingres, 265
Colour Plate 107: Dr. Peter Parker by Lamqua, 268

# Foreword

With the Act of Union in 1801, patronage fled Dublin, a compelling reason for a twenty-seven-year-old artist to seek his fortune elsewhere. A competitive London persuaded Chinnery to depart for the East Indies at the dawn of the Romantic Movement in art. Had he glimpsed the watercolours of Girtin, Francia or Turner in those few months in London, before he sailed away never to return? I feel a seed may have been sown. Although his portraits, and indeed his thousands of surviving pen and brown ink drawings (which have the fluency and feel of fine old master drawings) affirm his late eighteenth century and Royal Academy origins, his landscape art does not. In his watercolours in particular there is the touch of genius, a magical quality, all the more surprising when you consider that this man spent most of his adult life — half a century — in a mercantile community, about as far away as you could get from the mainstream influences of his profession. His art gives one a 'buzz' made all the more poignant and exciting when viewed against a background of his eccentric life and the romantic and adventurous spirit of the East India and China Trade.

An authoritative look at Chinnery has been long overdue, and here at last is a book which, to quote a favourite phrase of the artist, 'may be relied upon'.

Martyn Gregory

# Acknowledgements

Chinnery did not keep a diary, it seems, but he did leave behind him a tantalising record of a different kind: the shorthand annotation, of dots, dashes and curves, which appears on many hundreds of his drawings. They form a kind of running commentary on his thoughts and preoccupations, which may include dates, notes of form, colour and texture, identification of subjects, and proposals for further development of the picture; or they may refer to the weather, his family, his life, or art in general. A few other artists (such as his contemporary James Ward) made use of shorthand to some degree, but only Chinnery made it a central element in his artistic practice.

For many years after his death, his notation remained incomprehensible, like the hieroglyphs of an extinct civilisation. There is a key, however; for Chinnery was a faithful follower of the Gurney system, which was widely used in the late eighteenth and early nineteenth centuries (see Appendix ii). In the 1950s and 1960s several students of Chinnery's shorthand (notably Mrs. Moyra Baker of the Peabody Museum, Salem, Massachusetts) have made some progress in translating Chinnery's signs. But it has been the work of Geoffrey Bonsall, carried out in Hong Kong over a number of years, which has transformed the subject from a matter of more or less intelligent speculation into something approaching a scientific discipline. Since the 1970s Geoffrey Bonsall has proved himself the outstanding interpreter of Chinnery's shorthand, the Champollion of Chinnery studies. Almost all the translations of shorthand given in the present book have been at one time or another contributed or verified by him.

I have also been fortunate in having been given access to two substantial collections of correspondence concerning Chinnery: the letters and notes accumulated by Geoffrey Bonsall in Hong Kong, which are to be deposited in the India Office Library and Records, London; and the research materials gathered in England and South Africa by Randolph Vigne, which include the correspondence of W.H. Welply (the conscientious genealogist of the Chinnery family) from the 1920s onwards. I am indebted to both these Chinnery enthusiasts for so generously allowing me to plunder their copious files.

Of the many other people who have assisted in this project, I am grateful above all to Martyn Gregory for his encouragement, his unrivalled connoisseurship in matters regarding Chinnery and China Trade painting, and his gallery's excellent photographic library. Without the support and enthusiasm of Martyn and Penelope Gregory this book would not have been written.

My particular thanks are due to Alan Bradford, for the benefit of his special experience in conserving Chinnery's paintings, and of his excellent slides; and to Margaret Lee, Group Archivist of the Hongkong and Shanghai Banking Corporation, for her friendly assistance in obtaining photographs and information. I must also express my gratitude to the many collectors and curators who have made their pictures available and provided photographs: to Christie's, Sotheby's, Thomas Agnew & Sons, the Leger Galleries, and Spink & Son; and to the following individuals in particular: Mildred Archer, Robbie and Mabel Brothers, Dr. Iain Brown, Nigel Cameron, Frank Castle, Mrs. Kathleen Clark, Mrs. Bridget Colvin, Carl Crossman, Miss Catherine Cruft, John Curtis, Camilla Davidson, Bill Drummond, Harriet Drummond, Crosby Forbes, Sir Brinsley Ford, Sven Gahlin, Sean Galvin, Mr. and Mrs. A.M. Goodman, Mrs. Alison Goodwin, Charles Greig, Antony Griffiths, César Guillen-Nuñez, Anthony and Linda Hardy, Sir Stephen Hastings, Luke Herrmann, Tamsin Hitchens, Susanna Hoe, Malcom and Ursula Horsman, Dr. J.P.W.A. van Braam Houckgeest, Ralph Hyde, Ian Jenkins, Derek and Mary Jennings, Mrs. Anne Johnstone, Patricia Kattenhorn, Charles J. Kelly, Richard Kelton, Lady Keswick, Henry Keswick, David and Melanie Landale, Adrian Le Harivel, Deborah Lewis, Pat and Clayton Lewis, Lowell Libson, Richard Lockett, Biba McGuire, The Macnab of Macnab, Major Fergus Matheson, Sir Torquil Matheson of Matheson, Jorge Midorikawa, Dr. Charles Mollan, the late Lord Moyne and Lady Moyne, Richard Ormond, Alan Reid, Michael and Steven Rich, Mr. and Mrs. R.B. Richards, Pauline Lady Rumbold, J.W.M. St. Mawr Sheil, Bill Sargent, Ken Stubbings, Karen Taylor, Mrs. Bobby Teague, Peter and Nancy Thompson, Íde Ní Thuama, Giles Tillotson, Brigadier and Mrs. G. Viner, Major and Mrs. Anthony Watson, Paul Winfisky, Mrs. Marie-Louise Winkler, and Andrew Wyld.

# Introduction

Among British artists George Chinnery is a special case. Having left Britain at the age of twenty-eight, he spent the last fifty years of his life on the other side of the world — twenty-three of them in India, and twenty-seven on the China coast. If he had remained in Britain, or even in Europe, he would no doubt have been caught up in the changing fashions of art and taste; he would perhaps have allied himself with one coterie or another; his work would have been exhibited before professional critics and connoisseurs; he would have been extolled or ridiculed by Ruskin. Wealthy manufacturers would have patronised him and entertained him in their country houses; and a flattering account of his achievements would have been published by one of his disciples, if not by Chinnery himself.

As it was, Chinnery forfeited all these by spending the great majority of his working life in the Far East, and much of it in a small community of western expatriates. He certainly considered returning to England, at one point at least (see p.106), but if he had come home for the last years of his life, he might not have appreciated what he found. When Thackeray's Colonel Newcome returns to England after a tour of duty in India, with his brown face and unfashionably loose-fitting clothes, he is regarded with some amusement; when the Colonel revisits a meeting place which he remembers as the haunt of Sheridan and his fellow wits, he is astonished to discover instead a drunken singer of vulgar ballads. How much less would Chinnery, after a far longer absence than the Colonel's, have relished a Victorian Britain in which the cities were dominated by industry, the countryside by railways, and society by a virtuous and domesticated royal family. Would Chinnery have made common cause with the Pre-Raphaelites, or with the organisers of the Great Exhibition? One would guess not. Conversely, the style of Chinnery's oil paintings and watercolours, highly fashionable in the reign of George III, would have seemed as *passé* as Colonel Newcome's trousers.

Even Chinnery's personality, it is tempting to think, remained rooted in the London and the Dublin of the volatile 1790s, a time of violent conflict, outrageous boldness and folly. It is hard to imagine Chinnery playing out a respectable retirement in a secluded villa in the Home Counties. Perhaps it is fitting that his career was not chronicled by some worthy Victorian follower, for in the absence of a contemporary biographer his words and deeds became the subject of rumour and mystery. During the twenty-seven years which he spent isolated on a remote peninsula in the South China Sea, he attracted all kinds of speculation. After his death the myths proliferated, and extended to his pictures: for many years almost any eighteenth- or nineteenth-century oil painting of a Chinese subject was liable to be attributed to him, and to this day pictures from a great variety of sources are displayed or catalogued either as 'Chinnery' or, more cautiously, as 'Chinnery school'.

If one were to accept all that has been published about Chinnery in apparently reputable books and journals, one could construct a summary of Chinnery's career along the following lines:

> George Chinnery was born in 1748 near Tipperary; his family were small landowners. Showing signs of artistic precocity as a young child, he pursued his vocation despite opposition from his father. He left home at an early age, thereby forfeiting the affection of his parents, who transferred it to George's level-headed brother William.
>
> Alone in Dublin at the age of fifteen, he studied under Benjamin West and soon surpassed his master. He moved to London and enrolled at St. Martin's Lane Academy, although most of his time was spent in the taverns of Fleet Street. He became a pupil of Sir Joshua Reynolds, and was patronised by a family of wealthy industrialists. His particular friend was the artist John Raphael Smith; but when Smith joined forces with George Morland, the jealous Chinnery returned to his native Ireland.
>
> Having in due course found his way to Calcutta, Chinnery was declared an incurable lunatic, and had to be kept under restraint. He resorted to alcohol — or, according to other sources, opium — in large quantities. Throughout the East he led a clandestine existence, moving from city to city as he sought to escape from his wife, who relentlessly pursued him. In his desperation to evade her he travelled as far afield as Siam. On the China coast (which he had prevously visited as a member of Lord Macartney's embassy to Peking in 1793) he adopted Chinese clothing and surrounded himself with 'petites amies, obeissantes et habiles', although his dissipation earned him the censure of the missionary Dr. Morrison.
>
> Finally George Chinnery, 'the father of Impressionism', died peacefully on his terrace at Macao, or in poverty at Peking, in his hundredth or 103rd year.[1]

Regrettably perhaps, none of the statements in the above account has any basis in fact.

In the last quarter century the legend of Chinnery has acquired a new dimension, through the medium of historical fiction. He must be one of the few artists — perhaps the only one — to have played a major role, thinly disguised, in three recent novels, one of them also a film. In the first of these, James Clavell's *Taipan* (1966), he appears as the libidinous Aristotle Quance, 'half English and half Irish...the oldest European in the Orient', estranged from an 'Irish monster' of a wife. On the last page the elderly artist hails the new Taipan, and asks him for a loan. 'Women are the cause of all men's tribulations,' he is made to say. ' "Well", he added cautiously, "not all women. Not dear little Maria Tang. Ah, now, there's a luscious colleen if ever I saw one..." '

In *An Insular Possession*, by Timothy Mo (1986), the artist reappears as Augustine O'Rourke, a corpulent, brandy-swilling Irishman possessed of 'a terrible, unpredictable itch...for young female flesh'; he is known to the Chinese as 'the Fat Fornicating Red-Yanged Devil'. By contrast the central character in Katharine Odell's novel *Chinnery in China* (1971), a milder and more sensitive personality, abstains entirely from alcohol and the local women, although he does enjoy a brief and passionate affair with 'Charlotte Winters', a character clearly modelled upon the diarist Harriet Low.

Behind the myth-making lies Chinnery's art. If Chinnery's biography has been presented as a caricature of the artist as a wayward genius, a flouter of convention, it is partly because his painting invites it. It is always tempting to interpret a work of art as an expression of the artist's personality, and in Chinnery's case it is particularly hard to resist, when faced with the individuality of his painting, its touches of brilliance and flamboyance, its mannerism, and its occasional lapses into absurdity. Even the American China trader Gideon Nye, who had known Chinnery for many years, was led to believe that Chinnery had been expelled from Ireland for his activities as a nationalist revolutionary. For, according to Nye, 'Chinnery had some of the weaknesses of genius, with his geniality of disposition; and such an exuberance of imagination and fancy that there was a *gusto* in much that he did approaching the grotesque: ...his *gusto,* or exaggerated ideal, in colour, sometimes overmastered his hand, which in Art is scarcely a fault...'[2]

PART I:
# England and Ireland

# CHAPTER 1

## Scribes and Embezzlers: the Chinnery Family

*O: The Ostrich*

*The thoughtless Ostrich drops her eggs, nor cares*
*Who tramples on, or who her offspring nears.*

*Application:*
*Hard-hearted Parents are worse than Infidels.*

Sound in sentiment if weak in rhyme, this verse appeared in an elaborate writing manual of about 1760, which was largely the work of 'that able and experienced penman, Mr. William Chinnery senior'.[1] William Chinnery's remarkable mastery of the pen initiated a family tradition which was to culminate in the art of his grandson, George Chinnery.

William Chinnery's father (also named William) was, if not an artist, no doubt a man of some dexterity: in 1723 his trade was given as 'cordwainer' (shoemaker) in St. Botolph's parish, Bishopsgate, where he had been baptised in 1679. William the cordwainer's father was yet another William (1646-1709), who apparently came to Bishopsgate in London from his native East Anglia; the name of Chinnery, together with such degenerate forms as Gennery and Jenoyre, is strongly associated with East Anglia, where it is found as early as the fourteenth century, perhaps coming originally from the Low Countries.[2]

Returning to William Chinnery the penman (1708-1791), we find him apprenticed at the age of fifteen to Richard Ford, stationer; having served his time there, he went to live (and presumably to work) with Bernard Lintot the Fleet Street bookseller. 'It was whilst he lived in those places', a contemporary records, 'that he improved his natural genius for fine writing, to such a degree, as to become one of the celebrated writing masters in London.' By 1762, the same writer affirms, 'Mr. Chinnery employed his whole time in teaching abroad [i.e. in his clients' houses]; and instructing young gentlemen in his house, at the Globe in Chancery-lane.'[3]

William Chinnery's extraordinary flair can still be appreciated in a bound volume of his manuscript pages which has been passed down to one of his descendants. The (manuscript) title page offers 'Specimens of Natural Penmanship exemplified in all the usual Hands practis'd. Invented, and naturally perform'd, by William Chinnery.' The volume contains alphabets, book labels, bills of exchange and visiting cards, as well as specimens of calligraphy in the form of epigrams, mottoes and verses. The volume as a whole may have served as a pattern book which

*Plate 1. Portrait of William Chinnery the penman, by his son, William Chinnery Junior.* Private collection

presented a variety of styles and options available to clients. Its forty-eight pages demonstrate the remarkable virtuosity of William Chinnery not only in lettering but also in the freehand drawing of ovals and spirals, flourishes and embellishments of all kinds (Plates 2 and 3). Many of the pages are dated, the earliest date being 1736, the latest 1748, and the commonest 1738 (the year of the author-artist's thirtieth birthday). In a prefatory note of September 1738 William Chinnery states that this attempt at 'a Compleat BODY OF PENMANSHIP' was entirely 'Perform'd on a flat Counter and in a Publick Shop'.[4]

His major published work, *The Compendious Emblematist...,* is a splendid calligraphic pattern book which ran to several editions. On every right-hand page is a moralising couplet appropriate to a particular letter of the alphabet, such as 'O: The Ostrich' quoted above. Another couplet, which George Chinnery might have called to mind in the course of his marital difficulties, was:

*J: The Jay*

*The Jay is for his noisy nonsense priz'd*
*But the loud female Tatler is despis'd.*

*Application:*
*No torment like a Wedded Shrew.*

On each left-hand page is a corresponding illustration — in the last case entitled 'The Plagues of Wedlock' — for which no artist's name is given; there is no reason to suppose that William Chinnery Senior (as he was now known) was responsible for any pictorial work. He lived on until 22 December 1791, and would have been well acquainted with his grandson George, who was seventeen at that date. The church register of St. Bride's, Fleet Street, records the

*Plate 3. Manuscript preface of 'Compleat Body of Penmanship' by William Chinnery Senior. Written in pen and ink, 1738.* Private collection

burial there of William Chinnery, 'an eminent writing-master'.[5]

The only recorded son of William the penman was yet another William Chinnery (c.1740/1-1803), and George Chinnery's father. At least at the outset of his career (and perhaps throughout it) he seems to have followed his father as a calligrapher. He may well have contributed to *The Compendious Emblematist...*, for some of the plates carry the engraved inscription 'William Chinnery Senior' while others are entitled simply 'William Chinnery'. Moreover, two published journals independently describe him as a writing master.[6] Further evidence is to be found at the end of the sixth edition of Thomas Gurney's manual of shorthand entitled *Brachygraphy...* (1767), in which several practitioners of Gurney's shorthand testify to its speed and usefulness: first on the list is 'William Chinnery, Junior, Writing-Master and Accomptant, in Gough-Square, who for his own private Use has wrote in this Method the Book of Psalms, and the New Testament.'[7]

By this time William Chinnery Junior had tried his hand at portraiture. A drawing (Plate 1), which passed down through the descendants of George Chinnery's sister Frances Duncan, is (according to a long-standing family tradition) a portrait by William Chinnery Junior of his father, William the penman. Possibly this was the 'Portrait of a gentleman' exhibited by William Junior in 1764 at the Free Society of Artists, which (in the years before the Royal Academy was founded) was one of the two leading venues at which artists could display their work to the public. In 1766 he exhibited 'A portrait; in crayons', but there is no further record of pictures by George Chinnery's father.[8]

It has been supposed that once William Chinnery Junior (Plate 4) had abandoned his artistic ambitions, he became a 'Madras merchant' at Cuddalore, and thereby founded the family fortunes in India.[9] But this is far from certain, for no record of William Chinnery in India can be found. As a young married man he must have remained in England, since between 1764 and 1777 his wife Elizabeth Bassett — the daughter of a Cornish clergyman — gave birth in London at short and regular intervals to a series of children. If he then went to India after 1777, he must have returned by 1791, when the rates for 4 Gough Square were paid by 'William Chinnery'.[10] (His father had died that year, so that this entry must refer to the son.) However, no Chinnery appears in the lists of East India Company servants between 1777 and 1791. It remains possible that William Chinnery operated in India as an independent trader; records of such Europeans at this early date are very sketchy.

*Plate 4. William Chinnery Junior by his son, George Chinnery. Oils.* National Portrait Gallery, London

As regards the 'Chinnery Factory at Cuddalore', this may well have been the business not of William Chinnery but of his son John Terry Chinnery, who spent most of the years 1793-9 at Cuddalore (close to Fort St. David), and would almost certainly have had manufacturing and trading interests there. The agency house of Chase, Chinnery & Macdowell is recorded in the *East India Registers* from 1803 to 1805, but again it is John Chinnery, not his father, who was involved in this agency, together with two fellow servants of the Company, Thomas Chase and John Macdowell; Macdowell was appointed to the service on the same day (1 August 1792) as John Chinnery.[11]

So it seems likely that the artist's father did not, after all, go out to India. It is certain, however, that he and his wife Elizabeth had at least seven children, whose births are recorded in the registers of St. Botolph's Church. George, born on 5 January 1774, was their sixth child. Of the others two it seems died young; and John Terry Chinnery, who has been mentioned briefly above, is discussed in greater detail in Chapter 4. The other (and eldest) brother was William Bassett Chinnery (1766-1839). William Bassett's career was in its way as flamboyant and as erratic as George's, and deserves to be described a little more fully, both for its own sake and for the light which it casts on his younger brother.

From relatively humble beginnings, William Bassett Chinnery gained a position of power in the Treasury. He had received a position here initially through the influence of Lord Thurlow (Lord Chancellor from 1778 to 1792); Thurlow's daughters had been instructed in the arts of writing by William Bassett Chinnery's father, who had recommended his son to Lord Thurlow as a copier of papers. In 1783 the young man went to work under George Rose, Secretary to the Treasury and a close friend of William Pitt. He advanced quickly in the Treasury to become a Chief Clerk, a post which brought with it several lucrative agencies; by 1794 he was acting as agent for a number of Crown Colonies, including New South Wales and the Bahamas, and he was allowed a commission on the sums of money which passed through his hands.

In 1790 he married the lively and talented Margaret Tresilian. They lived in princely style, acquiring a succession of properties in London and elsewhere, the most splendid being Gilwell Hall near Walthamstow in Essex. Their dinners and concerts attracted a fashionable company, including the perpetual spendthrift William Spencer, poet and nephew of the Duke of Marlborough; the Irish-born Countess of Charlemont, 'that beautiful *blueish* stocking'; and the arch-gossip Sylvester Douglas, Lord Glenbervie, defender of Queen Caroline. Glenbervie likened the Chinnerys to the Johnstones, who entertained lavishly at Brighton: neither family had 'rank', he wrote,

> Yet, by a command of money, which Johnstone is said to have acquired by contracts and cards, and which nobody knows how Chinnery has acquired, the ambition of good company, good houses, excellent cooks, and excellent cellars, by knowing who *is,* or *wishes to be* with who, by frequent dinners and musical and dancing parties, in both which accomplishments the two young ladies, Miss Johnstone and Miss Chinnery excel, they contrive to purchase the society, or at least the presence, almost whenever they please, of all that is most distinguished for rank, beauty, youth, talents, and wealth in the highest or most fashionable walks of life. But the Chinnery parties seem to me more select and exquisite...[12]

And however parvenu, William Bassett Chinnery evidently had a certain style: 'Chinnery, though a coxcomb, and but ill-disguising under tolerable French and Italian, and a profusion of civility, the quill behind his ear, has a better *ton* and more vivacity and lightness of conversation, makes a better bow, and has a better address than Johnstone...'[13]

One of the Chinnerys' closest friends was Giambattista Viotti, the leading violinist of his day and a refugee from the French Revolution. Viotti became a frequent house guest of the Chinnerys, who also lent him money; in return he performed at their musical events, instructed their children and dedicated several of his compositions to them. In 1824 Viotti died at Mrs. Chinnery's house in Upper Berkeley Street, leaving her his Stradivarius.[14] William Chinnery also had contacts with the Royal Academy. When William Hodges died suddenly in 1797, Chinnery helped to find employment for the artist's widow and son. And when in 1806 the diarist Joseph Farington learnt that 'Artists though not Members of the Academy would be admitted to make designs or Models', his informant was the sculptor John Rossi, who in turn had heard it from 'Chinnery of the Treasury'.[15]

With his connections in society and in Government, William would surely have been of assistance to his younger brother George. It may have been William who introduced him to John Jeffreys Pratt, 2nd Earl of Camden, a teller of the Exchequer and a Lord of the Treasury; subsequently he became Lord Lieutenant of Ireland, where his ill-judged actions helped to provoke the uprising of May 1798. George Chinnery's portrait of Camden formerly hung

*Plate 5. Terminal bust of a young man, sold from William Bassett Chinnery's collection to the British Museum in 1812.* British Museum

in Dublin Castle, together with other portraits of Lords Lieutenant, but by the beginning of the twentieth century it had disappeared. Another likely acquaintance of William Chinnery's was Charles Long, later 1st Baron Farnborough, who was Joint Secretary to the Treasury in the 1790s; George Chinnery also painted his portrait, which was engraved by James Heath.[16]

William and Margaret Chinnery were assiduous collectors and patrons of the arts. At Gilwell they formed a notable array of porcelain, both oriental and European, and classical vases and statuary, some of which were later purchased by the British Museum. When the young portrait painter Marie Vigée-Lebrun came to London from Paris in 1802, one of her first visits was to Gilwell, where she was charmed by the elaborate floral decorations ('une féerie printanière') and delighted by the piano-playing of the ten-year-old Caroline Chinnery.[17] The French artist portrayed Margaret Chinnery seated with an open volume of the *Letters of Madame de Genlis*.[18] In the same year George Chinnery, who was about to leave England for ever, exhibited three portraits (perhaps miniatures) of his brother's children, Caroline, her twin brother George Robert, and their younger brother Walter;[19] the three children, and their mother (Plate 6), were also painted at about this time by Trossarelli.

Giovanni Trossarelli (or Gaspare — there is some confusion over his name[20]) would have known George Chinnery at the Royal Academy Schools, for in the year before Chinnery's arrival we find that a certain 'Gaspero Troparelli' was enrolled there.[21] Since the name 'Troparelli' does not occur again, it must be a case of the perennial inability of the British to pronounce and spell foreign names (at about the same time the mistress of the 3rd Duke of Dorset, Giannetta Baccelli, was known to the servants at Knole as 'Shelley', while the artist Anton Mengs appeared in a Royal Academy catalogue as 'Mr. Minx'). The subjects of portraits which Trossarelli exhibited at the Royal Academy ranged from Prince William of Gloucester to 'Mr. Price, dentist'; they included the composer-musician Cherubini, and Viotti, who was also portrayed by George Chinnery. [22]

In 1810 the William Bassett Chinnerys were at the peak of their fame and fortune. Their son George Robert Chinnery, in whom Marie Vigée-Lebrun had earlier observed 'une véritable passion pour l'étude',[23] had by now won himself a reputation for scholarship at Oxford; as the winner of the Newdigate Prize for poetry, he gave a public recital in the Sheldonian Theatre of his rousing if melodramatic poem *The Statue of the Dying Gladiator*.[24] But the extravagance of his father had now become so conspicuous that, as his protector George Rose put it, 'his integrity as a public officer was suspected'. William Chinnery was interrogated by the Prime Minister, Spencer Perceval, but managed to convince him that all was in order; he claimed to have been living 'with very exact economy', and to have been receiving money from 'some very old connexions formed at school'.[25]

Two years later, the truth was at last revealed. Perceval now realised that William Chinnery had deceived him 'most terribly', and that his misappropriations

*Plate 6. Miniature portrait of Mrs. Margaret Chinnery, by Giovanni Trossarelli. Pencil and watercolours on ivory.* Martyn Gregory Gallery

were on a scale far beyond what he had feared.[26] Whereas William Chinnery's legitimate income was £4,000 a year, he had succeeded in diverting some £70,000 of public money into his own operations. He was of course dismissed, together with another guilty official, but his debts were far more than he could pay. On 17 March 1812 it was reported that a writ had been taken out against him. By this time he had made his escape; in June the news came that he was living in Göteborg. Gilwell with its treasures was sold to raise money for his creditors. William Chinnery never returned to Britain, dying in Paris in 1834.[27]

It was a major scandal. In the House of Lords, Byron referred to Chinnery in his condemnation of the Government; in the Commons, George Rose had to defend himself, claiming that in the last fifteen years he had visited William Chinnery only to stand godfather to one of his children. Spencer Perceval's embarrassment was short-lived, since on 11 May of that year he was assassinated — by another bankrupt — in the lobby of the House of Commons. Joseph Farington heard the story of the Chinnery affair from the financier John Julius Angerstein, whose picture collection was to form the nucleus of the National Gallery; Angerstein told him that William Chinnery had also obtained many items from tradesmen on credit, and had left their bills unpaid.[28]

For the Chinnery family the blow must have been severe, especially as the talented Caroline died, at the age of twenty, within three weeks of her father's departure. It was said that 'she had the measles, and an incipiant [*sic*] consumption which followed was supposed to be forwarded by her attending at parties at late hours at the Prince Regent's Pavilion at Brighton last autumn'.[29] Her brother, George Robert, came to live with his mother in London; he was given a post as Clerk in the Treasury, and then entered the diplomatic service, travelling on the Continent as Private Secretary to George Canning. He died unmarried in his early thirties, while serving in Madrid as Commissioner for Claims.[30]

Margaret, who outlived her husband and all three of her children, survived until 1840. She was left with sufficient income to keep house in fashionable Charles Street, off Berkeley Square, with two maids and two manservants.[31] She and young George Robert seem to have maintained their place in London society: in July 1813 George Robert and Viotti were among the guests at a party given for Madame de Stael, newly arrived from Paris and the great celebrity of the season.[32] The Duke of Cambridge, the King's least scandalous son, remained on terms of close friendship with Margaret and her household, and at one time she hoped that the Duke might secure for her a position as lady-in-waiting at one of the royal palaces.[33] In 1818 Lord Glenbervie attended a concert at Mrs. Chinnery's, where the faithful Viotti (whom Glenbervie had once hinted might have been the father of the Chinnery children) was still entertaining a cosmopolitan gathering of noblemen and diplomats.[34]

A postscript may be added to the story of Gilwell. A century after the downfall of William Bassett Chinnery, the estate of Gilwell was acquired as the headquarters of the Boy Scout Movement. One can be confident that, had William Chinnery still been alive, *Scouting for Boys* would not have been his favourite book. The movement's founder, no doubt unaware that the house had once been maintained by large sums of public money fraudulently diverted, chose to be remembered by the title Baron Baden-Powell of Gilwell.

George Chinnery seems not to have been personally involved in his brother's affairs; he had by this time been in India for ten years, and in view of the debts which he had run up on his own account, was in no position to assist his brother or his family. He did however write to Lord Minto, whose portrait he had painted shortly before Minto's return from India, asking him to intercede on his brother's behalf. This plea had no effect, since (unknown to the artist) Minto had died a month after arriving in England, before George Chinnery's letter was even written. But the letter does indicate the extent of William's influence, making it clear that he had known Minto well before the latter's appointment as Governor-General of Bengal, and indeed had been responsible for the introduction to Minto of his brother George:

> Could I, my Lord, dare to ask it, I would in a point very near my Heart, request your Benevolence & Goodness now your Lordship is in England to be extended to my Brother — As a public servant I will not, I cannot defend him — I do it in the humblest Manner — I lay at your Lordship's feet my Supplication on the Score of this good Man, who in the Zenith of his Means, extended to many the most active and uninterested Benevolence — without my solicitation, I think he still holds a place in yr. Lordship's Friendship, & I have certain Accounts I think that the Royal Family bear him in kind recollection — His Worth must be great to balance his faults, & I hope most Sincerely so, that something may be done for him thro' means your Lordship's influence will greatly add to. My natural Affection would make me his Advocate — even without this his Introduction to your Lordship, the great distinction of my Life would engage alone all my best & grateful feelings...[35]

It is clear that the brothers William and George Chinnery had a good deal in common: charm, plausibility, and a capacity for spending other people's money. The family tradition was maintained by George's illegitimate son Edward, who was convicted in Calcutta of stealing a small quantity of groceries — a theft which the jury regarded as arising from high spirits rather than criminal intent (see p.154).

Frances Chinnery, the artist's youngest sister, sailed for India on the *Buckingham* in June 1796, to join her brother John. She was eighteen, and her companion Mary Payton was twenty-five. The two women had the misfortune to travel out not only with a pair of sisters (named Smith) who were apparently younger and more vivacious than themselves, but also with the tediously arrogant Lieutenant George Elers. In his *Memoirs* Elers dismissed them:

> Mamma Payton...was very quiet and matronly, and rolled about her fine black eyes at dinner in every direction. Without being absolutely vulgar, she had no polish or refinement, and had evidently not been used to fashionable company, which the two Miss Smiths clearly had. As to poor Miss Chinnery, no one ever thought of her. Poor soul! She had neither beauty nor talent; but she was good-natured and inoffensive, and thankful *when* she received attention. [36]

If they were overlooked on board ship, neither Mary Payton nor Frances Chinnery remained single for long. Very shortly after their arrival in India, Mary was married to John Chinnery, on 19 January 1797; three months later, Frances was married to John Duncan of the East India Company's medical service. The younger Miss Smith became the mistress of Colonel Arthur Wellesley. Elers himself cultivated Wellesley for several years; in later life he wrote a long and obsequious letter to the Duke of Wellington (as Wellesley had now become), reminding him of their long acquaintance and requesting a post on his staff. It is satisfying to relate that the Duke briskly refused. [37]

John Chinnery died in 1817, leaving three daughters and a son. The son, William Charles Chinnery (1805-1839), died unmarried as a Captain in the 4th Madras Native Infantry. Since the sons of both William Bassett Chinnery and George Chinnery also died young and childless, George Chinnery himself outlived not only his brothers but also his sons and nephews. With him was extinguished the enterprising male line which descended from the 'eminent writing-master', William Chinnery Senior.

# CHAPTER 2

# 'A new style of painting':
# London and the Royal Academy Schools

Nothing is known of George Chinnery's childhood. He was born on 5 January 1774 and baptised on 4 February, the sixth of seven children who were all baptised at St. Bride's in the City of London, the tallest of the churches built by Wren a century before. The Chinnerys lived in Gough Square, just across Fleet Street from the church, amid a warren of small courts overlooked by unostentatious but moderately prosperous households. Samuel Johnson lived in Gough Square from 1748 until 1759, and the rate books show that a 'William Chinnery' — either the father or the grandfather of the artist — paid his dues there throughout George Chinnery's early years.[1]

In December 1791 the senior William Chinnery died, but he had lived just long enough to see his grandson enter the public arena as an artist. In May of this year, at the age of seventeen, George Chinnery had his first picture displayed at the annual exhibition of the Royal Academy in Somerset House. It was evidently a miniature, as the catalogue lists it among the 'Miniatures, &c.' in the Great Room on the second floor. Described simply as 'Portrait', it has been said, perhaps unreliably, to represent his father.[2] Chinnery's name and address were omitted from the list of artists at the back of the catalogue — a fair measure of his obscurity.

In the following year's exhibition he had three portrait miniatures on show, this time in the name of George Chinnery of 4 Gough Square. They represented 'a clergyman' (identifiable as the Rev. J. Moore), 'a gentleman' (the artist's brother John), and 'an artist' (A.J. Oliver).[3] Perhaps these met with a favourable response, for soon after the exhibition was over, on 6 July 1792, Chinnery enrolled at the Royal Academy Schools. The Schools were free to applicants who could satisfy the Council of their abilities; they offered students the opportunity to copy from the cast collection, to hear the professors' lectures, and to attend the life classes, although a rule required that 'no student under the Age of twenty be admitted to draw after the Female Model, unless he be a married Man.'[4] Chinnery's age at entry is given in the register as nineteen, whereas he was in fact eighteen; possibly he felt that a small deceit would help to advance his artistic education.

The Schools were an informal institution, and although in 1792 the length of the course was set at seven years, many students, Chinnery included, attended for a shorter period. Nevertheless the Schools enjoyed considerable prestige, and were the starting point of many successful careers: William Blake, Thomas Daniell, Thomas Rowlandson, and (Sir) Thomas Lawrence were among Chinnery's predecessors, and J.M.W. Turner, a year younger than Chinnery, was his contemporary at the Schools, studying there from 1789 until October

*Plate 7. Academic study from an early Chinnery sketchbook. Pen and ink.*
Private collection

1793. Another artist whose friendship with Chinnery must have been formed at this time was Archer James Oliver, who entered the Schools in 1790, and had a fashionable portrait practice until his health failed in the 1820s. After Chinnery had exhibited his portrait of Oliver in 1792, Oliver in turn showed a portrait of Chinnery in 1794. In 1802 Oliver sent in a portrait of 'W. Chinnery senior', presumably George's father, who was to die in the following year of an inflammation of the bowel.[5]

Chinnery is often said to have been a pupil of Sir Joshua Reynolds, first President of the Royal Academy. In fact Sir Joshua died, after some years of failing eyesight, five months before Chinnery was admitted to the Academy Schools. Reynolds had employed numerous pupil assistants (especially in the 1770s) who painted drapery and accessories, and sometimes copied pictures by the master. But there is no record and little likelihood that a very young Chinnery was one of them. Of all Reynolds's pupils only the portrait painter James Northcote went on to distinguish himself as an independent artist.

Nor would Chinnery have heard Reynolds lecture, although he would certainly have known his lectures in their printed form, the *Discourses on Art*, which as a full series was first published in 1797. Later in Calcutta, while instructing his pupil Maria Browne, Chinnery referred her to 'Sir Joshua in his admirable and never enough to be admired Lectures',[6] and several of his remarks to her make it clear that the *Discourses* were familiar to him (see

Plate 8. Miniature portrait of an elderly lady. Pencil and watercolours, s. and d. 1 January 1793. Victoria and Albert Museum

Plate 9. Lady Elizabeth Stanley. Pencil and watercolours, s. and d. 1794. Martyn Gregory Gallery

Appendix i). Sir Charles D'Oyly's burlesque account of Chinnery's studio in Calcutta suggests that Chinnery at this later date encouraged the idea that he was Reynolds's natural successor:

> And we have seen Sir Joshua there — a gem
> Or two, within this storeroom of bijoux,
> The artist on his knees, adoring them,
> And swallowing greedily his tints and hues —
> Then standing back — then forward — loath to lose
> A moment in the ardent meditation,
> Then fancying that he stood in his great shoes,
> Tracing between them great assimilation,
> Except his knighthood merely, — and his reputation.[7]

The reference here to 'Sir Joshua' refers more probably to a portrait of Reynolds by Chinnery than to a work from Reynolds's brush; the Hong Kong loan exhibition of 1876 (see p.262) included 'a small study of Sir Joshua's head' by Chinnery.[8]

If Chinnery attended any lectures during his years at the Royal Academy Schools, they would probably have been those delivered each spring by James Barry, the Irish-born painter of historical subjects who was Professor of Painting at this time. A contemporary reported that 'as a Lecturer, his manner is awkward, cold, and unimpressive, but his matter is interesting, and fraught with information'.[9] Fiercely jealous of Reynolds, Barry initially conceived his lectures as a counterblast to the *Discourses...*, but he gave up his quarrel after the death of his rival, and on the traditional subjects of design and composition, chiaroscuro and colouring, Chinnery would have heard little from Barry which had not already been expressed more cogently by Reynolds

*Colour Plate 1. Miniature portrait of Charles James Fox. Pencil and watercolours, s. and d. 1794.* Private collection

*Colour Plate 2. Miniature portrait of a gentleman in a powdered wig. Pencil and watercolours, s. and d. 1795.* Brigadier and Mrs. Viner

and by other European theorists before him. And if Chinnery heard Barry's exhortations to undertake 'great subjects' in painting, he probably ignored them. Since even Barry himself was known to have difficulty in finding commissions for his grandiose scenes of history and mythology, what hope was there for young artists at the outset of their career? However fervently they might aspire to history painting, or long to paint landscapes, neither could be relied upon for a living. Only portraiture could offer a steady income.

By the Academy exhibition of 1793 Chinnery had found new lodgings at 1 Sackville Street, off Piccadilly, where he was to remain for the next two years. At the exhibition he showed three more portraits. One is described in the catalogue as 'a gentleman', which was apparently a misunderstanding of some kind, since the sitter is identified as Mrs. Oliver. The second, 'a lady', portrayed Jane Porter (sister of the artist Sir Robert Ker Porter), who was to achieve success as a romantic novelist; the third was of himself. To 1793 also belongs the earliest of Chinnery's reliably dated pictures to have survived — a miniature of an elderly lady (Plate 8), rather clumsily handled, and signed with a mock-heroic 'Georgius Chinnery'. The portrait is dated 1 January 1793; Chinnery was not quite nineteen years old.

The year 1794 must have brought confidence to the young artist. Not only could he now draw from the Female Model with a clear conscience, as he passed his twentieth birthday in January; he also submitted no fewer than twelve portraits to the Royal Academy exhibition, and had them warmly praised in a published review. These portraits were hung in the Antique Academy on the first floor, and were evidently not miniatures (which were listed in a separate section). It was under the heading of 'drawings' that they were noticed in the outspoken *A Liberal Critique on the Present Exhibition of the Royal Academy* published by John Williams under the pseudonym 'Anthony Pasquin'. Having scornfully dismissed the works of many more celebrated artists — describing a painting by Rigaud as 'an inexplicable daub', and a 'Bacchante' by Pellegrini as 'pleasing only to voluptuaries' — the critic turned to Chinnery's contribution: 'Mr. Chinnery has some portraits, which highly pleased me; among the budding candidates for fame this rising young artist is the most prominent. His progress has been rapid almost beyond example; he has rather adopted a new style of painting, somewhat after the manner of Cosway.'[10]

*Plate 10. A young lady by a pedestal. Pencil and watercolours, s. and d. 1795.* British Museum

*Plate 11. A young lady by a tall pedestal. Pencil and watercolours, s. and d. 1795.* Private collection

*Plate 12. A young lady playing the harp. Pencil and watercolours, s. and d. 1795.* Private collection

*Plate 13. A young lady in a woodland setting. Pencil and watercolours, s. and d. 1795.* Private collection

*Plate 15. Miniature portrait of Elizabeth, Lady Tuite. Pencil and watercolours, s. and d. 1796.* Victoria and Albert Museum

*Plate 14. An officer of the Royal Horse Artillery. Pencil and watercolours, s. and d. 1794.* Private collection

These pictures which Williams so much admired were probably small portrait drawings, a genre which Cosway had recently made fashionable, often adding watercolour to the whole or just to the faces, as Chinnery was to do in India. An appealing example painted in this year is Chinnery's watercolour of Lady Elizabeth Stanley (Plate 9), the second daughter of the ebullient and hospitable 12th Earl of Derby. The boxer dog shown beside her is a reminder of the family's affinity for animals: Lady Elizabeth's father founded the Derby stakes, and her brother Edward (later the 13th Earl) established at Knowsley Hall the famous menagerie whose inmates were painted by Edward Lear. On 15 January 1795, shortly after this portrait was drawn, Lady Elizabeth Stanley was married to Stephen Thomas Cole of Twickenham and Stoke Lyne; a dedication (on the backboard of this picture) to 'Mrs. Cole', with the date 9 November 1794, suggests that the drawing may have served as an engagement present to the sitter's prospective mother-in-law.

Several small full-length drawings by Chinnery carry the date 1795 (Plates 10-13): they depict young ladies in flowing, high-waisted dresses, hair hanging loosely over their shoulders, who pose beside pedestals or rockwork in gentle landscapes. In each picture the delicately stippled face is the most detailed element, the eyes are romantically dark, and the mouth yields a mannerly fraction of a smile.

The treatment of the faces in these drawings is similar to that seen in Chinnery's miniatures of the same period (Colour Plates 1 and 2 and Plates 14-16). In each case the face is characterised by lightly-drawn, individual lines, which are especially conspicuous at the chin and around the eyes; in the agreeable portrait of Elizabeth, Lady Tuite (granddaughter of Charles Cobbe, Archbishop of Dublin), this hatching technique occupies the whole face (Plate 15). The backgrounds in these early miniatures are made up similarly of short lines nearly parallel, but are plain in general impression — Chinnery

*Plate 16. Miniature portrait of a gentleman. Pencil and watercolours, s. and d. 1795.* Hongkong and Shanghai Banking Corporation

had not yet begun to experiment with the mottled, thundery backgrounds which he was to employ in Madras. The hair is drawn once again with discrete, wiry brushstrokes, curving or curling. Chinnery's miniatures of an officer of the Royal Horse Artillery (Plate 14) and of Charles James Fox (Colour Plate 1), both signed and dated 1794, are highly accomplished works by any standards, and a notable improvement on his 'elderly lady' of the previous year. In a more freely-handled portrait of 1795 (Plate 16), we see also the tousled hair which became a feature of many of Chinnery's portraits in various media.

In 1795 he exhibited two miniature portraits of gentlemen, one of them identified as 'the late Lord Ashburton'.[11] But these were his last contributions to the Academy for three years. At this point Chinnery travelled to Ireland, his first venture across the sea — a small sea, in this case, but a bold step for a young artist at a critical stage in his career. Hitherto he had been known as a skilful draughtsman on a small scale; in Ireland he was to extend his repertoire, and to begin to achieve a reputation in the more ambitious profession of oil painting.

*Colour Plate 3. Marianne Chinnery. Pencil and watercolours, s. and d. 1800.* Hongkong and Shanghai Banking Corporation

*Colour Plate 4. A young boy with a drum. Pencil and watercolours, s. and d. 1797.* Private collection

# CHAPTER 3
# *Ireland*

On the face of it, Ireland was unpromising territory for an English artist. It was common enough for ambitious Irish painters to seek their fortune in England; of Chinnery's contemporaries, Nathaniel Hone, Thomas Hickey, James Barry and Martin Archer Shee, together with many less celebrated painters, all left their native Ireland for London. London offered them the prospect not only of patronage but also of displaying their work in public. Since 1780 there had been no institution in Dublin at which artists could exhibit their paintings, and it was only after Chinnery's arrival (and, it seems, largely through his efforts) that a series of public exhibitions was established there.

Chinnery would have been aware that certain English artists had prospered in Dublin. In particular John Astley, who worked in Dublin in the 1750s, was said to have earned £3,000 there in the space of three years. Like Chinnery, however, Astley was a man of expensive habits and heavy debts who was supported only by a (second) marriage to a wealthy widow.[1] Often it was debt which induced English artists to cross over to Ireland in the first place. Francis Wheatley came to Dublin in 1779 to escape from his creditors, and to live with a fellow-artist's wife, whom he passed off as his own.[2] In 1787 the North American artist Gilbert Stuart also made Dublin his refuge from debts, and despite his great success there, further debts caused him to leave four years later. It is possible that Chinnery's visit to Ireland was prompted by difficulties of a similar kind.

There were positive incentives also. In the last decade of the eighteenth century the population of Dublin was greater than that of any English provincial city, and the Protestant Irish nobility and gentry were at the peak of their power and confidence. Henry Grattan's so-called 'Free Parliament', supported by the Irish Volunteer Movement, had won for the Irish a degree of self-government — although it was a parliament which was composed only of Protestants, and was ultimately subject to the English parliament at Westminster. Splendid houses had been built for the peers and commoners who attended the Parliament House on College Green. The Royal Irish Academy, founded in 1785, served as a focus for scientific and literary activity. Substantial libraries were formed, theatres were well attended, and from 1791 even the card players were provided with the fine rooms of Daly's Club in which to lose their fortunes. The large sums spent on decorations and entertainment in turn brought wealth to the makers and suppliers of luxury goods, such as Wedgwood, which in 1772 had opened its showrooms on College Green.

Chinnery arrived in Dublin in 1796.[3] He had relations there, but not close ones. A George Chinnery had gone to Ireland in about 1620, and although hardships and setbacks caused him to return to England, his eldest son John remained as an army officer; in 1660 he was rewarded with an estate in County Cork. From John descended a prosperous branch of the family. At the time when George Chinnery the artist arrived in Dublin, this branch of the Chinnerys was represented by Brodrick Chinnery, M.P. for Bandon and nephew of the late Right Reverend George Chinnery, Bishop of Cloyne. In Dublin Brodrick had a house in Mountjoy Square. It has been suggested that the artist came to Ireland specifically to paint Brodrick, but the prospect of portraying his distant cousin hardly seems a sufficient reason for the journey.

It turned out, however, that George Chinnery was just in time to witness a rise in his cousin's status. On 29 August 1799 Brodrick received a baronetcy — the first title to be held by a Chinnery, if one discounts the Bishop. His baronetcy was one of many inducements accepted by members of the Irish Parliament in return for their votes in favour of the Act of Union. He thus became Sir Brodrick Chinnery, and was assured of a seat in the House of Commons at Westminster into the bargain. George Chinnery painted two portraits (one of them a miniature) of Sir Brodrick,[4] as if to mark this notable elevation. When the 1st Baronet died in 1808, he was succeeded by his son, the second Sir Brodrick, but the title became extinct in 1867 when the 3rd Baronet, the Rev. Sir Nicholas Chinnery, was killed with his wife in a railway accident.[5]

*Plate 17. Marianne Chinnery (née Vigne), the artist's wife. Engraving by James Heath after Chinnery.* British Museum

George Chinnery did not lodge with the Chinnerys of Mountjoy Square, living instead in the house of the jeweller James Vigne and his wife Elizabeth (née Eustace), which was fashionably situated at 27 College Green. The Vignes had English relations, also watchmakers and jewellers, who may have been acquainted with the Chinnerys in England.[6] James Vigne of Dublin had a cousin in the Strand, London, who was also named James; the latter's son, Henry George Vigne, entered the Royal Academy Schools on 8 November 1782. He exhibited two miniatures at the Royal Academy in 1785 and in 1787, but died later in 1787 at the age of twenty-two.

James Vigne of Dublin had three sons and two daughters. It was the second of the daughters, Marianne (Plate 17), who married the lodger. The wedding of George Chinnery and Marianne Vigne took place on 19 April 1799, and soon they had two children, Matilda (born in October 1800) and John Eustace (born in September 1801). Tradition has it that 'the union did not prove a harmonious one',[7] and certainly it was a brief one, for George parted from Marianne shortly after — or perhaps even shortly before — the birth of their second child.

In his profession, on the other hand, Chinnery quickly made his mark in Dublin. The Royal Dublin Society had a Drawing School (broadly equivalent to the Royal Academy Schools in London) which in the year of Chinnery's arrival moved to new premises in Poolbeg Street. The artists working in Dublin were invited to elect a committee of 'directors', each of whom was to take charge of the life classes for four weeks at a time. Chinnery was one of the nine directors elected; the others included the landscape painter William

Ashford and the portrait painter William Cuming.[8]

By 1800 a Society of Artists of Ireland had been founded, and Chinnery was its Secretary. The Society reintroduced public exhibitions as an annual fixture, and despite splits and mergers on the part of the members, these exhibitions became a regular feature of Dublin's social life. Previously, the Royal Dublin Society had encouraged artists by awarding premiums (money prizes) to the leading performers in different aspects of painting. Now, however, Chinnery proposed in a letter that instead of offering premiums the Royal Dublin Society should buy from the annual exhibitions pictures which were judged to be outstanding; these would remain on display for the benefit of young students. The idea was adopted, and happily for Chinnery, one of his own paintings was selected in the first year — 'Attention' (see Plate 22 below), which the Royal Dublin Society bought for £62 11s. 3d.[9]

Chinnery's success in Ireland can be measured by the long list of portraits which he painted there, a list which includes many of the leading characters in this momentous period of Irish history.[10] This is not to say that Chinnery encountered all the men and women he portrayed; he would also have been required to reproduce portraits (often in a different medium or scale) which had been executed by another artist. But Dublin society was close knit, and an artist who had once gained *entrée* could expect to meet potential patrons without delay.

Perhaps the principal figure in Dublin's literary and artistic circles was James Caulfeild, 1st Earl of Charlemont, whose son's portrait by Chinnery was reproduced shortly after the Earl's death in 1799.[11] His spacious Dublin residence (now the Municipal Gallery of Modern Art) housed the fruits of a very Grand Tour which had extended to Egypt and the Levant. He was the first President of the Royal Irish Academy, and above all he is remembered as the Commander-in-chief of the Irish Volunteers, who were established to combat the threat of a French invasion and became a powerful political force in the movement for Irish independence. Chinnery may well have been personally acquainted with the 'Volunteer Earl', for the latter's daughter-in-law, Anne, Lady Charlemont, was later a guest at the house of his brother William Chinnery.[12]

Another of Chinnery's subjects was closely associated with Charlemont: William Conyngham Plunket, 1st Baron Plunket, who campaigned against the union of Ireland with England. He entered the Irish Parliament in 1798 as the Member for the Earl's family borough of Charlemont; later he became Lord Chancellor of Ireland, and was an influential advocate of Catholic emancipation.

Other notable figures portrayed by Chinnery achieved celebrity of a different kind. Thomas 'Buck' Whaley of the Hell-Fire Club (son of the priest-hunting 'Burn Chapel' Whaley) spent much of his time at College Green, some of it in the Parliament House but more of it in Daly's Club. In 1788-9 he travelled to Jerusalem to win a bet of £15,000. He was not always so successful in his wagers, however, and his gambling debts finally forced him to retire to the Isle of Man, taking with him the full-length portraits of himself and his wife which Chinnery had painted.[13] Chinnery may also have painted Whaley's unscrupulous companion John Scott, 1st Earl of Clonmel, who was known as 'copper-faced Jack' because of 'his unblushing effrontery, coupled with his somewhat bronzed visage'.[14] A ruthless opponent of the freedom of the Press, Clonmel pursued a vendetta against John Magee, proprietor of the *Dublin Evening Post*. In revenge, Clonmel organised a 'grand Olympic pig hunt' beside the Earl's lovingly nurtured gardens. The pigs were smeared with soap, and the hunters were plied with whisky. In the resulting mêlée Clonmel's gardens were ruined, and the enraged Earl was driven from his estate.

The first exhibition to be mounted by the Society of Artists of Ireland was held in June 1800 in Allen's Rooms at 32 Dame Street, Dublin. Chinnery contributed twelve pictures. One of these was a large, ambitious repesentation of 'Satan's arrival at the confines of light', a scene from *Paradise Lost* in which Satan appears in 'a glimmering dawn' at the edge of Chaos. This was the only subject picture ever exhibited by Chinnery, and one must regret that it has disappeared, for he would surely have painted a magnificently demonic Satan. A *Critical Review...* devoted to the exhibition regarded this painting as 'the first thought of a daring and vigorous mind', a bold attempt at a theme to which only a Raphael or a Michelangelo could do justice; in other words, a failure, but an honourable one, since 'the enthusiastic mind of a young painter ill brooks the confined limits of portrait painting'.[15]

Chinnery's other eleven exhibits did not venture beyond these limits, for all were portraits, eight in oils and three in crayons.[16] Among the subjects of the oils were Thomas Whaley (see p.34), depicted life-size in a cornfield, with dogs and a servant 'giving the sportsman's whistle'. This composition was thought to demonstrate 'powers of genius in a very singular degree and of the very highest kind.' The companion picture of the Hon. Anne Whaley already betrayed Chinnery's fondness for vivid reds: she was shown in a grove, with 'a rose and lilly [*sic*] in her bosom, and...flaming tints of the crimson and orange poppy which appear to bend their proud heads before her in homage to her beauty.' There was also a bust-length portrait of Thomas Whaley's sister, the Countess of Clare, whose husband John Fitzgibbon (Lord Clare) was Lord Chancellor of Ireland and the most powerful politician in Dublin. *A Critical Review...* reported that, although a graceful picture, 'it appears like a first or second sitting'[17]; the lack of finish in Chinnery's portraits was something on which his critics repeatedly commented.

Other figures portrayed by Chinnery in this exhibition included a certain Miss Price, Mr. Standford of Dame Street, and Mr. Vigne the jeweller, Chinnery's father-in-law. The latter, presented half-length and life-size, was shown holding a letter and wearing a 'holiday expression...it is such as we might expect from a man, who has just received good news or met an

*Plate 18. General Vallancey. Oils.* Royal Irish Academy

*Plate 19. 'Miss Vigne' (Marianne Chinnery). Oils.* National Gallery of Ireland

accession of fortune.' It was a picture which could 'challenge competition with the works of any painter of the English school',[18] and indeed *A Critical Review...* leaves its readers in no doubt that Chinnery was outstanding among the artists represented in the exhibition.

Two at least of his portraits shown at this event have survived. One of these, which was acquired from the artist by the Royal Irish Academy, is a portrait of the extraordinary General Vallancey (Plate 18). Although in his eightieth year when the picture was hung, Vallancey remained an energetic and influential figure in Dublin. Trained as an engineer, he has been credited with the design of Queen's Bridge over the Liffey, and in 1798 he drew up plans for the defence of Dublin in the event of a French invasion. He married three times, was involved in many of the activities of the Royal Dublin Society, and published a number of enthusiastic but ill-founded books on Irish archaeology and language, which gained him an undeserved reputation as an antiquary. 'The General had the energy of a bull, the ambitions of a Leonardo da Vinci, and talents of an ordinary kind.'[19] Chinnery's portrait of him shows a strongly-built man with (one fancies) an impatient expression, resting his brass-buttoned sleeve on a heavy folio, thus representing both the military and the literary aspects of his life.

The other surviving portrait, 'Miss Vigne', is now in the National Gallery of Ireland (Plate 19). It is a portrait of the artist's wife Marianne, whom he had married in the previous year: her wedding ring is conspicuously displayed. The pale expanse of her clothing and headscarf, which occupies nearly half of the picture's area, lends contrast to the vivid red of Marianne's book and lips; strokes of unmixed red also appear beneath her nose and ear — a mannerism that Chinnery was to maintain in many of his portraits, on one occasion to the great annoyance of the sitter (see p.122). It is an informal, domestic portrait, in which Marianne appears immersed in her book, seemingly unaware of the artist.

*Plate 20. Mrs. Eustace, the artist's grandmother-in-law. Oils.* National Gallery of Ireland

A related drawing, dated 1800 (Colour Plate 3), presents the same sitter in very similar clothing, once again with the dark hair on her forehead threatening to cast her eyes into shadow. The two portraits of Marianne repesent two divergent courses in Chinnery's art. In the drawing she is more conventionally posed, looking directly out at the artist, and situated at the foot of a column in keeping with the current tradition of formal portraiture. The face is delicately painted in watercolours: here we see the meticulous technique of the miniature-painter, as distinct from the broad handling and cavalier deployment of his oil paints.

Chinnery's portrait of Marianne's grandmother, Mrs. Eustace (Plate 20), must also have been painted at this time; as in the oil portrait of Marianne, the drapery is treated in summary style, and there is a certain vagueness about the outline of the face. The expression of Mrs. Eustace, is stern, even disapproving, as might befit the grandmother-in-law of the young artist. Her net and lace bonnet, like the caps worn by young girls in several of Reynolds's portraits, is defined by angular strokes of mixed pigment, and her gloved hand is no more than sketched, as if Chinnery had no patience with such an accessory.[20]

More ambitious is the portrait of Mrs. Conyngham, sitting at a piano or harpsichord, with sheet music at her elbow and a 'lyre guitar' beside her (Plate 21). The last was an exotic hybrid instrument which was briefly fashionable at the turn of the nineteenth century; the particular model illustrated by Chinnery is an 'Apollo lyre', so named after the stylised Sun god which conceals the tuning pegs.[21] Once again, the lack of confidence about the jaw line and in some of the drapery suggests an artist who is not yet in full command of his technique. Since Mrs. Conyngham left for India in 1801, her portrait must have been painted either before that time, or, possibly, in India; if the latter, it must have been during the few months in 1807-8 which Chinnery spent in Calcutta, before the sitter's death in September 1808.

She was born Charlotte Greer, the niece of Sir John Hadley D'Oyly, 6th Baronet. Sir John had returned from India in 1785 with his wife, a young family and a handsome fortune. He was a sociable man, a friend of George III and a loyal supporter of Warren Hastings. He spent the years 1800-3 in Ireland, where he had a brewery near Dublin. He may well have encountered Chinnery here, and even encouraged him to make the journey to India; Sir John himself returned to India with his family in 1804. Chinnery portrayed several members of the D'Oyly family in the ensuing years.

By all accounts Charlotte was an accomplished and attractive individual. The diarist William Hickey delivered a parcel to her mother in 1780, and described the mother as 'an uncommonly fine woman with three beautiful daughters,'[22] these being Harriet, Charlotte and Marian. By contrast, their father was 'an abominable sot' — William Greer of Keyhaven, who had been chief mate of the *Nassau* in which Hickey had recently sailed back from India. According to Hickey, William Greer had spent most of the voyage in his cabin, drunk and abusive, or else quarrelling with the second officer, John Pascal Larkins, whose son was later portrayed by Chinnery.[23]

Something of Charlotte's life in India is recorded in the journal of a young lieutenant, John Pester, who travelled out to India with her in 1801. Soon after her arrival she was married to Robert Conyngham, who had already spent ten years in the Bengal Civil Service. Pester often stayed with the Conynghams at Mynpoorie, tiffing with them on mutton chops with hock and water, and riding their Arab horses. Pester seems to have been deeply impressed by Charlotte, naming her as one of the three finest women in India, and admiring the musical talents which are indicated in Chinnery's portrait; with bravado he remarked that 'the harmony of her piano was a very different kind of music from that which we shortly expected to be amused with in the field.' Charlotte died in Calcutta four years later, however, while Pester survived the Maratha Wars and retired to England as a Lieutenant-Colonel.[24]

In 1801 the Society of Artists' exhibition was held in the Parliament House, and Chinnery supplied eleven more pictures. Although these cannot all be identified, a manuscript journal preserved in the Royal Academy of Ireland includes some illuminating remarks on the exhibition. The author's identity is unknown; from his journal we may gather only that he was a man of business, with Scottish relations, who sometimes played the flute before breakfast.

We first read of Chinnery in connection with a portrait of the author himself which was being executed in 1801 by the young miniature-painter Henry Kirchhoffer: on 16 June it was decided that the background was 'to be imitated from one of Chinnery, as the blue colour of my coat is scientifically denominated cold, it is to be warmed, by the vicinity of a crimson curtain'.[25] Although in the event the curtain was replaced by a clouded sky, we can infer that Chinnery's work was regarded as something of a model, and when on 6 July the anonymous journal records its author's impressions of the

*Plate 21. Mrs. Conyngham. Oils.* National Gallery of Ireland

exhibition (which he had last visited three weeks before), it is clear that Chinnery was noted as a flamboyant, original artist with a frustrating disregard for detail:

> Geo. Chinnery — 11 pieces — better finished I believe than those of last year, but still capable of much improvement. The manner of this painter possesses a peculiarity which would enable one any where to distinguish his works — They have a strong expression of original genius, bold but always either palpably unfinished or with as little as possible — it appears to be his wish to paint every thing in an uncommon manner, & of course to attract attention, which would otherwise be directed to more finished production of the common walk — Hamilton's pencil is by no means a tame one, but the designs of Chinnery finished by its critical minuteness would I should think produce capital pictures.[26]

The journal records some of Chinnery's subjects in the exhibition. There was a half-length portrait of 'Mr. Cooke of the Theatre Royal', presumably

Thomas Cooke, leader of the Dublin Theatre Orchestra ('attitude pleasing — the right arm thrown forward — an excellent likeness, but coarsely executed'); a view in oils from Glenna Cottage, Killarney ('well executed, if not in company with others much superior'); a watercolour of sunset at Killarney ('perhaps natural, but parallel stripes of scarlet, black, purple & yellow make but a tawdry appearance on paper'); and another of a ruined church at Casle Dermot ('the landscape well but the building such bright masses of white and green that it appears to have been cut out of something else and pasted into its present situation'). The landscapes were included by Chinnery, in the author's opinion, 'to display the versatility of his genius', although portraiture was 'his natural walk'.[27]

Of the portraits not specified in this journal, two more can be identified: 'Counsellor Plunket', the future Lord Chancellor of Ireland (see p.34); and Hugh Douglas Hamilton, the genial elder statesman of Irish portraiture.[28] A reviewer claimed that the latter picture had earned Chinnery 'a place in the Pantheon of British Painters'.[29]

One picture, however, stood out from the others contributed by Chinnery. Entitled 'Attention', it is a portrait of the other Miss Vigne — Miss Maria Vigne, who was now Chinnery's sister-in-law (Plate 22). She is pictured full-length, reclining in a Romneyish pose amid an ample supply of cushions, which together with the pointed slippers and exotically coloured fabrics

*Plate 22. 'Attention',  portrait of Maria Vigne, the artist's sister-in-law. Oils.* Royal Dublin Society

convey something of the atmosphere of an oriental harem. Like the 'Miss Vigne' of 1800 (Plate 19), she is absorbed by a book — the *Arabian Nights*, perhaps. The theme of a woman reclining on a sofa was itself a little *risqué;* visitors to the exhibition might have been reminded of William Cowper's recent poem *The Task*, in whose first book the sofa is taken as a symbol of urban artifice and dissipation, invented as it was for '...relaxation of the languid frame / By soft recumbency of outstretch'd limbs'. The anonymous journal, however, approaches this painting from a more formal point of view:

> *Attention* — A picture in which the most difficult attitudes & the greatest variety of drapery has like the motley penmanship of a Christmas piece, been assembled to display the powers of the artist — The subject is represented by a female figure, sitting or rather lying, upon a sofa — her head reclined over a book — the face handsome & well foreshortened, but the shades of too blue a tint & the arms as coarse as house painting — The robe bundled up over the legs, which are crossed in the careless manner which close attention to an interesting novel might be supposed to have effected — nothing that could contribute to richness was omitted in the colouring — yellow shoes — purple robe — ermine — muslin of all kinds & textures — crimson sopha gilding carving — the white fur capitally expressed by white blue and yellow tints — a scarf of embroidered muslin also strikingly natural — but another part of the muslin Drapery stiff in the extreme — the folds bearing a strong resemblance to flakes of ice — a frame on which the utmost extent of the carvers skill has been lavished.

The exhibition catalogue included eight lines of verse to accompany this picture, which began: 'The mind enamoured by some fancied tale, / Attention leads by magic force along...'

The theatricality of 'Attention' may have owed something to Henry Fuseli, who was perhaps the dominant individual among the artists working in London in the 1790s. Chinnery would surely have admired the eccentric, cosmopolitan Fuseli, who had lived in Rome and Venice, in Berlin and in Paris, where he had known Jean-Jacques Rousseau himself. Fuseli's enthusiasm for themes from Milton's *Paradise Lost* influenced a generation of painters, including Barry, Romney, Flaxman and Blake; in 1797 even the young Thomas Lawrence depicted 'Satan summoning his legions' on a canvas of 127 square feet, and three years later Chinnery likewise exhibited his 'Satan's arrival at the confines of light'.

Of course, Chinnery's portraits are far removed from the agonies and ecstasies which afflict Fuseli's muscular hero figures. Nevertheless Goethe's description of Fuseli as a 'mannerist'[30] could apply also to many of Chinnery's oil paintings. In his figures we repeatedly find wilful distortions of anatomy, exaggerated effects of light and shade, and dashes of violent colour which are displays of artifice, a kind of personal punctuation which expresses the character of the artist no less than that of his sitters.

When 'Attention' was shown to the public in Parliament House, an extra *frisson* was aroused by the gossip which the anonymous visitor heard and confided with relish to his journal:

> There is a likeness tho' very flattering between this portrait & that of
> Miss Vigne exhibited last year — it has occasioned some small talk for
> the timekillers while lolling on the forums at the exhibition — the lady
> is it seems an inmate of the same house, and being *admirably calculated*
> to inspire the tender passion. The enamoured artist has *painted* for
> love.[31]

Presumably the 'timekillers' were not aware that there were two Vigne sisters,
of whom the other was married to the artist. (If, on the other hand, they were
right — and Chinnery had indeed conceived a passion for his sister-in-law
Maria — the situation could account for his precipitate departure from
Dublin; but this is no more than speculation.)

Three months later, on 15 October 1801, the same journal writer attended a
dance at which he met 'the Messrs. Vignes, Jewellers of College Green &
beaus of the first water, to use a shop phrase in character'. He observed:

> 'Miss Vigne, otherwise 'Attention' viz the subject of Mr. Chinnery's
> picture with that title; she has a shining face, black eyes, not very
> genteel but without affectation of hauteur & not ill informed, as I
> gathered from a tête-a-tête at an interval of the dancing — a
> dissertation on the merits of Scotch & Irish music & of the dancing of
> different countries...'[32]

No mention is made of Mrs. Chinnery, who was no doubt at home with her
two small children, Matilda (who would have been a year old) and John
Eustace (aged one month). No mention, either, of the sociable George
Chinnery; had he perhaps left the country already?

In any case his reasons for leaving may not have been purely domestic. The
most bizarre suggestion is that he was 'compromised in the rebellious
movement of Lord Edward Fitzgerald, but was allowed to live in India and
China'.[33] It is difficult to envisage Chinnery as a cloak-and-dagger activist in
the republican cause; moreover, it was in 1798 that this abortive rising
occurred (and the popular hero Fitzgerald fatally wounded during his arrest),
whereas Chinnery remained in Ireland for three years more.

Indirectly, however, the failure of the nationalist uprising may well have
contributed to Chinnery's departure. In the aftermath of the attempted *coup
d'état*, which had been supported (albeit inadequately) by troops from
revolutionary France, the Government in London was able to abolish the Irish
Parliament. William Pitt promised stability, prosperity and (at first) Catholic
emancipation in return for the 'Union' of England with Ireland. The Irish
peers and Members of Parliament who were initially hostile were won over by
wholesale bribery. From 1 January 1801, the Irish people were represented
only at the English Parliament.

The effect on fashionable society in Dublin was considerable. The old
Parliament House on College Green, which had been a meeting place for
many of Dublin's most prominent figures, became the headquarters of the
Bank of Ireland. A minority of its former Members found employment at

Westminster, while others retired to the country, and their grand town houses were let out as lodgings. Membership of the Royal Dublin Society fell sharply. A contemporary caricature depicts a Dublin ballroom peopled only by the elderly and the idle. The eighty-two peers in the old Parliament were estimated to have spent £632,000 a year in Dublin;[34] now, as the rich departed, so did the prospects for hundreds of decorators and suppliers of luxury goods, including perhaps the Vignes, jewellers of College Green. For artists too, despite the activities of the Society of Artists of Ireland, it must have seemed that the once-glittering prospects of Dublin were now sadly dimmed.

Chinnery's contribution to the artistic life of Dublin did not go unrecognised. After the exhibition of 1801 he was awarded a silver palette, which has survived.[35] The engraved inscription reads: 'In Testimony of his Exertions in promoting the Fine Arts in Ireland, this Palette was presented to

*Plate 24. Figures by a sea wall. Pen and ink and watercolours, s. and d. 1801.* Victoria and Albert Museum

Mr. Geo. Chinnery by the ARTISTS of Dublin. July 27. 1801.'

There had been precedents for such a tribute — Martin Archer Shee had received a silver palette from the Royal Dublin Society in 1789 — but it was a rare honour. Possibly it was already known that Chinnery was leaving Ireland. There is nothing to suggest that the native Irish artists resented the intrusion of the energetic young man from London. One of them, William Cuming, paid him the compliment of painting a portrait in a manner very close to Chinnery's.[36] Another, John Comerford of Killarney, is said to have met Chinnery during a visit to southern Ireland, and to have been encouraged by Chinnery to come to Dublin: in 1802 he was staying with the Vignes on College Green.[37] Perhaps the jeweller and his wife gave lodging to Comerford in place of their recently-departed son-in-law.

By the age of twenty-eight Chinnery had achieved a degree of success in several styles and media. He was an accomplished miniature-painter in pen and watercolour on ivory or card, and he continued to portray winsome children and young ladies in gently sylvan settings (Colour Plate 4 and Plate 23). He had begun to paint topographical scenes in watercolour, although very few of these survive; his beach scene of 1801 (Plate 24), a weakly-drawn essay in the manner of Rowlandson, contains little sign of future genius. More promising is Plate 25, a portrait in crayons dated 25 August 1800, with Chinnery's characteristic instructions inscribed on the back: 'To be kept from damp & sun.' He has been credited with producing a series of lively female portraits, in gouache or a mixture of gouache with pastel, which appeared on the art market shortly before the First World War; but despite the flamboyant inscription 'G. Chinnery' on certain of these, their attribution to him must be regarded as dubious.[38] In his oil painting, above all, he had developed a broad, vigorous approach, and laid the foundation for a career as a portraitist.

Like many contemporary artists, Chinnery also tried his hand as a book illustrator. His drawings of scenes from Henry Fielding's *Amelia* can be dated to the years before his departure in 1802 for India, where there would have

*Plate 25. Portrait of a lady in a black shawl. Crayons.* Sean Galvin, Esq

been no prospect of publication. They are sketched in a casual, angular style, with figures posed a little stiffly against an impressionistic background, which is also to be seen in Chinnery's sketches made during his early years at Madras. His prison scene (Plate 26) from the first book of *Amelia*, depicts a young woman, convicted of stealing a loaf of bread, who supports her dying father, while the unjustly imprisoned Captain Booth (husband of Amelia) surveys them with pity and indignation. In Plate 27 Booth is seen riding off in his officer's uniform to join his regiment at Gibraltar; he pauses to look back at the house in which he has left his pregnant wife — a situation with which Chinnery may possibly have had some sympathy.

Chinnery's illustrations were never engraved, and indeed none of his sketches for *Amelia* are finished drawings fit for an engraver's use. The publishers of illustrated works at this period required detailed drawings of complex narrative scenes on a tiny scale, as demonstrated in the frontispieces to *Amelia* (and other works by Fielding) executed by Michael 'Angelo' Rooker, which were published by Cadell in 1783.[39] Chinnery's talents lay elsewhere.

In the months between his returning to England and his setting sail for India, Chinnery set himself up at 20 Brook Street, off Grosvenor Square; this, at least, is the address which he gave when submitting a portrait of his brother William's three children to the Royal Academy exhibition of 1802.[40] William himself wrote an ingratiating letter, which has recently come to light, to a member of the exhibition's Hanging Committee. Whether prompted by family pride or simply by a compulsion to exercise influence whenever possible, William Chinnery made a brazen attempt to prevail on the committee to favour his brother's portrait:

My Dear Sir,
You are I understand one of the three of the Council of the Royal Academy who are to have the Superintendence of placing the Pictures for the ensuing Exhibition, & I therefore venture to express an anxious wish to you about a single Picture painted by my Brother of my 3 Children; — it is the only Picture he has had time to paint since his return from Ireland, & it might therefore be very detrimental to his Pursuit in his Profession if it were to be placed in a bad Situation for View, especially as it [is] a large Picture, & I hope you will think worthy of a good one; — if therefore you could with perfect propriety stand his friend by arranging the thing so that the Picture in Question be placed in such a Situation as in your excellent Judgement may be most beneficial to his Interest, you will lay him & me under a great Obligation I assure you; — indeed the Object is so very material an one to him that I cannot avoid mentioning it anxiously to you, & will venture to trust to your friendship & kind Disposition on the Occasion, & that you will excuse the Trouble I give you.
Yours very truly<br>Wm. Chinnery

Treasury Chambers
April 10, 1802.[41]

It was in May 1802, while his pictures were on view both at the Royal Academy and in Dublin,[42] that Chinnery received permission (as the next chapter describes) to travel to India. On 2 June another artist left for India — Henry Salt, who had been working as an assistant to the portrait painter John Hoppner, and who now enjoyed the comfortable position of secretary-cum-draughtsman to Lord Valentia. At last on 11 June Chinnery himself, probably in less comfortable circumstances, sailed for the East on board the *Gilwell.*[43] It must have seemed to him a favourable omen that his ship bore the name of his prosperous brother's country house.

*Plate 26. Prison scene: illustration to Fielding's* Amelia. *Pencil and watercolours.* Yale Center for British Art, Paul Mellon Collection

*Plate 27. Captain Booth rides off to join his regiment: illustration to Fielding's* Amelia. *Pencil and watercolours.* Private collection

PART II:
# India — From Madras to Dacca

# CHAPTER 4
## *Madras*

To the enterprising artist India offered rich rewards — richer than Dublin, perhaps richer even than London — but the risks were correspondingly great. Illness, above all, was a constant threat to Europeans. The Prinsep family, with whom Chinnery was involved in various ways, was a typical case: of the seven Prinsep brothers who worked in India, four died prematurely, three of them in India and the fourth just after his return home. At the same period six Thackeray brothers came out to India; all of them died there, independently, at an average age of thirty-one.[1]

Chinnery himself suffered from many ailments, but as it turned out, his fifty years in the East far exceeded what he or anyone could have expected. In general British artists in India had a fair record of longevity. (Clergymen, by contrast, were a vulnerable species; as James Prinsep observed, 'there is something in the clerical life, or at least in the Episcopal, which prevents their standing our climate.'[2])

From a financial point of view, the artists who had preceded Chinnery in India had experienced mixed degrees of success. The pioneering Tilly Kettle (who worked in India from 1769 to 1776) and George Willison (in India from 1774 to 1780) both returned to England comfortably wealthy. Johann Zoffany's six years in India (1783-89) had also proved lucrative. On the other hand neither Thomas Hickey (despite his long residence), nor Ozias Humphry, nor A.W. Devis had prospered conspicuously in India; despite his stylishness and charm, Devis had returned to England with a newly-married wife and no money at all.[3]

Worse still was the case of John Alefounder, who arranged illicitly to sail to India, arriving in 1785 with neither introductions nor any great ability. As a contemporary guidebook explained, 'nothing can be more forlorn than the station of a mere adventurer, on his arrival in India. With money in his pocket, he may assuredly subsist; but without some friend to introduce him into society, he may remain for years without being noticed.'[4] This was exactly Alefounder's fate, and for an artist, 'to be noticed' was essential. More than once he tried to hang himself, but was cut down just in time. Eventually the miserable artist managed to kill himself with a penknife, in Calcutta on Christmas Day 1794.[5]

Chinnery was evidently not deterred by such stories, nor by the prospect of an uncongenial climate and an interrupted family life. But there were official obstacles also. The East India Company maintained strict control over personnel bound for India: every European resident in India was required to hold a licence from the Company, a licence which could be cancelled and which was not easy to obtain in the first place. Those who travelled out on an East Indiaman were generally employed either in the military or in the civil service of the East India Company; if the latter, they were often obliged to pay extravagant sums for their passage, in the expectation of even greater rewards when they arrived. To go out in any other capacity, such as 'free merchant' or 'painter', required the specific permission of the Directors of the Company. If the applicant could present a strong case and influential sponsors, he (or, much less commonly, she) might be granted leave to travel; he had then to strike his own bargain with a ship's captain.

The Court of Directors was inclined to believe, reasonably enough, that British India could support only a limited number of artists. In September 1784, when giving permission for John Smart and Ozias Humphry to travel out to work as painters, they resolved at the same time that no further artists should be allowed to follow them that season.[6] In 1802, when Chinnery applied to go to India, the situation was favourable: the two most talented European artists to have practised in India, Johann Zoffany and A.W.Devis, had both returned to England, and although Zoffany had been granted leave on 2 March 1798 to go out again for a further period, he was persuaded to spend his last years in Britain.[7] John Smart, the ablest miniature painter to visit India, had returned in 1795. Chinnery's principal competitors consisted of Thomas Hickey in Madras and Robert Home in Calcutta, but both were now elderly men.

One of Chinnery's immediate predecessors in the voyage to India was the miniature painter Edward Nash, who left Portsmouth on 9 January 1801 for Bombay, where he remained until his return to England in 1810. Bombay had the reputation of being a particularly unhealthy place for Europeans, and at this date the city had not attracted wealthy Englishmen to the same extent as had Madras and Calcutta. One of the few British artists who had attempted to work there was James Wales, who made a valuable series of drawings of the cave temples nearby, but died in 1795 of a fever which was attributed to the putrid air he had inhaled in the caves. There is no evidence that Chinnery, adventurous as he was in many respects, ever paid a visit to Bombay.

It was on 12 May 1802 that the Court of Directors of the East India Company, nineteen strong, considered the petition of George Chinnery for 'leave to proceed to Madras to follow his profession as a Portrait Painter'. The Court minutes contain a laconic record: 'It was moved that "Mr Chinnery's Application be complied with". And the question upon that motion being put to the Court, It passed in the negative.'[8]

No reason is given for this refusal. A week later the Court heard another letter from Chinnery asking that his case be reconsidered. He begged leave to proceed to Madras 'to follow his profession as a Painter, which he again begs to assure the Court is the sole motive for his wish to go to India'.[9] Some manoeuvring must have taken place behind the scenes, for on this occasion the Court gave its permission for Chinnery to travel out, making it clear that he was to work as a 'Painter'. Perhaps the Directors suspected that he was using the profession of artist as a pretext for joining his brother John in his business enterprises.[10]

Neither of Chinnery's applications referred to his wife. It would not have been impossible in principle for his dependants to have accompanied him;

when Thomas Hickey had sailed for Madras four years before, he had taken his two daughters with him.[11] But the majority of men who sailed to India were unmarried, and in the minority of cases in which married men made the journey, it was common practice for their wife and children to follow at a later date — although few had to wait for as long as sixteen years, which was the fate of Marianne Chinnery. A British wife in India was regarded as an expensive luxury:

> No lady can be landed there under respectable circumstances throughout, for less than five hundred pounds...Such is the encrease of domestics, of cloathing, of accommodation, and, particularly, in keeping a carriage, without which no comfort can be expected, that it is utterly beyond the means of full four persons in five to receive an European lady into their houses.[12]

European women were thus in short supply in India, there being fewer than 250 of them in Bengal and its dependencies in 1810, whereas there were some 4,000 European 'men of respectability, including military officers'.[13] It was only in the 1840s, after the institution of the 'overland route' through Egypt had made the journey to India a more attractive prospect, that young women were sent out in quantity from Britain to find husbands. When Chinnery arrived in India, a young expatriate was more likely to live with one or more Indian *bibis* than with a British wife. Many of his sitters, leading figures of British society in India, had children of mixed race; even Sir Charles Metcalfe, who became Governor-General in 1835, lived for many years with an Indian consort, who bore him three sons. Chinnery himself had two illegitimate sons by an unidentified Indian mistress (see pp. 153-4 ).

Even for a bachelor the cost of living was high. The minimum necessary for a man setting up in Calcutta, who was not in the service of the East India Company, was estimated at £600, which would cover rent, furnishings, servants, horse, and table expenses. In Madras costs were rather lower, but nevertheless daunting. Since furnished lettings were unknown, the new arrival had to furnish his house from scratch, and in a socially competitive atmosphere, many felt obliged to spend lavishly; William Hickey stated that he had equipped his house very handsomely 'at an expense of upwards of twelve thousand rupees, including plate'[14] (eight to ten rupees were then the equivalent of a pound). On the other hand, this demand for furnishings could operate to an artist's advantage, for a well-judged painting could help to confer upon a Calcutta dining room the prestige which was so strongly desired.

Social position was a matter of particular significance to any British artist in India. As an artist Chinnery would have been one of a small group of professional men whose status was not clearly determined, since they belonged neither to the military nor to the civil sectors of the East India Company, nor again to the independent community of merchants. During Chinnery's years in India, British society became increasingly stratified, and also increasingly exclusive of Indians. With a few striking exceptions, the British in India became less interested in Indian culture, while self-consciously celebrating their own; 'Every Briton seems to pride himself on being outrageously John Bull', observed Mrs. Maria Graham in 1810.[15]

This was true above all of the army officers, who tended to cultivate an ethos of hard-drinking, nationalistic philistinism, and to regard themselves as superior to all civilians. On the other hand, as a disaffected ex-soldier wrote, 'civilians have some undeniable advantages over officers of the service. They come out on average three years later, mix more in women's society, and what brains they have are not allowed to die utterly unemployed.'[16] The mutual antipathy between the two camps is clearly expressed in the letters written by the versatile James Prinsep, numismatist, linguist, musician, architect and chemist. Although a companionable man, Prinsep would not share his house at Benares with an officer 'on account of the continual lounging visitors'. Later at Lucknow he reported the reaction of a young officer to a copy of the *Asiatic Journal,* of which Prinsep was editor. 'Turning over the pages with a curled lip he hurled the yellow pamphlet across the room with a summary critique: "d——d nonsense".'[17]

Chinnery's natural associates were thus the civil servants, the doctors, lawyers and architects, who preserved such European culture as existed in British India, and supported the concerts, the theatrical events and the sketching clubs; Sir Charles D'Oyly (see Chapter 6) and the members of the Prinsep family come immediately to mind. However, Chinnery was a particularly sociable individual, and this was undoubtedly of benefit to his portrait practice, just as the careers in India of Thomas Hickey and A.W.Devis had been assisted by their genial temperament and popularity. Chinnery appears to have mixed as readily with soldiers as with civilians, and perhaps better still with their wives. He described the parties given by Mrs. Maria Browne, wife of Major Browne of the Royal Artillery, as 'without exception the pleasantest parties I go to'.[18] Taken as a group, his male portraits represent a cross-section of the different walks of Anglo-Indian life: middle-ranking civil servants and young officers painted during his early years in Madras, supplemented in Bengal by the wealthier merchants, judges, missionaries, generals, and governors-general.

**The Voyage to Madras**

Chinnery's voyage to India was long and probably tedious. The *Gilwell,* in which he sailed, must even then have seemed a perilously small vessel in which to undertake so great a voyage. She was a 400-ton ship of 17 feet draft, carrying eight 9-pounder guns and two 12-pounders.[19] The *Gilwell* had been built in India in 1800 for the firm of Law & Co., perhaps to take advantage of the recent lifting of the ban which had prevented Indian-built ships from trading at British ports. She was classed as an 'Extra Ship'[20] — that is, an East Indiaman of reduced size, which carried fewer men than the regular ships, and a smaller quantity of the 'privilege stores' allowed to officers; thus 'Extra Ships' were more profitable as transporters of cargo.

From a passenger's point of view, however, they left much to be desired. Because many of them had their guns below decks, they were obliged to keep their gunports closed when on the high seas, which left them defenceless.

*Plate 28. Masula boats and catamaran at Madras. Pen and ink and wash.* India Office Library

*Plate 29. Masula boat and catamarans in the surf, Madras. Oils.* Private collection

Some of them, a contemporary observed, 'have more the form of chests than ships, and detain every thing they are in company with.'[21] The voyage of the *Gilwell*, under the command of Captain Sheen, was indeed a slow one. Too late in the year to avoid the adverse north-east monsoon in the Indian Ocean, she was at sea for six and a half months, including a stop at Madeira; earlier in the year a four-month voyage might have been expected. On 21 December 1802 Chinnery at last reached Madras, accompanied by only two other passengers, who are listed as William Hall and M. Scott Moore. They disembarked at last on 21 December 1802.[22]

Arriving at Madras was a rude introduction to India. Since the city had no deep-water harbour, passengers were brought inshore on small boats, and then carried to dry land either in chairs or on the backs of the boatmen. Chinnery made several studies of these flat-bottomed masula boats, which were made from planks of mango wood sewn together with coconut fibres (Plates 28 and 29). As he observed in the text to his etching of the subject, 'to all appearance, any other kind of Vessel would be safer on the water; on the contrary no Boat of any other kind dare venture over the violent Surf.' The long oars seen in his drawing served as rudders held over the stern by the steersman: 'the Dexterity with which he balances himself in the heavy sea is perfectly astonishing.'[23]

Although travellers wrote of 'the dreaded surf', landing by masula boat was not as dangerous as it appeared, thanks to the flexibility of the craft and the skill of the boatmen, who were offered premiums for saving endangered Europeans. But no insurance could be obtained during the western monsoon season at the end of the year; if the flag on the flagstaff at Fort St. George was lowered, as it may well have been when Chinnery arrived on the *Gilwell*, this signalled to approaching ships that if they landed passengers or cargo, it was at their own risk.[24]

The narrow rafts seen in Chinnery's views of the Madras surf are catamarans, the original craft to be so called, which consisted of two (sometimes three or four) logs lashed together. They are given pride of place in his oil painting (Plate 29), their upswept lines emphasised by the dramatised curves of beach and breakers, while the boatmen launch themselves into the waves. Catamarans were particularly suited to stormy weather. It was customary for them to follow the masula boats in case of accident; alternatively they rode the surf in conditions which were too rough even for the masula boats. Their boatmen carried messages in their headgear, made of waxed cloth folded into a conical shape, out to the ships in the roads. When several catamarans were tied together they could transport heavy loads ashore, such as anchors or cannon.

Chinnery's etching of Fort St. George (Plate 30) presents the view as seen by the passenger who had at last reached dry land. A canopied bullock cart waits to carry him to his residence. This would be either in the Fort itself — the headquarters of a victorious army 60,000 strong, which, since the defeat of Tipu Sultan on 4 May 1799, held sway over a large area of Southern India; or in Black Town (renamed Georgetown in the twentieth century), which lay just to the north of the Fort, and was the residence of a number of British and Portuguese merchants, despite its reputation as a place infested with mosquitoes, rats, cockroaches, scorpions, and 'that most loathsome companion, the bug';[25] or else in one of the spacious 'garden houses' beyond the Fort along the Mount Road beyond the Cooum River, where the wealthier British could live in temperatures a few degrees cooler than those experienced within the walls of the crowded Fort. George Chinnery himself was probably able to lodge in conditions of reasonable comfort, since he had the great advantage of a brother — John Terry Chinnery — who was firmly ensconced in the Anglo-Indian community of Madras.

## John Terry Chinnery

Four years older than George, John Terry Chinnery had been appointed to the East India Company's civil service on 1 August 1792, at the age of twenty-two.[26] He may have owed his apppointment to the powerful connections of his elder brother William; such positions depended upon patronage, and were keenly sought after, as they offered the recipients not simply salaries but (in effect) licences to enrich themselves.

John Chinnery's career was typical enough. His first employment carried the intriguing title of 'Assistant under the Secretary in the Secret, Political and Military Department' (the 'Secret Committee' was chiefly concerned with information which affected the safety of shipping). In 1793 he moved down the coast to Cuddalore, as Assistant under the Resident and then, in 1796, as Deputy Commercial Resident. In 1800 he appears in the *Madras Almanac* as Collector in Colombo; finally in 1812 he is recorded as Commercial Resident in the Northern Division of Arcot. As a Commercial Resident he was allowed to trade on his own behalf; moreover, he was allowed a proportion of the investment which he provided for the Company, and for this reason a Commercial Resident's salary was set at a low level (500 rupees a month in 1805).[27] This entailed substantial rewards, but also risks, since his income depended to a high degree on the success or failure of the commodity in which he invested the Company's money.

For a number of years, including the period during which he was joined by his brother George, John Chinnery was listed as 'out of employ'. This was not by any means a disaster. In addition to the small allowance which the Company made to all its civil servants who were not occupying specific posts, it meant that he could devote himself to his own business interests. In the *East India Register* for 1803 John Chinnery appears as a Director of the Madras Bank, and a partner in the agency house of Chase, Chinnery & Macdowell. John Macdowell, who had been appointed to the service on the same day as John Chinnery, was in fact at home in England in the years 1802-6, leaving John Chinnery and Thomas Chase, a man of twelve years' seniority to his partners, to continue the agency's business in India.[28]

John Chinnery is listed also as Treasurer of the Male Asylum, a position of social rather than financial significance; his wife was likewise a Directress of the Female Asylum, together with the wives of several prominent men in Madras.[29] Most of the pupils of these charitable schools were the children of British fathers and Indian mothers. The graduates of the Female Asylum were

*Plate 30. Fort St. George, Madras. Etching, 1806.* Private collection

in strong demand as wives of Company officers, both military and civil; the children of such marriages were regarded as 75 per cent European, and were thus eligible for service in the Company.[30]

In the registers for 1806 John Chinnery's agency no longer appears, but by now he was Secretary of the New Madras Insurance Company, a post which in the previous year had been held by Thomas Chase. The names of Chinnery, Chase and others appear and reappear, constantly reshuffled, in the posts and committees listed in succeeding volumes of the *East India Register* and the *Madras Almanac;* all these civil servants were enriching themselves from as many different sources as possible. Thomas Chase was for a time earning £550 per year for his Government posts, and a further £4,000 per year as a banker and merchant.[31] One of his interests was shipowning; 'Chase & Co.', presumably including John Chinnery, owned several vessels in the early years of the century.

In 1805, the first year in which Madras merchant vessels are recorded in the *East India Registers*, Chase & Company are shown as the owners of four ships: the *Marquess of Wellesley*, the snow *Harington*, the *Matilda*, and the *Gilwell*. John Chinnery may well have been involved in the financing of these Madras-based ships, and perhaps invested on behalf of his prosperous brother William; it can be no coincidence that Matilda was the name of John Chinnery's eldest daughter (who was born in 1797 and sent back to England at the age of two), nor that Gilwell was the name of William's country house. As part-owner of the *Gilwell*, John Chinnery would have facilitated the passage of his brother George to India on the same ship. Harington was the name of a senior merchant at Madras, William Harington, who may also have been involved in the scheme; and the *Marquess of Wellesley*, loyally named after the Governor-General (who had received his marquisate in 1799), was the ship in which Mrs. John Chinnery, and four of the artist's nieces and nephews, travelled home to England in March 1805.[32]

A letter in the Jardine, Matheson archive reveals that the *Marquess of Wellesley* also carried, on behalf of John Chinnery, a consignment of particular value to

his brother: five cases of picture frames. These were dispatched from Canton on 25 December 1804, following an order placed by Captain Sheen in the previous season. The bill amounted to 1693 Spanish dollars (about £340), debited to Messrs. Chase, Chinnery & McDouall.[33] In Canton carved picture frames — as well as paintings and many other artefacts — were skilfully fashioned to suit western tastes; John Chinnery's order indicates that many of the pictures produced by his brother in India were placed in Chinese frames.

### Personalities of Madras

Clearly John Chinnery was in a strong position to introduce his brother George to potential clients. In 1803 the name of 'George Chinnery, Portrait Painter' first appears in the annual manuscript lists of non-official European inhabitants of Madras.[34] In the printed volumes of the *East India Register*, which were generally a year or two out of date, he is first listed in 1804, with the description 'out of employ', but in fact he had already undertaken a number of useful portrait commissions, several of them from colleagues (or wives of colleagues) of his brother.

One of these was Robert Sherson, who was three places junior to John Chinnery in the roll of 'covenanted civil servants on the Fort St. George establishment'; when George Chinnery arrived, Sherson was Deputy Collector of Government Customs, and in 1807 he became Joint Assay Master.[35] Chinnery painted a large and flattering[36] miniature portrait, dated 1803, of Mrs. Sherson in a high-waisted, décolleté dress (Plate 31); the background is a mottled pattern in shades of blue and grey, abstract but reminiscent of a stormy sky. Similar mottled backgrounds appear in some of Cosway's work, and another can be seen in Chinnery's miniature of the same year, depicting two girls beside a large urn (Colour Plate 5). 'To be kept from Damp and *Sun*', the artist has instructed beneath his signature on the reverse.

A high proportion of Chinnery's Madras portraits were in miniature, a

format which, for the expatriate, had the great appeal of portability. A miniature could be sent home without the trouble and expense of customs clearance, and preserved (if the artist's instructions were followed) from the extremes of climate. It could be embraced, literally, by relatives and lovers divided by ten thousand miles from the object of their affections; in the words of Sir Charles D'Oyly, they might '...Press the cold iv'ry to their hearts, and raise / The image of their lost one to their arms'.[37]

Chinnery also began to develop his talents as an oil painter. Colour Plate 6 is a watercolour study for a group portrait in oils, from Chinnery's initial years in Madras (a related sketch is dated 27 December 1804), but there is no record of the finished painting. Two early oils which have survived are the three-quarter length portraits of Mr. and Mrs. Hugh Lord. The Welsh-born Hugh Lord had entered the East India Company's service in 1796, four years after John Terry Chinnery, and was appointed Commercial Resident at Amboyna in January 1802, proceeding through the customary succession of civil and judicial appointments. In each of Chinnery's portraits of the Lords, an illuminated figure is set against a dark background relieved by glimmering traces of sunset. Hugh Lord stands with his arm upraised;[38] Lucy Lord (Colour Plate 9), her eyes heavily shadowed, stares intently at the spectator in the dramatic manner of a supernatural heroine presented by Fuseli or Romney. The portrait of Mrs. Lord in particular suggests the influence of the early works of Sir Thomas Lawrence, the rising star of Chinnery's student years, who between 1790 and the very early 1800s painted a number of portraits of men and women who accost the viewer with wide eyes, solemn mouth and challengingly direct gaze.[39]

By contrast the portrait of Charles May Lushington (Plate 32), dated 1803, is a closely-studied pencil drawing. The manner of this, and of numerous other portrait drawings executed by Chinnery during his years in India, follows the example of the London artist Henry Edridge, who was six years older than Chinnery. In Edridge's pencil portraits the face alone is painted with

*Plate 33. Lieutenant Fleetwood Pellew. Pencil and watercolours.* National Maritime Museum, Greenwich

*Plate 34. Rev. Richard Hall Kerr. Engraving by William Skelton after Chinnery.* British Museum

watercolour, or sometimes the face and hands, and the rest of the figure and the surroundings are precisely outlined and shaded in pencil. In the portrait of Charles Lushington the head is likewise coloured in Chinnery's miniature technique, while the tone of the remainder is built up of pencil shading in parallel lines of varying density. The sitter came from a distinguished Anglo-Indian family: one Lushington survived the 'Black Hole', another (the father of Charles) was Chairman of the East India Company, and a third (a brother of Charles) became Governor of Madras. Like most of Chinnery's sitters in these early years at Madras, Charles Lushington was a young man freshly out from England; he went on to make his career in the judicial service, retired from Bengal in 1827 and died in Brighton.

Madras was a garrison town, and several of its officers were portrayed by Chinnery. One of his miniatures of 1803 depicts a dignified soldier known as 'Colonel [*sic*] Armstrong' (Colour Plate 7),[40] but there seems to have been no one answering to this description at Madras during Chinnery's years there. Possibly the miniature represents Major Charles Armstrong, who was Military Secretary to the Governor-General in 1804. Major Armstrong had the misfortune to be passing through Vellore in his palanquin on 10 July 1806, the day on which a serious mutiny broke out in the town. The mutiny led to the death of Armstrong, and the recall of the Governor, Lord William Bentinck.

Another watercolour portrait of Chinnery's Madras years is that of Lieutenant-Colonel William Ormsby (Colour Plate 8), who was a military cadet at the time of Chinnery's arrival in Madras. Ormsby followed a career in the Company's army, becoming (as a Major) Superintendent of Police. He is pictured here as a young man in civilian dress. Chinnery's handling of his cravat and waistcoat is similar to that of many of his subsequent portraits in oils; but he has not added the dashes of red and blue which he was later to apply so freely.

One of the most distinguished naval officers to visit Madras was Edward Pellew, 1st Viscount Exmouth, who was renowned as an inspiring and humane commander. In April 1804 he was appointed Rear-Admiral and Commander-in-Chief in the East Indies, where one of his measures was to arrange that the Calcutta merchants' ships should sail in convoy, in order to reduce losses at the hands of the French. Chinnery may have drawn a portrait of Edward Pellew,[41] and he certainly portrayed his second son Fleetwood (Plate 33), who served under his father on the East India station between 1805 and 1812. The younger Pellew is depicted as a seventeen-year-old in action at Batavia, urging on his men (represented by a nervous-loking seaman) in the boat assault of 1806. Many years later Fleetwood Pellew was to return to the East as Commander-in-Chief on the East Indies and China station. He was recalled, however, after refusing to allow his men shore leave in Hong Kong.

No less active in his own sphere was Richard Hall Kerr, who began his career in Madras running a school for 'the better class Europeans and Eurasians' in Black Town. He then became a chaplain, at a time when chaplains were accepted only grudgingly by the Company (for many years the Directors were obliged by law to send out a chaplain with every ship of 500 tons and over; they took care to build ships of 499 tons, to avoid the expense).[42] Kerr made himself useful to the Company, however, by setting up a printing press in the Male Asylum, of which he was Superintendent.[43]

Encouraged by the growing evangelical movement in England, Kerr campaigned for more chaplains to be sent to India, for a 'native workhouse', and for free schools at which Indians should learn Christian principles and 'British virtue'.[44] He was also responsible for the building of the first church in Black Town. He aroused some opposition, and quarrelled in particular with Charles Ball, his fellow-chaplain, complaining that Ball treated him with 'gross rudeness'. But Kerr had a powerful ally in the Governor, and Ball was sent off to Trichinopoly.

Kerr died 'of exhaustion of mind and body' in 1808; in the following year his engraved portrait was published, after an original by Chinnery (Plate 34). His success in Madras signified the ending of a relatively tolerant, *laissez-faire* attitude towards Indian religious and cultural life, and a new zeal for imposing Christianity upon the Indians. At the beginning of the century there had been five chaplains in south-west India; by 1819 there were twenty-three.[45]

## The Kirkpatrick Children

One of the few full-length portraits to survive from Chinnery's early years, and one of the most memorable of his entire career, is the exotic portrait of the Kirkpatrick children (Colour Plate 12). At first sight it appears that these are English children dressed for a fancy-dress ball, but the gold-fringed Indian robes have a greater significance.

The boy and his younger sister were William and Katherine Aurora, children of Colonel James Achilles Kirkpatrick and his Indo-Persian wife. Kirkpatrick was an extraordinary individual. After serving as translator to the Nizam of Hyderabad, he succeeded his brother in 1797 as Resident to the Hyderabad court. He established a close relatonship with the Nizam, who formally accepted him as his adopted son; and he married Khairunnissa, the fourteen-year-old great-niece of the Nizam's chief minister, Mir Alam. In 1801 he was described by a British visitor to the court:

> Major Kirkpatrick is a good-looking man...he wears mustachios; his hair is cropped short, and his fingers are dyed with henna. In other respects he is like an Englishman...[At the durbar] he goes in great state. He has several elephants, and a state palankeen, led horses, flags, long poles with tassels, &c., and is attended by two companies of infantry and a troop of cavalry...Major Kirkpatrick behaved like a native, and with great propriety.[46]

He became extremely wealthy, and had a palatial Residency built for him in the Palladian style, with separate quarters for his wife and her *zenana*. Since she did not enter the main Residency, a large-scale model of it was erected for her in 'the Begum's Garden'.

Kirkpatrick's actions brought him enemies among the British, who accused him of bribery and abjuring his religion, but he proved too valuable an asset to be convicted. Together with Mir Alam, he persuaded the Nizam to transfer his allegiance from the French to the British side: in a bloodless coup, 14,000 French-trained sepoys surrendered, and the last stronghold of French influence in Southern India was eliminated.

James Kirkpatrick and Khairunnissa had two children, of whom the younger, Katherine Aurora — generally known as Kitty — is known to have been born in 1802. Chinnery probably painted their portrait in 1805, since on 10 September of that year the two children left Madras for England. (It was a common practice at that time for parents to send their children back to be educated in Britain, where they were more likely to live until adulthood; Chinnery's nephew and three nieces had been sent home only six months before.) As frequently happened, William and Kitty did not see their parents again. Their father died only a month after their ship, the *Hawkesbury*, sailed. By coincidence George Elers, who had come out to India on the same ship as George Chinnery's sister Frances, was returning on the ship which brought the Kirkpatrick children home. Elers described them in his condescending manner:

> A Mrs Ure, the wife of a Dr Ure of Hyderabad, [who] had two fine children of three and four years under her charge, the children of Colonel Kirkpatrick, of Hyderabad, by a Princess, to whom report said he was married. Her Highness would not part with her children until £10,000 had been settled upon each of them. They were a boy and a girl, and they had a faithful old black man, who was very fond of them, to attend upon them...It was my fortune to have this black and white party consigned to my care on landing in England.[47]

When the *Hawkesbury* arrived at Portsmouth, Elers's talents proved useful. He had learned that Mrs. Ure's luggage contained quantities of jewels and fine shawls, presumably belonging to the Kirkpatrick children. In order to prevent the customs from inspecting these, Elers placed a massive bribe of twenty guineas (which Mrs. Ure had given him) in the hand of a customs official, who duly passed the treasure-laden trunks unopened.[48]

Kitty Kirkpatrick grew up in England, and achieved a celebrity of her own through her association with Thomas Carlyle. She first met Carlyle in 1824, when the awkward young literary genius was newly arrived in London from Edinburgh; he was captivated by this 'strangely complexioned young lady with soft brown eyes and floods of *bronze*-red hair, really a pretty looking, smiling, and amiable, though most foreign bit of magnificence...';[49] the bronze-red hair, and perhaps the strange complexion, can be seen in the portrait. A little later he caught sight of her among the roses in the garden of her cousins' country home at Shooters' Hill — a vision which contributed to the character of Blumine, 'the Rose-Goddess', in Carlyle's perplexing book *Sartor Resartus*. Blumine is 'many-tinted, radiant Aurora', and 'the fairest of Orient Light-bringers'.[50] Carlyle escorted Kitty to Paris, together with her married cousin, and although he already had an understanding with Jane Welsh, whom he was to marry, he continued to enjoy the company of Kitty, and to tease Jane with references to the fortune of £50,000 which Kitty had inherited. But there was no serious prospect of Kitty's marrying him. Instead she married Captain James Winsloe-Phillips of the 7th Hussars. Carlyle later wrote of her dismissively in his *Reminiscences*, perhaps with a trace of jealous resentment:

> Amiable, affectionate, graceful, might be called attractive (not *slim* enough for the title 'pretty', not tall enough for 'beautiful'); had something low-voiced, languidly harmonious; placid, sensuous, loved perfumes &c; a half-Begum in short; interesting specimen of the Semi-Oriental Englishwoman. Still lives, near Exeter (the prize of some idle ex-Captain of Sepoys), with many children, whom she looks after with a passionate interest.[51]

Meanwhile the portrait had also came to England. After James Kirkpatrick's death, his former under-secretary Henry Russell, who was shortly to become Resident of Hyderabad himself, arranged for the picture to be sent to Khairunnissa, who had moved to Masulipatam. In some way the painting subsequently entered Russell's own possession, and it was hung on the walls of Swallowfield, the Berkshire house to which the Russells eventually retired. In 1846 Swallowfield was visited by Kitty Phillips, as she now was; Kitty 'shed floods of tears' when she recognised the portrait of herself and her brother (who had died in 1828). The elderly Sir Henry Russell was moved to leave Kitty the portrait in his will, despite protests from his family; it thus passed to Kitty and her descendants, before finding its way back to the East in the 1950s.[52]

It seems that when Kitty saw the painting at Swallowfield, she also observed that 'the staircase was the entrance to her beautiful home in India.'[53] If this last detail was rightly remembered by Kitty (and correctly reported by Lady

*Plate 35. The Banqueting Hall and Government House, Madras. Pencil, dated 21 Oct. 1806.* Private collection

*Plate 36. Women taking water at a well. Etching, 1806.* Private collection

*Plate 37. St. Mary's Church, Madras. Pencil, pen and ink, and watercolours.* Private collection

*Colour Plate 5. Two girls by a decorated urn. Watercolours. A version of this picture in oils on ivory (Hongkong and Shanghai Banking Corporation) is dated by Chinnery '1803'.* Martyn Gregory Gallery

*Colour Plate 6. Study for a portrait group. Watercolours.* Private collection

Russell), it would suggest that Chinnery had travelled up to Hyderabad to paint the portrait. But Kitty had not seen India since the age of three, and the patterned carpet in the picture does not suggest the Residency entrance; so it is more likely that the children were painted by Chinnery in Madras, a few weeks before they took ship.

### The 'Grecian City'

When the artist William Hodges had come to Madras in 1781, the place had put him in mind of 'a Grecian city in the age of Alexander'.[54] He was referring of course to the small proportion of Madras in which the British had erected buildings in the classical style. By the time of Chinnery's arrival in 1802 the classical impression must have been even more striking, for within the last two years Madras had been furnished with a group of majestic government buildings, complete with columns, pediments and friezes, which had been commissioned by the Governor, the 2nd Lord Clive. The East India Company's Directors disapproved of this expensive exhibition on the part of the Governor, and recalled him, but the new buildings and their imperial symbolism remained for all to see.

Chinnery's drawing of 1806 (Plate 35) shows the new Banqueting Hall, which had been inaugurated with a grand ball only two months before his arrival. The north and south pediments were ornamented with trophies commemorating the British victories at Plassey and Seringapatam; these were to be replaced in the twentieth century by the coat-of-arms of the Republic of India. Inside the Banqueting Hall was a series of portraits of commanders-in-chief and governors, including Eyre Coote, Cornwallis and Wellesley. These

*Plate 38. Street scene, Madras. Pencil, pen and ink, and watercolours, with scratching out.* Private collection

portraits — most of which were repainted by Thomas Hickey after Chinnery had moved on to Calcutta — performed much the same symbolic function as the trophies outside; and once Chinnery was firmly established in India, he was able to profit by the continuing demand for such symbols of British dominion.

If the public architecture of Madras was classical in form, then so — in Chinnery's eyes — were some of the native inhabitants. In the text which acompanied his etching of a trio of women taking water at a well (Plate 36), Chinnery referred to 'their Persons being often of a very fine shape...the simplicity of the dress they wear, and the style in which this is put on, give a great similarity of appearance in them to the Antique Figures...' The male Indian figures who appear in Chinnery's drawings of this period also have the air of Grecian heroes: his masula boatmen are mesomorphic and muscular (Plates 28-30), and some of their poses might have been derived from the casts in the Royal Academy. The proportions of his palanquin bearers (Plate 42), however, are clearly not classical, for the length of their sinewy limbs is exaggerated; nor are they caricatures, but possess a dignity and individuality which is rarely seen in other western drawings of Indians at this date.

Adjacent to the neoclassical buildings of Fort St. George was the remarkable church of St. Mary's, consecrated in 1680, the earliest Anglican church in the East (Plate 37). Built within the Fort, it was a soldier's church from the first: its designer was probably a master gunner, and the walls and roofs were constructed of solid masonry, to withstand bombardment as well as the equally destructive white ants. On several occasions during the wars against the French and Hyder Ali, St. Mary's was used as a store for water or grain. The steeple served as a lookout, until damage inflicted by French gunfire caused the steeple and tower to be dismantled. In the 1790s it was proposed that a new spire should be erected which could also be used as a lighthouse, but this scheme was rejected as irreligious, and in 1795 the church received a spire in the form of a fluted obelisk, which can be seen in Chinnery's drawing.[55]

*Plate 39. Temple and tank, Madras (perhaps the Kapaleshvara Temple in Mylapore). Pencil and pen and ink.* Private collection

It is clear from Chinnery's drawings and sketches in Madras that his draughtsman's technique was not yet settled. A number of his drawings of this period are executed in an abbreviated, angular manner which he abandoned soon afterwards (Colour Plates 10 and 11, and Plates 38, 39 and 40). In these rapid watercolours a kind of pictorial code is in operation: small spots of dark ink or watercolour are used to denote apertures in buildings (Colour Plate 10) or heads in a distant crowd (Plate 40); sometimes these spots have no representative function at all. Small horizontal lines may indicate tiling or brickwork, and trees are formed from summary dashings and dabbings with a

*Plate 40. The East India Company's 'Town Temple', Madras. Pencil, pen and ink, and watercolours.* Private collection

*Colour Plate 7. Miniature portrait of 'Colonel Armstrong'. Pencil and watercolours, s. and d. 1803.* Private collection

*Colour Plate 8. Lieutenant-Colonel William Ormsby. Watercolours.* Malcom and Ursula Horsman

*Colour Plate 9. Mrs. Lucy Lord (née Gahagan). Oils.* Martyn Gregory Gallery

wet brush. Where human faces are sketched on a small scale, they are sometimes marked by a sharp angle for the nose or chin, a short angled line to suggest eyes and eyebrows, and a dot or two for the other facial features. Indian faces are generally denoted by a hint of drooping moustache, and a couple of flat overlapping ovals to indicate a turban. The two races are distinguished more clearly still when watercolour is added — pink and white for European faces, light brown for Indian.

Employing his abbreviated style, Chinnery sketched the Hindu and Mohammedan architecture of the city and its environs, visiting the Dravidian *gopurams* of Tiruvarur to the west and the temples of Mahabalipuram (Colour Plate 11) to the south. Plate 40 depicts 'The Entrance to the Honorable Company's pagoda, Black Town' (1805), in which the crowd of Indian figures contrasts with the sparsely-populated classical clarity of Fort St. George half a mile away (Plate 30). The building depicted is the so-called 'Gentoo Pagoda' or 'Town Temple', a Hindu temple which was managed by the East India Company and supported by import and export taxes levied on all but Europeans and Armenians.

## The Palanquin

At the same time, Chinnery was experimenting with the more fluid and more disciplined style which he was to develop in Bengal and China. This process is illustrated in his drawings of palanquin bearers (Plates 41 and 42 and Colour Plate 13). In the quick sketch of 5 September 1805 (Plate 41), the bearers are token figures, squat and ill-proportioned, serving only to illustrate the means by which the lolling Englishman is transported. In the pen-and-ink sketch of bearers at rest (Plate 42), the purposeful curves of the figures' backs and legs introduce an element of dynamism and drama to the composition; and in the finished watercolour of 1806 (Colour Plate 13), the powerful, sweeping curves, drawn with great confidence, transform the bearers — not perhaps into individual personalities, but certainly into sinewy figures full of dignity and latent energy.

The palanquin, or palankeen, or palki (a dozen other spellings were current) was used by Europeans in India from an early date. In its original form it was little more than a cot slung from a bamboo pole, and was better known as a *dhooly* or *doolie*. Doolies were also widely used as stretchers, to carry away soldiers wounded in battle; one over-enthusiastic Member of Parliament, misunderstanding a report from India, is said to have passed on a story that after an engagement, the helpless wounded had been swept away by 'ferocious doolies rushing down from the mountain'.[56]

From this basic model the palanquin was developed in various shapes, sizes, and degrees of splendour; it might be rectangular or hexagonal, with windows and curtains or sliding doors, the woodwork plain or intricately carved, and the interiors upholstered with all kinds of ingenious displays of luxury. The palanquin was of course a symbol of status, and as such it aroused controversy. In the early seventeenth century a regulation (albeit widely ignored) was

*Plate 41. Sketch of palanquin bearers. Pen and ink and wash, inscribed 'Madras 5 Sept. 1805'.* Private collection

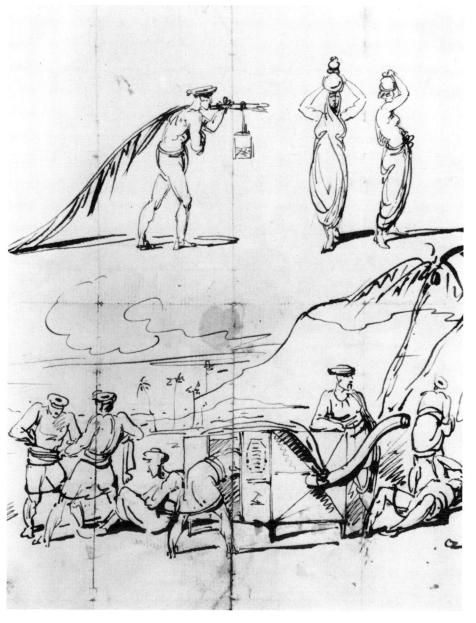

*Plate 42. Sheet of sketches with palanquin bearers at rest. Pen and ink.* Temple Newsam, Leeds

*Colour Plate 10. Ruined mosque near Madras. Pencil, pen and ink, and watercolours, s. and d. 1806.* Private collection

*Colour Plate 11. Shore temples, Mahabalipuram. Pencil, pen and ink, and watercolours, with scratching out.* Malcom and Ursula Horsman

*Colour Plate 12 William and Katherine Kirkpatrick, Oils, c 1805* Hongkong and Shanghai Banking Corporation

issued by the Portuguese Government prohibiting the male Portuguese inhabitants of Goa from travelling by palanquin, 'as in good sooth too effeminate a proceeding'; and efforts were made to prevent Portuguese women from going about in enclosed palanquins, which were thought to lend themselves to intrigue. In 1758 the Directors of the East India Company ordered that no Writer (junior civil servant) should keep 'either palanquin, horse or chaise, during his Writership, on pain of being immediately dismissed from our service', the objection apparently being that these 'afforded the Writers opportunities for rambling'.[57]

Nevertheless, when Chinnery reached India the palanquin was regarded by Europeans as an essential part of everyday life. Many of them complained in their letters of the discomforts of the palanquin, its confinement and its jerking motion; when D'Oyly's character Tom Raw travels in a palanquin, he contrives to fall through the bottom of it.[58] But whatever the drawbacks of travelling by palanquin, to travel without one was a great deal worse. When Richmond Thackeray arrived in Madras three years before Chinnery, he was dismayed to find that he had to venture out in the sun, because the army had taken the field, and all the palanquins and bearers had gone with the soldiers.[59]

In Calcutta at this time the palanquin was *de rigueur*:

> You must take it as universal and invariable that a Gentleman never *walks* in Calcutta, and even the wifes [*sic*] of common European soldiers sometimes ride in a hired Palanquin...an Elephant on London Bridge would not create more astonishment than a Gentleman *walking* about Calcutta in the middle of the day.[60]

By now the *dhooly* was going out of fashion, although it was 'still in very common use among the less opulent classes, and especially employed for the conveyance of women'.[61] It was being superseded by the *mahannah* or *meeana*, which is the model depicted in Chinnery's watercolour (Colour Plate 13). The *mahannah* measured some 6 x $2^1/_2$ feet, so that the traveller could lie back in comfort, often on chintz-covered cushions. Chinnery's *mahannah* has shuttered windows on all sides, as well as shuttered doors, and has four short legs on which to rest. Such a massive chest with its occupant was too heavy to be carried on long journeys outside the city, for which an alternative was the *bochah*, lighter and more upright than the *mahannah*. Women always travelled upright in a 'chair palanquin' of this kind, it being considered unseemly for a woman to recline. A gentleman might well keep both reclining and upright versions; when William Hickey left India, the auction sale of his effects included 'A very elegant chair finished in the first style' and 'A fashonable mehanna as good as new.'[62]

A palanquin could cost as much as 500 rupees, but 'a very good one may be had for 150 to 200 R[upee]s. They are are sometimes fitted up for travelling with shelves &c. and places for Bottles &c.'[63] Bearers by contrast were inexpensive, each receiving three to five rupees a month, although payment was regulated according to the caste of the bearer. A palanquin required at least four bearers, sometimes six or eight, in addition to the *jemadar* or principal servant who might walk alongside the palanquin, and *soontahburdars* to precede or accompany the palanquin holding symbolic batons, or perhaps a *chobdar* carrying a mace.[64] Often the bearers wore matching turbans and cummerbunds, but this livery does not appear on the bearers pictured by Chinnery. In his scene the pale blue turban perhaps marks the status of the *jemadar*, who holds a staff and leans back with both elbows on the roof of the palanquin (Colour Plate 13).

Soon after Chinnery left Calcutta for the China coast, the palanquin began to be superseded by the *palkee-garry*, or palanquin carriage, which was drawn by ponies posted along the route. Then in the 1850s the *palkee-garry* itself began to be superseded by the railway. By the 1880s the palanquin was 'used rarely, and only in out-of-the-way localities'.[65]

## The Bungalow

Among Chinnery's topographical work in Madras is a pair of watercolours of particular interest (Colour Plates 14 and 15). They illustrate an institution which was still something of a novelty, although it was to spread far beyond the confines of British India: the bungalow. Its origin lay in the *bangla* or *banggalo*, the village hut of Bengal which Chinnery was to sketch on so many occasions during his later years in India. The *bangla* was a single-storied, single-roomed structure raised on a shallow plinth, with walls made of bamboo and matting plastered with cow dung and clay. A pyramidal roof extended in some cases beyond the walls of the house to provide a shaded veranda — another term which was entering the English language by way of India.[66]

Even in its early manifestations, however, the Anglo-Indian bungalow was significantly different from its Bengali prototype. It was likely to be *cutcha* built (of sun-dried bricks), and provided with windows and doors. A canvas roof was often substituted for thatch, and the bungalow would probably be situated in a European cantonment with all amenities close at hand. Inside, a bungalow might well have no doors, but simply curtains (*purdahs*) of chintz. Often two or three bungalows would be used as a group; a contemporary of Chinnery had a pair of bungalows near each other, one for sleeping and dressing, the other for sitting and eating.[67]

Chinnery's watercolours are both dated 1805, but they illustrate quite distinct forms of bungalow, one a weekend retreat and the other a formal residence. The former (Colour Plate 14), with its pyramidal roof of striped canvas, is closer in its design to the *bangla*. The windows and entrance are protected from the sun by tatties, mats made from the roots of the fragrant grass *cuss* (or *khuss*) which was repeatedly wetted by servants so that the evaporation might cool the interior; the same grass was widely used as roofing thatch in the villages of Bengal. In addition the left-hand window is fitted with a *jhaump*, a heavy wooden shutter which was propped open by a pole. This was derived from the Bengali *jhanp*, a hurdle of woven straw and bamboo which covered the door of a hut. On the left of the bungalow can be seen a rudimentary veranda extending from the walls to a recently planted row of trees.

*Colour Plate 13. Palanquin bearers. Pen and ink and watercolours, s. and d. 1806.* Malcom and Ursula Horsman

This bungalow was situated in the fishing village of Ennore, a dozen miles north of Madras, which had become something of a weekend resort for the British in the settlement. Several bungalows were built along the strip of land seen here, between the sea and a lake or backwater, and a canal was constructed to link Ennore directly with Madras. When Maria Graham visited Ennore in 1810 she found:

> A small salt water lake, with abundance of fine fish and excellent oysters. These attractions have induced a party of gentlemen to build a house by subscription on the edge of the lake, where there is a meeting every week to eat fish, play cards, and sail about on the lake in two little pleasure-boats, a diversion which cannot be enjoyed anywhere else near Madras on account of the surf.[68]

It was probably in such a bungalow that Chinnery had 'his first experience in natural history'. Later he would provoke *frissons* in his listeners as he recalled a dinner which, soon after his arrival in Madras, he was enjoying with friends 'in the broad hall of a bungalow', when a snake slid in unnoticed from the veranda and wrapped itself around his ankle. But the reptile was no match for the artist, it seems:

> He signalled silence to every one, and in a voice scarcely above his breath, directed the servant to bring him a bowl of milk and a cane; his manner and look ensuring silence, he deliberately placed the former

*Colour Plate 14. Bungalow at Ennore. Pencil, pen and ink, and watercolours, s. and d. 1805.* Private collection

*Colour Plate 15. Crow's Tope, Madras. Pencil, pen and ink, and watercolours, s. and d. 1805.* Private collection

on the floor a short distance from his chair, and as quietly lowered the cane close to it, while still holding it by the handle. The odour of the milk attracted the snake, which immediately uncoiled itself from the ankle on [to] the stick. In another moment, while in the enjoyment of its unlooked-for feed, he sprang from his chair, jumped on the bowl and on the head of the uninvited guest, destroying it and its dinner in the twinkling of an eye.[69]

The more imposing Madras edifice pictured in Colour Plate 15 is no doubt *pukka* built of brick-fired bricks and mortar. It has a flat roof, a columned entrance, wooden shutters in the European colonial style, and a name — Crow's Tope (crow's grove). It stands within its own compound; servants' quarters are visible on the left, and a subsidiary bungalow on the right. The palanquin bearers who wait at the foot of the steps indicate the status of the occupant. Both this and the Ennore bungalow were the property of Sir Herbert Compton, who had switched early in his career from the military to the civil service. Having entered the East India Company's army as a private soldier, and subsequently received a commission, Compton had bought himself out of the army and articled himself as a lawyer in Madras. After a brief spell in England he worked his way up the Company's legal service, becoming Advocate-General in Calcutta and finally Chief Justice of the Bombay Supreme Court. Chinnery must have known him in Madras and later in Calcutta, for in 1816 the artist drew Compton's grand mansion in Calcutta's fashionable Garden Reach (Plate 65).

Although (or perhaps because) it was far removed from its Bengali origins, the second type of bungalow, with terraced roof and classical allusions, was adopted in India as a standard form of residence for British officials such as Compton. By the later years of the nineteenth century the bungalow was defined less in terms of its design or construction than according to its role in Anglo-Indian society — that is, as a substantial house in its own grounds which was built for a *sahib*. In 1891 it could be said that 'a cottage is a little house in the country, but a bungalow is a little country house'.[70]

Whether topographical drawing and painting would become a major element in Chinnery's career was not yet certain. He must have been well aware of the daunting example set by Thomas and William Daniell, who had returned to England in 1794 with quantities of precise drawings accumulated in the course of seven years' travelling throughout India; from these were created the meticulous plates known as *Oriental Scenery*. The project was a critical and a financial success — 'a feast of intellectual and unusual entertainment', as J.M.W. Turner described the series, 'bringing scenes to our fireside, too distant to visit, and too singular to be imagined'.[71] But the 144 aquatints of *Oriental Scenery* were the product not only of the Daniells' exhausting travels but also of another seven years of toil, in which William Daniell frequently laboured from 6 a.m. until midnight.[72]

Hard as Chinnery sometimes worked, he must have suspected that he had not the temperament for such an enterprise. He did, however, undertake to produce a series of etchings with explanatory text, which he grandly entitled

*Plate 43. Camels by the Cooum River, Madras. Pencil.* Helen, Lady Broughton

'The Indian Magazine and European Miscellany'. On 26 November 1806 it was announced that 'Mr George Chinnery as Joint-Proprietor of the work, will furnish an etching monthly. The first number will exhibit a view of Madras, from the beach; and every succeeding publication will contain either a landscape from nature or figures illustrative of the character, and occupations of the natives.'[73]

The series ran to nine issues, from February to October 1807, comprising four topographical views and five studies of 'characters' (see Plates 30 and 36). But half way through the series Chinnery abandoned Madras: in June he sailed for Calcutta, in pursuit of more lucrative employment. Presumably he left behind him four etchings which were published in his absence, to satisfy subscribers or to pay the printers' bills. Very few sets of these etchings survive. Although crude, they clearly show where Chinnery's talents lay. Even in the 'views of Madras', the interest is provided by the groups of figures, boats and incidental objects rather than in the buildings which are the nominal subjects of the plates. His preparatory drawings for these etchings depict groups of water carriers, or bearers, or boatmen, in many different attitudes and formations, with the signs '+' or 'x' beside them to indicate whether they were to be regarded as reliable or unreliable source material.[74] A charming sketch of this period depicts camels and their resting attendants at an encampment on the banks of the Cooum, with only the faintest traces of the Banqueting Hall and Government House on the far side of the river (Plate 43).

## The Madras Pantheon

Madras had only one place for social gatherings: the Assembly Rooms, also known as the Pantheon. Here Lord Clive gave suppers and balls in 1802, shortly before his recall to England, and here in 1805 a public entertainment was given in honour of Sir Arthur Wellesley. By 1810 the Pantheon contained 'a ballroom, a very pretty theatre, card-room and virandahs', and was used also as a masonic lodge.[75] Richard Kerr had been 'Provincial Grand Chaplain' of the six Madras and Vellore lodges on the Coromandel coast,[76] and Chinnery himself may have been initiated as a freemason here (see p.132).

In Chinnery's time the Pantheon was directed, and it seems owned, by a consortium.[77] When in 1821 the building was sold to an Armenian merchant, the group of men who assigned the property included several who had previously been portrayed by Chinnery: the advocate Herbert Compton, the naval officer Thomas Hoseason,[78] the cavalry officer Valentine Blacker (Plate

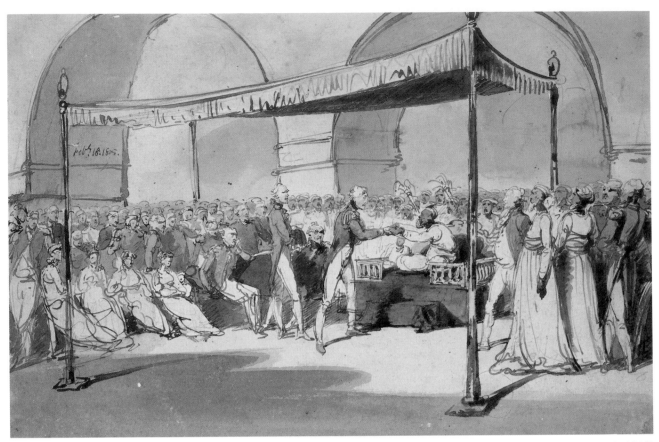

*Colour Plate 16. The durbar of Azim-ud-Daula. Pen and ink and watercolours, dated 'Feby. 18. 1805'.*
Private collection

67), who became Quartermaster-General at Fort St. George and later Surveyor-General of India, and the merchant Thomas Parry (see pp 81-2).

Chinnery may well have known these men through their connection with the Pantheon, since he would often have been requested to supply decorations for events held there. One 'entertainment' in which he was certainly involved was a celebration of the acquittal of Henry Dundas, 1st Viscount Melville, who had been impeached in London on grounds of misappropriating funds while Treasurer of the Navy. Dundas was a pugnacious Scotsman, hard-working and loyal to his allies — especially his close friend William Pitt. He was a hero of the Anglo-Indian community of Madras on two counts. In the first place he had held the ministerial post of President of the Board of Control, which had been set up in 1784 to supervise the activities of the Directors of the East India Company; this made him in effect the ruler of British India, although he never visited the East. And despite his several clashes with the various power blocs within the East India Company (notably the shipping interest), it was Dundas who, in a famous speech on 23 April 1793, persuaded Parliament to extend the Company's monopoly for another ten years. In the second place, Dundas was Secretary for War in the critical years 1794-1801. While others in Parliament advised caution, he encouraged Wellesley to pursue the aggressive campaign against Tipu which finally brought security to the British military and trading stations in the Madras Presidency. Dundas also received a good deal of credit for the defeat of Napoleon in Egypt, thus 'safeguarding India' for the British.[79]

The impeachment of Dundas took place in the early summer of 1806. He

On the drawing, handwritten annotations:

b mial
Diaw.g
for
the
Etch-
ing

The
Senator
offering
Security

Plenty to the widow
and British ...
(Sailor)

On the medal inscription:
·ET·PATRONUS·MULIERIS·VIDVATÆ·CONIVGE·BRITANNICO·
PATRE·EREPTO·AMICVS·
HVIVS·NEC·NON·NATORVM··IN·
·STAT·26·GEO·3·C·63·
·A.D.1786.

*Plate 44. Preparatory drawing for an etching published in tribute to Henry Dundas, 1807. Pen and ink and wash. Martyn Gregory Gallery*

was lucky to be acquitted, for money under his control was certainly misused, and on some of the charges the verdict was a narrow one. Dundas was restored to the Privy Council, but did not hold office again. Seven months after the acquittal, on 22 January 1807, the British in Madras held their celebration in the Pantheon. Chinnery designed a large transparency, representing Justice unveiling Truth to Britannia.[80] He also produced an etching, for which Plate 44 is the original drawing. The etching paid tribute to a popular and uncontroversial measure taken by Dundas: 'Providing for the widows and orphans of British seamen in the war against France and Spain, culminating in the Battle of Trafalgar.' A senatorial figure stands on the seashore, bestowing upon betoga'd widows the key of Security and the cornucopia of Plenty.

Security and plenty were commodities which Chinnery himself seems to have lacked during his four and a half years at Madras. He was by no means idle, but the lucrative commissions for portraits of Indian princes or British governors and commanders went not to Chinnery but to his rivals Thomas Hickey and Robert Home. If he had hoped to send home a comfortable allowance for his wife and children, it seems that he was disappointed, since in 1807 the prominent merchant Thomas Parry, together with some of his friends, sent the sum of £100 back to Marianne Chinnery in London — 'which although a small sum, will afford you some substance in the distressed state under which you suffer.'[81]

Thomas Parry was involved in the lives of the Chinnerys in several ways. A partner of Chase & Sewell in the early 1790s, he left to set up his own operations in banking, general trading and shipowning. In 1800 he was ordered home by the Governor, Lord Clive, probably because he had been raising fresh loans for Umdat-ul-Umara, Nawab of the Carnatic, although the Nawab was already heavily in debt to the East India Company. Parry did not comply with the order, however, and it was the Governor who returned to England, while Parry remained to make and lose several more fortunes. He was part owner of the *Marquess of Wellesley*, in which Chinnery's sister-in-law travelled back to England in 1805 (see p.57); in the following year the ship was gutted by fire, together with an underinsured cargo of grain. 1806 and 1807 were famine years in the Madras Presidency, and there were bankruptcies among the agency houses, notably Chase & Co., which failed to the extent of four million rupees; Parry was appointed liquidator. John Chinnery was no doubt affected, and indirectly George Chinnery also. By this time Chinnery had drawn a portrait of Parry, and was also renting a house from him, paying fifty rupees a month. Parry continued to support Marianne Chinnery, sending her £32 in 1808, and he remembered her in his will.[82]

## The Durbar

One further avenue lay open to Chinnery. In the few years preceding his arrival at Madras, an extraordinary sequence of military and diplomatic events had taken place, as the East India Company through conquest and alliance rapidly made itself ruler of south-eastern India. Such events were admirably fit to be commemorated in 'history paintings' (a genre much admired at that time in Academic circles in England), the 'history' in this case being extremely recent. Thomas Hickey, well aware of the opportunity, had planned an ambitious sequence of paintings commemorating the Third Mysore War, beginning with 'The storming of the breach at Seringapatam' and culminating in 'The placing of the Rajah on the Musnud of Mysore'. Between 1799 and 1801 Hickey made preliminary chalk drawings of the leading protagonists, but the series never materialised — it was surely beyond his capacities.[83]

Other artists accepted the challenge. Thomas Daniell exhibited at the Royal Academy in 1805 an elaborate durbar (audience) scene, based on sketches by James Wales, in which the British Resident at Poona was shown concluding a treaty with the Peshwa of the Marathas.[84] And Benjamin West had exhibited a painting which Chinnery would undoubtedly have noticed at the Royal Academy exhibition of 1795, in which the first Lord Clive was seen 'receiving the grant of the Diwani' — in effect, appropriating the revenues — of Bengal from the Emperor Shah Alam. West painted a stately and symbolic scene of apparent conciliation between eastern and western rulers, although a reviewer observed that the Muslim domes in the background of the picture bore a powerful resemblance to the dome of St. Paul's.[85]

Chinnery arrived in Madras just too late to witness the stirring events of the Third Mysore War, in which the artist Robert Home had accompanied Lord Cornwallis's victorious army. Perhaps Chinnery, whose belligerence was confined to domestic situations, was not greatly disappointed at missing the campaign. In February 1805, however, he did have the opportunity to sketch a notable durbar, and the date 'Feby. 18. 1805' inscribed on his drawing (Colour Plate 16) confirms that he was an eyewitness. On this day the new Commander-in-Chief, General Sir John Cradock, formally presented a letter from George III to the Nawab Azim-ud-Daula, congratulating the Nawab on his accession to the *musnud* — the cushion-throne denoting sovereignty. The letter was carried on an elephant in procession to the palace, along a route flanked by soldiers from the British garrison. When all the principals were assembled, the letter 'was read on the usual discharge of Artillery. These ceremonies being over, a most numerous company sat down to a Breakfast...'[86]

As a diplomatic event, the ceremony was something of a sham; since the East India Company's army controlled the Carnatic, Azim-ud-Daula was allowed to hold his position only after accepting the British terms; he was relieved of the debts incurred by his predecessors, and in return he handed over four-fifths of the revenues of the Carnatic to the Company, together with all powers of government.

Yet the occasion did bring together, by chance, several remarkable individuals. The Nawab himself is shown seated, as in Benjamin West's picture, on a raised divan beneath a canopy in the royal hall of audience. The figure with arms outstretched towards the Nawab is Sir Arthur Wellesley, who was passing through Madras on his way back to England where, as the Duke of Wellington, he would exercise his military genius against the French. Standing behind him is Lord William Cavendish Bentinck, Governor of Madras, who was later to be a courageous reformer and the first 'Governor-General of India'. Seated behind Bentinck, in a prophetic attitude of dejection, is Sir John Cradock, whose term as Commander-in-Chief was to be swiftly ended by the mutiny at Vellore, which caused him to be sent home in disgrace. Between the two standing figures sits the bespectacled Admiral Peter Rainier, who was retiring as Commander-in-Chief on the East India station. The veteran of many campaigns, Rainier had made himself hugely wealthy from the booty of captured ships; in a thoughtful gesture, he left the English nation a tenth of his estate in his will, to reduce the national debt.

Chinnery perhaps hoped that he might paint the scene as a grand tableau, fit to be sent back to the Royal Academy; but it was never done.

# CHAPTER 5

## *The Russell Commission*

Chinnery's great opportunity in India came in 1807. Although he had been active in Madras, he had received no major commissions, and he would have been well aware that the focus of Anglo-Indian society had now shifted from Madras to Calcutta; Calcutta was the metropolitan capital by whose standards all other Indian cities were seen as provincial. While Chinnery remained in Madras, he was regarded as no more than one of several artists who might be called on if required. But once in the socially competitive, fashion-conscious atmosphere of Calcutta, he was quickly recognised as the pre-eminent artist in India.

On 20 June 1807 Chinnery left Madras for Calcutta, on board the *City of London*,[1] in response to a 'special summons' to paint the portrait of Sir Henry Russell, who had just been appointed Chief Justice of the Supreme Court of Judicature of Bengal. It was to be painted at the request of 'several of the principal natives of the Settlement...that it might be exhibited in the Town Hall, a splendid building then in a considerable degree of forwardness.'[2] The choice of Chinnery as artist was no doubt Russell's — taken possibly as a result of his having inherited Chinnery's portrait of the Kirkpatrick children, which came into his possession after the death of their father (see p.63). In any event Russell received Chinnery as his personal guest, allowing him the use of two spacious apartments and a regular place at his dinner table. Since the Court was in recess when Chinnery arrived in July, he carried out the painting in the Court Room. Here he was often accompanied by the diarist William Hickey, who was Russell's attorney, and whose Memoirs give a detailed account of the commission: 'I generally passed two or three hours daily in observing the progress he made.'[3]

This over-life-size ceremonial portrait (112 x 74 inches) must have been an immense challenge to Chinnery, who was much more accustomed to working on pictures two inches high. As William Hickey testifies, the task occupied Chinnery from sunrise to sunset for nearly three months. Since Hickey had taken a close interest in the project, the artist asked him too to sit for his portrait; which on completion was given to Sir Henry Russell. Unfortunately this portrait of Hickey, which was last recorded as hanging in Sir Henry's dining room in the Court House, can no longer be traced.[4]

On 5 November 1807 Chinnery advertised in the *Calcutta Government Gazette* a proposal to publish an engraving of the Russell portrait. Subscriptions were to be received either 'at Mr CHINNERY's House, in Tank Square, Calcutta, where, after the 1st of November, the picture may be seen; or at the Bank of Hindoostan'.[5] William Hickey helped to raise subscriptions for the engraving, each subscriber paying three gold *mohurs* (nearly £5). Since it was not feasible for the engraving and printing to be carried out in India, Chinnery executed a smaller replica of the picture, which Hickey was to take back to be engraved in London. However, this second picture was not ready in time — Chinnery's clients were often to experience such difficulties — because the artist was afflicted with a debilitating inflammation of the eyes, causing him to shut himself up in a darkened room, 'his spirits being so depressed he would not admit Sir Henry Russell or any friend whomsoever', wrote Hickey, 'in which melancholy state I left him'.[6]

The portrait was displayed to the public in the Court Room, and was judged a great success. One of those who admired it was the Persian Ambassador, who was obliged by the rules of etiquette to pay a formal visit to the Chief Justice. Both Hickey and Chinnery accompanied Russell on this occasion, and Hickey claims that Chinnery was something of a 'Persian scholar', although not in the same class as the accomplished linguist Russell. 'The picture did Mr Chinnery infinite credit as an artist and must prove his genius so long as a particle of the canvas remains.'[7] As Hickey perhaps implied with these words, the picture surface did indeed deteriorate, and the composition is best appreciated today in the engraved version (Plate 45), which was finally carried out in London by Samuel Reynolds.[8]

In this picture Chinnery followed the example of Zoffany's portrait of a previous Chief Justice of Bengal, Sir Elijah Impey, insofar as Russell is represented (like Impey) with the regalia of Justice — long wig and robes, law books, mace and sword.[9] But in place of Zoffany's theatrically swaying figure, Chinnery portrays Russell seated and appropriately immovable in his judicial throne. Beside him lies the Great Seal of England attached to the patent of office. Above the mace is a group of allegorical figures, denoting blindfold Justice protecting Innocence in the shape of two naked children. (A figurine of Justice with her scales had been incorporated by Thomas Hickey in his portrait of Purniya, Chief Minister to the young Raja of Mysore;[10] Chinnery subsequently made use of such allegorical figures in several of his official portraits.) Beneath them the *fasces* of power are shown intertwined with a civic wreath, symbolising the high regard in which Russell's character was held by the people of Calcutta.

Although such a testimonial might seem to have been a standard tribute from obsequious officials, in this instance it represented a genuine respect. Unlike his immediate predecessor, Russell had earned the esteem of the Indian population as well as a considerable portion of the British. One case in particular, which occurred shortly after the portrait was finished, was regarded as establishing a new standard of equal justice for Indians and Europeans alike. John Grant, a young East India Company cadet, was found guilty of maliciously setting fire to a native's hut. Russell sentenced him to death, and in doing so he observed that 'the natives are entitled to have their characters, property, and lives protected; and as long as they enjoy that privilege from us, they give us their affection and allegiance in return.'[11]

Hickey had no such respect for Russell's predecessor as Chief Justice, Sir John Anstruther, who the diarist believed was 'almost always influenced by some interested or disgraceful motive.' Some time before he was due to depart for England, Anstruther had let it be known that he would appreciate a

*Plate 45. The Hon. Sir Henry Russell. Engraving by S.W. Reynolds after Chinnery.* British Museum

portrait of himself; but the hint was not taken. After several attempts he resorted to an address to the Grand Jury, 'one of the most disgustingly fulsome speeches that ever was uttered'. As a result the foreman of the Grand Jury proposed that Anstruther should be requested to sit for his portrait, but only six of the twenty-three jurors agreed to subscribe towards it. The resulting picture was, in Hickey's eyes at least, entirely appropriate: 'A sign-post whole-length likeness of him in his scarlet cloth robes, executed by Mr. Home, was five weeks later hung up in the Court room. Oh, what a wretched daub did it appear when in a few months Chinnery's picture of Sir Henry Russell was placed by its side!'[12]

Although William Hickey was twenty-five years older than Chinnery, the two men were to some extent kindred spirits, prone to self-importance and exaggeration, and Hickey was no doubt justified in claiming that 'Mr Chinnery was pleased to shew a very flattering partiality towards me'. His *Memoirs* contain an illuminating assessment of the artist, which makes it clear that even in his early thirties Chinnery suffered from fluctuating moods and bouts of depression:

> Mr. Chinnery, like many other men of extraordinary talent, was extremely odd and eccentric, so much so as at times to make me think him deranged. His health certainly was not good; and he had a strong tendency to hypochondria which frequently made him ridiculously fanciful, yet in spite of his mental and bodily infirmities, personal vanity shewed itself in various ways. When not under the influence of low spirits, he was a cheerful pleasant companion, but if hypochondriacal was melancholy and dejected to the greatest degree.[13]

It is possible, however, that Hickey's judgement was influenced by a story which reached him when he had returned to England, to the effect that 'soon after my departure from Calcutta Mr. Chinnery became determinedly insane, and has ever since been kept under restriction, being now pronounced a confirmed and incurable lunatic.'[14] Now this seems to be a case not simply of exaggeration, but of mistaken identity. For it is clear that after George Chinnery left his brother John in Madras, his brother became seriously incapacitated. By 1815 John Chinnery had been confined to the Lunatic Hospital in Madras, and there was little prospect of his recovery. His wife Mary appealed for relief from the Civil Fund, on behalf of herself and her four young children. Since her husband was still alive, she was technically ineligible; but the Trustees of the Civil Fund agreed to support Mary and her family, and recommended moreover that the principle should be 'adopted by the service at large'. The surgeon in charge of the Lunatic Hospital certified that 'Mr. Chinnery has entirely lost the use of his left side, and his judgement and memory are so impaired that he cannot recognise his nearest relatives — he is in fact in the most lamentable state of mental fatuity...'[15]

John Chinnery survived for two years more. George Chinnery meanwhile pursued his career in Calcutta and Dacca with increasing success. When he had completed the version of the Russell portrait which was to be engraved, he sent it off to Hickey in England, together with certain other portraits which

Hickey had commissioned. The letter which accompanied this consignment confirms that the artist's sanity (although not his hypochondria) was unimpaired. He tried to ensure that the pictures would come to no harm during the voyage:

Dear Sir,

I should have done myself the pleasure of sending you your picture properly rolled and packed before now, but that really and truly the smal [*sic*] painting from which the Engraving is to be made has occupied every moment of my time. Indeed for the last week I have been seriously indisposed with violent cough and pain in my face, and as if Hygrin [*sic*] had some spite against me I no sooner got rid of violent toothache, by retraction, but my right Eye is materially affected by the cold, so much so, that were not the Ships upon the Eve of sailing I should lay myself up entirely, and as it is, am by no means sure I shall not be obliged to do so, to my grievous inconvenience and loss.

You will find the warm Cloth and tin case an effectual Security. The pictures are rolled on a hollow Cylinder, and between each is put a piece of green silk to prevent their sticking to each other. You will be careful to have them gently warmed by a fire as you unroll them. In rolling them they were each made properly pliable by a regular heat. The picture you wished to bestow most attention to is the last rolled, in order that the circle might be the greatest, and of course the less chance of injury by rubbing or otherwise. All this puts you to some expense. The Silk cost me thirty-eight rupees and a half, and the tin case sixteen, making together sicca rupees fifty four and a half.

I am, My Dear Sir,

Your much obliged and faithful servant,

Geo: Chinnery

6th February 1808[16]

To Hickey's extreme annoyance, Chinnery's painstaking precautions were in vain, for when the tin chest arrived in England, the customs officers broke it open, tore the canvases from the roller, and charged him £40 duty for importing 'foreign pictures' — which were heavily taxed in accordance with an old Act of Parliament designed to encourage British artists.

# CHAPTER 6

## *Dacca and the D'Oylys*

In July 1808 Chinnery moved to Dacca (modern Dhaka, in Bangladesh), 180 miles from Calcutta. This step is hard to explain in purely economic terms, as Calcutta offered him far greater opportunities for patronage, especially following the success of the Russell commission. Possibly he hoped to recover his health; the climate of Dacca was regarded as one of the mildest in India. But a stronger motive may have been the prospect of working with Charles D'Oyly, who in February 1808 had been appointed Collector of the city.

Charles D'Oyly, seven years younger than Chinnery, was the foremost amateur practitioner of the graphic arts in Bengal. Born in Calcutta but educated in England, he had returned to India at the age of fifteen in the service of the East India Company. On reaching his majority he married his cousin, Marian Greer. As we have seen, Chinnery may have known his father, Sir John Hadley D'Oyly (Plate 46), in Ireland; and he certainly painted the portrait of Charlotte Conyngham (see pp.37-8 and Plate 21), Charles's cousin and sister-in-law, before coming to Dacca. The association between Chinnery and Charles D'Oyly must have begun in Calcutta, in the winter of 1807-8.

D'Oyly no doubt proposed to Chinnery, just as he later proposed in the prospectus for his *Antiquities of Dacca*, that 'the ancient Metropolis of DACCA, on the banks of the Ganges, [was] an interesting part of India not visited by the Messrs. DANIELL, nor, it is believed, by any European Artist.'[1] This was not strictly accurate, since Francesco Renaldi had been to Dacca in 1789, and Robert Home had paid a visit there in the summer of 1799.[2] But neither had tried to depict the architecture of the place, and Chinnery was evidently tempted by the project.

For an artist brought up in England at the height of the 'Picturesque' movement (as were both Chinnery and D'Oyly), Dacca offered a great wealth of architectural subjects. Many of the finest buildings dated from the seventeenth century, when the city, designated the capital of Bengal by the Emperor Jahangir, had been at its most prosperous. Later in that century Dacca had also become a centre of British trade in cotton textiles, but although the old British Factory still survived in Chinnery's day, no business was conducted there; the muslin industry, once a major part of Dacca's economy, was all but extinguished by European competition in the early nineteenth century. Substantial European-style houses, erected for a previous generation of merchants, could be obtained at a low rent — between sixty and 135 rupees per month[3] — while the palatial structures of the former Mughal rulers lay in picturesque decay. Bishop Reginald Heber, approaching the city by river in 1824, was impressed by 'the stateliness of the ruins...huge dark

*Plate 46. Miniature portrait of Sir James Hadley D'Oyly, 6th Baronet. Pencil and watercolours.* Private collection

masses of castle and tower...now overgrown with ivy and peepul-trees'.[4] He gave a vivid description of the city:

> Two-thirds of the vast area of Dacca are filled with ruins, some quite desolate and overgrown with jungle, others yet occupied by Mussulman chieftans...Of the three hundred thousand inhabitants who yet roost like bats in these old buildings, or rear their huts amid their desolate gardens, three-fourths are still Mussulmans, and the few English, and Armenians, and Greek Christians who are found here, are not altogether more than 60 or 80 persons, who live more with the natives, and form less of an exclusive society, than is the case in most parts of British India.[5]

The European population of Dacca was indeed a small one. Apart from a battalion of troops and a handful of the Company's civil servants, there were only twelve Europeans recorded in the city when Chinnery arrived: five merchants (three English, one French, one Danish), an Irish shopkeeper, a Hanoverian watchmaker, a pilot attached to the Dacca factory, a temporary visitor, two servants, and one man who was 'out of employ' following his discharge from the European Infantry.[6]

Chinnery arrived in Dacca in July 1808,[7] and went to live in the house of Charles and Marian D'Oyly. The D'Oylys had no children; in a letter to Warren Hastings, a close family friend, Charles wrote of 'the afflicting loss we have again sustained',[8] which may refer to the death of a child in infancy. These were tragic years for the D'Oylys. In 1807 Marian's brother-in-law Frederick Arnott, who had married her eldest sister Harriet, had ill-advisedly manhandled one of his indigo planters, and was killed in the fight which ensued.[9] In September of the following year her second sister Charlotte died; and in February 1809 the bereaved Harriet was returning to England in the *Calcutta* when the ship ran into a storm and went down with all hands.[10] D'Oyly wrote to Warren Hastings that he was devoting himself to art 'beyond perhaps what an amateur ought to be — It has had the good effect however of dispelling from my thoughts & pen a train of melancholy objects...'[11] As well as distracting him from his grief, the companionship and the advice provided by Chinnery encouraged D'Oyly to improve on his earlier drawings, some of which he had sent back to Warren Hastings in England for his approval:

> I certainly was satisfied with them [my drawings] at the time with respect to execution, but from my late progress in the more material & general principles of the art in consequence of some useful instructions I have recently received from a very able artist of the name of Chinnery I am led to apprehend there are radical faults in the disposition of Light & Shade as well as in color which would now make me condemn them as much as I formerly liked them — I am content however that you express yourself pleased with the Views — & shall some time hence please God offer you as Companions a few of the Ruins of the City of Dacca which I assure you are exquisite for their magnificence & elegance — & are calculated to tempt the pencil of an artist as much I

suppose if not more than most of the British Reliques — a visit which Chinnery has paid me at Dacca for some months past, has enabled him to collect more than 50 views of Ruins — & all are so beautiful I know not to which the preferance [*sic*] ought to be shewn.

All these I am drawing to supply me in future with materials for pictures — & I shall request him to allow me the selection of a Set — to finish for you — I mention this because it is his intention — if his means will allow him — to publish them to the world, & of course any anticipation of them might prove detrimental to his design — but he is so liberal & grateful for the small degree of patronage which I have had it in my power to afford him that he would willingly accord with any wish I might express. — & particularly when he knows it is for you. He is an enthusiastic lover of Sir Joshua & from holding him up as an example from his first entrance into the art he has acquired a considerable degree of his style — particularly in the force of coloring & the minute attention to the person whose portrait he designs & the expression of the Mind is the first beauty which rivets [?] the attention of the Spectator.[12]

Some of the work by Chinnery to which D'Oyly referred has survived: detailed topographical pencil drawings of the mosques and gateways of Dacca (Plates 47 and 48), with small groups of people at the roadside or at the water's edge.[13] Compass bearings are indicated by means of a small circle or globe pencilled in the corner, a device which he had begun to use in Madras. The artist made a feature of the luxuriant creeper overhanging the ruined domes and minarets, and the branches emerging from the fissures in the crumbling masonry — a combination much admired by contemporary English theorists in their quest for 'the fantastic strokes of nature working upon patterns of art, which all the refinement of magnificence cannot imitate'.[14]

Chinnery's projected publication did not materialise, however, and when the four series entitled *Antiquities of Dacca* were finally published (in England), at intervals between 1814 and 1827, all the topographical engravings were based on drawings by Sir Charles D'Oyly. As the prospectus had promised, the engraved views and historical text were accompanied by vignettes from drawings by Chinnery, but there were only three of these. The first, 'An Ancient Mosque and Modern Habitations of Dacca', was supposed to contrast 'present poverty with Mohammedan importance, and rusticity with architectural elegance'. The second was a more explicit comment on the decline of Dacca, showing (according to D'Oyly's text) the modern cottage 'of a poor muslin weaver, formed of bamboo, mud, and matting, thatched with straw: his umbrella and a few of his domestic culinary utensils, are lying about, and at the right hand corner is part of an old loom'. The third, 'Approach to Tungy', includes an elephant with a dead tiger slung across its back.[15]

Although these vignettes were composed for a specific publication, they set the tone for much of Chinnery's landscape painting and drawing in Bengal. After the early Dacca drawings he made little attempt to emulate the precise topographical draughtsmanship of Thomas and William Daniell; it was left to

Plate 47. *'Southern Gateway to the small Cuttra, with the Mosque in the Interior of the Square, Dacca, Oct. 26 1808.' Pencil.* Private collection

Plate 48. *'Mosque and Cuttra on the Banks of the Buragunga, Dacca, Oct. 31, 1808.' Pencil.* Private collection

D'Oyly to undertake a more or less systematic memorial of the Mughal buildings of Dacca, just as artists other than Chinnery were to delineate the stately architecture of Calcutta. It seems that at Dacca Chinnery decided to concentrate, in his 'finished' work, on intimate rural scenes of village life in Bengal (see Chapter 9), in which a limited repertoire of elements — thatched buildings, ruinous domes and minarets, cattle and goats, and certain figures — are deployed for pictorial effect in various patterns and combinations.

As D'Oyly's letter implies, there were also opportunities in Dacca for portraits, despite the small European population. Chinnery's portrait drawings of a youthful Charles D'Oyly (Plate 49), and of his first wife Marian (Plate 50), probably date from this period;[16] Marian died in 1814. He also portrayed George Cruttenden, the Commander of the Dacca Provisional Battalion, before he resigned his commission on 5 August 1809 in favour of commerce.[17] Others in Dacca whose portraits were painted by Chinnery, either at this time or subsequently, were Shearman Bird (Plate 51), Judge of the City Court of Dacca;[18] James Ruthven Elphinstone, who in 1809 was 3rd Judge of the Provincial Court of Appeal at Dacca (see p.105); and Charles Robert Lindsay, who was Assistant to the Commercial Resident at Dacca in 1810-11, before moving on to become Assistant to the Salt Agent in the 24 Parganas — the Salt Agent himself being Sir John Hadley D'Oyly, the father of Charles.

Both Elphinstone and Lindsay were younger sons of peers, and nephews of Directors of the East India Company. Their influence was perhaps not unconnected with Chinnery's subsequent commission to portray Elphinstone's brother-in-law, Sir John Adam; and when Chinnery's daughter Matilda applied to join her father in India, Lindsay's uncle Hugh was sitting on the committee which approved her application.[19] In British India relationships and personal contacts were still of over-riding significance in postings and promotions. Charles D'Oyly complained to Warren Hastings that 'Interest carries every thing before it, & L[ord] M[into]'s friends have the pickings of all the good Employments.'[20] D'Oyly at once admitted that he himself had profited from this system of patronage, but his observation was a fair one, and he might have extended it to portraiture; here too commissions were largely dependent on connections and personal recommendations. From this time onward, however, the system began to operate to Chinnery's advantage.

*Plate 49. Sir Charles D'Oyly as a young man. Pencil and watercolours.* Private collection

*Plate 50. Marian D'Oyly (née Greer), first wife of Sir Charles D'Oyly. Pencil and watercolours.* Private collection

*Plate 51. Judge Shearman Bird. Pencil and watercolours, s. and d. 1817.* Spink & Son Ltd.

It seems that Chinnery also received commissions from the Indian rulers of the province, for when Bishop Heber visited Shams-ud-Daulah, the Nawab of Dacca, he observed (among prints of Wellesley, Wellington and Lord Hastings) 'two very good portraits, by Chinnery, of the Nawab himself, and the late Nawab, his brother.'[21] Chinnery's delicately-drawn head of an unidentified Indian man (Plate 52), whose elaborate turban indicates that he was a man of standing, comes from the D'Oyly collection and is probably from his Dacca years; this, and his portrait drawing of a full-bearded Moslem (Plate 53), make one regret that so few of Chinnery's portraits of Indians are in evidence.

Chinnery was based at Dacca for some three years, making excursions into the neighbouring villages and towns. A miniature of this period is inscribed by Chinnery 'Comillah — Tipperah / Bengal / November 1809'[22] (the town of Comilla is fifty miles to the south of Dacca). Another miniature, dated May 1811, represents Thomas Colclough Watson (Colour Plate 17), who at this time was serving at Dinapore (near Patna) as aide-de-camp to his uncle, Major-General Samuel Watson. Subsequently he went to Java as extra aide-de-camp to Thomas Stamford Raffles, again probably through a family

*Plate 52. Portrait of an Indian. Pencil and watercolours.* Private collection

*Plate 53. Portrait of an Indian with full beard. Pencil and watercolours.* Private collection

connection — he was a cousin of Raffles's wife. Watson died in 1834 as a Lieutenant-Colonel. The portrait is as highly finished as any of Chinnery's miniatures, and shows no sign of the failing eyesight which is said to have compelled him to give up painting on this scale.[23]

On 1 May 1812 D'Oyly took up the new post of Deputy Collector of Government Customs and Town Duties at Calcutta; by this time Chinnery was also back in Calcutta. In 1817, three years after the death of his first wife Marian, D'Oyly married Elizabeth Jane Ross (Plate 54) who shared his artistic interests. Chinnery painted at least two portraits of D'Oyly with his second wife: an oil painting of the couple in Vandyck costume (Plate 55), painted in 1819 (according to an inscription on the back), and a miniature (Colour Plate 18) which has descended in the family of Shearman Bird.

In 1818 D'Oyly became Collector, and he also inherited the baronetcy on the death of his father. The D'Oylys' house in Calcutta became a meeting place of the many amateur artists in the British community. One of these was William Prinsep, who later recalled that 'many were the happy hours all lovers of the brush spent at the hospitable house of Sir Charles D'Oyly, himself an excellent artist, where Chinnery was a frequent and welcome guest.'[24]

Chinnery's letters to Maria Browne contain indications that he still regarded D'Oyly as his closest friend. 'All the Week I was dreadfuly ill', he wrote to her in August 1814; 'Friday I thought it was all over with me & Sunday gave D'Oyly a hint to be careful to recover my Sketches!!!' In November 1817 he excused himself from attending her, pleading pressure of work: 'Not a moment is left to me, even to go & see & breakfast with D'Oyly the last man on earth I would neglect...'[25]

Chinnery and D'Oyly parted company in 1821, when Chinnery went to Serampore (see p.157), and D'Oyly moved to Patna. By 1826 D'Oyly had set up a lithographic press in Bankipur, the suburb of Patna in which he and his family lived. This 'Behar Amateur Lithographic Press' produced several series of lithographed views and portraits, which were based on drawings by Chinnery, Charles and Eliza D'Oyly, and the Patna artist Jairam Das, who assisted D'Oyly

*Plate 54. Elizabeth Jane D'Oyly (née Ross), second wife of Sir Charles D'Oyly. Pencil and watercolours.* Private collection

in the running of the press, and whom D'Oyly encouraged to draw in a western idiom. Some of the lithographs are direct versions of Chinnery's work, while others are adapted ('Composition from Chinnery'), and others again are inscribed 'Chinnery delt. in outline', implying that one of the amateur artists supplied the tone.[26]

D'Oyly's own watercolours of his drawing room at Bankipur, in its winter and summer states, convey a lucid impression of the D'Oylys' artistic household (Plates 56 and 57). In each of the views (which are dated 1824) Sir Charles is occupied with his drawing books and his hookah, while his wife Eliza sits at the harp. (As William Prinsep observed of D'Oyly, 'his studio was always an attraction, for his pencil like his hookah-snake was always in his hand.'[27]) Among other family members is John Hadley D'Oyly, younger brother of Charles, who is shown at the billiard table on the far right (Plate 56).

According to a descendant of their sister Mrs. Snow, the pictures seen on the walls in these drawings were recognisable in 1907 as works which still belonged to the D'Oyly family.[28] Some of them were no doubt by Chinnery, and one may perhaps identify his portrait of Lord Hastings, which is hanging at an angle and is visible through the doorway to the left of the fireplace in Plate 56.

D'Oyly's two interior scenes represent his ideal of cultured domesticity, in which he and his wife are surrounded by pictures and music, family, friends and dogs. It is unlikely, however, that Chinnery was among the many visitors who sailed up the Ganges to call on the D'Oylys at Bankipur; the artist was now 350 miles away, struggling unsuccessfully to meet his obligations in Calcutta.

Of the many publications in which D'Oyly was involved, the most memorable is the long picaresque poem, *Tom Raw, the Griffin* (1828), a mild but often effective illustrated satire of Anglo-Indian manners. Its hero is a young 'griffin' or newcomer to India, who is introduced to the various institutions of British life in Calcutta. A central episode in the book is Tom's visit to Chinnery's studio. D'Oyly's illustration of this event exists in two versions: a watercolour (Colour Plate 19), which was not used for the printed work, and the published aquatint, 'Tom Raw sits for his portrait' (Plate 58).

*Plate 55. Sir Charles and Lady D'Oyly in Vandyck costume. Oils.* Private collection

*Plate 56. Sir Charles D'Oyly, The Winter Room in the D'Oylys' house in Patna. Pen and ink, watercolours and bodycolours, s. and d. Sep. 11 1824.* Yale Center for British Art, Paul Mellon Collection

*Plate 57. Sir Charles D'Oyly, The Summer Room in the D'Oylys' house in Patna. Watercolours, s. and d. Sep. 11 1824.* Yale Center for British Art, Paul Mellon Collection

*Colour Plate 17. Miniature portrait of Lieutenant Thomas Colclough Watson. Watercolours and bodycolours on ivory, s. and d. May 1811.* Martyn Gregory Gallery

*Colour Plate 18. Miniature portrait of Sir Charles and Lady D'Oyly. Watercolours and bodycolours on ivory.* Hongkong and Shanghai Banking Corporation

The watercolour represents a scene in stanza VIII (see Appendix iii), in which Tom is first introduced by his friend Randy to 'the ablest limner in the land, / With mild and gentle look inviting near, / Palette on thumb and maplestick in hand, / And saying, "Sirs — what may be your command?" '. A date is set for Tom's first sitting, and in the printed version, he is shown on the appointed day (stanza XXII),. with 'silver epaulette fresh scoured and polished', installed (stanza XXIII) 'on elevated floor..., / Calling up animated look and smile', while the artist 'flourished his charcoal ends'.

The artist, too, is more formally attired in the engraved version, wearing a cap and coat, but lacking the hair comb which can be seen in the watercolour (and in at least two of Chinnery's self-portraits); 'A semi-circular of tortoiseshell / Which, like Diana's crescent, tops his hairs / In inverse ratio...' (XVI). The engraving also contains a different selection of pictures on the studio wall. The watercolour includes once again the portrait of Lord Hastings (upper left, with unmistakably thick dark eyebrows), but it is omitted from the engraving, perhaps as being insufficiently respectful in a printed work by a civil servant; in a private letter written to the Governor-General's namesake, Warren Hastings, D'Oyly had complained that Lord and Lady Hastings were 'too enveloped in formality and grandeur, for there is no approach to anything like intimacy'.[29] A neat addition at the right of the engraving is the full-length portrait of the judge, who looks down at the scene with eyebrows raised, as if in disapproval of the artist's showmanship and the sitter's vanity.

Plate 58. 'Tom Raw sits for his portrait'. Etching and aquatint after Sir Charles D'Oyly. British Library

Colour Plate 19. Sir Charles D'Oyly, 'Tom Raw's introduction to Chinnery'. Watercolour. Hongkong and Shanghai Banking Corporation

PART III:
# Calcutta

# CHAPTER 7
## *Calcutta Portraits*

Considered in financial terms, the portraits painted by Chinnery in Calcutta represent the peak of his life's work. In aesthetic terms they do not place him in the first rank of European portrait artists; neither Chinnery nor any of his contemporaries in Britain can be regarded as worthy successors to Reynolds, Gainsborough and Lawrence. But Chinnery's Calcutta portraits have a special interest, which derives from the place and the circumstances in which they were painted — the capital of Britain's newly-unified 'Indian Empire', with its society of adventurous, acquisitive, occasionally philanthropic individuals who had chosen to join the tiny social minority of India's alien rulers.

*Colour Plate 20. A gentleman in a fur-trimmed cape. Oils.* Private collection

*Colour Plate 21. A member of the Pery family. Oils.* Private collection

For most of the eighteenth century, portraiture in India had been largely the preserve of the very wealthy, both Indian and British. In 1795 Robert Home had established himself in Calcutta, where he was well occupied with ceremonial portraits of the Wellesleys and Lord Minto, and also with half-lengths of East India Company officers. Home's work was in general capable rather than inspired, but his steady productivity and reasonable rates brought portraits within the reach of a wider stratum of the privileged classes than before. After ten years in Calcutta his commissions came more slowly, perhaps because of the competition presented by Chinnery and Thomas Hickey. In 1814, at the age of sixty-two, Home left Calcutta to take up a secure post as Court Painter to the Nawab of Oudh. Chinnery had by this time superseded Home as Calcutta's most fashionable portrait painter, but the younger artist's position was consolidated by Home's departure.

Chinnery's portraits of 1812-25 depict not only the pre-eminent figures of the time, but also a variety of middle-ranking civil servants and professional men, together with their wives and families. It would be absurd to suggest that Chinnery's portraits as a group represent a cross-section of Calcutta society; there are few artists in any society of whom this could be claimed. But collectively these portraits do offer some indications of the peculiar circumstances and attitudes which prevailed in the capital of British India.

In the first place, it is immediately apparent that the great majority of Chinnery's sitters were European, indeed British. This may be partly because his portraits of native Indians have remained in India,[1] and have not been publicised through the western network of auctions, galleries and exhibitions; and because Chinnery failed (or was unwilling) to secure a position as court painter to an Indian raja, as several of his predecessors had done. Yet it is also a sign of the times that Chinnery's subjects were predominantly British, and moreover that they were dressed as Englishmen in every detail — unlike their fathers and grandfathers in the East, who had sometimes had themselves or their families portrayed in oriental clothing, to commemorate their pioneering enterprise and, possibly, a sense of affinity with an adopted culture.

One of the last to do so was Colonel James Achilles Kirkpatrick, when in 1805 he commissioned Chinnery to portray his two Eurasian children in conspicuously Indian dress (Colour Plate 12). At that time it could still be said that Major Kirkpatrick 'behaved like a native, and with great propriety' (see p.62), but to most of Chinnery's British contemporaries in Calcutta, the suggestion that one of them had behaved like a native — or, to use the more common expression, had 'gone native' — was *ipso verbo* an insult. Chinnery's generation was increasingly concerned to eliminate any suggestion of 'going native' in costume, manners or cultural pursuits. If ever they chose to be portrayed in other than formal European dress, it was only to substitute a masquerade costume which was equally European (Plate 55). In certain cases the location of Chinnery's portraits is established by a pair of distant palm trees, or (in his portrait drawings) by a framed picture on the wall depicting the sitter's European-style mansion in Calcutta; in most instances, however, the sitters are presented amid the conventional properties of Georgian portraiture — billowing curtain and classical parapet, with a background of romantically swirling cloud, and a well-treed landscape which could as well represent Berkshire as Bengal.

By the same principle, there are no portraits in Chinnery's *oeuvre* in which a European is depicted together with his Indian wife or mistress. This represents a change in attitude rather than a radical change of social practice; many prominent men of Chinnery's time had an Indian wife or (much more commonly) an Indian mistress, but such an arrangement now excited sufficient disapproval to prevent its being openly acknowledged in a portrait — as had been done most famously in Francesco Renaldi's portrait of 1786 depicting Major (later General) William Palmer together with his *bibi*, her children by him, and the children's *ayahs*.[2] Chinnery did make pencil drawings of the illegitimate daughters of James Ruthven Elphinstone, born to him by 'Zebunissa, otherwise and more usually called Bunnoo Beebee', but he portrayed Elphinstone himself in a separate drawing.[3] No doubt Chinnery executed other such portraits of Indian mistresses and their Eurasian offspring, which have been subsequently discarded by disapproving grandchildren.

In the generation preceding Chinnery's, it had been common practice for Indians to be depicted together with Europeans in group portraits. Almost always the Indians occupied subordinate roles, appearing as *bibis, munshis* or *syces,* as musicians or dancers, as sepoys, hostages or vanquished enemies. In certain scenes, in which Europeans were depicted at the court of a nawab, the roles were to some degree reversed; perhaps only as participants in 'Colonel Mordaunt's Cock Match' do Indians and Europeans appear on equal terms.[4] But in most of Chinnery's portraits there is no notion of relating the European sitters either to the Indian environment or to the Indians with whose lives they were closely involved. Occasionally an Indian (or Chinese) *ayah* takes her place among the members of a family portrayed by Chinnery (Colour Plates 93 and 94), but most of his Calcutta portraits betray no trace of their Indian origin except the distinctive style of the artist.

Chinnery had returned from Dacca to Calcutta by the early months of 1812. The manuscript lists of European inhabitants in the city record that in 1812 he was residing 'to the eastward of Messrs. Fairlie Fergusson & Co.', this being an agency house in Old Council House Street.[5] Clearly his reputation had not suffered during his period in Dacca, for he was soon employed on two prestigious portrait commissions, from General Sir George Nugent, Commander-in-Chief of the British forces in India, and from Lord Minto, the Governor-General. Chinnery may have encountered Nugent in Ireland, where the latter was Adjutant-General from 1798 to 1801. But in India the initiative came from Lady Nugent: 'Saw Chinnery's paintings,' she wrote in her journal, 'the likenesses excellent — prevailed upon Sir George to sit for me.' As she recorded, the sittings began at 7 a.m. on 1 June 1812.[6]

In the following year Nugent was superseded, unfairly he believed, by the Prince Regent's friend Lord Moira, who subsequently became the Marquess of Hastings. Lord Hastings was appointed as both Commander-in-Chief and Governor-General, and was duly portrayed by Chinnery; but it was with his

*Detail of Colour Plate 22*

predecessor in the second office, Lord Minto, that the artist achieved the closer and more fruitful relationship.

Gilbert Elliot, 1st Earl of Minto, was a cultivated and versatile man. At school in Fontainebleau the young Mirabeau had been his friend and the philosopher David Hume his guardian. As an advocate he prepared, together with Edmund Burke, the case against Warren Hastings and Sir Elijah Impey. As a diplomat he was active in the war against France, and governed Corsica during its brief existence as the Anglo-Corsican Kingdom. By the time of his appointment to India he was a respected administrator, and a Fellow of the Royal Societies of London and Edinburgh. In India he did much to improve the finances of the East India Company; the military campaigns conducted during his term of office were not uniformly successful, but he earned particular credit as the conqueror of Java (formerly a Dutch colony), having accompanied the expedition himself. This achievement is celebrated in several of Chinnery's portraits of Minto.

It appears from Chinnery's letters to Lord Minto — if allowance is made for the artist's fulsome rhetoric — that Chinnery was on good terms with Minto and with other members of the Elliot family, to whom he sent his 'most respectful and affectionate regards', while passing on to Minto the respects of his friends Charles D'Oyly and James Atkinson.[7] Another contemporary described Minto as having 'a great deal of decided friendship whenever occasion called it forth', and 'a great share of that playful conversation which makes every man in company equally happy';[8] one can imagine that he found Chinnery a stimulating companion.

On a professional level, Minto's patronage brought both income and reputation to Chinnery, as his letters acknowledge at length. Moreover Minto held out prospects for Chinnery's future. In writing to Chinnery from Capetown on 21 February 1814 Minto had expressed a desire to see Chinnery in England, which prompted Chinnery to hint broadly that Minto might help him return there:

Had I the means (which I have limited to 6000£ over & above what would settle me in England & cover my passage wh. would amount to perhaps 1500 or 2000 £ more) I should enter the Lists with my Brethren unhesitatingly, should paint with my former Coadjutators now grown old in Expectation, & have a pleasure in referring to former Times when their Expectation was in Embryo, & my own distinction uncertain.[9]

*Colour Plate 22. Portrait of George Siddons with his hookah. Oils.* Hongkong and Shanghai
Banking Corporation

*Plate 59. Gilbert Elliot, 1st Earl of Minto. Oils.* National Galleries of Scotland

Lord Minto never received this letter, having died a month after disembarking in England. He may, however, have received a letter from Marianne Chinnery, conveying 'the ardent effusions of my most grateful heart' after hearing from her husband of the generosity shown to him by Minto and his family.[10]

Chinnery painted at least four portraits of the Governor-General. For Lord Minto himself he painted a full-length standing portrait in peer's robes and knee breeches, with his Earl's coronet behind him (Plate 59). His left hand rests on a map of Java, above which allegorical figures refer to his military and cultural achievements; other maps inscribed 'Bourbon' and 'Mauritius' lie on the ground. This painting was passed down to the 4th Earl, who himself became Viceroy of India a century after his great-grandfather; but the 4th Earl, mistakenly believing that it was not a portrait by Chinnery but a replica, presented it to the Town Hall of Hawick near his seat of Minto.[11] In 1815 the portrait was engraved in mezzotint by Charles Turner, who was said to have 'improved the figures &c greatly'.[12]

A second portrait was sent from Calcutta to Batavia, where it arrived on 18 July 1813. It was later given to Raffles, whom Minto had admired and promoted, and is still in the possession of his descendants.[13] Raffles was also with Minto in Malacca, which Minto visited *en route* for Java in 1811; and in 1814 a third portrait was sent to Malacca, commemmorating Minto in humanitarian guise. The Malacca waterfront appears behind the standing figure of the Earl, while a relief on a pedestal represents the public burning of various instruments of torture which had been discovered in a Malacca prison.[14]

A fourth portrait, now in the Rijksmuseum in Amsterdam, was commissioned by the Dutch inhabitants of Batavia. Chinnery had arranged that the painting be sent to Batavia in the care of the prominent Dutch administrator Jacob Andries van Braam, but — as so often in Chinnery's commissions — there were delays:

My business is so great & I have been pressed upon lately so much, as you are aware, that to put the last touch to the work has been out of my power —

To do this before you go is my intention — but time must be given for the picture to dry before it is packed, for if any dust or dirt gets on the picture before it is dry it will injure it very materially & I should feel most sensibly annoyed if any accident happened to a work, on which I build so much an increase of my professional reputation & to which such great commendation has been given.[15]

*Plate 60. Sir William Rumbold. Oils.* Private collection; on loan to the Fitzwilliam Museum, Cambridge

*Plate 61. Thomas Hooke Pearson. Oils.* Private collection

Perhaps predictably, the picture missed the boat. Van Braam sailed to Batavia without the portrait, and was obliged to postpone the speech which he had prepared for its unveiling. Chinnery had to write to van Braam in still more abject terms, proposing that the painting be conveyed on the next sailing of one of 'Mr Alexander's ships', and asking that van Braam explain the circumstances 'to the principal Inhabitants and to Mr Raffles...' 'It will be so very carefully packed that no fear can be entertained about it even should it not go in the hold & it is laid in the Deck for no wet shall get to it — could it go in the hold it would certainly be better.'[16]

Finally the portrait arrived, in the care of Dr. Robertson, in April 1814; van Braam was able to deliver his speech, and the picture — showing the robed Earl seated with a loyal address from the Dutch people of Batavia beside him — was received with acclamation.[17]

Having portrayed the Chief Justice, the Commander-in-Chief and the Governor-General, Chinnery was now in a position to receive commissions from the socially aspiring in all walks of life. Some of his most successful portraits of this period represent young men at the outset of their careers, who, as portrayed by Chinnery, convey a sense of confidence bordering on arrogance. The four young men represented in Plates 60, 61 and Colour Plates 20 and 21 stand with a slight sway of the hips, and a little more weight placed on their right leg than on their left. Their arms are nonchalantly deployed, and their chins are raised, or at least held up by their tight collars and cravats. There is no sign of the furniture which appears in Chinnery's family groups and couples, but the subjects are marked as gentlemen of standing and expectations by their personal accessories — top hat, gloves, seal at the waist — and by their stance: as Chinnery observed to his pupil, Mrs Browne, 'Expression' in a portrait lies rather in 'the *Shoulders* & *Hands* than in the face.'[18]

*Colour Plate 23. William Locker. Pencil and watercolours.* Hongkong and Shanghai Banking Corporation

Two of the young men (Plate 61 and Colour Plate 21) are fresh-faced teenagers, who call to mind the advice given by Robert 'Bobus' Smith to Lord Minto: 'You should always contrive to have some blooming youth fresh from England to sit next to you; the mosquitoes are sure to go to him.'[19] The demeanour of Thomas Hooke Pearson (Plate 61) in particular seems to anticipate a career distinguished by acts of reckless bravado. He can have been no older than eighteen when Chinnery portrayed him, newly returned from Eton to his native Calcutta, where his father had been Advocate-General to the East India Company. In March 1825, four months before Chinnery left India, Thomas Pearson joined the cavalry, in which he won renown for his courage and horsemanship; mounted on his thoroughbred, he charged the Sikh army at the battle of Maharajpore, his sword grasped between his teeth. He served as aide-de-camp to Lord Amherst on his mission to Ranjeet Singh, ruler of the Punjab, who presented him with a gold-inlaid sword after Pearson 'astonished and delighted the Sikhs by mounting and controlling an almost wild horse, which had never before allowed a rider to remain on its back'.[20] Surprisingly, Thomas Pearson lived into old age, retiring at the rank of General to breed racehorses.

*Colour Plate 24. Patrick Savage. Oils.* Hongkong and Shanghai Banking Corporation

Still more conspicuous, although in a different sphere, was the career of Sir William Rumbold, portrayed in one of Chinnery's most elegant small full-lengths (Plate 60). Rumbold is remembered particularly for his long-running disagreement with Sir Charles (later Baron) Metcalfe, who at the time was Resident of Hyderabad. The dispute arose from the fact that the Nizam of Hyderabad was heavily in debt to the banking house of William Palmer, of which Rumbold was a partner; as the Nizam continued to borrow, at a high rate of interest, so did the power of the bankers over the Nizam increase, becoming more significant (as it seemed to Metcalfe) than that of the British Government.

Underlying this controversy was a clash of personalities. Metcalfe was a conscientious civil servant with no great liking for Anglo-Indian social life; when he became Resident of Hyderabad in 1820, he expressed the wish that white ants might destroy the billiard table which, he felt, had turned the Residency into a tavern. By contrast the house of Sir William Rumbold was a centre of fashionable society, celebrated for its lavish entertainment, good music and beautiful women. Rumbold was moreover well connected, being the grandson of a former Governor of Madras, and the husband of a ward of Governor-General Lord Hastings, successor to Lord Minto. Much to Metcalfe's resentment, Rumbold and Palmer received more salutes, as they were borne along in their palanquins, than did the Resident himself.

Chinnery's portraits of Rumbold and Metcalfe reflect to some extent their differing temperaments. The portrait of Metcalfe[21] is a competent but

*Plate 62. Sir Charles Metcalfe. Oils.* National Portrait Gallery, London

*Plate 63. George Siddons. Oils.* Private collection

conventional head-and-shoulders study of a sober, correct and slightly over-fleshed man (Plate 62), whereas Rumbold cuts a flamboyant, almost swaggering figure, elevated on a decorative balcony overlooking Government House and a part of the south-east gateway. As India's leading portrait painter, Chinnery was not associated with any particular faction; he painted portraits of individuals on both sides of the dispute (which aroused strong passions in India and in England, and was eventually resolved by a compromise). These included Lord Hastings, who for the most part supported Rumbold; and on the other side, the wife and daughter of William Trant of the Bengal Civil Service.[22] Trant, who had succeeded Richmond Thackeray as Collector of the 24 Parganas, testified eloquently to the incorruptible character of his old friend Charles Metcalfe, whom he had known since they were boys together in the same house at Eton.[23]

It is notoriously tempting to judge a portrait in terms of what is known or believed about the sitter's personality. Thus the expression of George Siddons (Plate 63), which might otherwise be seen as one of friendly frankness, seems supercilious in the light of a contemporary description of the man as 'an empty Coxcomb, and consummate Puppy'.[24] The sitter was a son of the actress Sarah Siddons, and nephew of John Philip Kemble, whom Chinnery had portrayed in London. He spent six years in the small settlement of Bencoolen, in Sumatra, before being posted to Calcutta in 1818 as First Deputy to the Collector of Government Customs and Town Duties. The Collector was Sir Charles D'Oyly, who must have appreciated Siddons's artistic connections. In addition to this portrait, Chinnery produced a drawing of Siddons with his wife and two daughters,[25] and an unfinished painting of Siddons in his study, grasping the snake of his hookah (Colour Plate 22 and detail).

*Colour Plate 25. The Marquess of Hastings in Garter robes. Oils.* Hongkong and Shanghai Banking Corporation

## Judicial Portraits

Although Chinnery's clients in Calcutta represented a variety of occupations, judges and advocates formed perhaps the largest single group. Prominent among them were Sir Henry Russell's successor as Chief Justice of Bengal, Sir Edward Hyde East, whom Chinnery depicted in his judge's robes;[26] Robert Cutlar Fergusson, who acted as Advocate-General from 1816 to 1818;[27] and John Pearson, who became Advocate-General in 1824. Pearson was described by a visiting Frenchman as being 'plein d'esprit et de gaieté, et liberal comme nous, ce qui veut dire radical en anglais'.[28] Something of Pearson's wit and unorthodoxy is communicated in the relaxed pose and wry expression seen in Chinnery's portrait (Plate 64). A colleague was the Irishman James Hogg, who was appointed Registrar of the Supreme Court and Administrator-General in 1822, and returned to England ten years later to enjoy his fortune and a baronetcy. Sir James was the only member of the Calcutta Bar to become Chairman of the East India Company; a succession of Hoggs followed him with distinction in the legal profession.[29]

Another advocate well known to Chinnery was Sir Herbert Compton, whose Madras bungalow had been drawn by the artist in 1805 (see p.78 and Colour Plate 15). Compton was enrolled at the Supreme Court in Calcutta in June 1815, and at his marriage the following month, Chinnery was one of the four witnesses who signed the register.[30] In April of the following year Chinnery made a drawing of Compton's palatial house in Garden Reach (Plate 65), and in December he was again to be found 'on the road to Compton's'.[31] It seems that Compton was particularly eager to record his various residences, since in 1819 James Fraser was also 'at Mr Compton's', engaged in 'making a view of his garden house'.[32]

The major judicial commission of Chinnery's later years in Calcutta was undoubtedly the large portrait of Sir Francis Workman Macnaghten, Puisne Judge of the Supreme Court from 1816 to 1825. As a young man Macnaghten had been a close friend of William Hickey, and when Macnaghten was nominated High Sheriff of Calcutta in 1796, he had appointed Hickey his deputy. The diarist remembered Macnaghten as a warm-hearted but hot-tempered individual. On one occasion, infuriated by a persistent toothache, he had tried to hack out the offending tooth with a carving knife, thereby causing such serious and prolonged injury to his jaw that at one time three surgeons were in anxious attendance. He recovered, but the episode left 'an immense scar on the outside of his neck'.[33] The scar is obscured by whiskers in Chinnery's severe portrait, and in his pencil study for it (Plate 66).

*Plate 65. Holwell Place, the seat of Sir Herbert Compton. Pencil, dated April 21 1816. Private collection*

This portrait was commissioned in November 1822, nearly thirty years after Macnaghten's drastic attempt at self-surgery.[34] The judge was at this time involved in the various legal actions brought by the Government against Chinnery's friend and creditor, James Silk Buckingham (see pp.150-1); Macnaghten took a sympathetic attitude to Buckingham's case, but it was not enough to save the maverick editor from being deported.[35]

The Macnaghten portrait was a large one (88 x 60 inches), and it was probably the last major commission which Chinnery completed in Calcutta. It occupied him — although not continuously — for more than a year. On 26 January 1824 the *Calcutta Government Gazette* could at last report that 'the Portrait of Sir Francis Macnaghten is just finished, and placed in the Court House among the portraits of his predecessors.' As in the Russell portrait, Chinnery introduced blind Justice and other symbolic figures into the background. The head of Macnaghten was thought by the *Gazette* to be an exact likeness, 'acute and intelligent', and the handling and colour were said to be masterly. 'It is perhaps one of the finest specimens of Mr CHINNERY's talents, which are universally acknowledged to be rare and splendid, that we have seen.' There were objections, however. The black silk gown did not appear sufficiently contrasted with 'a warm and gleamy but well subdued offskip'. Moreover, in concentrating on the head the artist had neglected the 'inferior details' — a familiar criticism of Chinnery's work. The head alone was engraved by Savignhac and published in Calcutta in February 1824.[36]

Civilians formed the great majority of Chinnery's Calcutta sitters, but he continued to portray military officers, in oils or tightly-controlled drawings. Both Colonel Valentine Blacker (Plate 67 and see pp.79-80) and Captain William Locker of the 8th Light Dragoons (Colour Plate 23) are lent dignity by the artist's meticulous drawing of their shakos, scabbards and tasselled riding boots. These accoutrements are lacking

*Plate 66. Pencil study of Sir Francis Macnaghten. Hongkong and Shanghai Banking Corporation*

*Colour Plate 26. Mrs. Da Silva. Oils.* Private collection

*Colour Plate 27. Woman in black. Oils.* Spink & Son Ltd.

116

*Colour Plate 28. Mrs. Jane Pearson. Oils.* Hongkong and Shanghai Banking Corporation

*Colour Plate 29. Margaret Erskine. Oils.* Hongkong and Shanghai Banking Corporation

*Colour Plate 30. Woman in black. Oils.* Hongkong and Shanghai Banking Corporation

*Colour Plate 31. Woman in dark blue. Oils.* Kelton Foundation

*Plate 67. Lieutenant-Colonel Valentine Blacker. Pencil and watercolours, s. and d. 1819. Spink & Son Ltd.*

in the half-length oil portrait of Major (later Lieutenant-Colonel) Patrick Savage (Colour Plate 24), but instead a background is supplied in which evening sunshine emerges from swirling thunderclouds, as if to suggest a glorious victory won amid conflagration and cannon smoke.

The pinnacle of Calcutta society, the principal of both civil and military services from 1813 until 1823, was Francis Rawdon-Hastings, 2nd Earl of Moira, created Marquess of Hastings in recognition of his army's success in the Nepal war. As a young parliamentarian he had denounced the British government of India as 'founded in injustice, and originally established by force'.[37] This did not prevent him, when he came to power, from forcibly extending the British empire throughout India, and as far northward as the border with China, by means of campaigns against the Gurkhas, the Pindaris, and the Marathas. A veteran of the American and French wars, he was a ruthlessly efficient soldier and an unscrupulous politician. These attributes are not evident in Chinnery's portraits of Hastings, who was by now in his sixties. Chinnery presents him as an elderly patriarch, heavily-jowled, benevolent, even bucolic — far removed from the dashing young man whom Sir Joshua Reynolds had portrayed thirty years before.[38]

The small full-length of Lord Hastings in Garter robes (Colour Plate 25) is one of several portraits of the Governor-General painted by Chinnery. A three-quarter-length, showing Hastings seated and in military uniform, was in the Bengal Artillery Mess Room at Dum Dum in 1823, at which time it was engraved and published; it was later hung in the Viceroy's Residence at Delhi.[39] Another full-length in Garter robes, but with the addition of 'the emblems of masonry', was commissioned by the masonic lodge at Mauritius, where Hastings (then Lord Moira), in his capacity as a leading freemason, had laid the corner-stone of the new cathedral. In June 1816 this portrait was in progress, and the likeness was said to be 'already correct and striking'.[40]

What should have been Chinnery's grandest painting of Lord Hastings was an equestrian portrait commissioned in December 1822 as a memorial to the outgoing Governor-General. Subscriptions totalling 16,000 rupees were raised for Chinnery to execute the commission. His pen-and-ink sketch (Plate 68) depicts Hastings in military mode, astride a spirited charger, directing operations from a hilltop as battle rages below.[41] But the painting did not follow. When Chinnery sailed to China in July 1825, ostensibly as a temporary measure for the benefit of his health, there remained a possibility that he might return to fulfil his commission. In July 1827, however, it was observed at a meeting in Calcutta Town Hall that the artist had now been absent from India for two years, and there was still no sign of the portrait. The upshot was that, 'Mr Chinnery not having fulfilled his part of the engagement, the

*Plate 68. Sketch for an equestrian portrait of Lord Hastings. Pen and ink over pencil. Sven Gahlin, Esq.*

committee withdrew from it entirely.'[42]

Chinnery's relationship with Lord Hastings had nevertheless been fruitful. Shortly after Hastings's arrival, the artist wrote to Lord Minto to say that he had dined at Government House, and received 'invitations to many parties of other kinds there...Of my productions his Lordship, Lady Loudoune [*sic*] & Family speak most warmly & on their return from the Upper provinces there will be I believe a considerable Employt. from them...'[43]

It seems moreover that Chinnery asked Hastings whether a commission in the Bengal army could be found for his son, John Eustace Chinnery; and that Hastings promised that the boy should have a position in the 47th Regiment. John Eustace duly applied to the Court of Directors in London, stating that his father had obtained him this commission through the Governor-General. The Court, which included Neil Edmonstone and several others who had known Chinnery, agreed that his son should proceed to India, once the Horse Guards had given word that the appointment had been confirmed. But when John Eustace Chinnery enquired at the Guards, he was told that the vacancy had been filled by someone else. He applied again to the Court, asking to be allowed to go to Bengal 'for the purpose of residing with his father'. This was refused.[44] John Eustace nevertheless made his way out to India, where he was reunited with his father before succumbing to a fever (see p.152).

Lord Hastings finally returned to England in January 1823, having been compelled to resign as a result of his involvement in the case of the loans made by Palmer and Rumbold to the Nizam of Hyderabad. In his place the Senior Member of Council, John Adam, was appointed acting Governor-General. When the new Governor-General, Lord Amherst, arrived in Calcutta later in the year, Adam stepped down, and subscriptions were raised for his portrait to be painted by Chinnery. The subscribers included many of Chinnery's old friends and sitters — Fergusson, Larkins, Lushington and Palmer (contributing 200 rupees each), two Plowdens (150 and 160 rupees),

*Colour Plate 32. Vase in a landscape.*
*Watercolours.* Private collection

*Plate 69. Frances Plowden (née Erskine). Pencil and water-colours.* Private collection.

C.R.Lindsay (100 rupees), and three Prinseps (50, 100 and 150 rupees). By January 1824, 16,000 rupees had been promised — the same as the sum raised for Chinnery's ill-fated equestrian portrait of Hastings.[45]

Once again, Chinnery was unable to fulfil the commission. This was partly because Adam was obliged to leave India prematurely, setting off on the long journey to England in the hope of recovering his health; moreover, since Chinnery had already borrowed money against the completion of the picture (see p.155), he was perhaps in no hurry to carry out the task. As it transpired, Adam died on the voyage, and Chinnery absconded to China. But on this occasion the project was not abandoned. Chinnery's preparatory sketches were sent back to England, where Sir Thomas Lawrence completed the portrait — although without the spectacles which appeared in Chinnery's drawings. Lawrence's picture was brought to Calcutta in June 1828.[46]

**Portraits of Women**

'Nearly unmitigated *ennui* is the lot of the majority of luckless women,' wrote a General's daughter of her fellow-Englishwomen in India,[47] and there is little in Chinnery's portraits of individual women (Plate 69 and Colour Plates 26-31) to contradict this. His female sitters are sometimes posed as formally as their male counterparts, beside a draped column or a parapet, but in many cases a shawl or bonnet is placed beside them, together with a vase or nosegay of flowers. Chinnery's studies of minor stage properties (Colour Plate 32 and Plate 70) have a freedom and elegance which make one regret that he seldom indulged in this kind of decorative drawing for its own sake.

It is his female portraits which most strongly suggest the influence of Sir Thomas Lawrence, who during Chinnery's student years in London was already regarded as the leading exponent of society portraiture. Ever since his early works Chinnery showed a fondness for translucent effects and lacy trimmings in shawls and bonnets, collars and sleeves. Typical is the portrait of Margaret Erskine (Colour Plate 29). Diaphanous sleeves are suggested by thin applications of near-white, leading to crimped edgings marked by firm strokes of pure white impasto, in the manner of Lawrence's portraits of the 1790s.

Plate 70. Studies of ornamental vases. Pen and ink over pencil. Private collection

Chinnery's concern for such effects is communicated in his tutorial letters to Maria Browne. 'Keep the white drapery clean — the ribbon looks a little *cottony* — ribbons ought always to be rather drawn...the Frill is admirable...'[48] Or again, 'In spotting of muslin never put a shadow under the spot — leave the Light spots by themselves...'[49] In general Chinnery's female portraits depend upon accessories to a greater extent than the male (with the exception of the ceremonial full-lengths), and for him this was a matter of principle:

> With a half length of a Man in particular there must be always a good deal of Contrivance & its success must depend on the real Bricks and Mortar as it were for one can add no extraneous ornaments — With Women, Draperies of all kinds can & do assist us — Laces, shawls Gauzes come in so as to alter even the attitude — *certainly so as to make quite a different thing of the Picture to what it would be without them.*[50]

Chinnery's treatment of the head and hair of his female subjects becomes more mannered in his later years, when the forehead is raised and the hair is drawn tightly across the crown of the head, although allowed to curl in luxuriant ringlets at either side. This effect, sometimes disconcerting to modern taste, was again a matter of aesthetic principle: '...you might have helped the Forehead by making it a Line or two higher wh. is always a beauty — low Foreheads are *not* beautiful...'[51]

The liberal use of red in the shadows between the fingers, and also (in a lighter shade) near the tips of the fingers themselves, is another feature which Chinnery's portraits, both male and female, have in common with the early work of Lawrence. '*Red tips* to fingers (particularly in pretty Ladies) are a great beauty'.[52] Chinnery also shared Lawrence's habit of introducing a strong element of red into the shadows under the nose. When Lawrence's seated portrait of Queen Charlotte was exhibited at the Royal Academy in 1789, it was observed that 'Her Majesty's nose, indeed, appears to be sore from taking snuff'.[53] A similar objection was made to one of Chinnery's portraits, depicting

Major Herbert of the Royal Engineers. Shortly after this picture was delivered to him, Herbert returned it with a note saying that 'he had no notion of having such a likeness with a polypus under the nose'. William Prinsep, who received the picture in Chinnery's absence (see p.161), admitted that 'Chinnery's shadows were rather too forcible & here doubtless the Indian red shadow of the nose was rather strong.' Prinsep therefore painted out the offending shadow, and Major Herbert was content, although Chinnery understandably 'went nearly mad' when he heard that Prinsep had dared to touch his work.[54]

### Family Groups

Since an Anglo-Indian family could count itself lucky if both parents survived to middle age, the idealised state of domestic happiness suggested by Chinnery's group portraits was often short-lived. Both James Stewart and Richmond Thackeray, pictured in Plates 71 and 72, had worked their way through the junior ranks of the East India Company's services to a point at which marriage became feasible, only to fall victim to fever and climate while still in their early thirties. Stewart had begun his career as a fifteen-year-old Surgeon's Mate on board an East Indiaman, before gaining a Company appointment in India, and spending some time in the service of the Nawab of Oudh. In September 1820 he married Charlotte Fraser at Cawnpore, having reached the rank of Assistant Surgeon, and Chinnery's portrait was probably painted shortly after the beginning of the Stewarts' brief married life.[55]

Richmond Thackeray, too, was quickly rich and quickly dead. A notable member of a distinguished Anglo-Indian family,[56] he is depicted in an elegant armchair, surrounded by symbols of wealth, wisdom and — in the form of his wife and child — domestic contentment. He maintained a fine residence at Chowringhee, while holding a succession of judicial and administrative posts in Calcutta and the provinces, culminating in the collectorship of the 24 Parganas to the south of Calcutta. As Collector of a Bengal district he held daunting responsibilities, which included 'roads, ferries, bridges, river-floods, jails, lunatics, child-landowners, state pensioners and wards, education, epidemics, dispensaries, payments for killing snakes and tigers...'[57]

In the winter of 1809-10 Richmond Thackeray met the seventeen-year-old Anne Becher, newly arrived from England. She was herself descended from a staunch Anglo-Indian family: a dozen Bechers served in India during her years there. Richmond 'came courting her on a white horse',[58] and in October 1810 they were married. Anne Thackeray has been credited with every virtue of intellect, taste and piety; she and her sister-in-law are said to have possessed such beauty and dignity that 'when they moved to leave the room, any gentlemen who were present rose instantly to hand them to the door.'[59] Even in old age she had 'fine dark eyebrows',[60] which are conspicuous in Chinnery's portrait. Indeed, Chinnery has painted her in his most romantic manner, with distracted gaze, unkempt ringlets, and outrageously long legs.

The Thackeray family was not, however, as happily settled as Chinnery's portrait might suggest. Captain Henry Carmichael-Smyth, whom Anne had

*Plate 71. Dr. James and Charlotte Stewart. Oils.* Private collection

*Plate 72. Richmond and Anne Thackeray, and their son William Makepeace Thackeray. Pencil and watercolours, s. and d. 1814.* Harris Art Gallery, Preston

once loved but believed to be dead, reappeared in 1812 in Calcutta, to the discomfiture of Richmond; after the death of Richmond in 1816 (and a suitable interval of mourning), Anne and Carmichael-Smyth were married. Also missing from the family group are Charlotte, Richmond's Indian or Eurasian mistress, and Sarah, the daughter of this liaison, who would have been about ten years old at the time of the portrait. Like Chinnery's sons Edward and Henry, and the illegitimate children of many of his contemporaries (John Elliot, Richmond's close friend and brother-in-law, fathered eight), Sarah would have been condemned to live and marry within a group of people who were uneasily but sharply distinguished from both Indians and Europeans, and whose existence was seldom acknowledged in the correspondence or the portraits of the time. In 1820 Sarah married an illegitimate man of mixed race; after her death in 1841 she was finally recognised as 'the only daughter of the late Richmond Thackeray', on the tombstone which was placed next to her father's in the Park Street cemetery.[61]

The wide-eyed child in the family portrait is William Makepeace Thackeray, the future novelist, who had been born in Calcutta on 18 July 1811. Thackeray was later to return the compliment by referring to Chinnery in his novel *The Newcomes.* Colonel Newcome, returned from service in India, speaks fondly of a portrait drawn by his son, a student of art whom the Colonel believes to be an unrivalled genius: 'Why, the rascal, Sir, has drawn me, his own father; And I have sent the drawing to Major Hobbs, who is in command of my regiment. Chinnery himself, Sir, couldn't hit off a likeness better.'[62]

William Makepeace Thackeray was four years old when his father died. Two years later he was sent to England to be educated. As an adult he may not have retained much memory of Chinnery; he could only dimly remember his own

father, as somebody 'very tall, and rising up out of a bath'.[63] Nevertheless it is tempting to imagine that Chinnery may have had some influence on Thackeray's artistic proclivities. As soon as the six-year-old Thackeray arrived in England, he drew a picture of the family house in Calcutta, 'not omitting the monkey looking out of the window, and black Betty at the top drying the towels'.[64] Thackeray became a skilful draughtsman and caricaturist, who studied painting in London and Paris with a view to becoming a professional artist. He no doubt experienced the reaction which is expressed by Major Pendennis when he discovers that Colonel Newcome intends to make his son a painter: 'An artist! By gad, in my time a fellow would as soon have thought of making his son a hairdresser, or a pastry-cook, by gad!'[65]

India continued to affect Thackeray's life in England, for in 1833 he lost much of the considerable fortune which he had inherited from his father; it is probable that this money had been invested in Palmer & Co. or in one of the other Indian agency houses which were bankrupted during the early 1830s. In *Vanity Fair* Thackeray wrote with some bitterness of 'the great house of Fogle, Fake, and Cracksman', which 'failed for a million, and plunged half the Indian public into misery and ruin'.[66]

*Colour Plate 34. The children of Captain Thomas Powell Comyn. Oils.* Hongkong and Shanghai Banking Corporation

In common with Reynolds and many of his contemporaries, Chinnery was quite prepared to repeat compositions, and his double portraits of the D'Oylys (Colour Plate 18), the Stewarts (Plate 71) and the Larkins (Colour Plate 33) all follow the same pattern with minor variations. John Pascal Larkins came from a well-known Anglo-Indian family, who had been solid supporters of Warren Hastings. His grandfather, his father and his uncle were all sea captains and shipowners, and another uncle had been the Company's Accountant-General. In 1819 he was appointed Junior Member of the Board of Customs, Salt and Opium, of which he became Senior Member four years later. In 1813 he had married Mary Robertson (seen here), a cousin of W.E.Gladstone. Chinnery also made a portrait drawing of the couple in 1814, and drawings of their sons in 1819 and 1822.[67] In 1823 Larkins was Chairman of the committee which organised the subscriptions for Chinnery's portrait of Sir John Adam, a committee entirely composed of friends or patrons of the artist.[68]

Chinnery drew a number of group portraits in the manner of the Thackeray picture, painting the heads, necks and exposed limbs of the figures in fine-brush watercolour. In effect these are portrait miniatures, set within a precisely pencilled framework of tables and settees. Plates 73 and 74 depict the children of Neil Benjamin Edmonstone, Member of the Supreme Council and one of the most powerful individuals in India. It is evident that a greater degree of informality is regarded as appropriate to the girls, while the boy, although the youngest of the children depicted, is allotted the most adult and independent stance. Chinnery's portraits of children often have a particular charm, but he had little opportunity to practise this *genre* when he moved to the China coast, where very few western children were to be found. In Calcutta it was generally necessary to portray children at a young age, before they were sent back to be educated in Britain; the parents, and the portrait, remained behind.

An appealing example is the triple portrait of the Comyn children (Colour Plate 34). The three figures form the pyramidal shape which, as Chinnery advised Maria Browne, 'the eye is always satisfied with & almost looks for'[69] — as indeed do the three children who are pictured together in D'Oyly's caricature of Chinnery's studio (Colour Plate 19). The Comyn group was painted in 1815-16, when Captain Thomas Powell Comyn had returned to Calcutta after serving against the Gurkhas in the Nepal War. In 1805 he had married Jane de Courcy, the natural daughter of an officer in the Bengal army. She was at most fifteen at the time,[70] which was not an uncommon age for a girl to be married in the overwhelmingly male society of the British in India. (Looking at Chinnery's drawing of an unidentified group (Plate 75), it is easy to imagine that, once the music stops, the officer lounging against the piano will stand to attention and propose marriage to the teenage pianist.)

Jane de Courcy was almost certainly Eurasian, but no trace of Indian ancestry is allowed to appear in any of her three children. A similarly European pallor is also to be discerned in other portrayals, by Chinnery's predecessors in India, of children of mixed birth or ancestry. The racial impulse underlying this convention finds literary expression in the final paragraph of Rider Haggard's *Allan Quartermain*. Here a child is born to the African Queen Nyleptha and the Englishman Sir Henry Curtis; fortunately for Sir Henry, the child — whom he resolves to bring up as an English gentleman — has the looks of 'a regular, curly-haired blue-eyed young Englishman'.[71]

The group portrait of Lady Harriet Paget and her five eldest children (Colour Plate 35) is unusually well documented in General Paget's letters. These illustrate the significance of a group portrait at a time and a place in which illness and military service constantly threatened to disrupt a family. The picture was painted for Sir Edward Paget, a soldier who had risen

*Plate 73. Charlotte and Henrietta Edmonstone. Pencil and watercolours.* Private collection

*Plate 74. Neil and Susanna Edmonstone. Pencil and watercolours.* Private collection

through the officer ranks with amazing rapidity: commissioned at the age of sixteen, he had become a Major-General at twenty-nine, and at forty-six was appointed Commander-in-Chief of India. By this time he had fought on four continents, received a bullet in the neck at Alexandria and retreated with Moore at Corunna. Yet this battle-scarred veteran, who dealt relentlessly with the Barrackpore mutineers of 1824, was said to have been particularly fond of his children. On one occasion, at a christening party, he playfully threw up his youngest boy, but in his enthusiasm misjudged his trajectory, and sent his son flying over his shoulder; the child was skilfully fielded by a lady-in-waiting.[72]

In 1815 General Paget had married Harriet Legge, daughter of the Earl of Dartmouth. By 1822 she had given birth to five children (three more were to follow later), and was due to return with them to England. Chinnery therefore painted the group — without Paget himself — as a permanent reminder to the General of his absent family. Paget's letters to Harriet in England reveal his impatience to secure this memorial of her and the children:

8 February 1823: I have no tidings yet of our Chinnery acquaintance, but I do not think I shall have patience to let many days over my head without hunting him up.

11 February: I have set Mr. Hamilton to work to make me a small brass gilt frame for your little picture, and whenever Chinnery lets me have my darling group, I shall ask him to do something to the drapery of the miniature.

15 February: I have at length heard from Chinnery, and he of his own accord offers to bring home the picture of my darling group on

*Colour Plate 35. Lady Harriet Paget and her five eldest children. Oils.* Hongkong and Shanghai Banking Corporation

Wednesday next. I trust he will be as good as his word, and I am rather disposed to be confident that he will. You shall know more about it when he arrives.

19 February: Five o'clock, and my picture not arrived! Oh, fie, my dear Mr. Chinnery!

20 February: Upon my return from my drive yesterday, I found Mr. Chinnery in the act of hanging the picture of my beloved darlings. It is perfectly, perfectly lovely, and a comfort and pleasure to me not to be described. He has, in truth, done his interesting subjects justice, and I cannot say how pleased I am at his having stuck to the day of his engagement.[73]

Two years later, as Paget was himself preparing to return to England, Lady D'Oyly sent him some paintings by her husband, which Paget was to take back with him. 'I should not be surprised if Chinnery were to add a few of his to this little collection,' he wrote to Harriet, 'though he is so uncertain a fellow

*Plate 75. Sketch of a family group in a Calcutta drawing room. Pen and ink over pencil.* Private collection

*Plate 76. Two children of the Thornton family. Oils.* Private collection

that I have no dependence upon his promises. He likes landscape painting a thousand times better than portrait painting, except when he gets so fine a subject as (tell that to Caroline) me to study. Then he is quite inspired.'[74]

Two months after this letter was written Chinnery sailed for China, leaving behind many dissatisfied customers. One was probably Paget's niece, Lady Louisa Stuart, whom Chinnery drew after her marriage in 1823 to William Duncombe: although the drawing, which depicts Lady Duncombe on horseback, is squared up as if for transfer to canvas, no version in oils has come to light.[75] But Harriet Paget was more fortunate than most. At some point she managed to secure an album containing fifty pen-and-ink drawings by Chinnery; this album, containing her signature and bookplate, is now in the India Office Library and Records in London.[76]

The Paget group portrait is one of Chinnery's most highly finished productions. The general theme of the picture, in which the children gather around and climb upon their mother, is reminiscent of Reynolds's portrait of Lady Cockburn and her three daughters.[77] But the sense of intimacy is heightened by the small size of the picture (2 feet across), the clustering of the six figures, and the close attention paid to buttons, trimmings and tassels. In this and in Chinnery's other groups of children (Plates 73, 74, 76 and Colour Plates 34 and 35), the figures are identified as children not only by their size and their clothing, but also by their postures; they are allowed to recline, to tuck up their legs beneath them, and to embrace one another with a degree of physical intimacy which is not permitted to adults, even to married couples. On the other hand, their facial expressions are sophisticated and adult — calm, quizzical, mildly amused. In each painting there is at least one child who looks directly at the artist/spectator, and at least one who does not, as if the spectator is politely acknowledged without quite meriting the group's full attention.

# CHAPTER 8

## Freemasonry and the Theatre

Even in the minor British settlements in India, theatricals were a focus of expatriate social life; many people who had seldom visited the theatre at home would now become regular attendants or participants, as if dedicated to the duty of keeping alight the flickering candle of British culture. Writing from Benares in 1824, James Prinsep explained to his sister Emily: 'Here society is so constituted that all must partake of such gaieties as are set on foot. — The Ps [Prinseps] are not singular in their conspicuousness at 4 or 5 masques — All the world is there, all equally with their heads rivetted to the object of amusing themselves...'[1]

James and his brother William Prinsep were involved, as both actors and decorators, in the spectacles held in Calcutta Town Hall and in the theatre at Chowringhee, Calcutta's most fashionable district.[2] For major events,

*Colour Plate 36. Trevor Plowden. Oils.* Private collection

professional artists were liable to be pressed into service, to supply designs not only for stage scenery but also for the large back-lit 'transparencies' which had become fashionable in London, especially since the modifications introduced there by the ingenious Philippe de Loutherbourg; in India too they became a feature of many entertainments and celebrations. While Chinnery was in Madras, his rival Robert Home was providing designs for the theatre at Barrackpore, fifteen miles from Calcutta, where the governors-general of Bengal had a summer residence.[3]

There is no evidence that Chinnery worked for the stage in London or Dublin, although it was common enough for artists to take seasonal employment as scene designers for public or private theatres, especially in the early part of their careers. He had however painted the portraits of two of the leading actor-directors in Britain, William Thomas Lewis of the Covent Garden Theatre and John Philip Kemble of Drury Lane,[4] useful credentials if credentials had been necessary.

Chinnery's decorations for the Pantheon at Madras have already been noted (see p.80). The grandest theatrical events were at Calcutta, however, despite the fact that the city had no proper theatre between 1808, when the old theatre behind the Writers' Buildings was bought up and extended to form the 'New China Bazar', and 1813, when the new theatre was opened at Chowringhee.[5] The Town Hall was frequently used for

Plate 77. *Design for a transparency in honour of Lord Hastings, 1819. Pen and ink over pencil.* Sven Gahlin, Esq.

Colour Plate 37. *Design for a transparency in honour of Lord Hastings. Pencil, ink and watercolours.* India Office Library

entertainments, and for special festivals there were illuminations throughout the city. One such occasion was the commemoraton of the victory at Waterloo, which was held on 8 December 1815. On 30 November the *Calcutta Government Gazette* previewed the event:

> A magnificent transparency is in preparation for the 8th proximo, representing the immortal WELLINGTON on horseback, to be placed over the Northern Gateway of the Government house...the transparency is taken from a Design by Mr CHINNERY, executed with all the taste and genius of that distinguished Artist.[6]

The same celebrations included the work of one of Chinnery's pupils, for among the several private houses decked out with illuminations or transparencies was that of Trevor Plowden (Colour Plate 36), at Garden Reach. Plowden himself is said to have painted 'with great taste' a transparency of the meeting of Wellington with Blücher at Waterloo.[7]

Theatre of a different kind, but again involving Chinnery, was practised by the freemasons of Bengal. Freemasonry was taken extremely seriously by its initiates. William Hickey became a mason — reaching the position of Noble Grand Master of the 'Asiatic Bucks Lodge' — after seeing how highly the French at Trincomalee regarded the fraternity.[8] During the wars of the late eighteenth century, both in Europe and in India, there were numerous occasions on which patriotic loyalties took second place to the ties of the Brotherhood. Brigadier Matthew Horne, who had been Provincial Grand Master of Madras, experienced the bond of international freemasonry when, having been taken prisoner by the French, he was handsomely treated by his captors, who were also masons. Another prominent freemason was General Sir David Baird, who became a popular hero after his exploits at Seringapatam and elsewhere. Baird too was a prisoner of war, first under the French and then under Tipu Sultan, who was also it seems a freemason. But neither Baird nor any of his fellow prisoners received any favours from Tipu, which led subsequent masons to doubt whether Tipu could ever have been a true member of the Brotherhood.[9]

At this time no fewer than six of the seven sons of George III were freemasons, including the Prince of Wales, who was installed as Provincial Grand Master of the Freemasons of England in 1792. Directly beneath the Prince in the masonic hierarchy was his close friend the 2nd Earl of Moira, who later became the Marquess of Hastings. When Moira was appointed Governor-General in India, he received a farewell dinner in London which was attended by 500 masons, among them six royal dukes. On 4 October 1813 he arrived in Calcutta, where he took over the role of Acting Grand Master of India, and on 11 December he attended another masonic dinner, given in his honour at Government House by 120 masons representing the combined lodges of Calcutta.

An unusual feature of this event was the fact that the names of those masons present at the banquet were listed in the next issue of the *India Gazette*.[10] High on the list of the lodge 'Star in the East', the oldest and most prestigious lodge in Bengal, is the name of George Chinnery. The Secretary of the lodge was his close friend and patron, Sir Charles D'Oyly. The list of lodge members also includes the names of Charles Robert Lindsay (a Lodge Steward), George Cruttenden, Robert Cutlar Fergusson and John Pascal Larkins, all of whom, together with Lord Moira, and no doubt other masons of Calcutta, had their portraits painted by Chinnery. In a few cases Chinnery's status as a mason would have been of direct benefit to him — notably in his commission to provide the Lodge of Mauritius with a full-length portrait of Lord Moira in masonic robes.[11] More frequently the masonic network, and its strong tradition of loyalty to fellow masons, must have been useful to Chinnery as a source of introductions, and perhaps as a medium for the raising of subscriptions for the portrait of an honoured citizen.

Both Lindsay and Larkins became leading figures in Anglo-Indian freemasonry. Lindsay was appointed Provincial Grand Master of Bengal on 17 January 1818, but resigned when he was posted away from Calcutta in the following year. He was succeeded by Larkins, in whose honour a 'Larkins' lodge was established at Dinapore.[12] The senior freemason in southern India was (before his removal to Calcutta) Herbert Compton, Provincial Grand Master of the Coast of Coromandel,[13] whose houses in Madras and in Calcutta were depicted by Chinnery (see Colour Plates 14 and 15 and Plate 65); his Provincial Grand Chaplain was Richard Hall Kerr (Plate 34).[14]

Other freemasons who were patrons or associates of Chinnery's were Neil Edmonstone, Sir William Rumbold, Jacob Andries van Braam and General Robert Rollo Gillespie, all members of the 'Moira' lodge which the Earl of Moira inaugurated in Calcutta shortly after his arrival in India. The dashing deeds of Gillespie, sportsman and hero of campaigns in both East and West Indies, were well known throughout the British Empire. At Port au Prince he had swum ashore, evading an enemy fusillade, only to be captured and sentenced to death by the French commissioner. Just in time, Gillespie 'perceived some emblem of freemasonry about the person of the commissioner'. He made the appropriate masonic response, whereupon his captor cancelled the execution, prepared a sumptuous meal for Gillespie and his companion, and sent them back to their squadron with a guard of honour.

Through this and other exploits Gillespie advanced to the rank of Major-General. Finally in the Gurkha Wars he led an attack against such overwhelming odds that he was killed together with a very large number of his men. In due course his masonic brothers raised a 'Gillespie Monument' in his memory, in his native County Down; its unveiling was attended by the largest gathering of freemasons ever known in Ireland.[15] Gillespie's body was preserved in spirits, and his portrait (by Chinnery) was reproduced in popular history books, to inspire the schoolchildren of England.[16]

The laying of a foundation stone was often marked, appropriately enough, by masonic ritual. When the building of the new Custom House of Calcutta was about to start, the lodge 'Star in the East' forwarded to Provincial Grand Lodge an application from its Brother D'Oyly (who was also Collector of Customs) requesting that the foundation be laid with masonic ceremonies. A masonic procession was duly formed on 12 February 1819, in which an inscribed plate and a golden mallet, compasses, square, level and plumb were borne aloft to the corner stone, on which were poured wine, oil and corn from silver cups.[17] In similar fashion the foundation stone of the 'Hindoo College' was laid by Brother Larkins on 25 February 1824, an event which was commemorated in a drawing by George Chinnery.[18]

While the Earl of Moira (Lord Hastings) remained as Governor-General, freemasonry flourished in Calcutta. His departure from Calcutta was marked by another masonic banquet held in the Town Hall on 27 December 1822. The fully-robed freemasons proceeded from the Cathedral to the Town Hall, led by 'the Band of music playing the Entered Apprentice's tune'. As one might imagine, 'Crowds of Natives and Europeans hung upon both flanks of the Procession, anxious to get a passing sight of the sons of mystery.' Presiding at the dinner was Brother Larkins, who had now reached the rank of Provincial Deputy Grand Master; behind his chair was 'a large transparency, emblematical of Faith, Hope, and Charity, represented by three female figures, classically designed and spiritedly executed, nearly as large as life.' Above these figures a cherub held up a scroll, inscribed at one end 'HASTINGS...and at the other, the melancholy word FAREWELL'.[19]

Brother Chinnery was very possibly responsible for this design; he was certainly responsible for a similar design which was exhibited at a grand ball in the Town Hall three days later. The entertainment was again in honour of Lord and Lady Hastings, but the President on this occasion was the incoming Governor, John Adam. 'The extent of decoration was, we believe, greater than on any previous occasion', declared the *India Gazette:*

The bannisters on the grand staircase were hung with flags of various colors, and on the north side of the landing place was a large transparency emblematical of the present state of India, freed as it is from the scourge of war and the depredations of merciless robbers, and surmounted by a wreath enclosing the illustrious name of HASTINGS.[20]

Two of Chinnery's designs for this transparency have survived: an initial pen-and-ink sketch (Plate 77) (in a Prinsep family album), and a more developed watercolour (Colour Plate 37). In both versions loyal Indians pay homage to the Governor-General, while Peace and Prosperity — seen formerly in Chinnery's commemmoration of Henry Dundas (Plate 44) — stand in attendance. Several dramatic touches were added at the watercolour stage, such as the wreath enclosing 'Hastings', and various weapons of war, notably the blood-stained dagger held by the manacled 'robber', who glares up at the Governor-General's name as if bent on an act of personal vengeance.

Chinnery's own theatrical personality lent itself easily to satire, as D'Oyly demonstrated in his poem *Tom Raw, the Griffin*. It is fitting that, eleven years after he had quit Calcutta, Chinnery have been celebrated in a burlesque at the Town Hall. The organisers were William and James Prinsep, Parker Plowden and James Young, and Mrs. Plowden was the prima donna. One of the highlights was a scene at the Court of Peking, in which the Emperor received a message from the King of England, delivered by Lord Grey. Lord Grey refused to kowtow (always a controversial issue in Anglo-Chinese relations), and in retaliation the Emperor ordered a painting of the King to be brought in and turned upside down — a reference to recent events in Canton. At this point :

> ...the Court painter Chinnery (who was then in China) is ordered to paint the nose red, which he declines doing as contrary to all principles of his Art or his religion. He and the ambassador are ordered for instant execution. The one is to be Drawn and quartered, the other hung. The painter suggests that both may be done together in the Academy.[21]

*Colour Plate 38. A* chowkidar *beside his* thannah. *Oils.* Martyn Gregory Gallery

# CHAPTER 9
## Village Life in Bengal

When Chinnery's name appears in the lists of European residents in India, it is generally with the added description 'Portrait Painter'. Portraits were his livelihood; there was little prospect of his making a living from landscape painting, unless he had been prepared to embark on a major venture of topographical publishing. Nevertheless Chinnery preferred landscape painting to portraiture 'a thousand to one', it was said (see p.129); and once his portraits had won him a secure income, he was able to indulge his preference.

Whether in oils or watercolours, Chinnery's landscapes are quite different in conception from those painted before him by Thomas and William Daniell. The Daniells had travelled in search of the spectacular and the singular in Indian scenery and architecture — sweeping vistas, crashing waterfalls, the great Islamic monuments of the north, and the towering *gopurams* and rock-cut temples of the south. Chinnery's views, on the other hand, often encompass no more than one or two small buildings and their immediate environs; they are also small in size — smaller, for the most part, than the aquatints of the Daniells' *Oriental Scenery,* let alone their exhibition paintings. Chinnery's was a distinctive genre of intimate, informal views of village and

*Plate 78. A seated* chowkidar *with his dog. Pen and ink.* India Office Library

countryside, in some cases more akin to the so-called 'fancy pictures' of rustic cottages and woodland clearings painted in England by Gainsborough and Morland.

Yet these pictures of Chinnery's have little of the sentimentality that is associated with the English tradition of 'fancy painting'. In place of the woodman's daughter, artfully clad in a tattered shawl, is a Bengali villager, fetching water or tending a fire. A figure often deployed by Chinnery is the *chowkidar* or village watchman (Plates 78 and 79 and Colour Plate 38), responsible for guarding both premises and crops; he stands or sits by his *thannah* — a term which originally denoted a fully-manned fortress, but by Chinnery's time referred to a sentry box or, in a village, a small thatched hut. The *chowkidar* is identified by his shield, which he wears on his back or hangs up on his *thannah*.

The small dwellings, or *banglas*, pictured by Chinnery in these scenes are generally walled with mud over a bamboo frame, with a single doorway and a small window or none at all. The roof consists of thatch lying in irregular wads on a lattice of interwoven bamboo; there being no chimney, smoke could escape through the uncovered areas. The thatched roofs, extending well beyond the walls in order to throw the monsoon rains clear of the building, are often supported by posts at their outer limits, creating a feature which was recreated in European bungalows, using more durable materials, as the veranda.

Scattered around the *banglas*, in Chinnery's paintings and drawings, are the items of furniture and equipment essential to Bengal village life: *chattars* (broad umbrellas), cooking utensils, *charpoys* (cots for sleeping), long tobacco

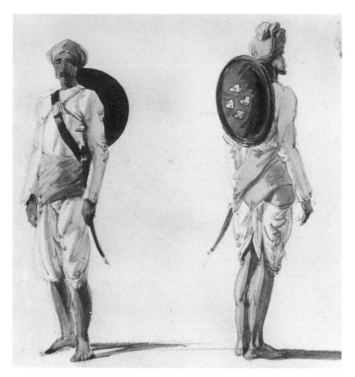

*Plate 79. Two studies of a* chowkidar. *Pencil and watercolours.* Private collection

pipes, and *jhaumps* (hurdles used as doors or shutters). In a letter of December 1814 he advised his pupil Maria Browne to make studies of such objects as 'Chatees [or chatties, round earthenware pots], Baskets, kedgeree [waterpots] & Brass Pots, Hubble Bubbles, pieces of Cloth &c'.[1] In Chinnery's village scenes there is often a *chattar* inserted into an aperture in the wall, and one drawing is inscribed 'the prising in of the chattar by the bamboo not to forget'.[2] In the foreground may be a pair of bullocks, whose smooth solidity contrasts with the ramshackle appearance of the hut (Colour Plates 39, 40 and 41).

Alternatively Chinnery depicted the overgrown ruins of monuments in brick or stone — also a fashionable subject for artists in Britain; but while his counterparts in England sought out the gaunt skeletons of decrepit abbeys or castles, Chinnery painted the remains of tombs and small mosques, which often appeared with fragments of *guldasta* strewn about, or an entire cupola lying intact on the ground. The Picturesque movement had been at its most intense during Chinnery's student years in England, and the artist never lost his relish for the much-prized attributes of varied texture and irregular outline. Colour Plate 42 is an eminently Picturesque composition, in which plant forms are mingled with the crumbling masonry, and a shaggy-roofed lean-to is juxtaposed with the polished domes of the tombs, while a bullock cart and a cooking fire add animation to the foreground.

Fire is included in many of Chinnery's village scenes, in which it fulfilled two pictorial roles. It gave him the opportunity to apply the touches of vivid red which he also found irresistible in his portrait painting; and moreover he could introduce from this point a curling stream of blue-grey smoke set against a shadowed area, thinning and expanding as it wafted upwards. In other instances smoke is supplied by a *nargila,* or (in his Macau paintings) from a blacksmith's portable furnace, in all cases with the effect of alleviating

*Colour Plate 39. Bengal village scene with cattle. Oils.* Private collection

a gloomy corner of the composition. On his drawings he reminds himself, in shorthand, to add smoke at a later stage: 'Smoke in the middle ground somewhere will be excellent,' or on another drawing, 'Smoke in the air in the dark parts would be beautiful.'[3]

Like other artists of his time Chinnery favoured the effects of late afternoon or evening sunshine; in many of his compositions a part of the foreground is seen in shadow, to point up the yellowing sunlight which falls laterally on a building or other feature in the middle distance. Less conventionally, however, his Bengal watercolours sometimes cast the whole foreground (or indeed the entire subject, figures and animals included) into deep shadow — often relieved only by the day's last ray of sunshine, which is allowed to pick out a branch, a boulder or a ripple of water (Colour Plates 43 and 44). In his 'Treatise' (see Appendix i) Chinnery lays great emphasis on the importance of 'general shadow' (that is, the shadow cast from objects outside the picture itself), and he recommends that such shadow should occupy a surprisingly high proportion of the composition:

> In Landscapes, General Shadow is the original & great Engine of Effect — it regulates the Conduct of the Picture entirely, & before anything else is thought of, the General Shadow must be *perfect* — in practice this General shadow ought for the most part to occupy 3/4ths or 2/3ds of the Whole picture — one 4th of light only may be too little; but a very striking Effect cannot be well preserved with more Light than *one* 3rd...[4]

Chinnery's shorthand had by now become a conspicuous addition to his drawings. Although he had begun to make shorthand jottings in Madras and Dacca, in Bengal he employed the notation more freely, so that it is often the vehicle of elaborate messages and *aides-mémoire* of various different kinds.

*Colour Plate 40. Bengal village scene with figures washing clothes. Pencil and watercolours.* Private collection

*Colour Plate 41. A bullock cart by an overgrown tomb. Pencil, pen and ink and watercolours.* Private collection

Plate 80. *Sheet of studies of figures in shallow water. Pencil,
dated April 18 1813.* India Office Library

Plate 81. *Substantial buildings in Bengal, with figure studies. Pen
and ink. Inscribed in shorthand (beside buildings) 'figures right size',
and (beside figures) 'The hubble bubble not upright enough. It ought
to be more upright so as to bring the mouth piece nearer to the stem.'*
Spink and Son Ltd.

Sometimes the shorthand simply indicates colour or texture, such as 'brick
and mortar', 'brown cloth', 'open scenery', 'mud', or 'rocks' (Edward Lear
was to add comparable notes to his drawings, but in his idiosyncratic
longhand: 'rox'). Alternatively it identifies errors of scale or draughtsmanship
— 'the figure too small', 'the pot ought not to touch the pole'; or it may point
out features of the drawing which had not been present in the scene as he
observed it — 'tomb added', 'some trifling additions to D[esign]', 'native
figure turned into an English one'; or it may recommend improvements —
'one animal ought to be eating'.

Sometimes again the message has no bearing on any future painting, but
records Chinnery's passing reflections and memoranda, as if his shorthand
functioned as a substitute for a daily journal. 'Enquiry to be made about the
situation of the man,' he notes beside a figure. On a drawing of an Indian
woman descending to a pool with a waterpot we read that 'the sketch of the
figure gives very ill idea of it at all. It was in nature by far the most beautiful
graceful and elegant thing I *ever saw*'. On a drawing of a headless cow, dated
October 1816, 'this was a very fine formed animal. It was a pity it moved.'[5]

If Chinnery's oil paintings of Bengal are generalised scenes, incorporating
elements from several drawings in the interests of a satisfying composition, the

*Plate 82. Title page of 'Lessons in Landscape'. Pencil.* Private collection

*Plate 83. A villager with a bullock. Pen and ink and watercolours, inscribed (not in Chinnery's hand)*
*'Hindoo costume from nature. Chinnery'.* India Office Library

*Colour Plate 42. Tombs and lean-to dwellings. Oils.* Private collection

*Colour Plate 43. An overgrown tomb at dusk. Pen and ink and watercolours.* Private collection

*Colour Plate 44. Bengal landscape with ruined building. Pen and ink and watercolours.* Private collection

*Colour Plate 45. Vignette of goats in a landscape. Pen and ink and watercolours.* Private collection

*Colour Plate 46. River scene. Watercolours.* Hongkong and Shanghai Banking Corporation

143

Plate 84. *The artist's dog, Squib.* Private collection

drawings themselves are closely observed from nature. The artist's concern with accuracy and authenticity is evident in his repetitions of particular figures or objects — which are drawn and redrawn with slight changes of posture or viewpoint — as well as in his shorthand notes. Drawings which he regarded as unsatisfactory were marked with a small diagonal cross 'x' (sometimes with an additional note to identify the shortcomings), and kept for comparison with 'correct' drawings, which he marked with an upright cross '+' (see Plate 80). When he came to ink over the pencil outlines, he inked over the 'incorrect' together with the 'correct', thus preserving the errors for future reference.

The drawing technique of Chinnery's Bengal period is assured and consistent; the staccato manner of his Madras sketches has now largely been superseded by smoothly curving lines. In certain cases the 'serpentine line' advocated by Hogarth threatens to take over the composition, extending in Plate 78 from the watchman's sandals to his luxuriant moustache — a reminder of Chinnery's dictum that 'straight lines and concavities should be avoided.'[6] He made numerous studies of Indian figures engaged in everyday activities: men and women bathing in the Hooghly (Plate 80), women carrying children on their shoulders or water pots on their heads, men carrying water bags or flasks suspended from a bamboo pole, women seated at a spinning-wheel, and men squatting by a cooking pot or puffing at a *nargila*

*Plate 85. Studies of water buffalo and other animals, from an album dated 1821.* India Office Library

*Plate 86. Study of a turkey cock. Pen and ink over pencil. Private collection*

(Plate 81). These accumulated drawings formed a body of reference material, which he was able to exploit in the production of finished oils or watercolours.

Alternatively the drawings were made up into presentation albums, known as 'sketch-books'. At the head of one of these books of drawings Chinnery would place a vignette with a title inscribed on an appropriate rock or wall: typical titles are 'BENGAL COTTAGE SCENERY 1822', or 'SCRAPS. POETRY AND DRAWING. 1823',[7] while Plate 82 is inscribed 'LESSONS IN LANDSCAPE'. There is no evidence that Chinnery intended to publish these sets in engraved form; rather, they would be commissioned by patrons, or else borrowed or hired by friends and amateur artists. An album of Chinnery drawings which formerly belonged to Lady Harriet Paget contains fifty drawings of the Indian people and habitations of Bengal, of which the first is a vignette entitled 'SCENERY IN BENGAL 1825'.[8] ('1825' must refer to the date of the album's presentation rather than that of the drawings' execution, since several of the drawings in the album are dated 1821.)

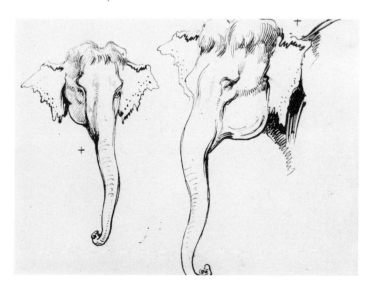

*Plate 87. Studies of an elephant. Pen and ink.* A. Fairbarns, Esq.

145

*Plate 88. Study of a* putelee. *Pencil, pen and ink, and watercolours, dated 26 Sept. 1813.* India Office Library

*Plate 89. Studies of boats on the Hooghly. Pen and ink, dated 30th August 1821, and inscribed in shorthand 'The chattar rather too long'.* India Office Library

Animals play a prominent part in Chinnery's drawings of Bengali village life. He drew bullocks from every angle, and the various operations involved in loading and emptying the large water bags which they often carried (Plate 83). Goats were a favourite subject of his: 'This was a perfect specimen of the fine form of the animal,' he observed in a shorthand note to a drawing of a plump she-goat with swelling udders. If any sentiment is allowed to enter Chinnery's village scenes, it is through the medium of animals — cows with their calves, or a young kid nuzzling against its mother (Colour Plate 45). He made numerous studies of dogs, including his own (Plate 84); another drawing of this animal is inscribed 'My poor little Squib who died June 25th 1808. He was the most attentive dog I ever saw — my true friend.'[9] The many dogs who appear in Chinnery's portraits, and especially the performing terrier in Plate 164, suggest that he continued to regard these animals with affection. In Bengal and Macau he made sketches of cats, chickens, horses, donkeys, deer and pigs; occasionally he also drew water buffalo, parrots, turkey cocks and elephants (Plates 85, 86 and 87).

The varieties of Indian boat which plied the Hooghly presented further subjects to Chinnery (Plates 88 and 89 and Colour Plate 46), although he found the craft of Bengal less absorbing than the sampans, junks and egg boats of Macau. One of the larger boats on the river was the *putelee*, seen head-on in Plate 88, with its steersman operating the immensely long oar at the stern. The *putelee* was a baggage craft with a long *choppar* or thatched roof, and a further bamboo platform built above it. This design was no doubt picturesque — Chinnery in a shorthand note to another drawing refers to 'the light seen through the flooring of the bamboos of the choppar' — but it was also unstable, causing 'frequent fatality...and great loss of time'.[10]

Chinnery also made studies of the *pulwar* and the *dengee*, passage boats with a narrow and sometimes detachable covering. Such small sailing craft appear in the background of some of Chinnery's Bengal watercolours, their sails forming the characteristic shape of a tall inverted triangle. When viewed at close quarters the sails can be seen to be a patchwork, the result of many *ad hoc* repairs; these repairs were frequently called for because the sails were made from jute or 'gunny', a flimsy material more usefully employed for sacking.

# CHAPTER 10

# *Sons and Rivals*

By 1817 Chinnery was established as the principal artist in the ever-expanding dominion of British India, with a wide and influential circle of friends and acquaintances. In the absence of his British family, he was in effect a bachelor — exempt, that is, from the social ordinance which obliged married couples to entertain on a lavish scale.[1] But in this year, within the space of three months, two arrivals in Calcutta — one an artist, the other his daughter — threatened to upset his social and professional equilibrium.

The first to arrive, on 4 April 1817, was the artist William Havell, a man six years younger than Chinnery. Havell's reputation had preceded him, and Chinnery, conscious of the damage which a fellow-artist could inflict upon his status and his income, prepared himself for combat. Havell had made his name in London as a watercolourist, and in the years 1805-9 he was perhaps the most impressive of the landscape artists who exhibited at the newly-founded Society of Painters in Watercolours. Like Chinnery, he did not underestimate his abilities. In 1808 the collector and connoisseur Sir George Beaumont wrote to William Wordsworth recommending Havell's work, but adding that 'if you can inspire him with a little humility, you will be of great service to him and facilitate his progress'.[2] In 1815 the *Examiner* claimed that Havell was 'a man of unquestionable genius...destined to be one of the great names of landscape'.[3]

At this point in his career Havell was appointed draughtsman to the British Embassy to Peking, which left England in February 1816 under the leadership of Lord Amherst. Amherst proved an inept diplomat, and the venture achieved nothing. As a final indignity, the embassy's ship *Alceste* was wrecked in the Java sea on the return journey, and all the embassy's possessions were lost. Havell had already quarrelled with the officers of the *Alceste,* and he now took the opportunity of parting company with the embassy, accepting a passage to Penang and on to Calcutta. The wealthy John Havell of Dinapore may have been a relation of his; in any case he arrived at Calcutta armed with 'good introductions'[4] and a considerable reputation. The amateur artist James Fraser, who took lessons from William Havell, wrote from Calcutta that Havell 'was I believe considered the best watercolour artist in England'.[5]

Chinnery's reaction to the news of Havell's arrival was a combination of excitement, alarm and aggression, expressed in a blustering declaration of war against the newcomer:

> About Mr H. he is not yet here — I believe he has not yet come up from the ship — Fear me not — you have no Idea how tough a Battle I shall make if there is any need of it — Any flourish of Trumpets preceeding king this or king that in any Tragedy you ever saw is a Child's rattle to

the ushering in of this Hero of the Art — I have the funniest story to tell you you ever heard — I have been sounded as to my reception of him more than once & have given my opinion just as I ought to give it — If he is a clever man I shall be really glad to see him — delighted indeed, for having to contend with sound masculine ability is always to be courted — it is only your pretenders & half wits that are annoying —

But I have a tolerably accurate notion of my own powers & to put me out of the saddle would be a Job not easily accomplished rest assured — there are not 3 people I would say this much to, & do not give it as my opinion — I wd. not seem arrogant for the whole world — I *feel rightly* wh. is enough — If I was not bothered as I am about *Finance* I would do more, rather I would shew my talent better — now I am shackled — but yet please God all will be well here in Time — There is such a thing as Galvanising Talent as well as other things, & if this Youngster comes in contact so as to have a chance of taking *a single picture from me* I shall get my Back pretty well up — from the *novelty* I must suffer something of course; but when this is over you shall find that if my Art (God knows I have nothing else to build on!) has been the means of my having such Friends as you & many others about me, I will shew myself worthy of attention & Distinction that are my greatest pride...[6]

In the event, Havell did not present the competiton which Chinnery had anticipated. In a letter written shortly after his arrival in Calcutta, Havell reported that he was fully employed, chiefly painting small watercolour portraits, and hoped to 'realise a purse for his return'. But he was frustrated by the expenses of living in India — or so it was reported by his contemporaries Richard and Samuel Redgrave.[7] Perhaps deterred by Chinnery's dominant position in Calcutta, Havell did not remain there long. He booked a passage to England for February 1819, but went to Madras instead; he travelled to Ceylon, back to Calcutta, to Hyderabad and to Bombay, working both in oils and in watercolours. Surprisingly few works done by Havell in the East can be traced today; Plates 90, 91 and 92 belong to a small group of paintings from these years which can certainly be attributed to him. He had managed to save a small sum when, following an attack of cholera, he left India for England on 14 January 1826, a few months after Chinnery's departure for Macau.[8]

Soon after William Havell came Chinnery's daughter Matilda, the first member of his British (or Irish) family to rejoin him in India. On 7 January 1817 she had obtained permission from the Court of Directors to travel out to her father in Calcutta. Shortly afterwards she sailed out on the *Minerva* by way of Madras; she arrived in Calcutta, together with six gentlemen passengers, on 18 July 1817.[9] At this time she was seventeen years old. She would have been with her father on 22 October 1818, when Chinnery noted in shorthand on a drawing of goats 'Matilda 19 years old today'.[10]

Chinnery thus began to resume the domestic life which he had left behind him in Dublin. After so long a separation, it cannot have been easy for Matilda to form a close relationship with a middle-aged man of eccentric habits, who

Plate 90. William Havell, portrait of Rous Peter of Madras. Pencil and watercolours, s. and d. 1819. Private collection

Plate 91. William Havell, portrait of a seated lady. Oils. Private collection

(as D'Oyly observed) was often subject to 'peevish humours'.[11] An entry in the diary of James Fraser, who frequently dined at the Chinnerys' house in the years 1818-19, gives an indication that their domestic life was often stormy:

> The evening of the day spent at Chinneries [*sic*] pleasantly enough, but there is always a fear of his temper flying out — & his poor Daughter is the first that suffers, tho it discomposes the whole company. The girl indeed has sufficient spirit to bear it and sometimes gives as good as she gets.[12]

On 27 September 1819 Matilda gained her independence from her father when she was married, in St. John's Cathedral, to James Cowley Brown of the Bengal Civil Service. The Browns then went to live in Benares (Varanasi), where James had been appointed Assistant to the Magistrate of the City Court. Three of the witnesses who signed the marriage register were George Chinnery, Sir Charles D'Oyly, and John Hadley D'Oyly, younger brother of Charles, who was to succeed him as 8th Baronet. Chinnery is also recorded as a witness at the wedding of the younger D'Oyly, which had taken place nine months before Matilda's.[13]

The fourth signatory to Matilda's marriage was James Silk Buckingham, a man who deserves a short digression, for it is appropriate that this enterprising and independent-minded individual should have been a family friend of the Chinnerys. He had gone to sea at the age of nine, and at twenty-one was captain of a West Indiaman. After extensive travels in the Middle East, Buckingham arrived in Bombay in 1815 with a commission to buy ships for Mohammed Ali, Pasha of Egypt. Since he had not applied to the East India Company for permission to come to India, the Company expelled him. He returned, and founded the *Calcutta Journal*, a successful publication which was

often critical of the Company's government; this caused him to be expelled again, in April 1823. Back in England he became a Member of Parliament, campaigned for temperance and the abolition of flogging in the armed forces, and finally won redress from the Company for the closure of the *Calcutta Journal.* In many respects Buckingham was a man ahead of his time, although his clashes with authority brought him a succession of financial losses. One further loss was incurred when he lent money to Chinnery in Serampore (see p.161), shortly before his second expulsion from India.[14]

Matilda's mother Marianne would also have attended the wedding, for in August 1818 she too had come to join Chinnery in Calcutta. She had not seen her husband for seventeen years. Later Chinnery would encourage the image of himself as a man hounded relentlessly by an unappealing and unforgiving wife. But this is a caricature; there are other circumstances to be considered. At that time it was customary for husbands to spend prolonged periods apart from their wives and children, especially if the health of either wife or children showed signs of suffering in the Indian climate. In the case of the Chinnerys, Marianne remained in England until both her children were old enough to look after themselves; then all three made their way, independently, to Calcutta.

On 3 March 1818 the Court of Directors had ordered that 'Mrs Mary Ann Chinnery be permitted to proceed to her husband at Calcutta accompanied by her daughter' — which was clearly a misunderstanding, since Matilda was already in India. Ten days later the situation was clarified, as the Court gave Marianne permission 'to take with her to Bengal on the ship *Henry Porcher,* a European female servant, named Anne Cavanagh, security being given for her return to England either on that ship or on the first that shall sail after there [*sic*] arrival, and the Company being at no expence thereby'.[15] So Marianne travelled out in some style. Was this a gesture of belated generosity on the part of her husband? Probably not, for Chinnery was already in debt, 'shackled', as he had declared to Maria Browne in the preceding March.[16] He was hardly in a position to finance his wife's passage, let alone a maid's.

An alternative sponsor may be suggested: Thomas Parry, Chinnery's patron and landlord in Madras. His relationship with Marianne remains a little mysterious. Their friendship developed at long range. As Parry had been in India since 1788, and never went home to Britain, he cannot have known Marianne personally when he sent her money in October 1807 (see p.81); in October 1808, when he sent her more, he would just have had time to receive (by return sea-mail) her acknowledgement of the first instalment. Parry arranged for Marianne to meet his wife Mary and their child, who were returning to England: 'You will, I know, be happy to see them.'[17] Perhaps Marianne looked after them; as it turned out, Mary Parry experienced as long a separation from her husband as did Marianne from George.

If Thomas Parry and Marianne Chinnery ever met, it must have been after her voyage to India in 1818. Parry was by now a wealthy man, well able to pay for two passages to India. In his will, dated 1823, Parry referred to 'my esteemed and excellent friend, Mrs Chinnery', and moreover entrusted his granddaughter, Emma Louise Gibson, to Marianne's care, with an appropriate provision.[18] In the following year, 1824, Parry died, and Marianne presumably took Emma Louise Gibson into her household.

By this time Marianne's husband was parted from her once again. George and Marianne had lived together in Calcutta, as is evident from a letter written by Chinnery to Maria Browne ('Mrs Chinnery desires me to thank you...') on 17 August 1820.[19] But within three years of Marianne's arrival in India, the artist was obliged to move on to Serampore, in order to evade his creditors. Marianne did not follow him there. She was living up-river at Chuprah when their son John Eustace Chinnery arrived at Calcutta in the spring of 1822. He could scarcely have remembered his father, who had left him as an infant in Ireland twenty years before. Since his father was living close to Calcutta, John Chinnery went first to see him. The events that followed were eloquently described in the *Calcutta Government Gazette:*

> ...after passing a few days of inexpressible happiness with his fond and delighted father, he embarked on the river to proceed to Chuprah, with the hope of gratifying, by his visit, an equally fond and expectant Mother and sister, whom he had not seen for many years...
>
> On his way up the river he was taken ill on the 3rd instant [June] at Berhampore...it pleased the Almighty to close his earthly career, after an illness of seven days, which no efforts were spared to conquer. The promising talent and accomplished understanding of this early victim to a baneful climate were such as to raise the most sanguine hopes of his future happiness and distincton...

As the *Gazette* concluded, John's premature death plunged his parents 'in one fatal moment from the pinnacle of human joy to the depth of human misery'.[20] They provided a memorial, in the Residency burial ground at Berhampore: 'To the memory of a most beloved and affectionate son, JOHN EUSTACE CHINNERY, who died, 10th June 1822, aged 20 years and 10 months.'[21]

Chinnery had two other sons, although Marianne was not their mother. The births of Edward and Henry Chinnery, in common with those of many other illegitimate children, are not recorded in the church registers of the time. But since their ages at death are stated with unusual precision, it can be inferred that they were both born in 1813, and that they were therefore probably twins.[22] Both were baptised in Calcutta on 19 March 1820, when they would have been six years old;[23] the baptisms took place shortly after the arrival in India of Chinnery's wife Marianne, and were perhaps performed at her request.

By the standards of the British in India, life would not have been easy for Edward and Henry Chinnery. It is certain that their mother was non-European, for in the directories their names are recorded in the list of 'East Indians' (also known as Eurasians) rather than in the list of 'European Inhabitants'.[24] As Eurasians they were excluded, by a directive of 1791, from the higher grades of the Company's civil service, from the officer ranks of the armed services, and indeed from all combatant positions in the army. This policy was based on the tenuous principle that Eurasians (who were generally the children of Indian mothers and British or Portuguese fathers) were despised by Indians, either socially or as a matter of religion.

When the East India's charter was renewed in 1833, Parliament stipulated that no discrimination in employment should be made on grounds of colour, religion, birthplace or descent. Nevertheless it was only a small number of well-connected Eurasians, such as the son of Sir Charles Metcalfe, who rose above the level of clerk or minor official. Among the British community there remained a strong prejudice against Eurasians, who were commonly said to possess the virtues of neither race but the vices of both. 'Are not the generality of Indo-Britons a class of poor weakly-looking persons, very sallow and unhealthy in their appearance, and very small in stature?' asked Lord Ellenborough at a parliamentary committee in 1853.[25] As the century progressed, racial prejudices on the part of the British became more pronounced and often more explicit.

Of Chinnery's two illegitimate sons, Henry at least was more fortunate than most of his Eurasian contemporaries. He became an aide-de-camp of the Nizam Humayun Jah who, in March 1836, sent him to England aboard the *Robarts* as his emissary to William IV. Among the many presents placed in Henry Chinnery's charge were 'a superb golden chair set with jewels in the most tasteful manner imaginable,' and a picture of the Nizam 'painted by Mr Hutchinson'.[26] Henry Chinnery seems to have carried out his duties satisfactorily:

> Mr Chinnery was, we hear, received with great kindness by their Majesties at Windsor, on the presentation of His Highness's presents, and the King was graciously pleased, as a mark of appreciation, to present him with a handsome gold watch and chain with the inscription: 'From His Majesty King William IV to Henry Chinnery, Esq.'[27]

It has been suggested that Henry Chinnery was an artist, who was responsible for copies of old masters, and for landscapes which have been described as 'by Chinnery' although they are clearly not by George.[28] But there is no evidence for this, and Henry could not have received much tuition from his father, who was confined to Serampore when his sons were eight, and left India altogether when they were twelve. The occupation of Henry Chinnery was given as 'Assistant, Police Office' in 1835, when he was living (as was his brother Edward) at 11 Government Place. In April 1839 he was a Clerk in the Civil Auditor's office, living in Collingah Lane; on 12 June of that year it was announced that Henry Chinnery was discharged from debt, in the Insolvent Debtors' Court.[29] He was employed as a Writer in South Collingah at the time of his death, which occurred in September 1841.[30]

Of Edward Chinnery's life little is known. In 1835 he was working as 'Assistant to A.Wright, Attorney'.[31] On 29 July 1836 he married Maria Elizabeth Murray in Calcutta, by licence, the bride being described as 'under age'.[32] Exactly a year later, he stood trial for larceny. It seems that on 28 June 1837, 'Kadur, a coolie' was bringing back some candles and tea from a shop to his employer, Mrs. Henderson, when he was intercepted by Edward Chinnery in a *palkee*. As he admitted in court, Edward Chinnery took the groceries, signed a receipt with the initials of Captain Henderson, sold the tea to another shopkeeper, and gave the candles to his mother (or so he claimed; his mother denied having received them). He was arrested by Perry, the constable, after he had been identified by the shopkeeper's assistant, who had seen him before at Isserchunder's wine shop in China Bazar.

In court Edward Chinnery pleaded guilty, but the jury, in confirming the verdict, 'recommended him to the mercy of the Court, because of his youth and because they imagined that when he committed the crime he did it under the impression that he was committing a frolic and not a larceny'. The judge responded with what was a light sentence by the standards of the time: three months' solitary confinement, so that Edward Chinnery would not be subjected to 'the contagion of the common felons in the jail'.[33] The experience cannot have improved either his health or his career prospects. Within four years of his conviction Edward Chinnery died, being 'out of employ' at the time.[34]

Thus the three sons of George Chinnery died prematurely and childless. The women of the family proved more robust, however. On 23 December 1865 Marianne, the artist's wife, died in her eighty-ninth year at 13 Charlotte Street, Brighton; since the householder at this address is listed as 'Mrs. Brown', it is likely that Marianne was cared for in her old age by her daughter Matilda Brown, who herself died in Brighton on 28 January 1879.[35] Matilda gave birth to at least five daughters and two sons, all of whom married; she was the source of the artist's many direct descendants, none of whom bear the surname Chinnery.

# CHAPTER 11

## *Escape from Debt*

The business of portrait painting, which brought Chinnery most of his income, was potentially a lucrative one. It was the custom for artists to set a scale of fees, and to charge their clients according to the size and scope of the portrait in question. A typical scale of charges made by a leading artist in India, such as Robert Home or Arthur William Devis, would range from £200 for a large full-length portrait to £40 or £50 for a head, with intermediate figures for three-quarter-length, half-length and bust portraits. These were high prices by English standards, equivalent to those asked by Sir Joshua Reynolds at the peak of his fame. Still larger sums could be expected in India from wealthy clients, whether European or Indian; on the other hand, when orders were in short supply, artists were obliged to reduce their scale of fees to attract new clients — Home lowered his prices by twenty per cent in 1809.[1]

Chinnery left no list of fees or sitters, and his charges are recorded only in isolated instances. He received £100 for his small (18 x 15 ins) three-quarter-length of the D'Oylys in masquerade dress (Plate 55), according to an inscription on the back of the canvas,[2] and 200 Spanish dollars (£40) for a portrait of a sea captain, probably a head, in 1830.[3] For a sketchbook in 1848 he charged $150 (£30).[4] Exceptional commissions brought exceptional fees, however. The subscriptions for Chinnery's portrait of Sir John Adam amounted to nearly 16,000 rupees (£1,600), and the same sum was set aside for his equestrian portrait of Lord Hastings (see p.118). Such fees are comparable with the 22,000 rupees subscribed in 1793 for A.W. Devis's portrait of Cornwallis, and the 15,000 rupees charged to Warren Hastings by Zoffany for the celebrated 'Cock Pitt', which incorporated some ninety figures.[5]

Chinnery's earnings in Calcutta were reckoned to be 5,000 rupees (£500) a month, or, by another estimate, nearly 50,000 rupees (£5,000) a year.[6] This was a very substantial amount — twice what a middle-ranking civil servant in India could expect. But in British India, success and a high income did not necessarily bring a settled prosperity; often the very opposite occurred, as in the case of A.W. Devis, whose portraits were much in demand in Madras and Calcutta, but who returned penniless to a debtors' prison in England. Chinnery fared little better. He was heavily in debt by 1814, repaying his loans at the rate of 1,000 rupees a month,[7] and he continued in this state, with (at best) temporary remissions, for the rest of his life.

How, then, were these debts incurred? Part of the answer must lie in the high costs of living in Calcutta, the domestic bills which D'Oyly observed 'forever running' in the artist's lodgings.[8] Housing in the city was notoriously expensive: 'It must be a very small, mean house, that does not, in Calcutta, let for 200Rs monthly, which is equal to £300 yearly.' For this amount, it was calculated, an entire family could live 'comfortably and genteelly' in any part of the British Isles.[9] There is no record of how much money Chinnery sent back from India for his wife and children, or provided for his Indian mistress and two sons in Calcutta. He was a famous eater and a regular smoker of the hookah, but not (it would seem) a heavy drinker, beyond 'the fiz of ripe pale ale' at tiffin (see Appendix iii, stanza xvii); he complained to Maria Browne that 'at one bout on Saturday one solitary Glass of Champagne half killed me and occasioned all the *real pain* I underwent...I declare I *will* be quiet, go nowhere, drink Tea & be stupid in private'.[10]

Illness continued to exacerbate his financial problems, although it is often hard to distinguish the physical symptoms from Chinnery's dramatisation of them. Penning a letter to Mrs. Browne at 7.30 in the morning — 'writing at nights hurts my Eyes so much that I feared to do it' — he declared that 'at 8 I must be before the Easel, unwell as I am & have been, with hardly the power of knowing one end of the pencil's stick from the other...'[11] Or again:

> I have been laid up these 4 last days, & am still so, with 30 Boils on my left Leg the Torture of wh. is excessive & mentally I am in misery from the necessary suspension of my Business! However Tomorrow well or unwell I *must* make the effort & go down stairs to my painting room.[12]

After his removal to China his health appears to have improved, possibly because he gave up drinking entirely; it is stated on good authority that, during his years on the China coast, he took no alcohol at all.[13] When a group of American visitors came to his Macau studio in 1839 they found him buoyant: '..."never was ill in my life...Our art is indeed meat and drink to us, elixir and medicine altogether".'[14]

Chinnery's professional overheads in Calcutta must have been considerable. In London in the early years of the century, canvas cost a guinea for a full-length, and certain pigments were very costly: up to £2 an ounce for carmine, and up to £5 for ultramarine.[15] In 1804 Thomas Lawrence ran up a bill for £14 in eight months for turpentine alone.[16] Chinnery moreover had to import most of his equipment from England — his pigments came from the old-established London colourman James Newman[17] — thereby adding to the cost, although he was able to obtain excellent frames from Canton more cheaply than from London (see p.58).

Yet these expenses do not fully explain Chinnery's chronic indebtedness. The state of debt, it could be said, was a contagious malady endemic in British India. The independent European merchants were accustomed to meeting triumph and disaster in rapid and unpredictable succession, as their fortunes depended to a large extent on matters beyond their control — storms at sea, the quality of harvests, or the solvency of their own debtors. Even the great house of Palmer, financiers to rulers and governments, was bankrupted in 1830, bringing down many smaller banks and agencies with it. For Company servants there was a greater degree of security, but many of them overestimated their expectations, borrowed heavily to establish themselves, and were burdened with debts for years afterwards.

One such was Chinnery's close friend Charles D'Oyly, who could only excuse himself on grounds of 'Youth — Indolence — an insuperable aversion to inspect my accounts'.[18] At Dacca D'Oyly was able to live on half his Collector's income which, although less than he had calculated, still amounted to 24,000 rupees. His father wrote to reassure their family friend, Warren Hastings, in England: 'Dacca is a cheap place, & the allurement of Calcutta shops is at an End, & he [Charles] has suffered so severely from former Imprudences, that I flatter myself he will in future persevere in his Intention of Devoting half his Income to the gradual Discharge of his Debts.'[19] As D'Oyly's house guest at Dacca, Chinnery may have resolved to make similar economies, but lapsed into 'imprudences' of his own once he returned to Calcutta.

If there were economic and social elements in Chinnery's perpetually mortgaged existence, we should also consider the psychological aspect of the case. As a species the colonial expatriate has been likened to a deep-sea fish, whose constitution has been adapted to withstand high pressures in its normal existence near the sea bed — but which, when brought up to the surface, becomes swollen and distorted. It is not only the new environment which causes the colonial, like the deep-sea fish, to behave in an extreme and abnormal fashion; it is also his or her internal (perhaps innate) attributes which create this susceptibility to unaccustomed pressures. According to this thesis, certain types of personality are attracted by the prospect of a colonial life, and once they have achieved it, they adopt the same excessive behaviour patterns as their predecessors in the colonial role.[20] Chinnery is perhaps a case in point — a man who was predisposed to extravagance and exhibitionism (if we may judge from the career of his high-living, spectacularly fraudulent brother William), and who found in the colonies an environment in which those traits could be most freely indulged.

A similar analysis of a 'colonial personality' occurs in a journal written in 1805 by a young Company servant of French descent. In composing this eminently plausible account the author might have had Chinnery himself in mind:

> An Englishman in India is proud and tenacious, he feels himself a Conqueror amongst a vanquished people and looks down with some degree of Superiority on all below him. Indolence, the disease of the Climate, affects him with its torpid influence, and to the present moment futurity is made subservient. A cool apathy, a listless inattention, and an improvident carelessness generally accompanies most of his actions; secure of today, he thinks not of tomorrow. Ambitious of splendor, he expends freely, & forms his calculation on Riches yet in perspective; *what* he wishes, that he procures, for it is seldom Prudence dares to say 'no', when desire says 'yes'.[21]

In 1821 Chinnery's financial situation had become so insecure that he moved fifteen miles up-river from Calcutta to the township of Serampore. Since Serampore was a Danish settlement, it lay beyond the jurisdiction of British civil law, and was thus a source of anger and frustration to many upright citizens:

> By its extreme proximity to Calcutta, Serampore embarrasses the course of justice. It is the haunt of all the big fraudulent bankrupts from the

*Plate 93. Village scene, Serampore. Pencil, dated May 26 1813.* India Office Library

*Plate 94. The banks of the Hooghly River at Serampore. Inscribed in shorthand 'Serampore' and dated September 1821.* Private collection

*Plate 95. An old wall and* bangla *at Serampore. Pen and ink over pencil, inscribed in shorthand* '*Serampore*' *and dated June 16th 1821.* India Office Library

capital of the empire. A few unfortunate and worthy men find a refuge here, to the satisfaction of all honest people; but for one man of that sort, whom one is glad to see escape the clutches of the law, there are a thousand rogues thoroughly fit for the pillory, who mock the misery of those they have ruined by their constant round of pleasures.[22]

Whether Chinnery is to be considered a rogue or an unfortunate, there is no doubt that it was debt which prompted his move to Serampore. The legal loophole which enabled him and others to evade their creditors was drawn tight shortly after Chinnery's visit: by an Act of Parliament passed on 19 July 1828, the mere act of absconding to a foreign settlement could be regarded as an act of bankruptcy, and the absconder's property could be assigned to his creditors.[23] But by that time Chinnery had found another refuge.

In addition to bankrupts and gamblers, the Danish colony was also a haven for missionaries, who for many years were forbidden to operate in the Company's territories. Here the Baptist missionary Joshua Marshman founded the Serampore College, and initiated the first Indian-language newspaper. An outstanding linguist, he published a Chinese version of the Bible and an English version of the works of Confucius, as well as many translations into Indian languages. There are several contemporary references to a portrait of Marshman by Chinnery, and it is tempting to identify these with Colour Plate 47: beyond the figure of the missionary appears the arresting face of one of his Chinese assistants, who stares impassively from the gloom like the imprisoned Count Ugolino in Reynolds's famous history picture. But on stylistic grounds the attribution to Chinnery cannot be upheld.

At Serampore Chinnery also knew Joshua's equally gifted and energetic son, John Clark Marshman, who spoke in later life of Chinnery's failure to finish his portraits: 'After having satisfied himself with a masterly representation of

*Plate 96. Preliminary drawing for the portrait of William and Mary Prinsep. Pencil.* Sven Gahlin, Esq.

the countenance, he turned to a new subject. Hence when he left Calcutta, more than twenty unfinished portraits were brought to the hammer.'[24]

According to William Prinsep, it was in June 1821 that 'our amusing and instructive friend George Chinnery, the painter, fell into such distress from heavy pressure from his creditors that he fled to the Danish settlement for protection, and took up his abode at Serampore.'[25] This date is to be relied on, for Prinsep was one of those creditors; there are also drawings by Chinnery which are inscribed in his shorthand 'Serampore' and dated 1821, as well as others which indicate that he had already visited the place in 1813 (Plates 93, 94 and 95).

Serampore in Chinnery's time was described by Bishop Heber as 'a handsome place, kept beautifully clean, and looking more like an European town than Calcutta or any of its neighbouring cantonments'. The Bishop also observed, however, that since the British had discontinued their annual grant of two hundred chests of opium, the Danish Government was no longer able to meet the expenses of the place, and little had been done to assist the sufferers from the recent floods.[26] For the small but cosmopolitan western community, lodgings were considerably cheaper than in Calcutta; and here Chinnery remained for three and a half years.

His exile did not prevent him from painting portraits, so long as his sitters could make their way to him. Two of those who did so were William and Mary Prinsep, who spent their holidays in a bungalow at Barrackpore, immediately across the river from Serampore. Every day William and his young wife would be ferried over the Hooghly to sit for Chinnery, as he worked on what Prinsep later described as 'that pretty portrait in oils which is the only painted likeness of either of us.'[27] This portrait (Frontispiece), which descended through the family of William's sister Emily, is one of Chinnery's happiest portrayals of European domestic life in India. Unusually, the husband is shown seated while the wife stands, holding up a watercolour which her husband has just completed. Chinnery's pencil sketch for this portrait (Plate 96) has survived in a Prinsep family album.[28] Here Mary Prinsep is made to hold out the paper in her right hand, with the result that William is left staring at the back of it. In the final version Mary is placed closer to her husband, and the two of them are enabled to consider the watercolour together.

This portrait commission led to Chinnery's release from Serampore. The sympathies of the young couple were aroused by the sight of the eminent artist in exile, and William Prinsep no doubt spoke for many others when he wrote that 'we all regretted the loss of his society and his brush from Calcutta.' He asked Chinnery for a list of his creditors, and the artist supplied him with a list of debts which amounted to about 20,000 rupees. An influential group of the artist's friends, led by John Palmer, James Silk Buckingham, Colonel James Young[29] and Prinsep himself, persuaded others to join them in advancing this sum to Chinnery, so that he could be installed once more in his Calcutta studio. As security for their loan the group took 'a formal lien on the public pictures for which he had orders in hand' — one of them being the subscription portrait of Lord Hastings on horseback; since this commission alone was worth 16,000 rupees, the lenders must have thought that their investment was secure.

Chinnery duly returned to Calcutta, where, wrote Prinsep, 'he was heartily welcomed back, and he resumed his active labours.' But to the dismay of his rescuers, the artist neglected the commissioned work which would have repaid their loan, and turned to fresh orders which brought in ready money:

*Colour Plate 47. Portrait, by an unidentified contemporary of Chinnery, of Joshua Marshman and one of his Chinese assistants. Oils.* Hongkong and Shanghai Banking Corporation

I had a most troublesome correspondence with him for it turned out that he had underestimated his liabilities full 10,000 Rs & when I urged that it was unfortunately necessary that he should devote at least half his day to the finishing of the works which were to repay his Benefactors he used to meet my remarks with such words as these 'Chain Lord Byron to a rock, could he have written such poetry as his free spirit dictates? Place my brush under coercion, do you think you will ever get a picture worth looking at?' The unpredictable fellow never touched one of them, & when he ran away to China we found ourselves losers of more than 30,000 Rs! & the public pictures were most of them never painted at all.[30]

Clearly Chinnery had now exhausted not only much of his friends' money, but also their goodwill. Prinsep found a message which the artist had left for him, empowering him to sell 'a few half finished portraits which the badness of his health rendered it impossible for him to do more to'. Prinsep also managed to secure some sketchbooks which Chinnery had left in the hands of a certain Monsieur L'Emerque.[31] But these were scant compensation. Chinnery himself was beyond his grasp, having boarded the Company ship *Hythe* at Calcutta on 13 July 1825, and sailed for Macau, leaving his wife and his creditors behind him in India.

PART IV:
## The China Coast

*Colour Plate 48. The western Factories at Canton, showing the American, English and Dutch flags. Pen and ink and water-colours.* Private collection

# CHAPTER 12
## *Canton and the Chinese*

When Chinnery sailed out of the Hooghly River in July 1825, neither he nor his friends and associates in Calcutta can have expected that he would not return. They must have anticipated that, after a diplomatic absence of a year or two, he would charm, bluster or cajole his way back into solvency and the fashionable society which he relished. Clearly he let it be known that he was making the voyage for the good of his health (and there may even have been some truth in this), for a year later it was reported in the Calcutta press that 'the Friends of Mr Chinnery will be glad to hear that his health has been re-established by his voyage to China'. But the same newspaper hinted at economic motives for his departure from Calcutta, 'where ere long we hope circumstances will admit of his returning'.[1]

The log of the *Hythe,* kept by Captain John Peter Wilson, gives details of the personnel and the voyage. The first mate was Robert Lindsay, who later became a Commander in the Company's regular service, and whose portrait (as a young man) was painted by Chinnery.[2] The artist was attended on the voyage by an Indian servant; the other passengers consisted of three officers, two of them accompanied by their wives and a servant each. The ship was carrying two detachments of sepoys and their officers bound for Penang.

The *Hythe* anchored in Penang roads on 16 August, and remained there for nine days. The troops and their baggage were landed, the decks were scrubbed, and the ship took on stores and water together with 'Betel Nut and Pepper'. Chinnery could presumably have done some sketching in Penang,

but if he did, the sketches have apparently been lost. Possibly he was deterred from going ashore by the frequent rain which Captain Wilson's log records.[3]

On 29 September 1825, five weeks after leaving Penang, Chinnery and his servant left the *Hythe* and landed at Macau, where he was to live — with brief sorties to Canton and Hong Kong — for the remaining twenty-seven years of his life.

Chinnery did not settle in Macau immediately, but divided his early years on the China coast between Macau and Canton. Canton (modern Guangzhou) was the fulcrum of the trade between China and the West. Until the Opium War forced the Chinese Government to 'open' other ports to the West, Canton was the only Chinese city in which foreigners were permitted to trade. A small strip of river frontage was allotted to the western trading nations, who set up their 'Hongs' or 'Factories', spacious western-style buildings often with columns and verandas, in which were offices, warehouses and living accommodation. Trading took place under conditions strictly regulated by the Chinese Government, and only during the winter season. In the spring, those merchants who did not sail homeward with their cargoes were obliged to withdraw in convoy to Macau, eighty miles to the south. If they had families or children with them in the East, these would reside in Macau all year, since western women were not allowed in Canton.

Within Canton, the movements of westerners were limited to the precincts of the Factories, with excursions across the river to Honam, to the Fa-ti gardens to the west, and to the deep-water anchorage at Whampoa. Occasionally westerners would venture into the Chinese city to the north, but there is no evidence that Chinnery did so. In Chinnery's views of Canton, the principal landmarks are the Chinese river forts, notably the obscurely-named Dutch Folly Fort (Plate 98) on the north side of

*Plate 98. The Dutch Folly Fort, Canton. Pencil, pen and ink, and watercolours.* Private collection

*Plate 99. The Red Fort, Canton, with a distant view of the western Factories. Pencil, pen and ink, and watercolours.* Hong Kong Museum of Art

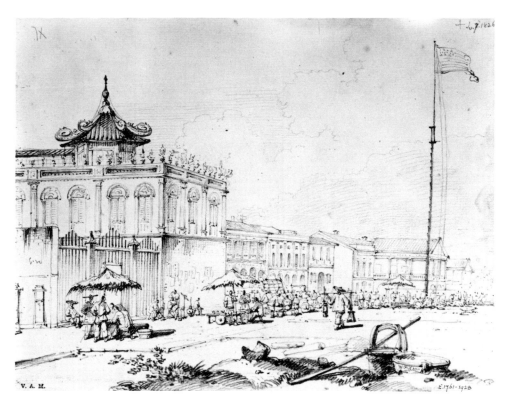

the river close to the Factories, and the Red Fort on the Honam side (Plate 99); the pedimented porticoes of the English and Dutch Hongs — the most imposing of the Factory buildings — at the eastern end of the concession (Plates 99 and 100 and Colour Plate 48); and, near the western end, the pagoda-roof of the Hong owned by the Cantonese Hong merchant Chung Qua (Plates 100 and 101).

The distinctive roof of Chung Qua's Hong was erected in the course of a general rebuilding which followed a disastrous fire in November 1822. On 9 July 1827 Chinnery made his detailed drawing of this roof (Plate 101) (which was taken down in the mid-1830s, following Chung Qua's bankruptcy and suicide). The drawing has extensive shorthand annotations which include 'Very light green porcelain', 'white over black', 'a kind of dragon's head', and 'fifteen flowerpots on all sides'. Chung Qua's Hong appears on the left of Colour Plate 49, an oil study *en grisaille* of Respondentia Square taken from a point near the English Hong. Even in this topographical subject, Chinnery's interest seems to lie in the groups of Chinese street vendors who frequented the Square; on the right is an itinerant barber, a figure depicted by Chinnery in many other drawings and paintings (Plates 109, 110 and 111).

Chinnery's dated drawings give some indication of his movements. He spent his first autumn (1825) in Macau, but he was evidently in Canton during the late summer and autumn of 1826, 1827, 1828, 1829, and 1832. It is clear that he made a prolonged visit in 1832, for a number of his drawings of Canton are inscribed with dates ranging from mid-April to the end of December of that year. In later years he seems to have kept largely to Macau. During his early

*Colour Plate 50. Junks and sampans: a misty morning.* Mr. and Mrs. P.J. Thompson

*Colour Plate 51. A junk at sunset.* Martyn Gregory Gallery

*Colour Plate 52. Junks and sampans off the China coast. Pen and ink and watercolours.* Malcom and Ursula Horsman

residence at Canton he lodged, according to the usually reliable William Hunter, at the Imperial Hong, the trading headquarters which operated under the Austrian flag.[4]

Although Chinnery was the only professional artist in the small western community on the China coast, he faced competition of a kind which he had not encountered in India. This came from the flourishing school of Cantonese artists who worked 'in the Western manner' — generally involving a combination of Chinese and European traditions — for the western market. These artists produced topographical views, showing the Factories at Canton, Macau, the anchorage at Whampoa, and other locations on the Pearl River; they also executed portraits, illustrations of the production of tea, porcelain and other commodities, and reinterpretations of western engravings. At first these 'export artists', as they are sometimes described today, worked in the traditional Chinese medium of water-based paint; but in the last years of the eighteenth century they began to employ the novel technique of painting in oils.

The best-known of the Cantonese 'export artists' contemporary with Chinnery was Guan Qiaochang, known to westerners as Lamqua. Many visitors went to the studio in China Street, Canton, in which he worked with a large number of assistants, following Chinnery's style closely and undercutting Chinnery's prices. Whether Lamqua was ever Chinnery's pupil in a formal sense is discussed in Chapter 17, but there can be no doubt that the two artists were already in close communication by the end of 1827. Writing from Canton on 12 December of that year, Chinnery sent a note to the Philadelphian merchant John Latimer, also resident in Canton:

Dear Sir,
Be pleased to pay to Lamqua Gent. on account of B.C.Wilcocks Esqre. for 200 (two hundred) Hair Pencils & 6 (six) Ivory Sheets for Miniature Painting, taken by him to the United States for Mr. Sully and Mr.Trot, the sum of Fifty Six SP.Dollars, & oblige
      Yours faithfully
        Geo. Chinnery[5]

The artists referred to are the history painter Thomas Sully and the miniature painter Benjamin Trott, who at one time was Sully's pupil. A letter from Chinnery to Latimer, also dated 12 December 1827, makes it clear that the brushes (at four to the Spanish dollar) were destined for Sully, and the ivories (at one Spanish dollar apiece) were for Trott. In the same letter Chinnery berates Latimer: 'I called on you this morning at 7 — but (Lazy Boots) you were Still in Bed...'[6]

Lamqua subsequently gained a reputation as a copier of Chinnery's original work. One of Chinnery's sitters, the Bostonian Robert Bennet Forbes, composed a tongue-in-cheek 'History of a Portrait', written as if from the portrait's point of view: 'In the winter of 1832 I underwent the infliction of a sitting to George Chinnery at Canton, for a half sized portrait, to be sent to my friends in the United States...' After a description of the artist and his habits, '...I found myself called into existence on a piece of canvas about 10 by 15 inches.' Then, 'as my master required a copy of me for a friend in Canton, I was transferred to the shop of Lamqua, where...after a few days' detention I was copied after a fashion and sent to my master.'[7] Nevertheless, Lamqua could do more than 'copy after a fashion'. He and the other export artists of Canton — their pictures are usually unsigned, and not easily distinguishable — were skilful practitioners, whose painting was not always markedly inferior to Chinnery's. They constituted a formidable threat to the English artist, and the study of Chinnery's work on the China coast remains beset by problems of attribution posed by Lamqua and his Cantonese colleagues.

### Whampoa

Ten miles below Canton on the Pearl River lay Whampoa, the deep-water anchorage at which the ocean-going East Indiamen ended their voyage. Here their cargoes were scrutinised by the Chinese customs, and then transferred to the smaller craft which operated between Whampoa and Canton. The anchorage offered an artistic set piece: 'No finer sight of the kind could be seen in any part of the world than the Company's fleet collected at Whampoa, with their inward cargoes discharged, and every ship in beautiful order, waiting for tea...everything indicated system, discipline, and force.'[8]

The mighty gathering at Whampoa was depicted by Thomas and William Daniell (who came here in 1785 and 1793), by William Huggins (who came in 1813), and by generations of Cantonese export artists. Yet it did not appeal to Chinnery, it seems. In the course of his twenty-seven years on the China coast he appears to have visited the place only once, not long after his arrival. A series of his slight sketches of Whampoa, which illustrate both the large and the small pagodas on Whampoa Island, belong to a series drawn on small buff sketchbook pages, with dates between 1827 and 1830.[9] The large pagoda on its eminence does, however, appear as a backdrop in certain of Chinnery's paintings, such as Plate 102, an oil study of a junk and sampans, with the Chinese custom house on the right.

Instead of the East Indiamen, Chinnery painted a series of understated and deceptively simple scenes of junks off the China coast, in morning mist or in

*Plate 102. A junk at Whampoa. Oils. Mr. and Mrs. R.J.F. Brothers*

placid evening sunshine (Colour Plates 50, 51 and 52). Gideon Nye, an early collector of Chinnery's work, admired these pictures in various media, showing 'junks at anchor and the water slightly rippling in the sun light...'; and in particular a painting of a junk in a dead calm, 'the air and sea's surface glowing in a white light...a triumph of art'.[10]

## Howqua and Mowqua

To a generation of western traders on the China coast, the best-known of their Chinese counterparts was Wu Bingjian, known by his Hong name of Howqua or Houqua (and sometimes, confusingly, as Howqua II).[11] From 1801 to 1826 Howqua was the nominated head of the Co-Hong, the association of wholesale merchants with whom the westerners conducted their official business; and although in 1826 he resigned from his position, his wealth and seniority ensured that he was still regarded as the Hong merchants' leader and representative.

In 1809 a Salem ship's captain noted that Howqua '...is very rich, sends good cargoes & is just in all his dealings, in short is a man of honour and veracity — has more business than any other man in the Hong...' In the margin the captain added 'Houqua is rather dear and can be coaxed'.[12] This tribute is typical of many which were recorded by those who came into contact with Howqua, especially the Americans Perkins, Cushing, Russell and the Forbes brothers, with whom he had close dealings. Such was his influence that, as the opium crisis deepened in the late 1830s, he forced the American firm of Russell & Co. to abandon their trading in opium, by threatening to withdraw his business from them.[13]

Howqua also traded abroad on his own account, chartering ships from Russell & Co. to take his teas to Europe. He had interests in tea plantations and rice fields, in property and in banking; when John Murray Forbes

Plate 103. *Portrait of Howqua. Pen and ink. Inscribed in shorthand 'December 26th [18]27. Canton'.* Private collection

Colour Plate 53. *Portrait of Howqua. Oils.* Hongkong and Shanghai Banking Corporation

returned home from the China coast, Howqua gave him a large sum of money to invest on his behalf in North American stock.[14] He was the richest merchant in China (possibly also in the world), with a fortune which he estimated in 1834 at 26 million Spanish dollars. He lent on a grand scale, advancing a quarter of a million taels (£86,000) to the East India Company in 1813. When six years later the Philadelphia merchant Benjamin Chew Wilcocks suffered a heavy loss, Howqua lent him the funds to continue in business; later, when Wilcocks seemed unable to repay him, Howqua tore up the promissory notes, freeing Wilcocks from the debt and enabling him to return to the United States.[15]

Howqua was not universally admired, however. Jardine and Matheson, who generally traded with Mowqua and other Hong merchants, were suspicious of Howqua's influence and his close relations with the American merchants. And whereas Howqua acted as a restraining influence on the Americans' opium dealings in the 1830s, William Jardine was advised by Mowqua that the Chinese Government would back down from confrontation and would legalise opium — a mistaken judgement which encouraged Jardine in his provocative policies.[16]

Most of the Hong merchants held titular ranks, which were denoted by the colour of their hat button. Thus the opaque blue hat buttons seen in Chinnery's portraits of both Howqua and Mowqua mark them as civil mandarins of the fourth grade. Ranks were also denoted by the species of bird embroidered on the surcoat; but even when these are decipherable, the coat badges painted by Chinnery and by his Chinese followers show little consistency and cannot be relied upon as accurate. These ranks were bestowed by the Government in return for payments (which might be either voluntary or compulsory), and carried certain privileges: holders of titular

*Detail of the portrait of Mowqua*

*Colour Plate 54. Portrait of Mowqua. Oils.* Hongkong and Shanghai Banking Corporation

*Colour Plate 55. Portrait of Mowqua. Oils.* Private collection

ranks were exempt from corporal punishment and torture. Recent investigation of the Chinese sources has revealed that Lu Yuankin (Mowqua) received his fourth-rank status in recognition of his contribution to the embankment of the Yellow River; he also earned a peacock's feather for hitting a target while accompanying the Emperor on a hunting exercise. These honours were taken away, however, when Mowqua was discovered to have bribed the local officials to install a tablet commemorating his dead father in the Temple of Worthies — a place of honour for which his late father, being of lowly birth, was not qualified.[17]

The position of Hong merchant was a prestigious one, but it also carried with it disadvantages which were so severe that few of the Hong merchants volunteered for the position; most were obliged to adopt it by the Hoppo (senior financial administrator) of Canton, who was able to exploit them and prevent them from retiring. When Howqua finally resigned from the Co-Hong, it was only after repeated applications and the payment of a large sum of money. Bankruptcy was a constant threat to all but the most affluent of the Hong merchants, and as each of them was held responsible for the good conduct of the western traders, as well as for their payment of duties, they came under increasing pressure from the Chinese authorities during the opium crisis. In 1839 Howqua and Mowqua were made to appear with iron chains around their necks, and stripped of their rank buttons, in order to induce the westerners to surrender their opium stocks. In 1841, when the British military force threatened to attack the city of Canton unless a ransom of six million dollars was paid, the Hong merchants provided two million dollars towards the ransom, of which $1,100,000 was contributed by Howqua, on behalf of himself and his family.[18]

Mowqua (Lu Yuankin) was the antithesis of Howqua. He was a large, robust man, and whereas the Wu (Howqua) family were renowned as painters, poets and sponsors of literary publications, Mowqua is remembered as an amiable character and an accomplished eater.[19] His father, known also as Mowqua, had also been a Hong merchant, who despite his humble origins had risen to be regarded as the richest of the Co-Hong in the first decade of the nineteenth century. From his father's death in 1812 until 1835 Mowqua was officially regarded as the second merchant, after Howqua, in the Co-Hong. But his path ran less smoothly than his rival's. In the great fire of Canton in 1822, Mowqua lost property to the value of 350,000 taels (£120,000), nearly twice as much as Howqua; this setback, exacerbated by reckless borrowing and the embarrassing episode of his father's tablet, meant that his financial state was often precarious.[20]

This antithesis is reflected in Chinnery's portraits of the two Hong merchants (Colour Plates 53 and 54). Each is surrounded by Chinese symbols of status — a mandarin's cap, fine porcelain and furniture, a spittoon and a hanging lantern — to which is added, incongruously, the European convention of a solid column. Beyond Howqua, however, are seen pot plants and shrubs (an allusion to his famous gardens), while Mowqua is supplied with the more mundane accessory of a goldfish bowl. A more striking difference between the two portraits lies in the sitters' postures. The weighty figure of Mowqua leans backward in a relaxed, almost sprawling fashion, while Howqua sits upright, a man whose 'person and looks bespoke that his great wealth had not been accumulated without proportionate anxiety'.[21] His pursed lips and gaunt cheeks, together with the expressive angles of wrists and fingers, put us in mind of some *fin de siècle* aesthete, a Max Beerbohm or a Comte de Montesquiou in Chinese guise. This intensity of expression is diluted in the later versions and imitations of this portrait, in which Howqua appears as a conventionally genial figure.

Both the pose and the lighting of the Howqua picture are wholly at odds with traditional Chinese notions of portraiture. Howqua is placed in the attitude which Chinnery was himself to adopt in his most celebrated self-portrait (Colour Plate 102): one leg is swung over the other almost at right angles to the head, which turns three-quarter face on to the spectator. It is noticeable that in the versions painted by Chinnery's Chinese followers, although the legs may still be crossed, the pose is nearer to the full-frontal approach typical of Chinese ancestor portraits. And these latter versions reduce or abandon the dramatic chiaroscuro of Chinnery's painting. Fully three-quarters of his composition is in shadow (a proportion which Chinnery had recommended in his projected 'Treatise': see Appendix i), while the face and upper body of Howqua are theatrically spotlit. One might suggest that the stormy sunset beyond Howqua's gardens was a symbol of approaching conflict, were it not for the fact that such backgrounds were a favourite device of Chinnery's, and one which he was liable to employ in the most inconsequential of contexts.

For Chinnery's portrait of Mowqua a small grisaille oil sketch survives (Colour Plate 55), an interesting example of his preliminary planning of a portrait in terms of light and shade. Although none of the detail is included at this stage, the balance of tones which is established here is preserved in the final picture; even the dash of white in the sky to the right of the column was evidently conceived at the outset as an element in the tonal balance of the composition.

This mannerism reappears in several Cantonese versions of the Mowqua portrait (Colour Plate 56). Again a more frontal pose is adopted. Changes have been made in the surcoat badge and hat button, and the porcelain, the latticework and the circular aperture have all been omitted. The artist has been unable to represent the transparency of the goldfish bowl, and has prudently left out the goldfish. The brushwork is less crisp throughout. Here the quality of the imitation is clearly inferior to the original — although in other cases the distinction is much less obvious.

While Mowqua was quickly forgotten, however, Howqua was commemorated across the world. After his death in 1843, an American clipper was named in his honour; a valedictory poem was composed by an American trading associate; a life-size clay figure of him was displayed in the 'Chinese Museum' set up in Philadelphia by the retired China trader Nathan Dunn; and an effigy of him was for many years on view at Madame Tussaud's waxworks in London. In the 1870 catalogue of Madame Tussaud's, Howqua appeared between the Duke of Wellington and George Washington, and was said to have been 'greatly distinguished among Hong merchants for his exceedingly cheerful disposition and for his great attachment to the English nation'.[22]

*Colour Plate 56. Portrait of Mowqua, by a Cantonese artist. Oils.* Hongkong and Shanghai Banking Corporation

*Colour Plate 57. Mah Chih Ping. Oils.* Hongkong and Shanghai Banking Corporation

*Colour Plate 58. A seated watchman. Oils.* Hongkong and Shanghai Banking Corporation

176

Yet the most enduring image of Howqua is undoubtedly that created by Chinnery, an image which was widely reproduced for the western market in various sizes, versions and media, in the studios of Canton. For westerners, this image of Howqua represented not merely an elegant Chinese dignitary in his picturesque robes and insignia, but also an individual who embodied those qualities of traditional culture, business acumen, courtesy and diplomacy which Europeans had for centuries attributed to the Chinese people as a whole. This western conception of China contained a large measure of fantasy, and it did not long survive the disillusioning experiences of the Opium Wars with their attendant propaganda; but the image of Howqua served as a reassuring sign that the stereotype of the benevolent, sophisticated Chinese was not entirely misconceived.

*Plate 104. Study of a bearded man smoking a pipe. Pencil, inscribed and dated 'Canton May 4 1826'. Cooper-Hewitt Museum, New York*

The initial portrait of Howqua by Chinnery, which gave rise to so many versions and imitations, is very probably the small full-length reproduced as Colour Plate 53. This is plausibly said to have been commissioned by W.H. Chicheley Plowden, the President of the Committee of the East India Company in Canton.[23] When Plowden sailed for home on 31 January 1830, he would have taken the portrait with him, and this was no doubt the 'Portrait of Howqua' by George Chinnery which was exhibited at the Royal Academy in 1831.[24] (The exhibition of the previous year had included another portrait of a Hong merchant by Chinnery, but his name was not stated.)

Chinnery's portraits of Chinese sitters were not restricted to the Hong merchants (Plates 104-111 and Colour Plates 57-60). His painting of an elderly man, shown seated with fan, book and spectacles (Colour Plate 57), has three Chinese characters inscribed in the upper right corner, 'Mah Chih Ping', but whether this denotes the figure's name or his rank is not clear. A man in a buttoned jacket, sitting on a bamboo stool with his dog beside him, is perhaps a watchman or a household servant (Colour Plate 58). Contrasting facial types, and contrasting styles of draughtsmanship, are to be seen in a sensitive pencil drawing of two young scribes (Plate 106), who can be identified as assistants of Robert Morrison (compare Colour Plate 150), and vigorous pen-and-ink sketches of bearded gentlemen, one wearing spectacles secured by means of a loop of string tied around his ear (Plates 107 and 108). Chinnery's portraits of a young Chinese woman seated by a circular window (Colour Plate 59) and a porter in a shaded landscape, pausing to draw on his slender pipe (Colour Plate 60) are scarcely less dignified than the Hong merchants portrayed with all their regalia and symbols of status.

One of Chinnery's most engaging portrait studies in oils is that of the Chinese barber (Plate 109), depicted in an alley off the square opposite the Factories at Canton. The itinerant barber, who advertised his presence by twanging his tweezers in a musical fashion, was a familiar figure in China. His chief role was shaving; since the head as well as the face was to be shaved, a Chinese man was unlikely to shave himself. The barber might also clean the ears of his customers, plait their queues, and massage their joints and muscles. In the words of William Alexander, who had sketched the barbers whom he had encountered while accompanying the first British Embassy to China in

*Colour Plate 59. A Chinese woman, with fan and birdcage, by a circular window. Oils.* Private collection

*Colour Plate 60. Chinese porter smoking a pipe. Oils.* Private collection

Plate 106. Studies of Robert Morrison's Chinese assistants. Pencil. Private collection

Plate 105. Studies of a boatwoman. Pencil. Cooper-Hewitt Museum, New York

Plate 107. Study of an elderly man with spectacles. Pen and ink. Victoria and Albert Museum

Plate 108. Study of an elderly man. Pen and ink over pencil. Private collection

1793, they 'tickle the nose, and play a thousand tricks to please and amuse their customers'.[25]

In Chinnery's painting, which is dated 1826, the barber balances himself on his characteristic pyramidal chest of drawers, surrounded by his equipment. His right hand rests on a tall tripod cylinder of bamboo, which held water, while the chest (as another witness described) 'contains the apparatus for shaving the head and beard, cleansing the ears, cutting the nails of the toes and fingers, and is easily converted into a seat for the welcome customer'.[26] Most of these operations are illustrated in Chinnery's sketches (Plates 110 and 111), in which the customer often co-operates in holding the barber's equipment while the latter's hands are occupied, and is made comfortable with a burning 'moon tiger' coil to ward off the mosquitoes.

Plate 109. A Chinese barber. Oils, dated 1826. Private collection

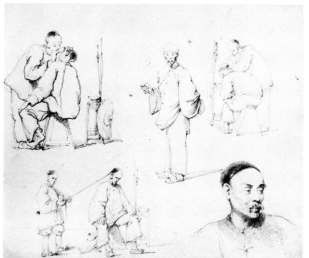

Plate 110. Studies of Chinese figures, including barbers and their customers. Pencil. Mr. and Mrs. P.J. Thompson

Plate 111. Barber and customer. Pen and ink over pencil. Inscribed and dated in shorthand 'correct September 8 [18]32 / At a shop door'. Private collection

*Colour Plate 61. The Praya Grande, Macau, from the south-west. Oils.* Private collection

*Colour Plate 62. The Praya Grande from the north-east. Pen and ink and watercolours.* Private collection

*Colour Plate 63. The Praya Grande from the east. Oils.* Hongkong and Shanghai Banking Corporation

# CHAPTER 13
# *Macau*

The peninsula of Macau, some eighty miles to the south of Canton, has served as a sanctuary for westerners ever since the Portuguese were allowed to settle here in the 1550s. The early Portuguese adventurers married Malaccan and Japanese women, and thus a heterogeneous Macanese race was created; in Chinnery's time they were often referred to as Macaistas, or simply as Portuguese. They were excluded from the Chinese mainland by a wall built across the isthmus, but their settlement prospered, largely through trade with Japan and Manila. They built forts on the hills, and installed cannon, for use against the marauding Dutch and English — the two nations which, by the early eighteenth century, had usurped Portugal's position as the leading western traders in the East.

The forts of Macau appear in many of Chinnery's drawings, in particular Fort Monte, dominating the centre of the peninsula; the hilltop forts of Bom Parto and Guia, at either end of the Praya Grande, or Great Bay; and the small battery of São Pedro near the shore between them. By the time of Chinnery's arrival the Praya Grande (Colour Plates 61, 62 and 63) was flanked by a shallow crescent of fine two-storied houses, often supplied with verandas and columns or colonnades, Many of these were rented by the foreign trading companies from their Portuguese owners, and for some years the East India Company occupied two of the most imposing structures, with pilasters and

*Plate 112. Gateway to the Seminary of São José, Macau. Pen and ink and watercolours.* Toyo Bunko, Tokyo

*Plate 113. Church of São Domingos, Macau, with street vendors. Pen and ink over pencil. Inscribed in shorthand 'figures correct right size'.* Victoria and Albert Museum

central pediments, which stood immediately to the south of the Governor's Palace. None of the buildings depicted by Chinnery on the Praya Grande survive today, and much of the bay itself has been reclaimed.

On the other hand, one may still see several of the great churches and seminaries founded by the Portuguese and the Spanish in the sixteenth and seventeenth centuries. These also appear frequently in Chinnery's pictures (Plates 112-116 and Colour Plate 64), either as the principal subject of a drawing or as an element in a street scene — a decorative gable or a raised pediment seen at an angle from the shadow of an alley, or one of the twin towers of São Lourenço glimpsed above the rooftops. The distinctive silhouettes of São Francisco, São Domingos, Santo Agostinho, São Paulo and São José, with their associated seminary and convent buildings, rise over the dwellings in Chinnery's townscapes, a testament to the power of the Roman Catholic Church or, more particularly, to the Jesuit order.

At the heart of the city, and adjacent to the senate house, stood the São Casa da Misericordia, a remarkable institution which embraced a hospital, a leprosarium, and an orphanage which took in abandoned infants and reared them until the age of seven. Its baroque doorway was surmounted by a relief of Our Lady of Mercy, and beside it stood a crenellated stone tower, which stands out in early views of Macau. Chinnery made many drawings from the street outside the Misericordia, showing the Spanish-built church of São Domingos on the opposite side, and the battlements of Fort Monte closing the view to the north (Plates 114 and 115).

Plate 114. View from São Casa da Misericordia towards São Domingos and Forte Monte, Macau. Pen
and ink and watercolours. Private collection

Plate 115. View from São Casa da Misericordia towards São Domingos and Forte Monte. Pen and ink
and sepia wash. Toyo Bunko, Tokyo

*Colour Plate 64. São Domingos Church,
Macau. Pen and ink and watercolours.*
Martyn Gregory Gallery

*Colour Plate 65. The Grotto
of Camões, Macau. Oils.*
Private collection

186

*Colour Plate 66. The inner harbour, Macau, seen from the Casa Gardens. Oils.* Private collection

The great emblem of Macau, and an evocation of its mingled cultures, is the façade of the Jesuit church of São Paulo. When it was completed in 1602 it was perhaps the most splendid church in Asia, with its roof of carved wood, richly painted and gilt. In 1633-5 the four-tiered stone façade was added, inspired by examples in northern Italy but built by local craftsmen, who included Japanese Christian refugees from Nagasaki. They created a rich assortment of reliefs in stone and castings in bronze: Christian symbols and Chinese pictograms, saints, demons, and references to Portuguese seafarers. In the centre of its third storey the Virgin Mary is accompanied by the peony, representing China, and the chrysanthemum, representing Japan. A Jesuit college was erected alongside the church, and a broad flight of steps was built in front, heightening the drama of the situation.

When Chinnery first came to Macau, São Paulo remained the pride of Portuguese Macau. In 1835, however, the wooden church caught fire during a severe typhoon, and much of it was destroyed. Chinnery's pen-and-ink drawing dated 18 October 1834 (Plate 116) depicts the church shortly before the fire; his sketches of the ruins, taken afterwards, are in the Victoria and Albert Museum.[1] Today the curving row of houses adjacent to the staircase has also gone, leaving the facade starkly silhouetted, a series of finely-fashioned

entrances leading to nothing — a symbol of the high aspirations of Christianity in the East, and of their ultimate frustration.

For the short-term visitor to Macau, one of the chief attractions was the Grotto of Camões (or Camoens), a cluster of granite rocks on a hilltop commanding a view over the Inner Harbour to the west of the peninsula (Colour Plate 65). According to deeply-rooted tradition, it was here that the one-eyed exile Luis Vaz de Camões composed his epic poem *Os Lusiadas,* in the first year of the Portuguese settlement. The 'grotto' formed a part of the large gardens of a fine house, generally known as the Casa (Colour Plate 66), which was occupied by a sequence of senior members of the East India Company until the Company's monopoly lapsed in 1834. These gardens also included a plot of land which was bought by the British in 1821 from the Portuguese owner, the senator and financier Manuel Pereira, to serve as a Protestant burial ground. Chinnery's tomb is here, together with those of many of his friends and associates.

A more spectacular rock formation which, however, is less impressive today, was situated at the southern point of the peninsula. Visitors would admire the 'enormous pile of rocks [which] lie tumbled together, as if thrown up by some dreadful convolution of nature', and the huge trees growing out of the fissures.[2] Beside it is the A-Ma or Ma-Kok temple, which lent its name to Macau; it was built on the site at which prayers were offered by the early Fukienese settlers to Ma Cho, the ancestral grandmother, guardian of fishermen. This place, a short walk from Chinnery's house, was the scene of some of his most satisfying drawings and paintings. Although he sometimes depicted the temple itself (Plate 117), he more often took up a position just

*Plate 117. The A-Ma (or Ma-Kok) temple, Macau. Pencil, dated April 16 1833. Inscribed in shorthand 'the good proportions may be depended upon', and 'fix'.* Private collection

*Plate 118. The sixteen-pillared house, Macau. Pencil, pen and ink, dated August 12th 1836 (pencil) and July 29th 1836 (ink).* City of Birmingham Museum and Art Gallery

*Colour Plate 67. The A-Ma temple. Oils.* Private collection

around the corner, so that, in the resulting pictures (Colour Plates 67 and 68), the temple gateway is only just visible, or not at all. The mass of dark rocks run down to the sea on the left, while on the right the light just catches the jetty in front of the temple, where two masts marked the Chinese customs point.

One of the grandest houses in Macau was that occupied by W.H. Chicheley Plowden, President of the Select Committee of the East India Company, and later by the American merchant Gideon Nye. Its street front, opposite São Lourenço, consisted of a screen with eight pairs of Corinthian columns, from

*Plate 119. Balconied house on the Praya Grande, Macau. Pen and ink and watercolours.* Private collection

190

which it was known as the sixteen-pillared house (Plate 118). Another distinctive house, illustrated in Plates 119 and 120, had a semicircular veranda which projected from the main building; it can also be seen in general views of the Praya Grande, behind a low wall near the southern end of the Praya. Among the tenants of this house were two of Chinnery's subjects, Captain

*Plate 120. Balconied house on the Praya Grande (from the west). Pen and ink and watercolours.* Private collection

191

Plate 121. Sketches of a western figure, a pair of hands, and part of the Praya Grande. Pencil and pen and ink, dated and inscribed with shorthand: (upper right) 'correct, December 6. 1847'; (upper centre, by pair of hands) 'May 12. '48, correct / both at home / correct'; (upper left by figure) 'At home May 12. '48 / correct, filled in'. Museu Luis de Camões, Macau

Plate 122. The Praya Manduco, Macau. Pen and ink and water-colours, dated ...17 1838. British Museum

Alexander Grant and Robert Bennet Forbes.[3]

Although Macau took on the outward appearance of a European colonial city, the majority of the population remained Chinese, and it was upon them that the essential economy of the place depended. In 1841 the Chinese population of Macau was estimated at 20,000-30,000, and the Portuguese/Macanese at something over 4,000, 'of whom above a fourth part are black slaves'.[4] In this same year the other foreign male residents numbered about 230, of whom only twenty-one are recorded as having 'family' with them. Over half were British; the group next in size was the Parsees, followed by the Americans.[5] The figures in Chinnery's street scenes are very largely Chinese, but pairs of Macanese women are also to be seen, with a servant holding an umbrella behind them (see Colour Plate 81). Following

192

*Colour Plate 69. Harriet Low.*
Mr. and Mrs. R.J.F.
Brothers (on loan to the
Peabody Museum, Salem,
Massachusetts)

the Malaccan custom, their heads are covered with shawls, which could be quickly drawn across the face if a man approached. Westerners seldom appear in Chinnery's Macau scenes; a rare instance is the tall-hatted figure who is placed by the sedan chair on the right of Colour Plate 63: a pen-and-ink drawing of the same figure (Plate 121), dated May 1848, suggests that the painting is also of that date .

In 1826 Chinnery took a short lease on a house in Macau; he was obliged to rent, like all his compatriots, as no westerners other than Portuguese were allowed to own property in Macau. The house was near the church of São Lourenço, towards the point of the peninsula. The archives of the Macau Senate record that on 17 June 1826, 'another request was heard from Rita Maria de Carvalho, wife of Manuel Honem de Carvalho, asking permission to rent her house, situated on the street of São Lourenço that descends to the Praia de Manduco [the bay facing the Inner Harbour (Plate 122)], to George Chinnery, a foreign businessman, for the time of six months'.[6]

This house was to remain Chinnery's home for the rest of his life. A 'Directory' of Macau in 1830, which survives in the British Library, lists some sixty locations with their Chinese names, including four lodgings which appear under the single heading (in Chinese translation) of 'behind São

*Plate 123. Robert Huddleston.*
*Oils.* Private collection

Lourenço Church'. These are 'Dr Morrison' (the missionary Robert Morrison: see Colour Plate 99); 'Mr Hudleston' (Robert Burland Hudleston of the East India Company, Plate 123); 'Mr Jackson' (John Jackson, also of the East India Company); and 'Mr Chinnery'.[7] The fact that these residences were bracketed together indicates that they were smaller than the independently-listed houses occupied by the leading merchants; possibly they shared a single entrance.

Chinnery's exact address is given in the Portuguese records of the Peking Mission held in the Bishop's Palace in Macau. The house was 8 Rua de Ignacia Baptista. (The street survives, although its houses have been rebuilt and renumbered; a parallel street has been named Rua de George Chinnery.) In 1843 it was taken over by the Catholic mission from its owner, Manuel Honem de Carvalho, until the debts incurred by Honem should be repaid by him or his heirs. The debts were never paid, and the mission retained the house. In 1847 the rent was reduced from $300 to $120, perhaps a sign of Macau's declining fortunes in the face of Hong Kong's rising prosperity. In any case Chinnery did not pay the rent for any of these years until his death in 1852, and only then was the money recovered from the artist's estate by the Mission Superior, Fr. Joaquim Leite.[8] Thus the statement made in the *China Mail*'s obituary notice of Chinnery, that he died in the house which he had occupied since 1827, is confirmed.

### Harriet Low

The non-Portuguese westerners kept largely to themselves, although one or two of the Portuguese families of Macau, notably the Paivas and the Pereiras, were included at their dinner tables. Their everyday activities are chronicled vividly in the journals kept by Harriet Low, who spent four years in Macau, and came to know Chinnery well. The Lows were a prominent New England family; Harriet's uncle, William Low, was a partner in Russell & Co., the leading American firm in Canton. In 1829 he and his wife Abigail (Plates 124 and 125) sailed from Salem for China, taking the twenty-year-old Harriet with them. She was to be a companion to Abigail Low in Macau during the winter months, while William Low would be occupied in Canton — where western women were forbidden. When Harriet arrived in Macau she found herself the only unmarried woman in the western expatriate community, and the centre of male attention.

The Lows landed at Macau on 30 September 1829. Like most of the other expatriates, they lived in considerable comfort. The house which they occupied near the Cathedral had a domed dining room ornamented with stucco, and a fine marble fireplace — 'a room that you would be proud of in America', in Harriet's eyes. She found that the bachelors, too, had 'everything in style, and plenty of servants'.[9] Formal dinners were given by the East India

*Plate 124. William Henry Low. Oils.* Peabody Museum, Salem, Massachusetts

*Plate 125. Mrs. William Henry Low (née Abigail Knapp). Oils.* Peabody Museum, Salem, Massachusetts

Company. On the occasion of Harriet Low's first Christmas in Macau, sixty sat down at the Company's table, each with their Chinese servant standing behind. 'The dinner consisted of every delicacy, served in the most elegant style...' Only the plum pudding lacked 'the home relish'.[10]

Music was to be heard, especially at the house of W.H. Chicheley Plowden, President of the Company's Select Committee. Chinnery's immediate neighbours, John Jackson and Robert Hudleston, played the violin and the hautboy, Robert Inglis played the flute, and in August 1832 Harriet Low heard the accordion here, 'a new instrument just come out'.[11] In the following spring an Italian touring company of singers came to Macau, and was much appreciated; Chinnery was in the Lows' 'box', which consisted of seven chairs in a row.[12]

There were also amateur theatricals, in which Chinnery was prominent. In one Macau production he played Mrs. Malaprop in *The Rivals*, a role for which he was qualified by virtue of his notorious puns;[13] and it was in another play that he first attracted the attention of Harriet Low, two months after her arrival. The name of Chinnery had already appeared (misspelt) in her entry for 17 October 1829, as one of seven gentlemen who called upon the Lows. At the theatre, however, he was recognised as 'Mr Chinnery, a famous portrait painter', who had been allotted a female part, although (as she noted) nobody could be less feminine than he. The part was that of Lucretia Mactab in *The Poor Gentleman* by George Colman the younger, a play which could well have been selected for the very purpose of giving Chinnery the role. Lucretia Mactab is 'a stiff maiden aunt', who is susceptible to flattery — 'how these tabbies love to be toaded' — and has artistic pretensions: she criticises her niece's embroidery, although the niece protests that she has copied from nature. Finally Lucretia is left destitute after the death of her debt-ridden brother. Chinnery's appearance 'made much sport', Harriet Low reported, adding that he had painted several of the scenes as well.[14]

Two weeks after this performance, Harriet Low paid her first visit to

Chinnery's 'room', as she generally described it; on one occasion she referred to his 'studio', but her inverted commas make it clear that the place did not deserve so dignified a description. 'He has some fine likenesses there. He is remarkably successful. How I wished that I had a little of the needful to put into the man's hand, that he might take my beautiful phiz...'[15]. Her wish was eventually granted.

During the next two years Harriet saw a good deal of Chinnery. She observed him in the company of the American merchants James Blight and Robert Wilkinson, the English merchant Thomas Beale, and the French Captain Durran; she encountered him at Mrs. Fearon's, at Mrs. Allport's and at Mrs. Morrison's, and she noted him among the players of card games at mixed social occasions — 'Old Maid', 'Old Bachelor', and 'Speculation'. She paid regular visits to Chinnery's lodgings, where she took instruction from him in sketching, and copied his drawings.

She disapproved of some of the artist's habits — 'taking snuff, smoking and snorting...were he not so agreeable, he would be intolerable'. (She held strong views on the subject: 'It is a great offence to smoke in a room where ladies ever enter.') Her journal makes no mention of Chinnery's smoking the hookah, and it seems that Chinnery had abandoned the instrument which he had so much enjoyed in Calcutta, for she comments in some detail on the few hookah smokers whom she encountered in Macau — Pereira, Beale and Clifton (see p.215).[16] But Chinnery was certainly fond of cigars. In a letter of 1827 he asked John Latimer to arrange for an incoming captain 'to let me have 500 of his Beauties of Cigars before they are all gone'.[17]

Moreover, Harriet complained of Chinnery, 'he is particularly disagreeable at breakfast, being something of a *gourmand* and not particular in his *manner* of eating.' Nevertheless she evidently enjoyed the company of a man whom she regarded as a 'droll genius', a man of 'excellent sense', really polite', and 'a great observer of human nature'. She in turn was 'one of his especial favorites',[18] and, it would seem, an apt pupil, not easily satisfied with her own work or with others'. When a miniature portrait of her sister arrived from America, she thought it failed to capture her sister's expression, and decided that its painter cannot have talked to her sister; it was Harriet's belief — surely inspired by Chinnery — that for a portrait painter to achieve a likeness, he or she must engage the sitter in conversation.[19]

In 1832 Chinnery dropped out of Harriet Low's social life when he paid a long visit to Canton. In his absence his role as Harriet's drawing master was supplanted by the skilful draughtsman and caricaturist William Wood. In the course of this year Wood gradually won a place in her affections; his sketching lessons sometimes occupied the whole day. In December he proposed marriage, and Harriet accepted him. But Wood was a controversial figure, who had made some powerful enemies during his brief career as editor of the *Chinese Courier;* a few months before his proposal, he had been challenged to a duel by the editor of the rival newspaper, the *Canton Register.* William Low would not allow his niece to be married to such a man, and the engagement was broken off. Harriet was sorrowful, but — to judge from the tone of her diary entries — not entirely devastated.[20]

*Colour Plate 70. Portrait of a Tanka boatwoman, with distant pagoda. Oils.* Anthony J. Hardy
Collection

Soon after this episode Chinnery returned to Macau, and was reinstated in Harriet's routine. On a visit to the artist's room, soon after the ending of her engagement, she saw 'a great attraction — a picture of my friend, which I was strongly tempted to pocket. It is a perfect likeness. I shall probably never see it again, as it is going to America. Well, I do not know why I should wish to, he is nothing to me.'[21] Presumably the portrait was of William Wood.

By now there were other distractions. As the Lows' period of residence in Macau was drawing to a close, it was arranged that all three — uncle, aunt and niece — should have their portraits separately painted by Chinnery. Harriet's portrait (Colour Plate 69) exhibits many of the mannerisms which are characteristic of Chinnery's female portraits of his Chinese period. The shoulders slope steeply, and the breasts appear constricted beneath a low-cut but shallow neckline. The great feature of the dress is the billowing sleeves, a fashion which had astonished Harriet when she had first encountered it three years before on a pair of new arrivals: 'They bring us the latest Calcutta fashions. Such sleeves I never beheld, — complete frights!'[22] The head is at an angle, and the lips are apart, a somewhat unconventional device: 'He requested me to have the mouth open, a thing I abominate in a picture, but he says it will never do to have it shut, as I generally leave it a little open.'[23]

A special interest attaches to this portrait, for the sitter recorded her reactions to it at various stages during its creation. Harriet's first sitting, on 10 April 1833, lasted for an hour, which she spent

> ...looking at one of the ugliest men in existence, but he makes himself so agreeable that you quite forget how ugly he is...Well, there I sat, with my head screwed and twisted in a strange manner, till after he had finished the first sketch, and then I looked at it. Oh, ye powers, what a thing! and yet I think it must be like me, because I saw mother's look about the eyes...The head appears about ready to take leave of the neck, the mouth is open as though I were snoring; there is a little something yclept nose, and a place where eyes should be. I suppose I must wait with patience for a few more sittings, but I think it will rather lower my vanity, though on the subject of personal appearance I never had much.[24]

Six days later she returned for a second sitting, this time of three hours, and found herself 'in better humor with my portrait, which will, I think, be an excellent likeness, and a little paint will make it better-looking than I am, I fear. You can make allowances for the paint. Chinnery said some good things, and we passed the morning very pleasantly.'[25] There were further sessions, during which Chinnery altered the composition by placing a book in his subject's hands; this alteration pleased Harriet, perhaps because the book partly masks the hands, which — as often in Chinnery's portraits — are painted in summary fashion. But the painting took longer than she had expected, and she grew impatient and hot; whereas Chinnery's sitters in Calcutta may well have enjoyed the benefit of a cooling punkah, there was no such luxury in his room in Macau, and Harriet complained that 'not a breath of air from out-of-doors is allowed to enter'. Her last sitting was on 15 May.

*Plate 126. Portrait head of a Tanka boatwoman. Pencil.*
Private collection

*Plate 127. Portrait of a Tanka boatwoman, standing. Oils.*
Private collection

She emerged exhausted and, finally, disappointed: 'The likeness is said to be perfect — but I think it is a very ugly person. It has not raised my vanity in the least.'[26]

In the same weeks Chinnery was painting the portraits of her uncle and aunt, and when the three of them went to the studio on 9 May, Harriet could write that 'we were all there also in effigy'.[27] On 19 November 1833 they finally left Macau aboard the Company ship *Waterloo*. Their portraits came safely to America.[28] William Low died at Capetown on the homeward voyage. Harriet was married in 1836 to a Bostonian, had eight children, and died in Brooklyn at the age of sixty-eight.

**Tanka Boatwomen**

'Macao was the asylum of the East, open to all, bond or free, and thus it became a proverb, Macao is the paradise of Debtors and Tan-Kas.'[29] Of the debtors, the most celebrated were Chinnery himself and Thomas Beale, keeper of a fine garden and aviary, who was finally driven to suicide. The 'Tan-Kas', on the other hand, occupy a special position in Chinnery's art. To an expatriate community which was very largely male, the image of the Tanka woman was a female symbol of the China coast (Plates 126 and 127 and Colour Plates 70 and 71). The China merchants would often complain, or boast, of their lack of contact with women; when the Philadelphia trader Nathan Dunn called on Harriet Low in Macau, she recorded that 'Dunn...has not seen a lady for eight years'.[30] For such as Dunn, a picture of a wistfully smiling Tanka woman served as a sentimental souvenir (Chinnery sent another client a 'picture of a little Tanka' to take home with him[31]) which carried a certain aura of romantic inaccessibility, similar perhaps to that of contemporary 'orientalist' pictures of women enclosed within a harem,

*Colour Plate 71. Tanka boatwoman by her dwelling. Oils.*
Hongkong and Shanghai Banking Corporation

*Colour Plate 72. Tanka boat dwellings raised on stones.* Mr. and Mrs.
P.J. Thompson

*Colour Plate 73. Tanka boat dwellings raised on stilts.*
*Pencil and watercolours.* Private collection

*Plate 128. Study of a Tanka boatwoman rowing. Pencil.* Private
collection

*Plate 129. Sketch of a Tanka boat at sea. Pen and ink, dated July 1st*
*1836.* Private collection

*Colour Plate 74. Fisherman carrying his net. Pen and ink and watercolours.* Mr. and Mrs R J F Brothers

although demure rather than erotic in effect.

The Tanka people were so named after their 'egg-boats' (Plates 128 and 129), broad, rounded sampans some fifteen feet long, with one or more curved roofs of rattan amidships. They formed a distinct ethnic group, which was discouraged from intermarrying with the mainland Chinese. They lived along the coast at Macau, Whampoa and Hong Kong, where in 1841-2 it was estimated that they made up a quarter of the local population, living in their moored craft.[32] On the shore at Macau they created makeshift dwellings by raising up the boats on stones or wooden stilts, and adding hurdles and thatch as required; Chinnery made many studies of these converted Tanka boats, often with children and women at a cooking stove, and clothing hung out to dry (Colour Plates 72 and 73), a picturesque equivalent in Chinnery's art to the *banglas* of Bengal, although more varied in the ingenuities of their architecture.

When a western ship arrived in the Macau roads, it would be met by a dozen of this

> ...class of athletic women, who..., standing in the bows of their neat boats, would importuningly beg the privilege of taking [the new arrival] over the shallow waters, and 'only for a dollar' — but during the opium *bobbery* these poor nautilae were forbidden to meet, or to aid foreign devils [i.e. westerners] in any way, and were suffering much from unprofitable idleness'.[33]

The Tanka women were closely supervised by the Chinese authorities, who required them to remain at night on the Praya Pequena, the beach opposite the official 'Hoppo-house'. This regulation was intended to prevent the Tanka boats from carrying prohibited items — a category which included western merchants who might wish to make a clandestine journey to Canton.[34]

Chinnery has been linked romantically with the Tanka women, especially two, known as Alloy and Assor ('The names of the girls are soft and pretty, and are in accordance with their very musical voices. Great numbers begin with an A, so that it would not be at all strange if you were to find Alloy, As-sou, As-say, and A-moy all in the same boat together'[35]). He did indeed portray both Alloy and Assor: the shorthand on a drawing of a Tanka woman reveals that on 18 July 1842 he began the new picture of Alloy',[36] and a portrait of Assor was exhibited at the Royal Academy in 1844. But the notion of a liaison between the elderly Chinnery and the boatwomen is a legend of recent origin.[37] Possibly it gained credence through a contemporary account of a trip in a Tanka boat rowed by two Tanka women:

> They were good-natured, pretty-looking young women, and smiled frequently, exhibiting beautiful teeth. One of them seemed to have taken a good deal of pains in adorning herself, and had arranged some artificial flowers in her hair. As I sat close to her, in trying to make myself understood, I happened to catch hold of her arm. This appeared to give her great uneasiness, as she immediately drew back and turned her eyes, with much anxiety, towards the shore, saying, 'Na! na! Mandarin see; he squeegee [fine] mee!'...Upon my enquiry whether the Mandarins were always so strict, she replied with great expression, 'Na, na! nightee time come, no man see!'[38]

The mystique was heightened by the fact that it was invariably women who rowed the Tanka boats — 'Where the men live, and how, I do not know.'[39]

Chinnery's paintings and drawings of the boatwomen (to use his own word[40]) range from portraits in oils to near-abstract sketches, which are composed of the curves of hull and roof, the angular forms of cloak and hood, and the long straight lines of the oars. Their faces often appear more western than Chinese, and some have been mistaken for Eurasians or Parsees; this is not entirely attributable to the preconceptions of the artist, for it seems that the Tanka women were indeed markedly different from the Cantonese. Their hair was worn long, parted at the front and plaited at the back. Their feet, which are conspicuous in Chinnery's pictures, were left unbound, and their characteristic dress was blue nankeen, either with a hood attached or worn with a red patterned headscarf; in Colour Plate 70 the headscarf has been removed and placed over the rock on which the subject sits. In many instances they are depicted smiling (which is unusual in Chinnery's portraiture, but was by all accounts entirely typical of the Tanka women themselves), sometimes revealing the teeth which so impressed the visitors from the West. Sentimental as they may be, Chinnery's portrayals of the Tanka boatwomen come close to the literary image of them as 'picturesque, white-teethed, laughing-mouthed, bandana-kerchief-headed nymphs'.[41]

Plate 130. *Fishermen on the beach, Macau. Pen and ink, dated January 13th 1843.* Private collection

Plate 131. *The Praya Grande, Macau, with sketches of creels and architectural details. Pencil, pen and ink, inscribed and dated in shorthand 'all these details May 13 [18]40'; also (by the upper figure) 'correct. Proportions right'.* Private collection

## Macau Street Scenes

In the opinion of Gideon Nye, the artist's contemporary and an astute critic of his art, Chinnery's genius did not lie in portraiture, nor did he take much pleasure in that aspect of his work. Rather, 'His greatest delight was his early sketching every morning of scenery, with groups of Chinese and animals in and around Macao...his groups of Chinese in all their various avocations and of animals, are inimitable'.[42] It is impossible to disagree, as one looks through his tireless sketches of Chinese figures drawn from every angle and captured in every gesture, that Chinnery's heart lay here, in what Nye described as 'the poetry of life'. In addition to the barbers who had attracted his attention in Canton, Chinnery's subjects included fishermen and shrimpers (Plates 130 and 131, and Colour Plate 74), vendors of vegetables or sweets, fortune tellers, beggars, money changers, and groups of figures eating and drinking at food stalls (Plates 132 and 133, Colour Plates 75, 76 and 77). Then as now, games of chance and skill were often in evidence: fantan, dice, cards, and shuttlecock played with the feet (Plates Plates 134 and 135).

If there is one figure subject which epitomises Chinnery's art, it is surely the blacksmith at work (Colour Plates 78 and 79). The artist repeatedly studied the action of hammering (with the blacksmith's thumb pressed against the handle of the hammer), the characteristic shapes of anvil and bellows, and above all (in the oils and watercolours) the effects of fire and smoke. Like the barber, the itinerant blacksmith carried a pyramidal chest; on this was placed the wooden bellows, which, as the sketches show, could be either rectangular or cylindrical. Inside this was a close-fitting piston made of iron, which the blacksmith moved back and forth, thereby forcing air through a small opening at the side, which gave on to a charcoal fire raised up on a stand beside the bellows. A supply of charcoal was kept in a basket close by, and often a very large bamboo umbrella provided shelter for the operator and his fire. 'In this manner the Chinese effects with a slight alternate motion of his elbow, what requires

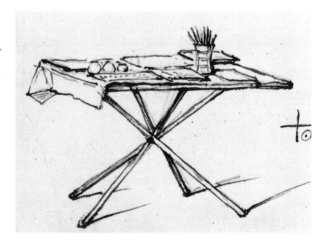

Plate 132. *Fortune teller's table. Pen and ink over pencil.* Mr. and Mrs. P.J. Thompson

Plate 133. Study of a Chinese man seated on a bench. Pen and ink over pencil. Anthony J. Hardy collection

Colour Plate 75. Street traders. Oils. Hongkong and Shanghai Banking Corporation

Colour Plate 76. Street scene, Macau. Oils. Private collection

*Colour Plate 77. Street market outside São Domingos. Oils.* Private collection

*Colour Plate 78. Blacksmiths at work. Oils.* Hongkong and Shanghai Banking Corporation

*Colour Plate 79. Blacksmiths at work. Pen and ink and watercolours.* Mr. and Mrs. R.J.F. Brothers

Plate 134. *A group of Chinese card players. Pen and ink.* Private collection

Plate 135. *A tradesman and customers, with distant shuttlecock players. Pen and ink with sepia wash, dated Feb 14. 1841. Inscribed in shorthand 'DSS' [drawn in simple state] and 'excellent'.* Private collection

Plate 136. *Studies of Chinese men in wet-weather dress. Pencil.* Private collection

Plate 137. *Cattle at a pool. Pen and ink over pencil. Inscribed with artist's shorthand 'Part incorrect part design. Grey part incorrect'. Dated April 7th [18]34.* Private collection

an exertion of almost all the muscles in the body of an European.'[43]

Agricultural workers also appear in Chinnery's sketchbooks, leading or tending cattle, or watering their produce. The wet-weather dress worn by the Chinese in the fields is sometimes illustrated (Plate 136). Thomas and William Daniell described it as 'a cloak and waistcoat, composed of the leaves of the cajam [cajan] tree, which, like the plumage of aquatic birds, have the curious property of repelling water'.[44] The wide-brimmed hats seen in Chinnery's drawing protected the wearer against rain and sun, both of which could be severe. Harriet Low experienced the torrential rains of August, when the streets of Macau reminded her of Venice, and the sedan chairs of gondolas.[45] Two hundred years before, this form of dress had caught the attention of Peter Mundy, perhaps the first Englishman to bring back drawings of China

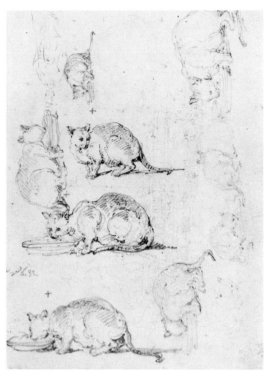

Plate 138. Studies of horses with grooms, and a dog. Inscribed in shorthand 'Mr. Smith's h[orse] correct November 10th 1840'. Private collection

Plate 139. Sheet of ten studies of cats. Pencil, dated March 6 1833. Private collection

Plate 140. Study of a pig. Pen and ink over pencil. Private collection

Plate 141. Study of a pig. Pen and ink over pencil. Mr. and Mrs. P.J. Thompson

and its people; Mundy sketched one of the boatmen wearing 'a coat of leaves...to keepe them from the Raine'.[46]

Cows (Plate 137) were of considerable significance to the expatriates in Macau, many of whom had been brought up on a diet rich in milk and cheese. Cattle were imported to the China coast from Britain and North America; the American firm of Wetmore & Co. had kept 'an old English cow for 7 or 8 years' by May 1844.[47] Chinese cows were smaller than the western imports. Rebecca Kinsman observed that they provided a supply of milk which was rich but short lived, as the Chinese animals were not accustomed to milking. Her friend Mrs. Ritchie bought a Chinese cow for 100 Spanish dollars, but it died a month later.[48] Most of the cows depicted by Chinnery

*Colour Plate 80. Farmers in a land-scape. Oils.* Private collection

*Colour Plate 81. Outside São Lourenço Church, Macau. Oils.* Hongkong and Shanghai Banking Corporation

208

Plate 142. *Sketches of a figure with watering cans. Pen and ink over pencil, dated 7 August and 8 August 1834.* Private collection

were of the Chinese variety, to judge from their size and leanness; often they are accompanied by their calves.

Chinnery also sketched horses and cats (Plates 138 and 139), and the exotic birds in Thomas Beale's aviary.[49] But Chinnery's finest animal creations are undoubtedly the magnificent pigs (Plates 140 and 141) which make an appearance in so many of his Macau scenes. Perhaps he experienced some fellow-feeling for these gross but splendid specimens. Dark-backed and heavy-bellied, with short legs and tail, the Chinese pig was a fleshier creature than its western cousin, and was much sought after in Europe for breeding and eating. 'The Chinese or Black breed will always be valuable', wrote an English agriculturalist at the end of the eighteenth century. 'They fatten amazingly fast, and afford the sweetest bacon; which has gained the preference everywhere amongst the nice-eating people.'[50] Pork was esteemed by western ships' captains, as it took salt better than other meats, and also by the Chinese. Harriet Low observed with regret that for marriage processions in Macau 'poor piggy was murdered, roasted, and lacquered for the occasion, and carried along on cars.'[51]

Chinnery sold a number of his sketchbooks, and lent others out for copying, but their primary function was to serve as raw material for finished watercolours and oil paintings. The shorthand notes beside his sketches often indicate whether he regarded them as suitable

*Plate 143. Outside São Lourenço Church, Macau. Pencil.* Geographical Society of Lisbon

*Colour Plate 82. Macau from
the north-east. Pencil, pen and
ink and watercolours.* Mr.
and Mrs. P.J. Thompson

*Colour Plate 83. Macau from
the north-east. Oils.* Anthony
J. Hardy Collection

for inclusion in a painting. In many cases the studies can be linked to the
subsequent pictures. The sketched figure who carries an ingenious yoke of
two watering cans (Plate 142) reappears in a painted landscape (Colour Plate
80); the group of men drawn in the act of hauling up water by pulley beside
the lower wall of São Lourenço (Plate 143) are depicted in an oil painting of
the same event seen from the other side of the well (Colour Plate 81). In
Colour Plates 82 and 83, a bird's-eye view over the roof-tops of Macau, looking
southwards from the hill above the Franciscan Fort, is represented in three
successive stages and media. In the upper part of Colour Plate 82 is the

pencilled outline of the distant houses; this has been redrawn below, in ink and watercolours; Colour Plate 83 is taken from the same viewpoint, but is painted in oils. In the last version the field of vision has been extended westwards, to include the whole Praya Grande as far as Penha Hill, and an East Indiaman framed in a rock arch on the extreme left. This oil painting and its companion (Colour Plate 84) also illustrate Chinnery's penchant for casting a high proportion of the foreground into heavy shadow, a practice he had advocated in the Treatise (see Appendix i) and continued to adopt in many of his drawings and watercolours (Colour Plate 85). The long, deep shadows are naturally accompanied by an evening sky — or rather, in the Praya Grande views, an early morning sunlight, illuminating the elegant façades along the east-facing beach.

# CHAPTER 14

# *China Traders*

The foreign community on the China coast was an extremely small one. A census taken at Canton in 1836 recorded 307 adult non-Chinese males, including sixty-two Parsees; of all these, twenty-three had a wife or family resident at Macau.[1] Such a small group, even when augmented by the Chinese Hong merchants of Canton, could scarcely be expected to support a professional artist. In fact Chinnery's livelihood depended in no small measure upon the efforts of William Jardine and James Matheson; the founders of a great trading empire, the two men acted as the artist's patrons, agents and financial advisers. It was only after their departure from the China coast that Chinnery, by now in his late sixties, ran into difficulties once again.

## Jardine and Matheson

William Jardine had begun his career as Assistant Surgeon, and later Surgeon, aboard several East Indiamen on the China run. In these positions he was entitled to 'privilege tonnage', that is, goods which he could bring back to Britain as a personal speculation — a much more lucrative business than medicine. In 1817 Jardine left the East India Company and bought a part share in a trading vessel. For the next fifteen years he participated in a succession of trading ventures based in Canton and Bombay. He became a partner in the prominent firm of Magniac & Co., as did a fellow-Scotsman, James Matheson; when the last of the Magniacs withdrew, the firm of Jardine, Matheson & Co. came into being, and began to trade on 1 July 1832. As shipowners, agents, and traders in tea, opium and other goods, they dominated the 'China trade' together with the rival firm of Dent & Co. A period of confusion followed the abolition of the East India Company's monopoly in 1834; but Jardine chartered several of the Company's ships and stengthened his firm's position. In the same year the firm bought its first steamship, a bold (and, as it transpired, premature) experiment. When relations between Britain and China became increasingly strained in the later 1830s, both Matheson and Jardine were in a position to exert a forceful influence on the actions of the British Government and its representatives in China.

William Jardine was ten years younger than Chinnery, and James Matheson was twelve years younger still. From the letters and notes contained in the firm's archive it is clear that the two men acted with consideration and generosity towards the elderly artist. They assisted him in various ways, one being to act as his literary agent. Matheson wrote in 1832 to the London publishers Smith Elder & Co. of Cornhill: 'By the Company's ships sailing in October or November I confidently expect to be able to send you one or two of Mr Chinnery's sketches, that you may perhaps deem worthy of a place in your Annual.'[2] This was perhaps a reference to *Friendship's Offering*, a series of annual volumes containing such literary gems as 'Lines on the Dandelion' and 'An Adventure with an American', with small engravings to match. But despite Matheson's efforts, no illustrations after Chinnery appeared in this insipid publication.

When one of Jardine's captains, George Parkyns, commissioned a painting from Chinnery, Jardine arranged for it to be shipped home on completion and for payment to be made.[3] On another occasion Matheson sent back to England a portrait of his niece Harriet Lyall with her husband Charles and their children, although he found the picture on the whole disappointing; 'Charles' likeness is however good, and as such it will no doubt gratify you all.'[4]

A number of portraits of William Jardine have survived, at least two of them by Chinnery (Colour Plates 86 and 87) and others by his Chinese imitators. It is likely that portraits of the Mathesons are among the numerous portraits by Chinnery whose sitters can no longer be identified with certainty; a pencil study of hands and the arm of a chair carries Chinnery's shorthand 'Mr Matheson (Alexander) at home'.[5] When William Prinsep visited Chinnery's studio on 13 November 1838 he found that 'Jardine was sitting for his portrait',[6] and a fortnight later Chinnery was supplying a sketchbook to James Matheson, addressing him in the most cordial terms:

My dear Mr Matheson,
I need not say that on my coming home yesterday I selected the Volume of my sketches for which you flatter me so highly by wishing to have. How gratified I am to give it to you you may suppose! knowing me as I believe you do — I *hope* you do.

But you know what my Sketch Books are — all full — but many in each Volume, with the embryo of design — many filled in partially — and many in their completed state of pen and sepia. The Vol. in question is one of my best I am happy to say; and there are *many* in fully, excellently, but they must *be all* so filled in before you get it, and altho' I say it that should not, it will be the Sketch Book of a Painter and some 50 years hence may be interesting — here and there I'll leave one in an unfinished state that G.C. may be seen more clearly, when it may come under the eye of a Brother of the Pencil.

Today or tomorrow kindly look in on me — most happy I'll be to see you and will explain myself better — I have written your name in the Volume. Monday I reckon on you and in this case I'll be punctual at $8^1/_2$ — but at all events tomorrow I'll come and see you some time.

Up till half past one at our delightful party! but I was out at 7 and got some good drawings, but business today I fear for! You are quite well I most truly hope.[7]

Despite Chinnery's cheerfulness, however, there were worries about his finances. He had not been forgotten by his creditors in India, who from time to time continued to press for repayment. In April 1829 Jardine opened a

letter addressed to Matheson 'in consequence of
Chinnery's anxiety about it';[8] the letter in question is
lost, but presumably it concerned the artist's debts.
The creditors finally obtained a court order
requiring Chinnery to pay to an appointed trustee
'the moiety of his gross earnings for five years from
11 March 1836'. Five years later the money had not
been paid, and Chinnery stood to lose all that he
had. At this point Matheson (the senior partner,
since Jardine had finally returned to Britain) wrote
to his agent in Calcutta, George James Gordon:

> My dear Gordon,
> I duly received your two kind letters about Mr
> Chinnery's affairs the purport of which is so
> very unexpected & disheartening that I did
> not venture to communicate it to him all at
> once, and not entirely until after he had been
> made aware of all by your note to Mrs Brown
> [Chinnery's daughter]. The object is of such
> vital importance to him that I trust you will

bear with us and give us your assistance in making one more effort for
his deliverance. With this view we now write to Lyall Matheson & Co. re-
establishing the credit on them for sixteen thousand (16,000) Rupees
with a request that they will pay it either to a receiver regularly
appointed who will grant a discharge or to you...[9]

Matheson argued that Chinnery could not have been expected to pay his debt
before the end of the five-year period, since his earnings could not even be
calculated until this period had elapsed. In any case the creditors had failed to
appoint a trustee to receive the money; moreover, many of the creditors had
by now left India and were unrepresented. Matheson referred to a credit of
16,000 Rupees which he had authorised in March 1841 to be made available
to Chinnery's creditors in Calcutta; he now instructed Lyall Matheson in
Calcutta (the Matheson concerned being his nephew Hugh) to renew that
credit 'till cancelled by us'.[10]

So it seems that some at least of Chinnery's debts were paid by Jardine,
Matheson & Co. It is unlikely that Chinnery could ever have repaid to the
firm the large amount demanded, and there is no evidence that he attempted
to do so. He continued to supply pictures to James Matheson, and to be paid
for them. Matheson's personal account books for the years 1840-2 survive, and
they record three payments to Chinnery for unspecified work: $150 on 31
October 1840, $250 on 31 January 1841, and $100 on 31 March 1842. On the
last occasion there were also payments of $18.50 to Chinnery's Chinese
follower and rival, Lamqua, and 'Expences of finding a small Dog $20'; one
can only speculate whether these three items were related — possibly the dog
was to appear in a portrait — or whether the payments reflect the relative
status of the two artists.[11]

*Colour Plate 87. William Jardine, seated. Oils.* Private collection

Several of the sea captains associated with Jardine and Matheson were portrayed by Chinnery. One of these was Captain Henry Gribble, who was temporarily abducted by the Chinese during the opium crisis (see p.249), and later became the first British Consul in Amoy (Xiamen). A second was Captain John Hine, formerly of the East Indiaman *Earl of Balcarres*, who became a close friend of William Jardine's, and organised a public dinner in his honour at the London Tavern in 1840; this portrait was exhibited at the Royal Academy

Plate 144. Portrait of a Parsee merchant and his Chinese secretary. Oils. Hongkong and Shanghai Banking Corporation

in 1831. Four years later Chinnery's portrait of Alexander Grant, another close associate of Jardine's, was also hung at the Academy. Grant commanded the *Hercules,* Jardine's opium receiving ship at Lintin, and continued to act for the firm after retiring to England. When Jardine called on Palmerston, to enlist the Government's support for the China traders, it was Alexander Grant who accompanied him.[12]

Another member of this group was Henry Wright, known as 'Old Wright' to distinguish him from his son. He served as purser of the *Castle Huntly* before joining Jardine in 1826 at Magniac & Co., and subsequently became a partner in Jardine, Matheson from 1835 until 1841. Chinnery's image of Wright (Colour Plate 88) was reproduced in several versions; although Wright is shown seated at his writing desk, his windswept hair and genial expression might seem to suggest that he was more at home on board ship than administering the mercantile empire of Jardine and Matheson.

Chinnery also portrayed the younger Wright (generally known as Harry)[13], and the resourceful Captain Clifton (Colour Plate 89), whose enterprise made a large contribution to the prosperity of Jardine, Matheson in the 1830s. Clifton resigned from the East India Company in 1825 in order to experiment with new ship designs and routes to China. He was not at first successful; his ship *Louisa* was launched in 1828 at the twenty-third attempt, and was wrecked a year later. Undeterred, Clifton built a new ship, the *Red Rover,* basing her lines on those of a celebrated American privateer. With this rapid, purpose-built vessel he proposed to carry the East India Company's opium from India to China three times a year; until then, once a year had been the rule. The Governor-General, Lord William Bentinck, was persuaded to advance the necessary funds. On 11 December 1829 Lady Bentinck christened the *Red Rover* at Howrah, and the first in a long line of 'opium clippers' was launched, with Clifton as Captain and principal owner.[14]

Clifton was succeeded as master of the *Red Rover* by Harry Wright, who captained the ship on a series of voyages selling opium along the Chinese coast; subsequently he retired to become a clergyman in Gloucestershire.

### Sir Jamsetjee Jeejeebhoy

The single largest constituent in the trade of Jardine, Matheson was the business which they conducted with the firm of the eminent Parsee, Sir Jamsetjee Jeejeebhoy; in the 1830s this was worth over £1 million a year. Jamsetjee's first employer had been a Bombay dealer in empty bottles, Framjee Nusserwanjee Bottlewalla. From this modest beginning he had built up a huge trading empire based on cotton and opium. He became a public benefactor on a grand scale. Bombay's first charitable dispensary, its first hospital for the poor, the Mohim Causeway, an art college and many other public institutions were initiated through Jamsetjee's generosity. He became the first Indian to receive a knighthood (in 1842), as well as a baronetcy (in 1857).[15]

In these circumstances, it is not surprising that a number of China coast paintings of Parsees have been assumed to be portraits of Sir Jamsetjee Jeejeebhoy by Chinnery. But Chinnery could not have known the great philanthropist personally. After five return voyages from Bombay to Canton (on one of which his ship was captured by the French, and he lost all his goods), Jamsetjee remained in Bombay from 1807 until his death in 1859. He did not revisit Canton, nor did Chinnery go to Bombay. Jamsetjee was, however, portrayed on at least two occasions by a certain John Smart — not to be confused with the miniature painters, father and son, of the same name; and on the basis of a lithograph of one of these portraits, a version in oils (Colour Plate 90) was produced by Lamqua or another Cantonese artist.[16]

Jamsetjee was by no means the only Parsee merchant involved in the China trade. At Macau the Parsees formed a conspicuous group, and were much admired by the young Rebecca Kinsman: 'Their dress is very strange, but graceful — and they are most of them fine looking, athletic looking men. They are from Bombay, and live here without their families, it being contrary to their religion to bring their wives from their own countries.' As a Quaker Mrs. Kinsman approved of their simple clothing, white in summer, and in winter 'long coats of drab or brown cloth', with no collar, but 'the ugliest imaginable caps upon their heads made of *calico* & glazed highly'.[17] Plate 144, a portrait of an unidentified Parsee with a Chinese servant, was evidently painted by Chinnery on the China coast. The picture seen hanging to the left of the column, in which two Parsees offer alms to an elderly and infirm Chinese man, alludes to the sitter's contribution to some charitable venture, possibly Doctor Colledge's dispensary (see p.221), to which several of the Parsee merchants contributed.

Chinnery must have been well acquainted with many members of the Parsee community. One of them, Hurjeebhoy Rustomjee, was described as an old friend of the artist, and remained with him on the last night of his life.[18] A pencil drawing (Plate 145) of the head of a Parsee — possibly a sketch for Plate 144 — carries the somewhat obscure observation in shorthand 'this is wonderful. More such things could be done'.[19] Nevertheless, a number of the surviving portraits of Parsees involved in the China trade must be attributed, on grounds of style, to Chinese 'export' artists working in Chinnery's manner. Further evidence is to be found in the frame plates on two Chinneryesque portraits of Parsees, members of the Patuck family, which are in the Prince of Wales Museum, Bombay. These are said to have been 'painted from life at Canton China in 1833' and '...in 1835' respectively. Chinnery is not recorded as being in Canton in either of these years, and the portraits are no doubt by Chinese artists.

*Plate 145. Portrait sketch of the head of a Parsee merchant. Pencil, inscribed in shorthand 'Mr H-R-J S-K-J October 12. [18]43. This is wonderful. More such things could be done'. Martyn Gregory Gallery*

*Colour Plate 88. Henry Wright. Oils.* Private collection

*Colour Plate 89. Captain Clifton of the* Red Rover. *Oils.* Private collection

### Families and Amahs

Chinnery's portraits of westerners on the China coast pose further problems of identification. A typical case is the portrait of a seated woman reproduced in Colour Plate 91. In style the painting is close to that of his Calcutta portraits, and the location is established by a painting of the Praya Grande and São Pedro fort on the wall behind. The piano, the slim novel in her hand and the open sewing box represent the limited activities available to expatriate women in Macau.

The sitter has been identified tentatively as Julia Baynes, wife of the leader of a rebel faction within the East India Company at Canton, who in single-minded pursuit of improved trading conditions had forced the moderate William Chicheley Plowden to resign from his position as President of the Select Committee.[20] It was Mrs. Baynes who, in 1830, accompanied her husband to Canton, in defiance of the Chinese regulation which forbade western women to enter the city; after protests from the Cantonese authorities, and counter protests from the Company, she was allowed to remain, but the episode aggravated the tension between the two sides.[21] Shortly after the Baynes returned to Macau they learned that the East India Company in London had dismissed William Baynes from the Committee at Canton. Harriet Low declared that 'Mrs Baynes is a heroine, and bears it all beautifully. She is a charming woman, and a pattern for all wives.'[22]

The identification of the piano-playing sitter as Mrs. Baynes is far from certain, however. Pianos were in short supply in Macau, and it is possible that the sitter is the Mrs. Daniell who (Harriet Low records) had a piano in her house, and lent it to the Lows when they held a party on 11 April 1832. There were two Mrs. Daniells in Macau at this time. One was Jane, wife of James Frederic Nugent Daniell, a senior Company colleague of Baynes. Daniell remained loyal to Plowden when the latter was forced by Baynes to resign, and

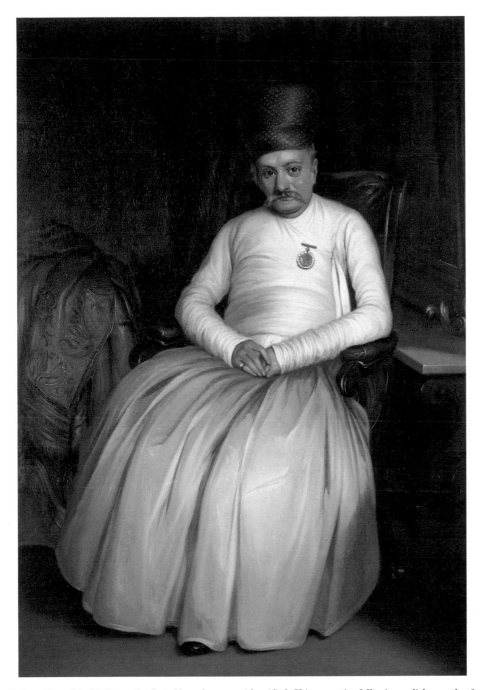

*Colour Plate 90. Sir Jamsetjee Jeejeebhoy, by an unidentified Chinese artist following a lithograph after J. Smart. Oils.* Private collection

when Baynes was finally demoted, Daniell was appointed above him. The other was Harriet, wife of James's younger brother Anthony. Both had children in Macau, and one of these — Harriet May — is portrayed in Colour Plate 92, adorned with a welter of pink ribbons.

Harriet Mary Daniell was one of a small group of children in Macau's British community. According to the register which was kept by the East India Company chaplains in Macau, some forty children were baptised between 1820 and 1833. A few of these were the children of ships' officers who were passing through, but many of the others spent at least their early childhood in Macau. During these years five children were born to Alexander and Maria

Teresa Grant; William and Julia Baynes had two sons and a daughter; a son and two daughters were born to John Francis and Emily Davis, and a son and two daughters again to William and Catherine Chicheley Plowden.[23] Chinnery painted several family groups in Canton, but it is not always clear which portrait represents which family, especially since some of the children whom he portrayed would have been born in the less well documented years after 1833.

The family group in Colour Plate 93 contains many of the elements of the 'piano-player' portrait: symbols of music and literature, a shawl and a vase of flowers, a patterned carpet and a glimpse of landscape. In this instance the location is indicated not by a painting on the wall but in the person of the Chinese amah on the left, who leans outwards to keep an eye on her younger charges. Her angled stance also has the effect of dissociating her from the members of the European family; it is they, with their raised chins and confident expressions, who are presented as the proper subjects of the portrait. The eyes of the three children are directed towards the artist, while the parents look upwards and outwards, as if preoccupied with weightier matters.

This portrait has been given the title of 'Charles Marjoribanks and his family'. Marjoribanks had joined the East India Company's establishment at Canton in 1813, and in the autumn of 1830 he found himself President of the Select Committee following the deposition of William Baynes. It can be confirmed that his wife was with him, for Harriet Low records a walk taken with 'Mrs and Mr Majoribanks' [sic], after watching the gentlemen all playing at Cricket...a famous English game'.[24] On 17 January 1832 Marjoribanks was invalided home on the *York*, after a farewell dinner which Chinnery attended. Moreover, it is clear that he took with him a picture of Chinnery, for his shorthand inscription on a drawing of the Factories at Canton (dated December 26th 1832) reads 'Mr Marjoribanks' picture taken home on the York January 1832'.[25] But I can find no evidence that Mr. and Mrs. Marjoribanks had children with them in Macau.

This formal portrait may be compared with the more freely-handled composition, perhaps a trial project, shown in Colour Plate 94. In the absence of the children's mother, the Chinese amah appears at the centre of the picture, with her right hand resting on the shoulder of the elder of the girls — although once again the amah is distinguished from the western figures by her angled head and custodial gaze. Quite apart from the sketchier technique employed here, the atmosphere is more homely and relaxed; a potted plant replaces the classical urn, and instead of the allusions to music and literature, a lop-eared terrier emerges from the shadows beneath the settee. Only the small boy in his tartan outfit seems a little isolated. Since the China trade was dominated by Scotsmen, the boy's kilt is of limited help in identifying the sitters, but it is worth noting a remark of Rebecca Kinsman's on 17 March 1846: 'Mrs MacQueen called. She brought her little boy David with her — a remarkably fine boy of 8 years old — dressed in Highland costume — kilt & tartan.'[26]

The amah or ayah played an important role in expatriate family life. (Although 'amah' referred, strictly speaking, to a wet nurse, the two Portuguese terms were used interchangeably, by foreigners in India and on the China coast, to mean a female servant responsible for her employer's children.) Rebecca Kinsman thought highly of her Chinese amah: 'She seems exceedingly fond of the baby, and these Chinese nurses are remarkable for their patience and kindness to children.' Sometimes Macanese amahs would be employed in addition, but their role would be purely supervisory, on the grounds that 'both from temperament & habit they are too lazy to work themselves'.[27]

## Dr. Colledge's Hospital

In the mind of Harriet Low, and of many others also, one individual stood out from amongst the westerners on the China coast. 'On Wednesday our good friend Dr. Colledge called', she wrote a fortnight after their first meeting. 'He is the best man I have seen yet. Everybody loves him and speaks well of him.' She added, disingenuously, 'It is a shame that he is a bachelor.'[28] Three years later, on 6 January 1833, her admiration was undiminished. 'He is continually going about doing good; he makes every one love him, he is so universally kind and obliging, and exerts himself to make all happy who come in his way. We call him "the sunbeam", for everything smiles when he approaches...'[29] By 1 February her ardour had cooled somewhat: 'He is thoroughly English [not a compliment], somewhat aristocratic, and fond of old customs...We talked a little about Unitarianism. He is prejudiced like all the others...'[30] Perhaps she was by now aware of the understanding between Colledge and her friend Caroline Shillaber, the only other unmarried western woman in the community. Five days later she had to record in her journal that Dr. Colledge and Caroline Shillaber were engaged to be married. The wedding took place within six weeks. Chinnery was commissioned to paint the bride's portrait, and it was diplomatically arranged that he should also paint the portrait of Harriet.[31] According to family tradition, Colour Plate 95 represents the Colledges in the early years of their marriage.

Thomas Colledge had been educated at Rugby, and studied at the United Hospitals in London under the eminent surgeon Sir Astley Cooper. In 1826, after six years as a shipboard surgeon for the East India Company, he became surgeon to the Factory at Canton, following the death through ill health of his predecessor. In 1827 he rented two small houses in Macau and set up a dispensary, which was open to all, but catered particularly for the victims of eye disease — a common complaint in China. In the six years of the clinic's existence Colledge treated some 4,000 Chinese sufferers. Sir Anders Ljungstedt, who wrote an account of the venture, regarded it as an important step in overcoming Chinese prejudice against westerners; he implied that money was better spent on such an enterprise than on religious missionary work.[32] This view was evidently shared by many of the leading residents on the China coast, for the list of subscribers includes Howqua (who contributed $500 a year), Mowqua, three other 'Hong merchants', several of the Parsee traders, Jardine, Matheson, Forbes, the Dents, and (collectively) the East India Company.[33]

According to Ljungstedt, Chinnery's portrait of Dr. Colledge with his patients (Colour Plate 96) was painted at the artist's own request. The subject was to be 'an act of his practical humanity...which would at once combine portrait with history'.[34] Chinnery probably intended this painting as his contribution to the venture (his name does not appear in the list of

*Colour Plate 91. A woman seated at a piano, said to be Mrs. Baynes. Oils.* Hongkong and Shanghai Banking Corporation

subscribers), and perhaps even as a means of raising funds when the picture was exhibited and engraved in England. He was at work on the painting by 30 March 1833, as a dated drawing attests.[35] On the following day Harriet went with Caroline and some others to Chinnery's studio, to inspect the picture. She made a careful scrutiny:

> It is a most interesting thing, a group of five figures, — but first for the likeness, which, I am sorry to say, is not so striking as in many of Chinnery's pictures, the face is in profile, which is, perhaps, the reason. The figure, a full length, is perfect. One hand is resting on the forehead of a China-woman whom he has restored to sight from total blindness. He has lifted her spectacles and is turning to Afun, his Chinese servant, and telling him to explain to the woman how she is to proceed in future. Afun's likeness is excellent. The son of the woman is on his knees before Colledge, presenting a chop (or letter of thanks, always

*Colour Plate 92. Harriet Mary Daniell (later Mrs. Masterman Williams). Oils.* Private collection

written on red paper) for his kindness. The fifth figure is a poor old man sitting on the floor in a corner, with his eyes bandaged, waiting for attention. It is a most interesting and touching picture. I hope to have the pleasure of bringing an engraving of it home with me.'[36]

A similar account is given by Ljungstedt, who adds that the painting within the painting, seen dimly on the right, shows Colledge's Ophthalmic Hospital.[37] The figure seen beneath the painting on the wall is Afun, Colledge's Chinese assistant and translator, with whom Harriet Low was acquainted. She asked Chinnery whether Afun had been able to keep still while sitting to the artist. '"Ma'am", he said, "the Rock of Gibraltar is calves'-foot jelly to him."'[38] When Harriet was in London the following summer, she was able to see the picture again (together with the portrait of Caroline) in the studio of William Daniell, who executed the mezzotint engraving. The Lows had with them Ayok, son of Afun, who 'burst into quite an hysterical laugh when he saw his father's face in Mr Colledge's picture'.[39] The two paintings had arrived too late to be included in the Royal Academy exhibition of that year, but were shown in 1835.

Comparing the portrait of Colledge at his dispensary with that of Morrison translating the Bible (Plate 150), it is difficult to resist Ljungstedt's view that the former enterprise was the more worthwhile. But western medicine did not always prove capable of curing Chinese maladies. Leeches were a recurring item of expenditure at the dispensary, and the supply was unreliable; one of Colledge's successors, Dr. Thomas Boswall Watson, reported that the cost of leeches had risen from $1 per thousand to $1 per hundred, and some were 'fastening with difficulty'.[40] Nor could Colledge cope with major surgery. When in 1830 a Chinese patient, Hoo Loo, came to him with a huge scrotal tumour, Colledge arranged for him to travel to England. An operation was performed at Guy's Hospital, attended by the leading physicians and surgeons of the time. But despite Hoo Loo's heroic endurance, he died on the operating table.[41]

In 1832 Colledge's fellow surgeon retired, and he had to close the infirmary. Before leaving the China coast, however, he acquired and fitted out a new, brick-built hospital building,[42] which was sketched by Chinnery (Plate 146);

*Colour Plate 93. Family group (perhaps the Marjoribanks family). Oils.* Hongkong and Shanghai Banking Corporation

this was opened in July 1838, under the auspices of the recently-founded Medical Missionary Society. The society's first chairman and principal sponsor was William Jardine, who sometimes assisted in his capacity as a former surgeon. The hospital's director, and in effect Colledge's successor in Canton and Macau, was the American medical missionary Peter Parker. A further link between Chinnery and the western medical venture at Macau and Canton is discussed on p.266.

*Plate 147. Sir Anders Ljungstedt. Oils.* Peabody Museum of Salem, Massachusetts

Sir Anders (Andrew) Ljungstedt, chronicler and sponsor of Colledge's ophthalmic hospital, was portrayed twice by Chinnery.[43] Ljungstedt came out to China on behalf of the Swedish East India Company, and when it ceased to trade, he remained in Macau as Swedish Consul. He made the first systematic (albeit anti-Portuguese) study of the history of Macau, based on early Portuguese documents, which was published in Macau in 1834; an enlarged edition was produced in Boston in 1836, but in the previous November he had died, at the age of seventy-six, and was buried in Macau's Protestant cemetery. Chinnery's portrait (Plate 147) depicts Ljungstedt towards the end of his long life, a dignified figure wearing the green ribbon of the Royal Order of Vasa.

## Tea Tasters

While Colledge was sending back anatomical specimens to London — a female Chinese foot aroused particular interest at Guy's in 1829[44] — John Reeves was providing a similar service in the field of natural history. An exact contemporary of Chinnery's, Reeves came out from England in 1812 at the age of thirty-eight. This was a relatively advanced age at which to begin a career on the China coast, but Reeves had recently been widowed, and in addition his expertise as a tea broker commanded a respectable salary from the East India Company; by 1829 his salary as Inspector of Teas was £2,000 a year, as much as the earnings of Dr. Colledge and the Rev. Robert Morrison combined.[45] Harriet Low regarded him as 'a very superior young man.'[46] The task of assessing the quality of the teas to be exported required a fine discrimination and a strong stomach. 'I have been tasting and comparing until I was almost sick', complained a fellow tea taster in 1848.[47]

Chinnery's portrait of Reeves (Plate 148) must have been painted during the latter's last tour of duty in China, which occupied the years 1826 to 1831. When he finally returned home in 1831 he brought with him numerous specimens of the diverse species of fish which had been collected for him in the region of Macau and Canton; some of the specimens were dried and mounted, while others were preserved in alcohol. By other ships he had sent back seeds and samples of Chinese plants and flowers — azaleas, camellias, chrysanthemums, peonies, roses. Most remarkable of all were the thousands of meticulous watercolours which Reeves commissioned from Chinese artists in Canton and Macau. These represented species of plants, and of insects, fish and birds, and (in smaller quantities) mammals, reptiles, crustaceans and molluscs. Many of these pictures are now held in the Natural History Museum, the Lindley Library and the Zoological Society of London. Most of the species are identified by Chinese ideograms, which were translated by

J.R.Morrison.[48]

Back in England, John Reeves kept in contact with the China coast through his son, John Russell Reeves, who followed his father as a tea inspector at Canton in 1827. In 1829 he became Secretary of the newly-formed museum of art and natural history, which was grandly entitled 'The British Museum in Canton'.[49] But the younger Reeves was not immune to the attractions of commerce. He soon joined Dent as a partner, having incurred official disapproval by openly engaging in private business while in the Company's employ.[50]

## North American Traders

Well before Chinnery arrived in China, a group of merchants from the north-eastern seaboard

*Plate 148. John Reeves. Oils.* Fitzwilliam Museum, Cambridge

of the United States had become a powerful element in the China trade. One of the artist's first patrons at Canton was the Philadelphian merchant Benjamin Chew Wilcocks, a man of Chinnery's own age and temper. Wilcocks had been a pioneer in the importation of Turkish opium into China, and it appears that he was also the first American merchant to trade in opium from India; in the early 1820s he was dealing on a large scale with the Parsee opium shippers in Bombay. On the China coast his opium shipments were facilitated by his status as American Consul, a post which he held from 1813 to 1822.[51]

Wilcocks retired to America in 1827, having commissioned a portrait of his Chinese associate and benefactor Howqua,[52] and also a portrait of himself (Colour Plate 97). The two portraits are of the same size, but the American merchant is seen standing — he was a man of commanding height, nicknamed 'the High Devil' by the Chinese.[53] Chinnery arrived in Canton two years before Wilcocks's departure. According to Hunter, 'Mr. B.C.Wilcox [*sic*], of Philadelphia, then an old resident, and like Chinnery always wearing the high white cravat and corresponding coat collar then so much in vogue, took to him immensely, and they became the best of friends.'[54] The portrait exhibits the high white cravat (as indeed does Chinnery's self-portrait, Colour Plate 102), and it also displays the artist's penchant for vermilion, which is introduced not only in the face, but in the coat lining, the watch string, and the ribbon which binds the scroll of papers on the desk. The painting is signed and dated, an unusual feature in Chinnery's oils and in his later work in general. The date '1828' indicates that the portrait was not finished until after Wilcocks's departure, and was sent on to America after him.

Wilcocks was one of several prosperous Philadelphia traders of Quaker stock who operated on the China coast. Unlike him, most of them made a point of abstaining from the opium trade. A leader among them was Nathan Dunn, whose widowed mother was a well-known Quaker minister in Philadelphia.

*Colour Plate 94. Family group. Oil sketch.* Hongkong and Shanghai Banking Corporation

The solid figure of Nathan Dunn was portrayed by Chinnery (Plate 149) in Macau, where Harriet Low observed the portrait in Chinnery's studio, and pronounced it 'a most perfect likeness'. Dunn was no ascetic, however; 'He is very fond of good living, and will have everything of the nicest kind', she commented as Dunn left China in January 1831, after twelve and a half years on the China coast.[55] He took back with him a large collection of Chinese artefacts, which he had gathered in Canton with the aid of his Chinese

*Plate 149. Nathan Dunn of Philadelphia. Oils.* Philadelphia Museum of Art (given by Mrs. Joseph H. Gaskill)

*Colour Plate 95. Dr. and Mrs. Colledge. Oils.* Hongkong and Shanghai Banking Corporation

colleagues. In December 1838 he opened his 'Chinese Museum' to the public, in the newly-built Philadelphia Museum.

The Chinese Museum was enormously successful. In the catalogue, which sold 50,000 copies within two years, Dunn expressed forcefully his views on opium: it was a poison, and to trade in it was both immoral and contrary to Chinese law; he wished the Chinese Government well in their efforts to suppress the traffic.[56] The museum included life-sized figures of Chinese men and women engaged in their various occupations, with appropriate costumes and furnishings. By all accounts it was a most impressive display. James Silk Buckingham, who had been Chinnery's friend in Calcutta, urged Dunn to exhibit his Chinese collection in England, and in 1842 it was placed on display in London, in a pagoda-style building erected at Hyde Park Corner. Again the exhibition was well attended, but if Dunn had hoped that it might influence public opinion and thus divert the British Government from its aggressive policy towards China, he was disappointed. The Chinese collection toured the English provinces, returned to New York, and was finally sold, in depleted form, at Christie's in London in December 1851.

Boston merchants were also strongly represented on the China coast. The Sturgis, Perkins and Forbes families were at the centre of a group of families based in eastern Massachusetts, who were linked by partnership and marriage, and whose financial operations were known as 'the Boston concern'. These families formed a succession of different companies and combinations in order to remain the controlling element in the American China trade. They had close links with Baring Brothers in London; at Canton they worked with Jardine and Matheson until 1834, and they had an indispensable ally in the Chinese merchant Howqua. Opium, imported largely from Turkey, formed a significant part of their business, although they dealt on a smaller scale than the British, whose opium was brought from India. But in the 1820s the American traders, led by the firm of Perkins & Co., expanded their opium trade rapidly, more rapidly indeed than the British, who responded by extending their cultivation of the poppy in Bengal.[57]

James Perkins Sturgis spent over forty years on the China coast, leaving the year before Chinnery's death; he supervised the opium receiving ship at the island of Lintin until the arrival of Robert Bennet Forbes in 1830. Sturgis then retired from the trade. In addition to his town house in Macau he occupied a bungalow on Penha Hill, at or near the point from which Chinnery's view across the rooftops (Colour Plate 84) was taken. Two portraits in oils of Sturgis were included in the Chinnery exhibition at the Peabody Museum, Salem, in 1967.[58] Two of his nephews formed the firm of Russell Sturgis in 1834, and merged with Russell & Co. in 1840; when a group of American visitors called at Chinnery's studio in 1839, they were pleased to see 'a truly excellent likeness of Mr Russel [*sic*] Sturgis' (as well as 'an equally correct one of the artist himself'[59] ).

**Missionaries**

Of Chinnery's contemporaries on the China coast, the most celebrated — among the British public, if not among the merchant community itself — was Robert Morrison, the first Protestant missionary to China. In physique Morrison was similar to Chinnery, but in temperament he was at an opposite extreme, a dedicated man who 'had no sprightliness or pleasantry, no versatility or wide acquaintance with letters, and was respected rather than loved by those who cared little for the things nearest his heart'.[60] Morrison devoted himself to the impossible project of converting the Chinese to Protestant Christianity. The Roman Catholic missionaries who had preceded him in China had faced daunting obstacles, but for Morrison the task was made even more desperate by the hostility of the (Catholic) Portuguese establishment in Macau, and the indifference — at best — of the East India Company. When Morrison had applied in London for a passage to China, the Company had rejected him, and he had to make his way via New York, in an American ship.

When Chinnery arrived in Macau, Morrison was temporarily back in Britain, having already put in a stint of seventeeen years on the China coast. Although he had made few conversions, Morrison had done a great deal to make his religion available to Chinese readers, establishing the Anglo-Chinese College at Malacca in 1818, producing his *magmum opus,* the *Dictionary of the Chinese Language* (1815-23), and completing, with William Milne, the first Chinese translation of the Bible, whose twenty-one volumes were published in Malacca in 1823. In London he was welcomed by large congregations, and the King gave the missionary his personal encouragement. Then in September 1826 he returned to his exertions in Macau, where the people were 'all deceived', he believed, 'and sunk in stupidity, respecting vain idols'.[61] In Macau he found that the political situation was deteriorating, and white ants had eaten their way through his library.

Morrison's great asset, so far as the East India Company was concerned, was his mastery of the Chinese language. He accepted a salary from the Company as its Translator and Interpreter, which helped to support his wife and children, although he was uneasy about his increasing involvement in Company affairs. He was asked to lend his expertise to the *Canton Register*, the first English-language newspaper in China, which made its appearance in 1827, printed on a hand-press lent by Alexander Matheson; again Morrison agreed, while privately disapproving of the *Register's* unashamed advertising of the current opium prices.[62]

Morrison lived in close proximity to Chinnery (see pp.193-4), but he seldom left his quarters, and would not have been a natural associate of the artist's. Describing himself as an 'anti earth-treasure hoarder',[63] the missionary perhaps experienced some fellow feeling for the artist, who was chronically lacking in 'earth-treasure'. In any case, Morrison was much gratified by Chinnery's portrait of him (Plate 150), and by the British Factory's response to it:

> Mr. Chinnery, the artist here, has painted a portrait of me, and of two Chinese assistants, forming a group, with reference to my Dictionary, translation of the Scriptures, Prayer-book, and the College. [The charter of the Anglo-Chinese College can be seen in Morrison's hands.] It has been much admired; and the gentlemen of the Factory have sent it home to be engraved at their expense, as a token of regard and esteem for an old friend.[64]

Morrison expressed his gratitude to Chinnery in another letter, sent to John Jackson, Secretary of the British Factory, who was then in Canton:

> As Mr. Chinnery has taken the utmost pains with the picture, and produced a painting which is, I believe, gratifying, as a work of art, to all who have seen it; instead of accepting more than a few copies of the engraving, I would resign those you suggested appropriating to me, to Mr. Chinnery's disposal.[65]

Robert Morrison's second wife, Eliza Armstrong, had been married to the missionary during his interval in England. Eliza came out to live with him in Macau, where she bore him several more children, and having outlived him returned home to edit his letters for publication. Chinnery's small three-quarter-length portrait of her (Colour Plate 98) presents a lively individual who displays a more lavish array of bonnet ribbon than one might expect in a missionary's wife. She wears a blue dress in the wide-sleeved fashion which had amazed Harriet Low when she first encountered it in August 1830 (see p.98 and Colour Plate 69). Chinnery's characteristic vermilion shadowing is

*Colour Plate 96. Dr. Colledge in his surgery. Oils.* Private collection, on loan to the Peabody Museum of Salem, Massachusetts

applied firmly beneath the nose, and also along the line of the hand. The portrait must have been painted before December 1833, when, in poor health, she sailed for England with six of her children and stepchildren.

Her husband, whose death occurred eight months after his wife's departure, is portrayed by contrast (and perhaps appropriately) in black and white (Colour Plate 99), with a minimum of flamboyance in the face. In painting Morrison's collar, and many of the collars displayed in Chinnery's portraits of western men from his Madras years onwards, the artist has followed his own advice to Mrs. Browne: 'Do not lay down the Collar of the Shirt but stick it up as upright as it can almost — it will give an amazing Smartness...'[66]

Morrison's last years were unhappy ones. In 1833 he was instructed by the Company, under pressure from the Portuguese, to issue no further publications from his house in Macau. In the following year the 9th Baron Napier arrived, sent out from England by Palmerston to impose a new trading

*Plate 151. Robert Morrison's grave in the Protestant cemetery, Macau. Pen and ink and watercolours, inscribed in shorthand 'April 23 1838. To remember the light...'* Private collection

*Colour Plate 97. Benjamin Chew Wilcocks. Oils, signed and dated 1828.* Hongkong and Shanghai Banking Corporation

regime upon the Chinese; for this ill-considered enterprise Morrison was appointed Interpreter, with the promise of £1,300 a year and 'a vice-consul's coat, with king's buttons'.[67] His health was already poor, but it deteriorated under the strains of his new task, and a fortnight after receiving his commission he was dead.

Robert Morrison was buried beside his first wife and an infant son in Macau's Protestant cemetery, which he had been instrumental in establishing. Chinnery sketched his tomb (Plate 151).[68] The artist was himself to be buried in the same graveyard, but his body was laid — fittingly or not — at the opposite end of the cemetery to the Morrisons.

Lord Napier himself died two months later. After an ineffectual show of force in the Canton River, he was obliged to withdraw to Macau, suffering from a fever from which he never recovered. His abortive policy is remembered as 'the Napier fizzle'. It is unlikely that Napier, in his brief visit to Macau, had the leisure or the inclination to sit for his portrait, but it seems

that he did commission a painting which is unique in Chinnery's *oeuvre*. It is a view of Napier's Scottish home, Thirlestane House near Selkirk in the Ettrick valley, which had been built in 1820 for Napier's father (Plate 152). Chinnery never visited Scotland, and he must have used a print or drawing supplied by Napier or by his wife and daughters who accompanied him to China.

In the light of Lord Napier's miserable end, the painting carries a special poignancy, with its contemplative figure wearing a plaid and tam-o'-shanter,

who seems to reflect Napier's nostalgia for his Scottish homeland. (Chinnery's drawing of the figure survives (Plate 153); it was presumably added by Chinnery to the original composition.) After Waterloo, Lord Napier had interrupted his naval career to marry and settle in Scotland, where he wrote a treatise on sheep farming, and is credited with introducing the white-faced Cheviot sheep into the Ettrick district. He would perhaps have preferred sheep to cattle in Chinnery's composition, but sheep were not to be found within the artist's tropical repertoire.

Robert Morrison's eldest son, John Robert, was born in Macau (to the missionary's first wife) in 1814, and educated in England. Returning to the China coast, he divided his time between missionary activity and interpreting for the business community in its less spiritual activities. Before his father's death he had been appointed 'Chinese Translator in the pay of the British free merchants in China'. A more popular character than his father, he adopted an increasingly secular role, as is reflected in Chinnery's portrait of him (Plate 154) with an unidentified figure — conceivably one of the

234

Chinese converts, who, as a contemporary observed, dressed 'a l'Européenne'.[69]. Whereas his father had been portrayed by Chinnery in clerical robes, with a globe to signify his missionary calling, the portrait of John Robert Morrison makes no allusion to religion. The weighty volume on the left of the portrait is Morrison's Chinese dictionary, his father's great achievement; John Robert's principal publication was the *Chinese Commercial Guide* of 1833. He lent his linguistic skills to the British Government's representatives in China, and during the hostilities of 1839-42 was attached to the British forces; the Chinese placed a price of $50,000 on his head. In 1841 he was given a major role in the initial Government of Hong Kong, but two years later he succumbed to malarial fever, while still in his twenties.[70]

Another case of divided loyalties is that of the Prussian missionary Charles Gutzlaff, a former protégé of Robert Morrison's, who arrived in Macau on a coastal junk in 1831. He was an extraordinarily gifted linguist; since leaving his native Pomerania he had learned Malay, Turkish and Arabic, and in China he soon mastered Mandarin, Cantonese and Fukienese. His entertaining and persuasive personality kindled a flicker of enthusiasm even in the down-to-earth Harriet Low.[71] In order to bring the Gospel to the Chinese masses, Gutzlaff agreed to act as interpreter in the coastal operations of Jardine's opium vessels — the *Sylph*, the *Colonel Young* and the *Red Rover*, all of them well-armed clippers. (He was also in need of income, since the Netherlands Missionary Society, which had financed his journey to Thailand, would not sponsor him in China.) As Robert Morrison had briefly done, Gutzlaff adopted Chinese dress during his travels, and he had the added advantage of

*Colour Plate 98. Eliza Morrison (née Armstrong). Oils.* Private collection

*Plate 155. 'Portrait of the Reverend Charles Gutzlaff, the Chinese Missionary, in the dress of a Fokien sailor...' Lithograph by R.J. Lane after Chinnery*

possessing 'a somewhat similar cast of features to the Chinese', or so a fellow-missionary claimed.[72]

Gutzlaff was aware that his policy would arouse criticism. He undertook his journey on the *Sylph* only 'after much consultation with others, and a conflict in my own mind'. He denounced opium as a horrible vice which led to derangement and a premature grave; on the other hand, he took the view that the opening up of China to western trade would be a valuable step in preparing the Chinese for Christianity.[73] So Gutzlaff travelled along the China coast as an undercover agent for both Jardine and Jesus.

In the Opium War he too interpreted for the British, and in 1843 he succeeded John Robert Morrison as Secretary of Trade at Hong Kong. As a civil magistrate in Ningbo and Zhenjiang he dispensed summary justice, raised a native police force, and organised a network of informers. As a missionary he remained an energetic preacher and distributor of tracts, but received little support from the missions in Europe, who distrusted his unorthodox methods. He died in Hong Kong in 1851, less than a year before Chinnery.

Portraits of missionaries are often elaborately staged affairs, intended for engraving, and calculated to inspire toilers in remote mission houses to greater efforts. Such a

*Colour Plate 99. Robert Morrison. Oils.* Private collection

picture is Chinnery's depiction of Robert Morrison and his assistants (who are evidently converts) (Plate 150), and it is not surprising to find that, in addition to the engraving, a number of copies were made in oils.[74] But Chinnery's portrait of Gutzlaff is in a different category. The oil painting was sent to London and exhibited at the Royal Academy in 1835, with the title 'Portrait of the Reverend Charles Gutzlaff, the Chinese Missionary, in the dress of a Fokien sailor, under which disguise he visited many parts of the Chinese Empire in 1831'.[75] This painting cannot be traced, but it was clearly the source of the lithograph of the same title (Plate 155), which was printed in London after an original 'painted by G. Chinnery at Canton'.

Moreover, a related drawing[76] carries the following inscription in shorthand: 'Mr. Gutzlaff in the dress of a Fukienese sailor. For Mr. Lindsay. September 27th 32. Fix.' Hugh Hamilton Lindsay, on whose opium clipper Gutzlaff sailed in 1832, may well have commissioned the portrait in oils. This is surely the definitive image of Gutzlaff, the entrepreneurial evangelist striking a Byronic attitude against a Chinese backdrop. His fluency in the dialects of Chinese is emphasised by his disguise, although one fears that his identity as a westerner would have been revealed at once by his luxuriant moustache.

*Plate 156. Self-portrait, c.1810. Oils.* Royal Academy of Arts

# CHAPTER 15

## *Images of the Artist*

In 1839 a group of American visitors called on Chinnery in Macau, and saw a painting of the artist himself.[1] Other visitors at other times probably also stood a good chance of finding a more or less recent self-portrait in his studio. The number of Chinnery's surviving self-portraits testifies to his vanity, and also suggests that they were marketable. The unmistakable visage of George Chinnery functioned, as did those of Howqua and the tanka boatwomen, as an icon of the China trade, a representative image fit to be commemorated in portable portraits and taken home by traders returning to the West.

The image which they took home with them was not simply the work of a skilful artist, but the portrait of a legendary personality, a great raconteur, and a survivor from a bygone age. His obituary in the *China Mail* claimed that he had 'held a distinguished place among the notables of the East, not less on account of his great conversational powers than of his accomplishments as an artist',[2] and many tributes were paid to his wit and repartee. Inevitably, reports of specific Chinnery anecdotes or *bon mots* do little justice to the original delivery, which by all accounts was achieved with skilful timing and dramatic emphasis, exploiting his 'deep-set eyes with heavy brows, beaming with expression and good-nature'.[3] The butt of Chinnery's stories — several of which were relayed by the American merchant William Hunter, who spent over twenty years on the China coast with the artist — was often himself, or else the absent Marianne Chinnery; also pilloried were the obsequious young officers of the East India Company, who suffered from 'curvature of the spine' to such a severe degree that it was sometimes 'a matter of doubt if the new-comer would ever again be able to resume the upright position'.[4]

Chinnery's terror of his wife has become an essential element in the Chinnery legend, and indeed it seems to have been a favourite subject of his conversation. According to Hunter, the prospect of Marianne joining her husband in Macau prompted the artist to move to Canton, where western women were not allowed.

> 'Now,' I heard him say, 'I am all right; what kind of providence is this Chinese Government, that it forbids the softer sex from coming and bothering us here. What an admirable arrangement, is it not?' he asked. 'Yes, Mr Chinnery,' I replied, 'it is indeed;' he rolled up his eyes and exclaimed 'Laus Deo'.[5]

There are many other such references — to his wife's purported ugliness, or to the trunk which he kept packed in readiness to flee if she should attempt a surprise visit. On one occasion she was on the point of sailing from India to Macau, we are told, but at the last moment the cabin which had been allotted

*Plate 157. Self-portrait with hookah. Pencil.* Mr. and Mrs. R.J.F. Brothers

to her was taken by a certain 'Blow-hard Brown'; on reaching Macau, Brown began to apologise to Chinnery for depriving his wife of the passage, when Chinnery interrupted him with a warm handshake and an invitation to breakfast: 'Chin-chin and good luck to you. May your shadow never grow less and your Patna [opium] yield you 1,000 per cent.'[6]

None of this can be taken very seriously. Marianne and her husband had lived apart in India, and there would have been little reason for her to leave the security of the large Anglo-Indian community in Calcutta, where she received annual payments from Chinnery.[7] The long-running saga of Chinnery's wife was largely a dramatisation on the part of the artist; his stories about his marriage were (in Hunter's words) 'as rich as a play', forming a standing joke which Chinnery would present, with small variations, for the amusement of his visitors. It became customary for them to enquire after Mrs. Chinnery, in order to elicit some outburst of theatrical misogyny. In this spirit Mrs. Davis, the wife of the Chief Superintendent of Trade, prompted Chinnery:

> 'Really,' said Mrs Davis, 'you say Mrs Chinnery is such a fright. It is not very gallant, at least. Now tell us, is there the least bit of exaggeration in what you say of her appearance? Be candid.' Dropping his knife and fork and looking steadfastly at her, he replied, 'Mrs Davis, Mrs Chinnery's appearance cannot be exaggerated. She was an ugly woman thirty years ago; what in the name of the Graces must she be now?'[8]

This theme of his wife's supposed unattractiveness is bound up with his own consciousness of himself as an unusually ugly person. A pencil sketch of a young man is inscribed in shorthand '50 years ago when I looked something like a gentleman',[9] and his self-portraits in general show little sign of self-flattery; on the contrary, he flaunted his heavy jowl and pouting lips both in his life and in his art. Harriet Low, who described him at the age of fifty-nine as 'fascinatingly ugly', also referred to 'a habit he has of distorting his features in a most un-Christian manner'.[10] A few years later he was described in slightly milder terms as 'a portly figure, set out in a rather French air, with a long, blue, thin frock on. He wore a mouth of goodly size, and eyes smilingly smothered in ruddy flesh, and pleasant humour...'[11] He was sometimes compared with the American William Wood, who worked with William Hunter in the firm of Russell & Co. Wood was the first editor of the *Canton Register*, an able draughtsman, and — until her uncle intervened — the fiancé of Harriet Low. He was severely pock-marked, however, and as a result Chinnery and Wood enjoyed a mock rivalry for the title of Macau's ugliest man.[12]

It is possible that Chinnery, who 'used to say that he followed Sir Joshua Reynolds in portraiture',[13] was also aware that his great mentor had been a man of unpolished appearance, who was regarded in his lifetime as florid and somewhat coarse in his facial features.[14] Several of Chinnery's self-portraits call to mind Reynolds's portrait (now in the Royal Collection) of himself late in life, with heavy nose and cheeks, and wearing the spectacles which had

*Colour Plate 100. Self-portrait. Oils.* Private collection

*Colour Plate 101. Self-portrait. Oils.* Hongkong and Shanghai Banking Corporation

become necessary to him in old age. Chinnery's eyesight began to fail at an earlier stage in his career, and all his self-portraits (apart from slight pencil sketches) include spectacles, attached a couple of inches above the ears.

One of Chinnery's first exhibits at the Royal Academy was a self-portrait, displayed in 1793, but this can no longer be traced. Perhaps the earliest of his self-portraits to survive is a small oval (Plate 156) which is now in the Academy's permanent collection;[15] to judge from the comparatively youthful appearance of the face, it was painted during Chinnery's early years in Bengal. Unlike the later self-portraits, it presents the subject almost full face, and deeply shadowed above the eyes, with a purple tint below them. Colour Plate 100, in which the rounded features of the sitter are set against an apparently unfinished background, can also be dated to his Calcutta years. So may a head-and-shoulders pencil study in which the mouthpiece of a hookah is inserted above a protruding lower lip (Plate 157);[16] it seems that when Chinnery moved to China he abandoned the hookah, although he continued the disagreeable habits of 'taking snuff, smoking, and snorting', as Harriet Low noted with disapproval. A pencil drawing of himself at the easel, in the collection of the British Museum, is dated 23 July 1824, a year before his departure from India.[17]

Shortly after arriving on the China coast Chinnery must have executed the small oil self-portrait which is now in the Metropolitan Museum in New York (Plate 158), and which was brought back to North America by Benjamin Wilcocks in 1827.[18] Once again the background seems to have been left unfinished, perhaps as a deliberate effect. To this group belongs Plate 159, whose reverse is inscribed in shorthand 'own portrait this for Mrs. [?]Morrison's' — the final name is tantalisingly unclear.

The self-portraits of his China years tend to follow a pattern. They are generally small, 9 or 10 inches high, and with a dark background, which is in

*Plate 158. Self-portrait, c.1826. Oils.* Metropolitan Museum of Art, Rogers Fund

*Plate 159. Self-portrait, c.1830. Pencil.* Private collection

keeping with the dictum expressed in the Treatise: 'Chinnery says "I patronize light Grounds Except in Very Old People — With them Dark [—] it adds to the Sobriety of Age".'[19] In most cases he presents himself in three-quarter right profile, turning his head towards the spectator, as though pausing for a moment from his work. An easel or sketch pad is often depicted, or else implied by the positioning of the body. An exception is Colour Plate 101, in which the face is seen in left profile, from behind the shoulder; this is perhaps the painting which Gideon Nye recalled as 'one of himself by himself painted by using two mirrors'.[20]

The self-portrait at the National Portrait Gallery in London (Colour Plate 102) is the most celebrated, the largest (28 x 21$^1$/$_2$ inches), and the best documented of the series. The scene is set in the artist's studio, where two characteristic paintings are on display. On the easel is a landscape depicting an overgrown tomb, and Indian figures in the foreground. On the wall behind is a view of the Praya Grande, Macau. Colours are arranged on his palette, the most prominent being white and vermilion. A folio of drawings is propped up against a table, and a pair of Chinese porcelain cups constitute a further clue to the location of the artist. Taken as a whole, the picture represents Chinnery's career, or the great majority of it which he spent in India and China. It was painted near the end of his life; even allowing a few years' interval between its execution and its exhibition at the Royal Academy in 1846, he must have been nearly seventy at the time of painting.

In the late self-portrait oils the artist's expression has grown more severe. In the Peabody Museum's picture (Plate 160) any inkling of amusement in the lips is contradicted by the sharp twist of the eyebrow and the dark eye glaring over the spectacles. The painting in the National Portrait Gallery goes further

*Colour Plate 102. Self-portrait, early 1840s. Oils.* National Portrait Gallery, London

*Plate 160. Self-portrait, c.1840. Oils.* Peabody Museum of Salem, Massachusetts

*Plate 161. Preparatory sketch for Colour Plate 102, squared up for transfer. Pencil and sepia ink.* National Portrait Gallery of Ireland

still: here Chinnery presents himself as the legendary curmudgeon of the China coast, with lips thrust forward and thick eyebrows twisted quizzically upward. No attempt is made to alleviate the bulbous nose and heavy jowls. Again one might detect a trace of a smile in the mouth, but again this is countered by the forbidding aspect of his furrowed forehead.

The National Portrait Gallery painting can be compared with its preparatory pencil study, squared up for transfer (Plate 161). Like the other self-portrait drawings,[21] it is less expressive than the corresponding painting, in that many of the signs of age and personality — the fine texture of the hair, the sagging cheeks, the creases about the eyes — can be conveyed only through the application of the oil paint. But in this case we can also see that, in progressing from the drawing to the painting, Chinnery has turned the body a little further towards the easel and away from the viewer, thus heightening the sense that the viewer has intruded, and will not be tolerated for long.

The portrait was taken back to Britain by Lancelot Dent, an old friend of Chinnery's and the senior British merchant on the China coast, who presumably had commissioned the picture. Chinnery's parting letter to Dent makes it clear that he expected the portrait to serve as a memorial to him: 'I believe I mentioned to you my particular wish that it should not be engraved during my Life Time — but after my Death I can have no objection.'[22] The letter expresses a typical mixture of irritability and pathos. 'I should have felt extremely obliged had you kindly kept your promise of seeing me before your final departure from Macau; but I can quite understand how much hurried you must have been at the moment of your going away...'

The letter and the picture were duly taken by Chinnery's friend Durran to Hong Kong, where Dent was staying in readiness for his voyage home. These were accompanied by the artist's certificate of authorship (works by British artists were not liable for customs duty), and instructions for varnishing when the picture reached England. The portrait was shown at the Royal Academy exhibition in the following year. The *Art-Union Monthly Journal* wished that 'the

*Plate 162. Self-portrait sketch. Pen and ink over pencil, dated September 20 1848.* Yale Center for British Art

extremities had not been so much neglected'[23] — the same criticism which had been expressed when Chinnery had first exhibited his oil paintings in Dublin forty-six years before.

This was not quite his last self-portrait; a pen-and-ink study dated 20 September 1848 (Plate 162) depicts the artist at the age of seventy-four, an apparently cheerful figure, although his face has grown thinner, and the painting on the easel is now a small one; the draughtsmanship shows little sign of failing powers. But the self-portrait taken home by Lancelot Dent was the last of his works to be publicly exhibited in the artist's lifetime. It was presented to the nation in 1888 by John Dent, nephew of Lancelot.

### The Memoir of William Prinsep

The published accounts of Chinnery in Macau present, inevitably, a somewhat glamorised picture of an eccentric genius and his endearing foibles. Even the journals of Harriet Low are circumscribed by her strong sense of propriety, and when she writes that Chinnery 'speaks well of every one',[24] it seems likely that she has only encountered the artist on his best behaviour. But these reverential reports are balanced to some extent by an account which has only recently come to light. This is the manuscript memoir written by written by an aggrieved creditor, William Prinsep, who had been closely associated with Chinnery in Calcutta, and later sought him out in his Chinese refuge.[25]

According to this memoir, it was in 1818, soon after Prinsep's arrival in Calcutta, that he 'became very intimate with George Chinnery, the only painter we had in those days worth having'.[26] Like Chinnery, he was involved in the amateur theatricals of Calcutta (as a designer of scenery and costume, and sometimes as an actor), and he was one of the group which met regularly to sketch at the house of Sir Charles D'Oyly. When Chinnery decamped to Serampore to escape his creditors, Prinsep was among those who settled the artist's debts and enabled him to return to Calcutta. When Chinnery sailed away to China, his debt to Prinsep remained unpaid.[27]

In 1830 William Prinsep experienced financial difficulties of his own, when the agency house of Palmer, in which he was a partner, went bankrupt. He recovered, building up a new business, and was able finally to retire to England in 1841 with a comfortable income. In 1838 he made a journey to the China coast, carrying dispatches to his trading associate, Lancelot Dent; but he also intended to visit Chinnery, for he brought with him a packet of Chinnery's sealed wills, which the artist had made out in India many years before. Sailing to Canton on the opium clipper *Water Witch,* he reached Macau on 5 November, and lodged with Dent's partner Robert Inglis.

Chinnery was not eager to meet Prinsep. Apart from the matter of outstanding debts, Chinnery believed that Prinsep had cheated him in appropriating and selling a group of sketchbooks which Chinnery had left behind in Calcutta. Prinsep's account of his approach to Chinnery reveals long-harboured resentments on both sides. He sent the packet of wills, together with a note in which

> I expressed as kindly as possible the hope that we might meet, all old
> differences being forgotten & as anxious to see his excellent work as

244

ever — but here I found there was to be no response — I was told by Mr Inglis and others that ever since Chinnery had resided in China on running away from Calcutta, he had never ceased to vilify me as a robber of the poor artists, an extortioner who had seized even his tools! meaning that having discovered several of his sketch books of considerable value made over to a French merchant surreptitiously when indebted to us so largely. I had of course impounded them & finding him not inclined to redeem them I sold them as payment of our claim. I found that none of the Residents had given the slightest credence to his bitter charges, but I took care they should know the truth & found that Chinnery's character was well known before he went there. He was only tolerated for his painting.[28]

There was no reply. Prinsep had only nine days before he was due to leave on the *Ariel* for Singapore. A week passed with no further communication. On the day before Prinsep's departure he was paying his farewell visits when Hugh Hamilton Lindsay, an associate of Jardine's with whom Prinsep had travelled from Canton, brought an offer of reconciliation from the artist. Certain conditions were set down:

He was to be seated in a room at Inglis' with his back to the door. I was to be introduced by two friends round to his front when he would rise & receive my proffered hand without any reference to the past. This was carried out to the letter amidst the laughter of all present who were highly amused at the scene after all his vapouring and abuse of me. The fact is that they had told him that if he did not accept my handsome offer of forgetfulness of all bygones which told entirely against himself, they would exclude him from their society.

I followed him afterwards to his studio to which he had invited me & found him surrounded by (as he described) tons of sketches, for he declared that he had adhered to his fixed principle of adding 7 new ideas every morning to his stock. Jardine was sitting for his portrait but I observed that though his pencil was as true for design as ever, his painting had certainly gone off. His former faults of exaggerated lights & shades were more prominent than ever & this was especially the case with his painted landscapes. While admiring one of his China paper sketch books with the observation that the trick would never pass from him 'Do you like it Sir — accept the book Sir as a peace offering from George Chinnery'! I have the book still & by artists it is considered a most valuable acquisition — it is of Chinese subjects entirely.

He offered me a cheque for 1000 dollars for the sketch books which had been signed in Calcutta. I told him that the assignees of his debt had already realised their value to the credit of his account. He declared he had left 12 books with M. L'Emerque, but only 11 had been handed over — so ended my communications with this extraordinary man whose talents were in the highest class & who if he had but been honest might in Europe have made a great name for himself.[29]

*Colour Plate 104. Murray Barracks and Old Church, Hong Kong. Oils.* Hongkong and Shanghai Banking Corporation

*Colour Plate 103. J.A. Durran. Oils.* Hongkong and Shanghai Banking Corporation

*Colour Plate 105. Canal and bridge, Honam. Oils.* Mr. and Mrs. R.J.F. Brothers

# CHAPTER 16
## *The Opium War, and After*

Since the turn of the nineteenth century, opium had been the mainstay of the China trade — the one import from the West which consistently found a ready market in China, and thus counterbalanced the ever-increasing exports of Chinese tea to the West. The Chinese Government, aware that opium was damaging its economy, outlawed the importation of opium, but corrupt local officials ensured that the trade continued to flourish. The East India Company, for its part, did not permit opium to be carried in its own ships, but connived at the transporting of its opium from India to China in licensed 'country ships'.

It has been suggested that Chinnery was himself an opium smoker,[1] but this is unlikely, for the western merchants seldom smoked the drug from which they profited so handsomely. In general they took the view that opium was in itself no more objectionable than alcohol (perhaps less so), and that its use and abuse were the responsibility of the individual consumer. They pointed

*Plate 163. James Holman, 'the blind traveller'. Oils.* The Royal Society, London

out that opium and its derivative laudanum were already widely used in the West for medicinal purposes. Chinnery himself, in conversation with Harriet Low, spoke of the beneficial effects of laudanum and salts, when taken in moderation; 'but take too much...and you know the consequences, exceedingly dangerous, and extremely disagreeable'.[2]

On the China coast opium provided an occasional diversion for western visitors: in 1830 the blind traveller James Holman (Plate 163) smoked two pipes at Jardine's house, in company with some others of the party, and experienced a headache;[3] and Duncan Macpherson, who served as a surgeon with the 37th Madras Native Infantry during the Opium War, reported that he had 'had the curiosity to try the effects of a few pipes upon myself'.[4] For westerners the smoking of opium was a matter of experiment and novelty rather than a habit. The opium pipe was perceived as a peculiarly Chinese indulgence, and it was not adopted, as the hookah had been in India, by the expatriate community. The notion that Chinnery was a habitual consumer of opium is based largely on an unpublished essay by the American trader Robert Bennet Forbes, who wrote that in Calcutta Chinnery's wife 'became aware of certain peccadilloes to which he had become addicted'.[5] But it is hard to believe that in Calcutta the hookah-smoking Chinnery would have also taken opium on a regular basis, or that if he did, that such eccentric behaviour could have gone unremarked. The 'peccadilloes' referred to, in the context of his wife, were more probably sexual than narcotic.

**The Opium Crisis**

In China, however, the consumption of opium continued, and the Peking Government became increasingly concerned to eradicate the trade and the consequent outflow of Chinese silver. In 1821 it had attempted to enforce the anti-opium laws at Macau, but the western merchants had responded by moving their stocks of opium to store ships off the island of Lintin in the Pearl River estuary; Macau forfeited much of its prosperity, but the opium trade went on.

After many further efforts, which were largely frustrated, the Emperor adopted a fresh tactic at the end of 1838, appointing an energetic and incorruptible man, Lin Tse-hsu (Zexu), as Imperial Commissioner for Canton, with a mandate to halt the opium trade by whatever means. At first Commissioner Lin was spectacularly successful. By blockading the western factories at Canton, he obliged the British merchants to surrender over 20,000 chests of opium, which under his supervision was then mixed with lime and salt and washed out to sea. From the Chinese Lin had confiscated 40,000 opium pipes by mid-May, and in June a series of statutes was passed, stricter than any previous opium laws, which extended the death penalty to foreigners (as well as Chinese) who dealt in opium.

Faced with this formidable opponent in Canton, the British Superintendent of Trade, Captain Charles Elliot, proposed that the British should conduct their trading operations through Macau instead. Lin therefore put pressure on the Portuguese Governor to expel the British from Macau. On 26 August 1839, the British residents — presumably including Chinnery — were evacuated from the Praya Grande, and were taken to quarters in the merchant ships which were anchored in Hong Kong harbour. Some of them returned shortly afterwards (Chinnery was certainly back in Macau by February 1840), but the situation remained explosive. On 3 November 1839 two British naval vessels severely damaged a fleet of war junks in the Pearl River, and the two nations were effectively at war.

At this point Chinnery became personally embroiled in the hostilities. Since Captain Elliot was still seeking to land cargoes at Macau, a *taotai* (senior Chinese official) ordered placards to be posted in the streets, announcing the imminent seizure of Elliot and five others named, 'who had taken foreign women with them, and gone to reside permanently in the town'.[6] For some unexplained reason, Chinnery was one of those cited. James Matheson wrote on 2 February 1840 to Andrew Jardine in Manila:

> Two days ago a high Tartar Mandarin named the Tow Tae entered Macao under a Salute...He has issued a Proclamation ordering away several English chiefly Elliot & his suite, Thom [Eliot's Secretary and interpreter], & (to the amazement of all) poor old Chinnery who is in great tribulation, & talks of going off in the next Ship for India. I fortunately am not named...[7]

Chinnery had every reason to be nervous. A few weeks before, Henry Gribble (one of Jardine's sea captains) had been captured, taken to Canton for interrogation, and released only after the British had threatened naval action. Elliot responded to the new proclamation by sending his wife and son to Singapore, but for Chinnery there was no such option. During February Elliot learnt from Palmerston in England that a naval and military expedition was making ready to assist the traders in the East; he was not allowed to make this letter public, however, and in any case Chinnery would have derived scant comfort from the news that the British navy was still four months away. On 23 February 1840 he wrote, in panic, to James Matheson:

> My Dear Mr. Matheson,
> All, & my *kindest* thanks! I will not detain your servt. to receive back Mr. R's Letters; wh. I see are long & wh. will require my attention (& great attention) in reading — Could you not do me the *great* favour of looking in *any* time to day at your own perfect Convenience? *Most* happy I'll be to see you — I am at the Top of my Stairs! Living in great Misery I assure you. To be away is every thing to me — I should like to paint a good few Pictures (at least try at it) before I'm put to the Sword — *rely* on it something serious if not dreadful is coming — I feel it as

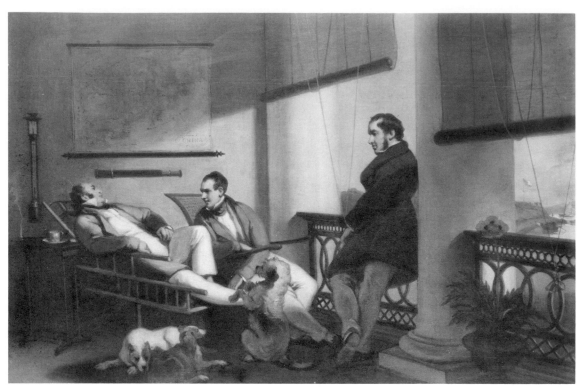

*Plate 164. 'On Dent's veranda'. Oils.* Private collection

certain, & am in a state of Anxiety beyond expression — I admit it —

I need not say how happy I'd be to come out if I *dared*. I dare not — I was at Breakfast *last* Sunday at Mr Leslie's & was accosted coming home 'Mr. C. you are a bold man to be walking about!!' For Capt. E it is all very well — the Head of the 7 prescribed [*sic*] — *he is safe* — poor sick G...[illegible] me is left for any thing that may happen —

Kindly pray do look in on me. If there was a Ship going to Bengal, I would lock up my House *today* & be away could I most certainly! *I passed a night of horror & presentiment not to be told* — I ran down to Dr. Anderson's last night with fear & trembling; & do not go out again till I cross the Beach.

I am always
My dear Mr Matheson
Most gratefully & cordially yours
Geo. Chinnery[8]

Sunday
Feb.23.1840

'Crossing the beach', which Chinnery anticipates at the end of the letter, must refer to the prospect of evacuation — although, in his state of terror, he might almost be alluding picturesquely to his own demise. He survived the crisis, however, and in June the British naval force began to gather at the China coast. First to arrive was the wooden paddle steamer *Madagascar*, which, after many difficulties at sea, reached Macau on 16 June, carrying the Commodore of the expeditionary force, Sir Gordon Bremer. Chinnery expressed his relief in a shorthand note on a drawing: 'June 16th 1840. Half an hour before the arrival of the first steamer!!! The most important day that the English have ever experienced in China.'[9]

### On Dent's Veranda

In the context of the Opium War, Chinnery's painting 'On Dent's verandah'

(Plate 164) takes on a particular significance. At first sight it is a scene of pleasant out-of-season relaxation — an illustration of Chinnery's famous remark that the servants of the East India Company 'spent six months in Macao, having nothing to do, and the other six months in Canton, sir, doing nothing'.[10] Beyond the veranda in the distance a Portuguese flag flies above the fort of São Francesco, at the northern tip of the Praya Grande. On the wall a telescope and a barometer suggest the marine interests of the three figures. The mild sunshine, slanting in beneath the partially-rolled rattans, illuminates the word 'China' in the corner of a map on the wall. A light breeze is just sufficient to agitate the spiral of smoke from an incense burner on the extreme left. The informality of the occasion is emphasised by the antics of one of the dogs, although its performance fails to distract the gentlemen from their conversation.

*Plate 165. Portrait drawing of J.A. Durran. Pencil. Inscribed and dated (not in Chinnery's hand) 'G. Chy. August 5th 1832 / Canton'. Mr. and Mrs. P.J. Thompson*

Yet there is more to the picture than meets the casual glance. The figures are not Company officials, but two merchants — the Frenchman J.A. Durran, and the American William Hunter — and an English naval officer, William Hall. All three were involved, in their different ways, in the hostilities of 1839-42. This picture was painted at the conclusion of that war, after three momentous years in which the fundamental assumptions underlying the relations between China and the West were changed for ever.

The veranda itself was the property of Dent & Co., the great rivals of Jardine, Matheson. Their house was situated on the Praya Grande, just to the north of São Pedro fort. After the departure of William Jardine in November 1838,

*Plate 166. Sketch for Plate 164. Pencil, dated October 29 [18]42 (see pp.253-4 for other inscriptions).* Private collection

Lancelot Dent was regarded as the senior member of the foreign community, a position which proved onerous as the opium crisis deepened. Lancelot Dent seems to have remained on good terms with Chinnery, commissioning drawings from him, and allowing the artist to draw money on his account.[11] When Lancelot Dent returned to Britain in 1845, taking with him Chinnery's self-portrait (see p.242), the artist wrote to him expressing 'the assurance that I have a due sense of my many obligations to you'.[12]

Dent is absent, however, from the scene depicted by Chinnery, and the role of host is played instead by the extravert Durran (also spelt Duran, Durant or Durand), who adopts the near-horizontal position favoured by 'East Indians'.[13] Durran had been Captain of a Bombay-based country ship which regularly brought opium and raw cotton from India to China. In January 1832 he was disembarking at Macau with his wife when he was injured in a dispute with the Chinese customs officials on the Praya Grande — an event which was indicative of the increasingly tense relations between western traders and Chinese authorities.[14] Chinnery's pencil portrait of Durran (Plate 165) was taken a few months after the incident. The Captain's wife was probably the 'Mrs Euphemia Durant' who lies buried in Macau's Protestant cemetery, having died on 13 July 1834.[15]

An explanation of Durran's lounging presence on Dent's veranda is supplied in an account of a voyage around the world made by the French ship *Bonité* in the years 1836-7. In January 1837 the French travellers were entertained at Canton in the house of Dent's partner Robert Inglis, and here they were pleased to meet their fellow-countryman Durran, 'qui arrivait de Calcutta et qui s'occupait particulièrement du commerce d'opium'.[16] They learned that Durran had on a previous occasion docked at Calcutta with a cargo which it seemed he would have to sell at a loss; but he was rescued by Dent, who, with no guarantee other than Durran's word of honour, had advanced him a substantial sum of money, so that Durran could postpone his sale until the market improved.

Since then Durran had remained attached to Dent's company, and probably resident in Dent's stately house on the Praya Grande,[17] while continuing to speculate on his own account. He was owner of the opium schooner *Lyra*, which entered trade in the inauspicious year of 1841; on a coastal voyage later that year, two men on board the *Lyra* were murdered.[18] When the war was over Durran continued in business, and in Macau he could be relied upon to introduce a little drama into the lives of the residents. To celebrate the fourth of July in 1845, he set off a firework display from the deck of the *Sylph,* one of the earliest and fastest of the opium clippers. At a party in the following year, when the guests were enjoying the luxury of ice-cream, it was Durran who left the doors of the ice-house open, and melted the precious store of ice.[19]

The figure seated next to Durran on the veranda is William Hunter, a native of Kentucky, who had first arrived on the China coast in 1825 at the age of twelve, but went back in 1827 when his firm failed. In March 1829 he returned to Canton, and was engaged by Samuel Russell. A few months after this, Russell & Co. merged with the previously dominant firm of Perkins & Co., and became the largest American dealers in opium. Hunter was made a partner of the firm in 1837. To judge from the two books in which he described his experiences (including several anecdotes involving Chinnery), Hunter was a capable businessman and a sociable character. He was also a passable amateur sailor, who on one occasion steered John Dent's 34-ton cutter *Gypsy* to second place in a race held in the Macau roads.[20] As part-owner of the *Midas*, he shared Captain Hall's interest in steam propulsion; in 1844 the *Midas* became the first American steamship to operate in the China seas. Several surviving portraits by Chinnery are said to represent Hunter.[21]

William Hunter had the particular distinction of being, for several years, one of only three foreigners on the China coast who were able to converse in Chinese — the others being the missionary Robert Morrison (who was Hunter's examiner at the Anglo-Chinese College in Malacca in 1827) and the diplomat John Francis Davis (whose conciliatory attitude towards the Chinese often set him at odds with the British merchants). Hunter too seems to have been disillusioned with the activities of many of his contemporaries in promoting what he called 'one of the most unjust [wars] ever waged by one nation against another';[22] for at the end of 1842, while still only thirty years old, he gave up his place in the Russell factory. At the time when he was pictured on Dent's veranda, Hunter was playing out the last months of his career on the China coast, from which he finally returned to North America in February 1844.

The third figure on the veranda, seen leaning against a column a little apart from the other two, is Captain (later Rear-Admiral) William Hutcheon Hall of the Royal Navy. Hall was a man of action, an engineer, an inventor, and — to many of the western community — the hero of the war. On 25 November 1840 Hall arrived at Macau in command of the sensational ship *Nemesis*, the first iron-built vessel to be seen in China. She was driven by steam, and her flat bottom (with movable keels) allowed her to penetrate close to the shore. She was armed with two pivot-mounted 32-pounders and a rocket launcher; during one operation an ignited Congreve rocket was jammed in its launching tube, threatening to blow up the *Nemesis*, and Hall himself pushed the rocket out, severely injuring his arm.

The *Nemesis* proved devastating to the Chinese, who were unprepared for such a deadly combination of versatility and fire power. After playing a major role in the military victory of the British force, Captain Hall was allowed to attend the signing of the Treaty of Nanking which formally terminated the war, 'as a mark of especial favour, although not of the prescribed rank'. On 23 December 1842 the *Nemesis* finally 'bid adieu to Macau', as a British chronicler put it, 'regretted by all',[23] except presumably the Chinese.

It is unlikely that Chinnery would have finished the painting by that time, for a drawing of the upper part of the barometer at the left of the picture survives, and is dated 2 December 1843.[24] Indeed the inclusion of Hall in the composition may have been an afterthought; he does not appear in Chinnery's preliminary sketch of 29 October 1842 (Plate 166), at which time he was away at Chusan where the *Nemesis* was undergoing repairs. This drawing shows Durran and Hunter side by side in their chairs, with shorthand inscriptions as follows: 'The part on poles out at the end...must be taken out

Plate 167. *Sketch for J.A. Durran lying on a sofa. Pencil, dated Oct. 13 1842.* Private collection

Plate 168. *J.A. Durran, smoking. Pen and ink over pencil, dated November 29 1843.* Private collection

Plate 169. *J.A. Durran at his easel. Pencil, pen and ink, dated May 26 1843. Inscribed in shorthand 'Monsieur Duran painting Monsieur T-st's portrait'.* Private collection

and done over again...Mr Durran white trousers...and Nankeen coat...Mr Hunter grey dressing gown...and white pantaloons...correct...October 29th. [18]42'. The chair is duly redrawn below, with shorthand 'broken[?]...all white'; and at the foot of the drawing, after the sign for 'correct', the longhand inscription 'Durran [?-indistinct] and Hunter. Bamboo Chair'.

Chinnery took sketches of Durran on several other occasions, one of them (Plate 167) a fortnight before the drawing for 'On Dent's veranda', although here he is caught in too undignified a position to be commemorated in an oil painting; in other portraits (Plates 168 and 169 and Colour Plate 103) Durran's balding head is protected by a variety of flamboyant headgear. Durran was himself an amateur artist, and he is portrayed in this role in Plate 169, with the shorthand inscription 'Monsieur Duran painting Monsieur T-st's portrait' — a possible reference to the British merchant Charles Twist. Eight months later Durran sketched Chinnery himself 'at dinner'.[25] Some of Durran's drawings and tracings after Chinnery are to be found in an album presented to Thomas Boswall Watson in 1847;[26] and Durran is mentioned in two letters from Chinnery of 20 and 25 February 1848, passing on instructions and pictures on Chinnery's behalf.[27]

Hunter and Durran were perhaps Chinnery's two closest friends during the last fifteen years of his life; Hunter was with him at his death-bed, and Durran was made trustee of Chinnery's estate.[28] To this extent the picture 'On Dent's veranda' is Chinnery's tribute to their congenial fellowship and support. But the presence of Captain Hall, above and a little apart from the two traders, lends an extra dimension to the picture, painted as it was at the close of an acrimonious war which threatened not only their own lives but the entire China trade. With the inclusion of Hall, the picture becomes an expression of relief, gratitude even, that the convivial, traditional existence of the western community on the China coast had been preserved. This impression is reinforced by one further element of the composition, which would never in reality have appeared in such a situation, but is here included purely for its symbolic significance: a large opium poppy, the economic basis of the western trade with China, is seen flourishing on Dent's veranda.

## Hong Kong

Until the Opium War, the small island of Hong Kong was regarded by westerners as little more than a watering place. Of greater significance was its sheltered harbour, far enough removed from Canton — some eighty miles — to provide a secure base for the opium store ships. Under the terms of the Chuenpi Convention, negotiated by Captain Charles Elliot, Hong Kong was to be ceded to Britain. A British force accordingly took possession of the island on 26 January 1841. James Matheson, who generally regarded Elliot as too lenient and conciliatory in his dealings with the Chinese, expressed his satisfaction to William Jardine in London: 'Elliot says that he sees no objection to our opium there, and as soon as the New Year holidays are over I shall set about building.'[29]

The agreement was not ratified by the Chinese Government, however, and hostilities recommenced; peace was not finally established until the signing of the Treaty of Nanking on 29 August 1842. By this time a township had developed, with the loyal name of Victoria, on the north side of the island. There were numerous commercial buildings and private bungalows, a four-mile road running parallel to the shore (Queen's Road), and a jail. On 17 March 1842 the first issue of the Hong Kong newspaper, the *Friend of China*, described the place as 'henceforth a part and parsel [*sic*] of the wide spread British Empire[,] that Empire on which the sun never sets, and with whose aggrandizement is linked the regeneration social and political of the vast Empire of China...'[30]

In these early years of the settlement there was little in Hong Kong to tempt an elderly artist away from his home in Macau. Despite the bravado of the soi-disant *Friend of China*, it was by no means clear at this stage that Hong Kong would become the new centre of the China trade. The acquisition of Hong Kong had not been a part of Elliot's brief, and Palmerston, in relieving Elliot of his post, referred to it sarcastically as 'a barren Island with hardly a House upon it'.[31] He was not far wide of the mark; the plant hunter Robert Fortune, arriving in July 1843, was surprised by the desolation of the hillsides of granite and red clay, the lack of animals, the fir trees reduced to stunted bushes.[32]

Building continued, however, much of it in defiance of official instructions from London. The population of westerners grew rapidly, and the Chinese population more rapidly still, attracted by the prospects of employment: by 1845 there were some 600 'Europeans', nearly 400 Indians, and an estimated 22,000 Chinese (including boat dwellers). But the settlement had a reputation for crime — the colonial government tried to outlaw the Triad societies, with little success — and it was notoriously unhealthy. In the summer of 1843 a hundred men of the 55th Regiment died of 'Hong Kong fever' within two months, and there was talk of exchanging Hong Kong for a healthier location.

The fever was at last kept in check through a programme of sanitation and drainage. By 1844 the leading merchants had transferred their headquarters

to Hong Kong. Moreover, the Chinese had relaxed the regulations which had confined the merchants' families to Macau; the result, according to a visitor to Macau in November of this year, was 'the removal of nearly all the British and American residents; and only a few American families now remain at Macao'.[33] This was an exaggeration, but a number of Chinnery's friends and clients had indeed moved to the new colony, and the departure of Lancelot Dent in 1845 must have been a severe blow to the artist. In the winter of 1845-6 Chinnery himself made the forty-mile steamer voyage to Hong Kong.

In the preceding ten years Chinnery had seldom stirred from Macau. A drawing of Lintin Island, dated 6 May 1837, indicates that he paid a visit to this opium depot twenty miles to the north-east of Macau.[34] (This was perhaps no more than a holiday excursion: five years before, Harriet Low had spent three weeks at Lintin, where she had danced quadrilles beneath a full moon on the deck of the *Red Rover*.[35]) In 1839 he may have taken refuge, together with most of the western inhabitants of Macau, in the ships anchored in Hong

Plate 171. Street scene, Hong Kong. Pencil, pen and ink. Toyo Bunko, Tokyo

256

*Plate 172. Murray Barracks and Old Church, Hong Kong. Pen and ink and watercolours.* Peabody Museum of Salem, Massachusetts

Kong harbour. But the journey of 1846 was Chinnery's only visit to the colony. On 18 February 1846 the naval surgeon Edward Cree, who was temporarily stationed at Hong Kong, had 'a pleasant chat with old Chinnery, the artist' in the bungalow of John and Wilkinson Dent, who perhaps provided him with lodgings.[36]

Unfortunately Chinnery was unable to make the most of his opportunity. 'I was there 6 months only: at the time so very unwell, not to say ill, that I had the power of doing but very little,' he wrote later to Captain D'Aguilar, son and aide-de-camp of General George D'Aguilar, Officer Commanding at Hong Kong. It appears that Chinnery had mistakenly sent some drawings of Canton or Macau to the younger D'Aguilar, who had wanted views of Hong Kong to take home with him. The artist wrote apologetically: 'Those views I made there I have commissions to execute Pictures from for particular parties whose names are written for the most part *in their own hand writing* on the several pages of the respective sketches.' Chinnery offered to make copies of 'any of the Views I have of the town of Victoria...I have in all but 15 (fifteen) views — and of these I now enclose you a list. — they are large and full of detail...' He proposed that any drawings selected could be forwarded by Wilkinson Dent to D'Aguilar in England.[37]

Chinnery's drawings of Hong Kong (Plates 170-173 and Colour Plate 104) depict a settlement whose buildings were functional rather than decorative. An impressive row of godowns had been erected by Jardine, Matheson at East Point, and the other structures of the new colony were likewise substantial and rectangular: barracks, officers' quarters, jail, military hospital, and residences for the leading officials, soldiers and merchants. Many of these utilised the local granite, which lent an unmistakable air of permanence. At the time of Chinnery's visit there were no church towers or Chinese temples to enliven the skyline, although there were (to the dismay of the Protestant missionaries) a well-attended Roman Catholic chapel and a mosque. The temporary matshed building in which Anglican worship was held appears in the foreground of one of Chinnery's compositions (Plate 172 and Colour Plate 104), with its bell visible at the east end. It was built on the parade-ground of

*Plate 173. Spring Gardens, Hong Kong. Pen and ink and watercolours.* Peabody Museum of Salem, Massachusetts

Murray Barracks, which is shown on the left, with General D'Aguilar's quarters, known as Headquarters House (later Flagstaff House), just behind.

The Hong Kong recorded by Chinnery was not so much a community as a grandiose building site. In 1846 the western settlement consisted of a scattering of imposing blocks isolated from each other on a rugged hillside. The streets seen in Chinnery's drawings are evidently still under construction, with boulders by the roadside and — in some cases — Chinese stonebreakers at work with hammers or pickaxes. 'Go where you would', a visitor observed, 'your ears were met with the clink of hammers and chisels, and your eyes were in danger of sparks of stone at every corner.'[38]

From the first, commerce was the ruling principle of the colony. The missionary George Smith recognised that in Hong Kong he faced an uphill struggle against Chinese and westerners alike; such was their disregard for the Sabbath, Smith complained, that even the congregation in the makeshift church had to contend with a din of hammers outside.[39] Today the site of the modest church depicted by Chinnery is occupied by the Hongkong Hilton Hotel.

**Final Years**

In the last years of his life Chinnery remained for the most part active and sociable, as can be judged from a journal kept by his friend and doctor Thomas Boswall Watson, together with his wife Elizabeth. Watson had practised medicine in his native Scotland, but had been faced with heavy costs and strong competition; at the suggestion of an old college friend who had visited the East, he sailed to China in 1845, at the age of thirty, and was joined there by his wife in the following year.[40]

Their journal, which is still in the possession of the Watson family, runs intermittently from October 1847 to February 1851. There are frequent references to Chinnery as a guest of the Watsons or as a fellow diner with friends such as the Middletons and the Stewarts. On 3 November 1847, St. Andrew's Day, the Watsons went to dinner at the Stewarts, and met Chinnery

V. A. M.

*Plate 174. Canal and bridge at Honam. Pen and ink, squared up for transfer, dated July 30 1832, and inscribed in shorthand 'Monday morning'.* Victoria and Albert Museum

there: 'the latter, in great spirits — sang two songs after dinner'. On 5 January 1848 Watson called on Chinnery in order to congratulate him on his seventy-fourth birthday. On 4 December of the same year 'Mr Chinnery and Mr Stewart dined with us off Turtle soup made from a turtle kindly sent us by Mrs Forbes.' (Another source records that in the preceding August, Mrs Forbes — the wife of the Massachusetts trader Robert Bennet Forbes — was 'getting her likeness taken by a Mr. Chinnery'.[41]) By this date the western residents of Macau formed a small but cosmopolitan group; other individuals observed in Chinnery's company were the Frenchman Paul Durran,[42] the Portuguese Governor Amaral (whose murder on 22 August 1849 is also noted), Mr. and Mrs. Paiva (also Portuguese), as well as the Parsee merchant Hurjeebhoy Rustomjee.[43]

One may fairly assume that Dr. Watson's medical services to Chinnery were paid for, in part at least, in the currency of drawings or drawing instruction, but the journal also records that on 11 September 1848 Watson 'paid Mr Chinnery for a book of sketches'; the sketchbook arrived seven weeks later. In the following year Watson's eldest son Jamie went to Chinnery to sit for his portrait. On another occasion Watson was at Chinnery's, looking through the artist's old sketches: 'I asked him to paint me a picture from one of them (an old bridge near Canton) — when I may get it is another thing.'[44] This subject is probably the horseshoe bridge over a creek in the suburb of Honam, across the river from the western factories at Canton; at least two Chinnery drawings of this bridge survive,[45] one of them squared up as if for transfer to canvas (Plate 174), and an oil painting which may perhaps have been the fulfilment of Watson's commission (Colour Plate 105).

Chinnery's dated drawings show that he was still sketching in the last year of his life. But he was finally incapacitated by illness. 'The confusion and swimming in my head I the most complain of — my sight is somewhat better', he wrote shortly before his death. 'I had my palette set this morning, but I could not use it! However, I by no means despair — I am certain (I think) that, with a change of weather, I shall get myself [well], as much as a man can be at near 80!...What my sufferings have been these last three months (my only source of daily bread being prevented me) Providence only knows! But I hold up in mind — if I get well I will fear nothing — there is enough to do, and more than enough, if my physical powers are restored to me. Please God, all will come right! May it be so!'[46]

On his last night Chinnery was accompanied by three old friends, Patrick Stewart, Hurjeebhoy Rustomjee, and the American William Hunter. Hunter recorded that Chinnery died at 4.30 in the morning on 30 May 1852. His body was left in the charge of 'his servant Augustine and several Chinese', until Hunter and Stewart returned at ten o'clock with Dr. Watson, who had attended the artist in his last illness. Watson then performed an autopsy. Why an autopsy should have been thought necessary is not clear, and perhaps it was no more than the remarkable length of Chinnery's life which aroused the doctor's curiosity. Since Chinnery had been celebrated for his powers of eating, it was supposed that his stomach might have suffered, but Watson declared that it had been perfectly healthy; his examination of the brain revealed that Chinnery had died of 'serious apoplexy', in modern terms a stroke.[47]

He was buried in the Protestant cemetery. A fund was raised for a memorial tablet to his memory, but twenty years later it had 'not yet been received from England'.[48] At some point before the end of the century an imposing monument was erected at the top of the graveyard, with the words 'George Chinnery' inscribed on the frieze. Further inscriptions were added in 1974, in English, Chinese and Potruguese, to mark the bicentenary of his birth. Among the sentiments expressed here at length is the somewhat cryptic message: 'We hope he found a sweet refuge against the tribulations and anxieties of his youth.'

No will was discovered, although Watson and Hunter searched through the artist's effects, at the request of Judge Carvalho. They found several camphor wood chests full of sketches and oil paintings. Among the latter Hunter described a carefully finished picture of the Bund at Calcutta, with a ship ready to sail, and 'a European, with a serious curvature of the spine [see p.238], a portfolio under one arm, and a sola [sic] topee in his hand, bowing towards the city, while at the top of the painting was a scroll, in which were the words "thermometer 200", evidently "too hot for me".' Hunter recalled that this picture was bought by John Dent; there is no record of it in recent times.[49]

Chinnery's paintings and sketches were sold at auction in Macau on 28 July, and those who had claims on Chinnery's estate were invited to apply to the court.[50] Whether by accident or design, the sale coincided with a regatta at Macau, and the sale became something of a social event; on 27 July it was reported that 'a Regatta, a Ball, and the Works of the late Mr Chinnery at Macau have taken away the elite of Hongkong society for the present week. The people who remain here wander about in disconsolate dullness, ashamed to shew themselves, as not to be at Macau argues them unknown.'[51]

Meanwhile several obituaries were published in the English language newspapers of India and China. Their leading theme was the late artist's reckless squandering of wealth and opportunities. A judicious article in the *Bengal Hurkaru* observed that Chinnery could have 'shaken the rupee tree' and accumulated an enormous fortune in Calcutta, if only he had been a steady and prudent man. He had resembled Coleridge 'not only in idleness and procrastination, but in his preference of conversation to work'.[52] The *Friend of India* made some interesting claims: that the artist had earned nearly half a lakh of rupees a year (i.e. 50,000 rupees) while in Calcutta; that he had not the patience to complete the drapery of his portraits, and left between fifty and one hundred unfinished portraits in his Indian studio; that 'he had that complete indifference to the value of money which so often accompanies artists of genius.' The newspaper believed that Chinnery had died 'under circumstances of painful destitution', something which the *Friend of China and Hongkong Gazette* implicitly confirmed, in stating that at the time of his death, measures were in progress to provide him with 'several additional comforts' and to relieve him from 'anxiety as to the means of living'.[53]

Fifty years had elapsed since Chinnery had left Britain. He outlived most of his contemporaries at the Royal Academy Schools, and almost all of his close relations. But he was not entirely forgotten in his homeland. His wife Marianne did not follow her husband to Macau, but sailed back to Europe from India and lived on until 1865, when she died in Brighton at the age of eighty-eight.[54] Many others whom he had known in India and China returned home with paintings and drawings of Chinnery's. A total of fourteen of his paintings, sent back from China, were exhibited at the Royal Academy between 1830 and 1846. The *Calcutta Monthly Journal* of August 1826 reproduced a letter written by Samuel Prout in England ('the celebrated PROUT') to an unidentified gentleman in Calcutta:

Mr R— J— has this day favoured me with a sight of some of Mr CHINNERY's drawings, through the indulgence of Mrs S—.

To say I have been gratified, would be saying nothing to express my admiration of them — they are the best specimens of powerful sketches I have ever seen, and the best in colour, management, and execution.

Chinnery responded in the same spirit:

I cannot express how much I am gratified by your good opinion: I am sure you have the best motive in urging me with such a stimulus; but when I recollect your talents and high character in art, I am a little perplexed, and scarce know what I ought to say.

Mr R— J— favoured me with a sight of the drawings belonging to Mrs S., with which I was DELIGHTED:- they brought my poor works instantly to the ground, and I suffered for the vanity of daring to think of myself in comparison with them. Their colour and energy appeared to me quite perfection. So you must allow me to be among your sincere and enthusiastic admirers.

Will you do me the kindness to accept two slight sketches for your portfolio of scraps, and when you have a broken boat or a tumble down fragment to give to the wind, pray remember me, and I shall value it exceedingly.[55]

In Macau and Hong Kong Chinnery's paintings and sketches continued to change hands for some years after the artist's death. Dr. Watson acted as unofficial agent. In 1856 he sold his practice to Dr. William Kane and became part owner of the Hong Kong Dispensary. When an American visitor to Macau learnt that Watson had 'some fine Chinnerys', Dr. Kane supplied him with an introduction to Watson in Hong Kong.[56] Watson also received a request from John Middleton in Calcutta to secure

One or two of Chinnery's works from Paul Durant's collection. He has a good many exquisite gems and they may go, as you say, cheap, for poor Chinnery's works are not now appreciated as they once were. Kindly manage this for me if you can. I don't want any of the common unfinished things but some one or two of those earlier productions some of which are exquisitely finished...[57]

In 1858 Watson suffered from attacks of pleurisy and of the Hong Kong fever which killed so many of his contemporaries. In January 1859 he left the China coast and returned to Scotland, where he died a few months later. His 'case of Chinnerys' was sent home after him.[58]

In 1876 a loan exhibition of pictures and works of art was organised in Hong Kong, perhaps the first public exhibition of art to be held on the island. A committee was formed of fourteen influential citizens, who appealed for contributions; they were 'astonished to find that over 250 paintings and drawings, all above mediocrity and many of high merit, were in the Colony'. The exhibition was set up in the City Hall, and formally opened by the Governor on 18 July. On the two following days Europeans were admitted, and Chinese visitors were allowed to enter on the two days after that.

The exhibits consisted of both locally-painted scenes of the China coast and contemporary paintings imported from Britain. At the far end of the hall was placed the large portrait of George IV which had formerly hung in the English Factory at Canton; further dignity was lent to the occasion by Winterhalter's portrait of Queen Victoria, lent by Government House and 'recently renovated by a local gentleman'. The committee had intended to bring together a collection of pictures by Chinnery, and to have made this a self-contained feature of the exhibition. But it became evident, as the *Daily Press* reported, that a large number of works by Chinnery had been removed from Hong Kong:

Most possessors of them have, during the twenty-five years that have elapsed since his death, returned to their native lands, and carried with them such records of his genius as they had been enabled to acquire. The few that remain, however, have been generally forthcoming, and abundantly testify to the talent of the man.[59]

CHAPTER 17

# *Chinnery and Lamqua*

Of Chinnery's Chinese followers, one man stands out: Guan Qiaochang, known to westerners as Lamqua or Lamquoi. The American Toogood Downing described him as 'having been a pupil of Mr. Chinnery, of Macao, and from him received instructions sufficient to enable him to paint in a tolerable manner after the European fashion...Lamquoi stands at the head of his profession.'[1] Several other contemporaries affirmed that Lamqua started his career as a pupil of Chinnery, or that he had taken lessons from him.[2] On the other hand, a visitor in 1843 reported that Chinnery was 'stoutly denying' that Lamqua had been a pupil of his.[3]

Pupil or not, Lamqua developed a great facility for painting portraits in Chinnery's manner. He became a serious rival to the English artist, undercutting his prices and gaining a considerable celebrity among visitors. Several of them left accounts of his premises at China Street, Canton, where he catered for his western clients. On the ground floor was the shop, hung with finished pictures for sale. Above was the workshop, in which eight or ten painters worked, some of them making copies of western prints in oils or watercolours, others painting miniatures on ivory, others again producing brightly-coloured mandarin figures, landscapes, boats or birds on pith paper, known mistakenly as 'rice paper'.[4]

On the third level, above the workshop, was the studio of Lamqua himself, a small room lit by a skylight (Plate 175). According to one source, he would offer

*Plate 176. Lamqua, self-portrait. Oils. Inscribed on back of frame 'Lamqua, age at 52 [sic], painted by himself, Canton, 1853'.* Hong Kong Museum of Art

to paint his sitters either 'English fashion' for £10, or 'China fashion' for £8,[5] but none of his portraits 'China fashion' can be identified today. Visitors to his studio would find numerous portraits in varying states of completion: most were of westerners, but some represented 'the intelligent Parsee', and others 'the unassuming head of a Chinaman'.[6]

The artist himself was said to be 'a stout, thick-set man, about the middle size, and bearing a considerable degree of intelligence and urbanity in his countenance',[7] a description which is borne out by his self-portrait in the Hong Kong Museum of Art (Plate 176). On the back of the self-portrait's frame is an inscription which presents crucial evidence: 'Lamqua, age at 52 [*sic*], painted by himself, Canton, 1853'.

It follows that when Chinnery came to the China coast, Lamqua was in his early twenties. Probably he was already practising as an artist. Since the middle of the eighteenth century, Cantonese artists had been painting 'in the Western manner', for export to Europe and North America. The best-known of these earlier artists was Spoilum, a portrait painter in oils, who it seems came from the same family as Lamqua.[8] A list of Cantonese 'outside merchants' in 1820, five years before Chinnery's arrival, includes 'Lamqua' of New China Street, who is described as a man of good character and 'no. 2 standing', and as a painter of ships and likenesses.[9] There are also examples of portraits, signed 'Lamqua', whose style belongs to the Spoilum tradition of portraiture, and lacks the dramatic chiaroscuro, the liberal use of vermilion, and the other mannerisms which Lamqua's later paintings borrowed from Chinnery.[10] Unless, therefore, some other 'Lamqua' was at work in these early years — a possibility which cannot be ruled out[11] — then Guan Qiaochang was already established as an artist when Chinnery arrived, and there is no truth

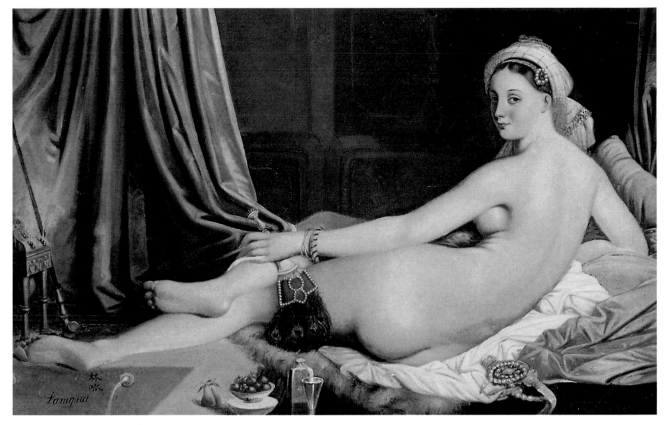

*Colour Plate 106. Lamqua after Ingres, 'Grande Odalisque'. Oils. Signed in Chinese and western script.* Private collection

in the story that he was a houseboy who took his first steps in art under Chinnery's supervision.[12]

There is documentary evidence of some association between Chinnery and Lamqua in the former's early years on the China coast. Two letters of December 1827 from Chinnery to the merchant John Latimer, requesting that Lamqua be given the sum of $56 in payment for a consignment of brushes and ivories (see p.169), indicate that Lamqua was acting as an agent or intermediary for Chinnery, and one can imagine that, as a member of a well-established family of Cantonese 'export' painters, he could have been of considerable assistance in many practical matters to the newly-arrived English artist.

In the early 1830s Lamqua's name appears in Latimer's cash books: 'Paid Lamqua for Copy of Portrait... $26.50', and 'Paid Lamqua — 1 book 12 paintings ($8) — 1 picture Joss house ($15) [probably the A-Ma temple in Macau]'.[13] According to the *Canton Register* of 1835, $15 was Lamqua's standard charge for a portrait head.[14] It is clear from several reports that his prices were a good deal lower than Chinnery's, and that this was a source of friction between them, in later years at least. The account books of Jardine, Matheson seem to bear out this discrepancy in fees: in 1840-3 Lamqua was paid (for unspecified services) $18.50, $34, and (by Alexander Matheson) $138, while Chinnery in the same period received payments of $150 and $250.[15] In the late 1830s Lamqua was said to be 'always happy to take your likeness for the small consideration of twenty dollars', and, although fully employed, earned 'no more than about £500 a year';[16] this would seem a respectable sum, but it is not clear whether it included the expenses of his studio and his many assistants.

*Plate 177. Lamqua, Woman with a facial tumour. Oils. Gordon Museum, Guy's Hospital*

Lamqua himself made a speciality of portraits in oils — 'I have not heard that he has attempted any other than portrait painting,' wrote Downing in 1838.[17] But it is not easy to identify a particular style which can be taken as characteristic of Lamqua. Several paintings carry the signature 'Lamqua' in western script or in Chinese; Colour Plate 106, a creditable copy of the engraved version of Ingres's 'Grande Odalisque', is signed in both scripts. But these paintings do not coincide with those which are closest in manner to Chinnery. Moreover, the signed pictures do not all appear to be the work of the same hand. It seems that the signature 'Lamqua' — like that of other leading export artists such as 'Sunqua' and 'Chow Kwa' — identifies the studio in which the picture was painted, but does not guarantee the authorship of an individual artist.

Nor is it necessarily true, as is sometimes assumed, that while Chinnery painted from the life, Lamqua was a mere copyist. For Chinnery too was prepared on occasion to copy a picture which was supplied to him (see p.234); and there are many accounts of Lamqua painting portraits at first hand. It is not even possible to make a clear distinction between Chinnery and Lamqua according to the pigments which they used. A French visitor to Lamqua's studio in Canton watched Lamqua sketch a portrait of an English friend ('The English seem to have been born to sit for their portraits'), and made a careful note of the brushes and paints used by the Chinese artists: 'The Chinese colors are much inferior to the European. They scarcely succeed in manufacturing any beside vermilion, lazulite, carmine of the plant carthame, and orpiment. The best painters, especially portrait painters, buy other paints of the English.'[18]

One painting which can confidently be ascribed to Lamqua is the portrait of the medical missionary Peter Parker, with a Chinese assistant attending to a patient (Colour Plate 107). This assistant is in all probability Guan (Kwan) A-to, who performed a number of successful operations on cataracts and tumours in the early 1840s; he was also the nephew of Lamqua. Lamqua took a close interest in Parker's medical activities, and offered to provide, as an expression of gratitude for Parker's labours in Canton, a series of portraits (see Plate 177) illustrating his individual patients, with their various medical conditions. One hundred and ten of these small oil portraits survive (some thirty being duplicates), most of them in the Yale Medical Library, and many can be related directly to the case notes written by Peter Parker.[19]

It is possible that members of Lamqua's studio may have been involved in this remarkable project, but it is difficult to doubt that the picture of Parker and Guan A-to was painted by the hand of Lamqua himself. Lamqua's picture is moreover a thoroughly Chinnerian composition; several of its details are based on Chinnery's portrait of Dr. Colledge in his surgery (Colour Plate 96), and the figure of Dr. Parker is shown in the cross-legged posture in which Chinnery had presented Howqua (Colour Plate 53) and himself (Colour Plate 102). But there is a significant departure from the Colledge picture: it is now the Chinese surgeon, rather than the westerner, who is conducting the operation.

Although Lamqua did not leave the China coast himself, his paintings were exhibited in both Britain and North America during his lifetime. At the Royal Academy in London he was represented by a 'Head of an old Man' (1835) and a portrait of Captain W.H. Hall of the *Nemesis* (1845). 'Portrait of Moushing, Tea Merchant' was hung at the Apollo Club in New York in March 1841, and three more of his portraits appeared at the Pennsylvania Academy of Fine Arts in 1851, 'a gentleman', 'Napoleon and his son' and 'Sir Henry Pottinger'. In the same year five further portraits by Lamqua, of Chinese sitters (including Howqua), were exhibited at the Boston Athenaeum; they had been shipped by the China trader Augustine Heard of Ipswich, Massachusetts. Two of these, which were given by Heard to the Union Club, were identified as 'Ke Yaing' and 'Lin Chong': they probably represent the commissioners Ch'i ying (Keying), signatory of the Treaty of Nanking, and Lin Tse-hsu (also known as Lin Wen-chung), scourge of the opium dealers.[20]

Commissioner Lin was also represented in Madame Tussaud's exhibition in Baker Street, London. Advertised as 'the Destroyer of £2,500,000 of British Property', with 'his Small Footed Wife', the fully-robed figues were said to have been 'Modelled from Life, by the Celebrated LAMB-QUA, of Canton'.[21]

At least one of Lamqua's sons followed his father as an export portrait painter. A letter of 1844, sent by Major-General D'Aguilar (the Lieutenant-Governor of Hong Kong) to the Chinese General Zhao Changling in Canton, enquires after 'the artist who has done your portrait...I have heard that he is Guan Yan, son of Guan Lamqua. I want to invite him to come to Hong Kong to draw me a portrait, which I could send to you as a gift.'[22]

This interesting letter indicates that portraits had a diplomatic function, serving as gifts between representatives of the Chinese and British Governments. It also suggests that by the early 1840s 'Guan Yan' had reached an age of responsibility which enabled his father to leave the Canton studio for prolonged periods. Lamqua spent several months in Macau in 1843; in December of this year Rebecca Kinsman recorded that 'as a very *great favour* and it certainly was one, *he came here* to paint Ecca [Rebecca's daughter], as it would have been inconvenient for so *many of us* to have gone to his room.' She added that, despite his portly appearance, Lamqua had 'a great deal of genius', and was highly regarded among the Chinese; 'he has painted Sir Henry Pottinger, Admiral Parker, and various other distinguished men.' (Subsequently Rebecca Kinsman visited Chinnery, whose art she admired, but not the artist: 'he is a remarkable old man, a very disagreeable one however, on account of his vanity.'[23])

In 1845, as it became clear that Hong Kong was superseding Macau as the centre of the China trade, Lamqua opened a studio in Hong Kong at 3 Oswald Building, Queen's Road.[24] Chinnery was now in his seventies, and although he paid a visit to Hong Kong in 1846, he was sick for most of the time and achieved little. Thus Lamqua and his family were strongly placed to win commissions from westerners, and may well have been responsible for the majority of export portraits executed in the 1840s and 1850s.

*Colour Plate 107. Lamqua, Dr. Peter Parker, with his assistant Guan A-to performing an operation on the eye of a patient.* Private collection

# Appendices

# APPENDIX i

# *Technique and Theory: the Treatise*

For all his sportive manner, Chinnery took himself extremely seriously as an artist, a teacher, and a theoretician. It was his intention, in Calcutta at least, to write a book about the principles and practice of painting. He had this in mind by December 1814: '...my Book *when I write it!* is to have each Theory, *practically* illustrated...'[1] The book was never completed, but an initial draft survives in the British Library.[2] Although this draft has become known as the 'Treatise', it is not a coherent or systematic work, but a disorganised collection of notes and recommendations written down at various times, partly by Chinnery and partly by his pupil and correspondent, Maria Browne. (Chinnery was nevertheless the sole author; the sections in Mrs. Browne's hand are often prefaced by 'Chinnery's Remarks', or 'Chinnery says...') Three dates — 1814, 1816, 1821 — appear at different points of the manuscript, and the project seems to have foundered in the latter year, when Chinnery went to Serampore. Mrs. Browne returned to England shortly afterwards, and died there in 1828.

The Treatise can be considered together with Chinnery's letters to Maria Browne, which cover much the same period (May 1813 to July 1821), and which contain applications of many of the principles enunciated in the Treatise. Twelve years younger than Chinnery, Maria Roberts came out to India at the age of nineteen, and married Lieutenant (later Lieutenant-Colonel) Marmaduke Browne of the Bengal Artillery. Marmaduke Browne is said to have made a preliminary test of Maria's character by refraining from speaking to her;[3] if so, she received some compensation in her friendship with the effusive Chinnery. She was a talented amateur artist, who completed over a hundred miniatures and crayon portraits, together with a number of copies of miniatures by other artists; the list of her works includes the names of many of Chinnery's friends and patrons — Elliott, D'Oyly, Atkinson, Compton, Edmonstone, MacNabb, Rumbold, Hastings.[4]

The subject matter of both the Treatise and the letters ranges from theoretical principles to the practical handling of materials and pigments. Some of Chinnery's observations apply only to miniature painting on ivory, while others refer more broadly to oils and watercolours also. There are intriguing glimpses of studio practice and the use of accessories: the portrait painter is advised to sketch the attitude of a seated subject by placing him or her on a stool — 'Unless it be an Elderly Person who you Wish to Appear Lounging [;] in that case always Shew the back of the Chair or Couch'. In painting drapery, he suggests that a piece of fabric of the appropriate texture be kept close at hand, 'as the folds will be more Natural'. And when painting a miniature in which a sky background is intended, 'a Table Cloth placed immediately behind the Sitter' will show the true colour of the head.[5]

To preserve pencil drawing, Chinnery explains the process known as 'fixing' or 'egging' (the instruction 'fix' often appears in shorthand on his drawings). His recipe for 'egging' runs as follows:

> The Egg (the white of it) is to be beat up into a thick Froth — so thick that when the plate or other Vessel it is beat up in is turned over it will not move — This is to be sloped a little & from it a *Glaze* will run & this is to be used only — The Glaze above is to be used with a flat broad Brush, & to be put over in Ribbands...[6]

When Chinnery moved to the China coast, he often resorted to congee (rice gruel) as an alternative fixative; congee is mentioned in several shorthand notes on Chinnery's later drawings.

While egg whites were used as a preservative, the yolks could serve another useful function, in the process of 'stopping out'. The yolks should be mixed with hair powder into a paste (the Treatise proposes), and the paste may then be applied to the paper in the exact shape which the artist wishes to remain white. When the paste has dried hard, watercolour can be painted on to the paper as a whole; then the area of hardened paste is removed with a sharp knife, and any remaining marks are rubbed away with a clean piece of bread, leaving a white area of the required shape.[7]

Bread, in Chinnery's view, was the only means of removing pencil cleanly. No doubt he recalled that, during his years at the Royal Academy Schools, the students had had their bread removed, because 'they have a practise of throwing the bread, allowed to them by the Academy for rubbing out, at each other, so as to waste so much that the Bill for bread sometimes amounts to Sixteen Shillings a week...' The President, Benjamin West, had proposed that without bread the students would 'pay more attention to their outlines'.[8] As a teacher Chinnery adopted a less severe attitude, but he did insist that the bread must be perfectly clean, as clean as the paper itself.[9]

Tints and colours form a major theme of the Treatise and the letters to Mrs. Browne. In a letter of 5 June 1813 Chinnery sketches a diagram to illustrate his theory of the radiation of colours, in which 'things get lower, duller, *cooler* & weaker' as one moves from yellow to orange, red, violet and purple. A portrait head which is painted in warm colours will appear to stand out, if the background is painted in colours which are progressively cooler as the artist moves away from the head.[10] (Here Chinnery follows Reynolds, who, taking the great Venetian artists as his model, had recommended the use of 'warm' reds and yellows for the principal, illuminated subject, set against a background of 'cool' blues, greens and greys.[11]) That Mrs. Browne did not understand all the ramifications of Chinnery's principles is clear from his letters to her, and not at all surprising, since his instructions are often elliptical and obscure. For particular effects, however, he makes specific proposals: 'Lake & Lamp black — A Beautiful Shadow Color for Water Color Drawings — Indigo Lake & Burnt Sienna a More beautiful Color for Ivory Pictures or *very* delicate paper ones'.[12]

Chinnery was strongly attached to vermilion, as many of his portraits and landscape paintings demonstrate. Possibly he was aware that Reynolds, after using carmine for much of his earlier career, had come to realise its fugitive nature and turned to vermilion instead.[13] 'There is something about Vermilion very curious', he wrote to Mrs. Browne,

'Vermilion is Vermilion — but Newman does contrive to make *his* cakes of a very different Colour to all others — I have now a bit this big ☐ only & for a Cake would willingly give 100Rs — it is the only colour wh. does for Coats at all...'[14] The Treatise offers specific advice on its use: for flesh colour in watercolours, use a solution of vermilion in portraits of the majority of children and women; for certain others, and for fair men, use a mixture of vermilion with a little carmine; for darker men, lake and 'Burnt Terra di Sienna'.[15]

The colouring of drapery poses special problems (the Treatise observes), and white drapery is the most difficult of all, for its treatment must be in accordance with the particular face depicted. 'Mrs A's white Drapery who has a red face will differ Exceedingly from Mrs B's Face with only a beautiful Bloom — & so on to pale & Sallow...' Transparent drapery acquires a pinkish hue where the flesh is seen through it. Drapery and curtains of coloured silk or velvet call (in miniature painting) for the colour to be laid on in a very thick wash mixed with gum; then, before this is dry, 'the light Parts Representing Folds to be taken off with a Dry brush'.[16]

On a theoretical level, Chinnery's principles follow in the tradition of the *Discourses* of Sir Joshua Reynolds. He advises the portrait painter to follow 'general forms' characteristic of a class, rather than individual idiosyncrasies; and while a close study of nature is necessary, it is not sufficient, for the artist must view the subject with 'a poet's eye'. Moreover, the artist should be prepared to depart from nature in order to achieve a masterly effect. 'Nothing can be well done *from* nature that is not equally well done without it — Colouring most particularly.'[17]

An allied proposition is that the single-minded pursuit of 'likeness' is liable to lead an aspiring painter astray. 'It is air, Grace, & something not very describable, wh. makes pictures.'[18] More specifically, if a ball is represented as perfectly round, it will look vulgar; one must consult 'that *feeling* and *Conception* of Picture which regulates the Painter's Eye...Nature is not picture altho' picture is Nature.'[19] This is once again a theme of the *Discourses*, in which Reynolds had insisted that 'a mere copier of nature can never produce any thing great; can never raise and enlarge the conceptions...', and that the grace and the likeness of a portrait lay more in the 'general air' than in 'the exact similitude of every feature'.[20]

On other occasions Chinnery's recommendations

lead in an apparently opposite direction. Genius is all very well, he warns, but method and patient application are the essential elements — '9/10ths of our Art is Mechanical'.[21] Such changes of emphasis, hedging and qualification are also reminiscent of Reynolds, who was well aware of the treacherous ambiguities inherent in the terms 'imitation', 'genius' and 'nature'. Reynolds observed that art involved 'perfections that are incompatible with each other', and 'contrary excellences' which cannot be united.[22] As Chinnery instructed Mrs. Browne, 'Sir Joshua in his admirable, & never enough to be admired, Lectures, observes that the Art is full of apparent Contradictions — whether this is the fault of the Art itself, or from the want of Language to express ourselves rightly one can't say...'[23] Chinnery felt this difficulty keenly, since he was obliged to bring his theoretical pronouncements to bear on the particular strengths and weaknesses of Maria Browne's work.

Chinnery prided himself on his teaching. 'There is not so great an *Art* as teaching', he wrote complacently to Mrs. Browne, justifying to her his light-hearted approach and misquoting Pope in defence of his methods.[24] Judging from his letters to her and from Harriet Low's Macau journal, one can at least infer that he was a stimulating tutor of those whose company he enjoyed. He was informal, flexible in approach, and inventive in vocabulary, urging Maria Browne to achieve 'pulpiness' in a portrait, to represent hair as 'wirey' rather than 'cottony', to capture the 'Snug Cosy Attitude' of a child on a sofa, and give a 'soft fleshy look' to a woman's cheek.[25] To Maria Browne he offered a good deal of encouragement, mixed with occasional outbursts of forthright censure which, if they had not been presented in a spirit of good-humoured raillery, might have been difficult to accept. Susceptible to flattery himself, Chinnery was not inclined to flatter fellow artists. In January 1819 another dedicated amateur, James Baillie Fraser, took his paintings to Chinnery, 'and of course got them criticised', he reported in his diary, with a touch of wounded pride.[26]

Both for teaching and for his own reference, Chinnery developed a system in which the various processes involved in creating a watercolour were divided into nine steps. These were arranged in a diagram of squares, three rows of three. 'He divides Said rules into nine stages — & makes his Scholars Draw nine Squares & numbers them...', wrote Maria

Browne. She drew nine squares herself and began to fill in the rules, but evidently found that they would not fit into the diagram, and so started afresh without the squares, under the heading 'Landscapes'. The instructions are long and sometimes difficult to understand, as Mrs. Browne herself confessed. (To complicate matters further, a single square may contain two or more parts, so that the division into nine is somewhat arbitrary; on certain of his drawings Chinnery substitutes a diagram of eight squares, two rows of four.) A tentative summary follows of Chinnery's nine stages, as set out by Mrs. Browne,[27] with some adjustment in the light of the notes accompanying Chinnery's drawings.

1. Slight charcoal sketch, followed by a firm outline in medium lead pencil, drawn as accurately as possible.

2. Add half tints, using neutral tint for the sky and distance, and lake and lamp black for the foreground; each plane should be darker as the painter advances to the foreground. Then add a darker tint of the same colour. At this stage all the objects in the landscape should appear white, as if they were made of chalk or ivory.

3. According to Mrs. Browne, the most important stage, but the hardest to comprehend. According to 'Chinnery's Theory of Air & Vapour', particles of daylight are compressed in the middle of the picture (in the horizontal plane of a picture), and thinly scattered at the outer edges. This effect is applied in grey tints over land and sky (water is to be left alone). Then add 'General Shadow over all but the lights, and darken the foreground to throw back the distant objects. After this, the last of the 'grey stages', the scene will appear as if viewed 'through Spectacles covered with Crape'.

4. Colouring now begins. Wash the whole composition, except for any lake or sea, with yellow ochre (deeper for sunset than for daylight), using a broad, flat brush, starting with the light parts and radiating towards the darker areas.

5. This stage, described by Chinnery as 'the crude state of coloring', consists of a number of detailed instructions related to particular elements in the composition. For instance, apply indigo washes to the sky; touch clouds with yellow in the light parts and pink lake in the dark parts; colour hills and foliage in yellow ochre and burnt sienna.

6. Wash the whole with a large camel brush and clean water. Where necessary, remove surplus colour with a fitch, and smooth off rough edges with a sponge brush. Then 'Wash up the whole picture so as to have the Effect of a Crayon Drawing'.

7. Create 'forms' in the sky, using Prussian blue and indigo, and tinting clouds with chrome yellow and red lead. Add highlights in foreground foliage with touches of chrome and yellow ochre. Many more specific recommendations follow here, including the various colours required for different areas of shadow, such as 'for Shadows of Earth & Building — Lake & lamp black mixed with the local colors *chiefly* burnt Siena'.

8. Indicate shadowed 'cavities' in open scenery by neutral tint. Indicate other kinds of cavity — in enclosed scenery, or apertures in huts, or the spaces between adjacent rocks — by means of sepia and gum; for cavities in lighter parts of the foreground, use a mixture of brown pink and burnt sienna.

9. General retouching throughout the picture. Use a fitch to soften all parts which require blending, and remove unwanted elements with a sponge brush. To create an effect of gravel or irregularity in the foreground, paint forms in sepia on waxed paper, 'then before it dries press it Smoothly over the part with your finger & the impression will Come off beautifully'.

Chinnery continued to use this system (or a system very similar to it) during his later career on the China coast. Although the instructions noted by Maria Browne refer to landscape, they were also applicable to portraits, with only minor modifications. A page of portrait sketches dated 12 and 19 March 1847, in the Victoria and Albert Museum, is inscribed in a combination of shorthand, numbers and letters. Following Geoffrey Bonsall's translation of the shorthand, this reads:

Portrait ought to have three distinct stages.

1. DSS.OL — BOC. BOC.CS. black only bold and exactly squared and decided.

2. 34 *full black and white only* (body colour). 2345671 [last numeral indistinct] (AC.CP.SS.)

mosaic squared bright tinting singly to each not hurriedly.

3. R.&.C. as sparingly as possible.

These stages which have a reference to the head apply to every part of the picture.[28]

Chinnery's abbreviations are not always decipherable or consistent. The numerical sequences clearly refer to the successive stages in producing a picture. 'DSS.OL' seems to mean 'Draw simple sketch outline', and 'BOC' perhaps 'Basic original colour'. 'R.&.C.', which appears frequently on Chinnery's drawings, means 'Repair and Completion'. Other abbreviations which are sometimes found are 'PO' (Perfect Outline), 'FGS' (Full General Shadow), and 'Cavs.' (Cavities). Abbreviations for individual pigments, which occur frequently in the Treatise, are more straightforward: 'Y.O.' for Yellow Ochre, 'B.U.' for Burnt Umber, 'B.T.S.' for Burnt Terra de Sienna, 'B.P.' for Brown Pink, 'N.T.' for Neutral Tint, and 'M.T.' for Middle Tint.

All the instructions above refer to watercolour painting; topics which apply only to oil painting — such as varnishing — are not raised. But the matter of a final coat of varnish, so essential to the preservation of an oil painting, must have caused Chinnery some anxiety. Both in India and on the China coast, he was often asked to supply portraits of individuals who were about to return to Europe or North America; if, however, an oil painting was varnished shortly after the paint had been applied, there was a danger that the turpentine content of the natural resin varnish would combine with the fresh paint layer, causing discoloration and making it difficult for the varnish to be cleaned off at a later date. An interval of six months or a year between painting and varnishing was often recommended. So it seems likely that some of Chinnery's paintings were still unvarnished when they were shipped back to the West. On the back of one picture — of a Tanka boatwoman (Colour Plate 70) — his instructions survive, a forlorn appeal written on a piece of paper (with the year torn off at the right-hand margin) attached to the back of the stretcher: 'Mr Chinnery begs the favor of any artist into whose hands this picture might be put to varnish it with a coat of strong mastic *varnish* — Macao China Decr. 6th...'

# APPENDIX ii

## *Chinnery's Shorthand*

The use of shorthand in England can be dated to Elizabethan times. Charles I wrote letters in shorthand, and by the middle of the eighteenth century a dozen different systems were in circulation. Of these the Gurney system became pre-eminent. Thomas Gurney developed his notation in the 1720s, adapting a system which had been set out by William Mason fifty years before. The earliest surviving edition of Thomas Gurney's manual, entitled *Brachygraphy: or Short Writing made Easy...*, is dated 1753.

By this time Thomas Gurney had been appointed Shorthand Writer of the Old Bailey lawcourts, and his system gained official recognition as the shorthand employed in the Houses of Parliament, in government committees, in lawsuits and in courts martial. Many momentous judicial and parliamentary events were recorded in Gurney shorthand, including the trials of Warren Hastings (taken down by Joseph Gurney, son of Thomas) and of Queen Caroline. The physician and poet Erasmus Darwin, a friend of Thomas Gurney's, commemorated the system in verse ('...Gurney's Arts the fleeting Word congeal...'), and Byron referred to it in *Don Juan*, contriving to rhyme 'journey' with 'Gurney'.[1]

By the end of Chinnery's lifetime the Gurney system faced a strong challenge from two other methods, those of Samuel Taylor and Isaac Pitman; but Gurney's textbook was still in print in the 1880s, and his notation was in use in legislatures as far afield as Victoria and New South Wales. The parliamentary committees on the Indian mutiny, the Jameson raid and the O'Connell trial were all recorded in Gurney shorthand.[2]

The Gurney system is based upon spelling rather than phonetics (although there is a phonetic element), and was thought to be easier to read than its rival systems, but more difficult to learn. The early Gurney handbooks are as daunting as Latin primers, with their tables of persons, moods and tenses. In addition to the basic vocabulary, the eighteenth-century student had to memorise long lists of arbitrary signs for such words and phrases as 'tabernacle' and 'world without end', which assisted the shorthand writer in taking down sermons and biblical texts.[3] William Chinnery, the father and presumably the teacher of the artist, used the Gurney system to write out the New Testament and the Book of Psalms, and so did a certain Josiah Lewis, who completed the New Testament in a hundred hours and the Psalms in thirty.[4]

The Gurney system was gradually streamlined by omitting the more obscure moods, tenses and ecclesiastical references. Some shorthand writers developed their own modifications, but George Chinnery kept closely to the prescribed Gurney system, which he wrote neatly and fluently, with a minimum of correction. Little shorthand is to be found in his early drawings; it was not until his second decade in India that he saw the full potential of the discipline which he had learned as a child.

During his years in Bengal and on the China coast, Chinnery's shorthand became an essential aspect of his drawings. When he sold or gave away a drawing, he did not rub out his shorthand notes; when he reinforced a pencil sketch with an ink outline, he often went over the shorthand at the same time, and sometimes added further annotations in ink. He seldom signed his drawings, but the shorthand in itself functions as a kind of signature, since it was not used by his followers (although it has been found in a series of deceptive modern fakes, which are drawn on old paper).

Considered as an element of a picture, shorthand is generally less intrusive than orthodox script; only the most practised readers of Gurney shorthand — an extremely small proportion of his potential audience — could take in its meaning at a glance. Chinnery did not arrange his shorthand notes in any particular spatial pattern, but in some finished drawings he took care to deploy the signs in such a way as to minimise their disruptive effect. Yet one cannot conclude that the shorthand is entirely neutral in its contribution. To the uncomprehending viewer it adds a dimension of mystery and exoticism, as might a hieroglyphic inscription on an ancient Egyptian obelisk.

# APPENDIX iii

# *Chinnery's Studio, as described in* Tom Raw, the Griffin

A visit to Chinnery's studio in Calcutta, from Sir Charles D'Oyly's illustrated poem *Tom Raw, the Griffin* (1828), Canto V, pp.113ff.

### I

HAIL, graphic art! The prototype of Nature
In all her varied forms most exquisite,
That stamps a duplicate of face and feature,
As penna-polygraphs, now doubly write;
That death of its obliterating might
Plunders, and brings before us our progenitors —
It matters not how long obscured from sight, —
Adam and Eve, Augustus, or the senators
Of Rome; — though dead for centuries, once more
 rise up monitors.

### II

E'en the snug parlour, twelve by ten, displays
Europe and Asia, Afric and America,
Their scenes, their clime, and customs to our gaze,
Or favourite towns and counties, — Ayr, or Kerrick, or
Whatever you most wish to contemplate,
But which ne'er fail to put you in a merry key
And in the reach of all, — at moderate rate,
For who can't buy a drawing, may secure a plate.

### III

But chief to absent lovers dear, who gaze
Hours, days, and years, on imitative charms,
Press the cold iv'ry to their hearts, and raise
The image of their lost one to their arms.
Oh! how imagination the heart warms,
And how delightful is fond fancy's flight —
Yet after all — what is it thus disarms
Absence of pain? — Four inches — no, not quite
Of ivory — a little carmine, — red, and white!

### IV

Touched by a tiny brush of camel's hair,
A little water, and — But oh! not these
Alone could seize the heart; — they have their share;

But 'tis the efforts of the mind that please,
And raised to eminence unrivalled Greece. —
'Hands paint not — 'tis the working of the brains!'
As Opie said to such as came to tease
Him, — asking how he coloured eyes and veins?
*Multum in parvo* — much in little — for their pains?

### V

'But what's the meaning of this declamation
'On art?' we think we hear the eager cry,
Why, gentle readers, 'tis a proclamation
Before we usher in great Ch—n—y![1]
Whom Tom knew not — (the greater sinner — he,)
That giant man in face and scenery,
Whose works have pleased alike in East and West,
Who looks at nature with an eye bold and free,
And steals her charms more keenly than the rest,
Who, with less real merit, better line their nest.

### VI

'You have not been at Ch—n—y's, I think?'
Said Randy to his friend, one afternoon.
'No,' replied Tom, 'that is a wanting link
In my career, which I must add, and soon.' —
'Well then,' cried Randy, 'I will grant the boon
'Of shewing you to this most skilled of painters:
'You'll be delighted with him — if in tune;
'He's always in his shop, and will not stint us
'In hearty welcomes, as his lungs will soon acquaint us.'

### VII

In Garston's Buildings,[2] opposite the church,
Formed of the overplus of Town Hall brick,
And just behind the houses of John B—ch,[3]
Up a vile lane whose odour makes one sick
Resides this famous limner — never stick
At vain preliminaries of rapping knockers,
To see if he's at home — go in, and kick
The peons, that, slumbering on the stair-case, look as
(But yet they are not) barriers in your way. Odd
 zookers!

### VIII

Laugh as you please, till in his atelier
You see the ablest limner in the land,
With mild and gentle look inviting near,
Palette on thumb and maplestick in hand,
And saying, 'Sirs — what may be your command?'
'We would not interrupt you! — Mr. Raw!' — .
'Your most obedient — Do I understand
'Your friend desires to sit? — Pray, does he draw? —
''Tis a great art — and always practised with a
    claw!¹⁴ (*éclat*)

### IX

'What! always at your punning?' — 'Pon my honour,
'My good friend Randy, I delight in puns,
'I relish them as epicures a konnah,
'They *go off* just as sharp as *Mantons guns.*
'Talking of fire-arms, I remember once
'A friend informing me he could command
'Four of them always ready to advance.
'*I* said immediately, — You understand —
'Then, certainly, you always have a *stock in hand!*

### X

'But did you ever hear the pun I let off
' 'Bout Wellington and the Green Man and Still?' —
'Phoo! Phoo!' said Randy; 'when you're fairly set off
'There's no controlling you till you've had your fill. —
'Come shew us all your portraits — Where's Miss
    Frill? —
'Raw's gazing on your half-done things like mad.'
'*Is he quite raw?*' the punster whispered, — 'Will
'He *bear a dressing?* He's a comely lad,
'*Raw, dressing, — palate, — taste, eat up.* Faith, not so
    bad!'

### XI

At every word an equivoque was wrought,
And conversation hobbled on in quirks,
Or grave or merry — still it mattered naught,
Bad puns ensued with nostril moving jerks,
With notes and annotations, snorts and smirks,
When conversaton failed their sense to take in.
He drew them, even, from his beauteous works
From which the friends were all the beauties raking,
And observations on his excellences making.

### XII

Their ready recogniton of those faces
That nightly grace the course, or public ball,
Or mix, among the concourse at the races,
The conversazioni at the hall,
Or at the burrah konnahs — quite enthral
Th' enthusiastic artist — 'Aye, sir, these
'Are likenesses that make observers call
'Out — such alone my greediness appease;
'But pray just look at this chef-d'oeuvre, if you
    please.'

### XIII

So saying, from the wall, turned right about,
A kit-cat of a lady he displayed,
'Now if this does not make you both cry out
'I'll burn my palette, and give up the trade —
'What! — not one word nor observation made?
'Perhaps you're not acquainted with the lady?' —
'I — think — I've seen her,' — Randy cried, — afraid
Of a wrong guess, — 'it is not Miss — Makeready,
'She's pale and thin — this like a country-girl on
    May-day.'

### XIV

'Delightful! — charming!' — with sarcastic grin,
Uttered the man of paint — ' 'tis *so* agreeable
'When praise unqualified one hopes to win,
'To find folks sorely puzzled when they see a belle,
'So much admired, and — all well knowing me able
'To draw to life the hardest countenances,
'To hear my works — (reckoned inimitable),
'Hem'd at and haw'd at — Can't account for fancies! —
'To satisfy the world — Oh, Lord! how great the
    chance is!!!'

### XV

'Nay! Nay! my friend — the fault no doubt is ours —
'Tell us at once, who is it?' — 'Why — Miss Shuffle,'
'Miss Shuffle! — so it is — What monstrous powers
'You have — but we must not your temper ruffle,
'Nay — what a face you make — Come no more
    scuffle,' —
'I *live by making faces* — that you know,
'So never mind — mine I will strive to muffle —
'And now, in faith — as public pictures flow
'Like *bores* — (they're *bores* indeed!) I must to
    painting go.'

### XVI

And off he marched, with, 'Gentlemen, good day,
'I'm sorry that my duty interferes
'With inclination — hast'ning me away,' —
And then he tuck'd his locks above his ears.
Dids't ever mark the monstrous comb he wears,

A semi-circular of tortoiseshell?
Which, like Diana's crescent, tops his hairs
In inverse ratio — once it graced the swell
Of crinal horrors that adorned an Indian belle!

### XVII

Meanwhile, within our hero's breast arose
The wish to have his ruddy face portrayed,
With apprehensions how to pay for't — Those
Who've pros and cons can judge the fuss it made;
But, he to his friend, his wish no secret made.
The crash of crock'ry ware, and knives and forks,
Shewed that the artist at his tiffin played,
The fiz of ripe pale ale, and sound of corks,
That he was then employed on very *sparkling works.*

### XVIII

Just at that moment, a fine clear bass voice,
Warbling out, — 'Huntsman rest,' was heard to quaver,
The tones were deep, the execution choice,
Though much of the bassoon it seemed to savour.
'Now,' — Randy said ' 's the time to ask a favour,'
And it was proffered in the very nick;
Such times are chosen by the groaning slave, or
Appointment seeker — practised in the trick,
When, after meals — Great men their teeth,
    contented, pick.

### XIX

For there was never mortal, yet, succeeded
In any boon upon a stomach empty,
By peevish humours is a meal preceded,
And growling pshaws! and pishes! that ne'er tempt ye
To make their suit — Reflection will exempt ye
From this restraint, — when tired jaws have taken
Their utmost, and the finish'd bowl's redempt. — Ye
Then may gain it — or I am much mistaken;
They, who act otherwise, may never save their bacon.

### XX

'Talk not of price, dear Randy, — when a friend
'Whispers a wish — We'll settle that at leisure;
'Meanwhile, to time, I must, perforce, attend.
'Where is my book? — I'm pressed beyond all
    measure, —
'Days growing short — ships sailing — giving
    pleasure
'To all — but — let-us-see. — Monday? — that's full, —
'Tuesday, to finish Mrs Roundhead's *treasure,*
'A little ugly knave. — A young John Bull —
'Wednesday, — Miss Fribble — Thursday', —
    (reading), 'if it's cool.'

### XXI

'Lady Hysteric — reasonable condition!
'when hours to me are just great heaps of gold! —
'Friday, at ten, Miss Frill, — elev'n Ram Kishen —
'We'll put the baboo off — *He* will not scold —
'Friday, at half-past ten, then, — hot or cold,
'I shall expect to see you — Mister Raw —
'At two I have another sitter — hold —
'The second sitting Thursday sennight — pshaw!
'That's full — well — Friday — Next month I have
    time to draw!'

### XXII

The day and hour arrived, — Our hero went,
In full apparel, to be fairly typed,
The comb and brush had done their parts, and lent
Charms to the flowing locks — his face was wiped,
From every soorky stain[5] — his belt was piped,
And silver epaulet fresh scoured and polished,
A white silk handkerchief with yellow striped,
(The red, by constant friction, being demolished.)
And stock aspiring — which was nothing of the
    smallest.

### XXIII

On elevated floor, young Thomas sat,
Calling up animated look and smile;
The limner had his canvas, and all that,
Flourished his charcoal ends, and snuffed a while,
Then talked — Tom's *mauvaise honte* to reconcile,
'The body more in front, — not — *so* — much —
    quite,'
And up he stept, — 'just so — the very style, —
'Now look at me, I beg — more full the sight,
'The figure straighter — head turned sharply to the
    right!'[6]

### XXIV

But, as the sitting to a painter's irksome,
We'd rather seize upon the opportunity
To roam about his room, and try to work some
More animating sport for our community,
For spice of former dulness some immunity;
It is an olio, certainly, of oddities,
And we ought, long ere now, to have shewn it t'ye,
Passing the furniture, and such commodities.
To have such useful things — the due of every body
    'tis.

### XXV

*Imprimis,* o'er the walls are charcoal dashings
Of sudden thoughts — or imitative keys,[7]

Hung on a nail — and various coloured splashings —
The shape of frames, of houses, horses, trees,
Prismatic circles[8] — five dot effigies;[9]
Notes of short hand — a card for five o'clock,
Lord M. desires the honour of Mr C.'s
'Company,' in conspicuous station stuck,
To shew the deference paid his talent — or his luck!

### XXVI

Close to the window is a dressing table
Where, erst, in miniatures engaged, he toiled,[10]
And near a chair and hookah, when he's able
To contemplate the canvas he has oiled:
In this enjoyment were he ever foiled,
Adieu to talent — 'Tis his next great pleasure
To painting, he has often said (and smiled),
The sitting over, to devote his leisure
In smoky meditation o'er his new wrought treasure.

### XXVII

A teapoy groaning with odd tomes and scraps
Of undigested journals, stands behind,
Sketch books, surmounted by his flannel caps,
Loose prints, and notes — some very far from kind,
With pretty little chits from dames that wind
Him round their finger — lawyers' letters, dunning,
For clients, most solicitous to grind,
And drafts of letters, full of wit and punning,
And house accounts that still keep on forever running.

### XXVIII

In one damp corner — stewed without reflection,
Because 'tis never wanted — pines a Vatican,
And, of the finest plates, a rare collection. —
(Can he so thoughtless be? — ay, can he? — that he
    can! —
And, when I tell you plainly — you'll see what he can
Neglect), — they're mostly borrowed from collectors,
And buried in this motley graphic catacom',
Eaten by rats and white ants — no respecters
Of Raphael, Titian, Rubens, — Ajaxes and Hectors.

### XXIX

What lovely face is that which hangs among
Th' unfinished pictures — in a faded frame? —
Oh! we could gaze, nor think that gazing wrong,
Though rumour has been busy with her fame:
Romney portrayed those matchless charms — a
    name
That next to Reynolds sparkles in the art,
Whose sweetness merits that superior claim,
Which meretricious glare can ne'er impart,
Driving his matchless colour brush right through the
    heart.

### XXX

And we have seen Sir Joshua there — a gem
Or two, within this store room of bijoux,
The artist on his knees, adoring them,
And swallowing greedily his tints and hues —
Then starting back — then forward — loath to lose
A moment in the ardent meditation,
Then fancying that he stood in his great shoes,
Tracing between them great assimilation,
Except his knighthood merely, — and his reputation.

# APPENDIX iv

# *Artists and Amateurs associated with Chinnery in India and on the China Coast*

**Henrietta Mary Alcock (d.1853)**
Daughter of the sculptor John Bacon, Henrietta was married to John Rutherford Alcock (see below) in May 1841, and accompanied him to China. A collection of her drawings and watercolours of Chinese subjects (together with a smaller number drawn by her husband) also includes views derived from Chinnery.[1] She died in Shanghai in March 1853.

*Henrietta Mary Alcock, British Consulate at Kolungsoo (Gulangyu), Amoy. Pencil and watercolours, signed with initials, inscribed as title and dated 1844.* Martyn Gregory Gallery

**Sir John Rutherford Alcock (1809-1897)**
While enrolled as a medical student, Rutherford Alcock also practised in the studio of the sculptor Sir Francis Chantrey, and his wax models won two medals awarded by the Society of Arts. He was forced to abandon his surgical career when illness caused a partial paralysis of his hands; instead he became one of the first British Consuls in China, following the Treaty of Nanking. Alcock was appointed Consul at Fuzhou (1844) and Shanghai (1846), serving subsequently as Minister Plenipotentiary to Japan (1859). On his travels he was able to make a number of sketches, although these were less accomplished than his wife's (see above). His biography[2] is illustrated with several drawings by the Alcocks and by Chinnery, and copies after Chinnery.

**James Atkinson (1780-1852)**
Atkinson made his way to India as a medical officer of the East India Company. In 1805 he was appointed assistant surgeon at Backergunge, to the south of Dacca, where he may first have met Chinnery. Atkinson's proficiency as a Persian linguist attracted the notice of Lord Minto, who invited him to Calcutta in 1813. Here he served as Assistant Assay Master of the Calcutta Mint. A poet, a translator and an amateur artist, he produced a number of small watercolour portrait heads of notable British figures in India.[3] His portrait of Lord Minto in the National Portrait Gallery is almost certainly a copy after Chinnery.[4]

In 1815 his own portrait in miniature was painted by Maria Browne, Chinnery's pupil.[5] In 1817 he became Superintendent of the *Calcutta Government Gazette*, in whose pages Chinnery's name frequently appeared. He was a member of the D'Oyly circle (see D'Oyly below): on 26 December 1818 he and Chinnery were fellow witnesses at the marriage of John Hadley D'Oyly, and he collaborated with Sir Charles D'Oyly in the creation of *Tom Raw, the Griffin* (see Appendix iii).[6] Atkinson served as superintending surgeon in the first Afghan War, and retired from India in 1847; he survived Chinnery by two months.

His wife Jane was a student of Chinnery, as is clear from a sketchbook formerly in the possession of J.S. Maas & Co., London. Their son, George Franklin Atkinson of the Bengal Engineers (1822-59), was also an artist, and the author of the well-known illustrated book *Curry and Rice* (1860).

**Marciano Baptista (1826-1896)**
Born in Macau and educated at the seminary of São José, Baptista was copying drawings by Chinnery in the 1840s. By 1857 he had moved to Hong Kong, where he advertised himself as a pupil of Chinnery, and produced topographical watercolours of locations on the China coast (see colour illustration

p.285); in his treatment of sky and clouds, in particular, he remained close to the example of his mentor. In Hong Kong he also practised scene painting and photography, and occasionally painted in oils. A number of his descendants, in succeeding generations, have also practised as artists.[7]

### Walford Thomas Bellairs (c.1794-1850)
Lieutenant Bellairs came to the China coast in 1845 as an Admiralty Agent in the Contract Mail Steam Service. His topographical drawings, in a sharply linear style, record his travels to China via Egypt and India (see colour illustration p.285). His visit to Hong Kong in February 1846, aboard the P. & O.'s paddle steamer *Lady Mary Wood,* coincided with Chinnery's period of residence on the island, and Bellairs was the owner of at least one Chinnery drawing.[8]

### Auguste Borget (1809-1877)
A pupil of Jean-Antoine Gudin and a close friend of Honoré de Balzac, the French-born Auguste Borget arrived at the China coast in August 1838, in the course of a journey around the world, and remained for nearly a year. In the autumn of 1838 William Prinsep (q.v.) went sketching with Borget in Macau (see colour illustration p.288); he found the Frenchman's portfolio 'rich with scenes from South America, Sandwich Islands and China, and he was a pleasant fellow into the bargain'.[9] In the following year Borget fell ill in Calcutta, where he was nursed by Mary Prinsep. His drawings of Bengal strongly suggest the influence of Chinnery, although his paintings maintain a distinct style. After his return to Paris he exhibited paintings of eastern subjects, and his drawings were published in several books (see Bibliography; see also Sotheby Parke Bernet (Hong Kong) sale of 4 December 1978, lots 1-15).

A friendship between Borget and Chinnery is indicated by an informal portrait drawing of Borget by Chinnery,[10] and a painting of Macau by Borget, in Gideon Nye's collection, which had been 'an interchanged gift to Mr. Chinnery'.[11] Borget also supplied some ideas to the older artist: two sketches by Chinnery each bear the shorthand inscription 'a design of Mr. Borget'.

### Maria Browne (1786-1828)
In 1805 Maria Roberts sailed to India with her brother, an East India Company agent, and on 14 March 1806 she was married in Calcutta to Marmaduke Browne (later Lieutenant-Colonel) of the Bengal Artillery. She was a dedicated amateur

*Auguste Borget, Tanka boat people. Pencil, inscribed and dated 'Macau n.bre 1838'.* Private collection

painter of miniatures and crayon portraits, who kept a list of her work from the year of her arrival until 1821[12]; shortly after this she returned to England, suffering from ill health, and in 1828 she died at her family home in Somerset.

In India her sitters included members of the Elliot and D'Oyly families, and many other prominent figures in the British community. When Chinnery came to Calcutta, Maria Browne received instruction from him, and they became close friends; a group of Chinnery's letters to her, extending from 1813 to 1821, are preserved in the British Library, as is the draft 'Treatise' on the theory and practice of miniature, watercolour and oil painting, which was written down at different times by Chinnery and Maria Browne together.[13] (See Appendix i for a discussion of Chinnery's methods and principles, as revealed in these letters and the Treatise.)

### James Thomas Caldwell, R.N. (d.1849)
Commissioned Lieutenant in 1834, Caldwell served in the West Indies and the Mediterranean before participating in the first Opium War; he became Flag Lieutenant to Rear-Admiral Cochrane, and was promoted Commander in 1844. He was a companion of Edward Cree (q.v.) at Canton in 1846. For an adaptation in watercolour by Caldwell of a Chinnery composition at Macau see Hong Kong Museum of Art, 1983, no.50.

### Edward Hodges Cree, R.N. (1814-1901)
As a naval surgeon Cree spent much of his career on foreign stations, including the Far East, where he was

posted during the years 1840-6 and 1848-50. As an artist he received some professional tuition in Portsmouth and in Malta, but he developed a highly individual and appealing style of his own, with which he vividly illustrated his journals. Cree encountered Chinnery at Hong Kong in February 1846 (see p.257), and two ink drawings included at this point in Cree's MS journals are evidently copies of Chinnery's work.[14]

### Mary Dalrymple

An album dated 1834, whose contents have now been dispersed, contained a series of copies by Mary Dalrymple of Chinnery's Macau drawings — some of them deceptively close to the originals — together with other drawings (including views of Madras) in her own manner. See Martyn Gregory Gallery catalogue 41, 1985.

*Sir Charles D'Oyly, Cattle in a landscape. Watercolours, inscribed on the reverse 'a failure by C. D'Oyly'.* Private collection

*Mary Dalrymple, Macau landscape. Pen and ink over pencil, inscribed 'copied from Chinnery'.* Private collection

### Sir Charles D'Oyly, 7th Baronet (1781-1845)

D'Oyly arrived in India in 1797, and probably met Chinnery late in 1807, in Calcutta. In February 1808 he was posted Collector of Dacca (Dhaka), where Chinnery joined him a few months later. The two men became close friends (see Chapter 6). Chinnery instructed and encouraged D'Oyly in his drawing: 'If you have watched my progress', D'Oyly wrote to Warren Hastings on 30 August 1813, 'you will be convinced how much improvement I have acquired under the able superintendence of Mr. Chinnery.'[15] In 1812 both D'Oyly and Chinnery moved to

Calcutta, where their association continued.

Some of D'Oyly's drawings and watercolours are recognisably copies or pastiches of Chinnery's work. The illustration above, a Chinnerian composition complete with a distant wisp of smoke, is inscribed with regretful honesty 'a failure by C. D'Oyly'. Nevertheless most of his work is clearly distinguishable from Chinnery's. He employed a variety of media, including detailed drawings, small watercolour vignettes, topographical oil paintings, etchings and lithographs.[16] Although under Chinnery's tutelage he declared himself opposed to 'littleness and minutiae of hand',[17] many of his

*Sir Charles D'Oyly, Bengal landscape. Etching.* Private collection

drawings of Bengal are highly worked with areas of dense cross-hatching or crowded with figures and animals; details vie for attention, often at the expense of the composition as a whole.

From 1821 until 1832 D'Oyly lived at Patna, initially as Opium Agent of Behar province and finally as Commercial Resident of Patna itself. Here (as in Calcutta) the D'Oylys welcomed amateur artists, and he founded an art society, mock-heroically entitled 'The United Patna and Gaya Society, and Behar School of Athens'.[18] In 1833 he went back to Calcutta as Senior Member of the Board of Customs, Salt, and Opium, and President of the Marine Board. He retired in 1838, and executed a number of drawings of Cape Town on his return journey to Britain.

Many sketchbooks by D'Oyly survive. A group of ninety-nine coats-of-arms, each set in an imaginary landscape and dated between August and October 1807, was sold at Sotheby's on 18 March 1986 (lot 6); in the same sale were two other albums of D'Oyly's Indian scenes, dated 1820 (lot 4) and 1829-32 (lot 5). A series of eighty-two drawings in the India Office Library, among them the original drawings for his publication *Sketches of the new road in a journey from Calcutta to Gyah* (1830), and a similar sketchbook is in Patna Museum. He was a witty interpreter of the human figure, as can be seen in his illustrations to Thomas Williamson's *The European in India* (1813) and *Tom Raw, the Griffin* ( see Appendix iii).

Other members of the D'Oyly family were also active as amateur artists, including Sir Charles Walters D'Oyly, 9th Baronet (1822-1900), whose Indian scenes are sometimes confused with those of the 7th Baronet.

### Lady Elizabeth Jane D'Oyly, née Ross (fl.1815-40)
The second wife of Sir Charles (q.v.), Eliza D'Oyly was a cousin of the Countess of Loudun, who married Governor-General Lord Hastings. A visitor to the D'Oylys' house at Patna praised her 'large and elegant mind, her taste, her sensibility; all others seem as beings of an inferior order'.[19] Her drawings are often to be found in albums together with her husband's, and some of her work was reproduced on his lithographic press.

### J.A. Durran (fl. 1830-55)
The French sea captain and opium trader Durran (also spelt Duran or Durand) was a close friend of Chinnery in the 1840s. Chinnery portrayed Durran at his easel, and Durran in turn sketched Chinnery at dinner (see p.254). Copies of Chinnery's work by Durran are to be found in an album presented to Dr. Watson (q.v.) by his friends in 1847 (Watson family collection).

### Hon. John Edmund Elliot (1788-1862)
The third son of the 1st Earl of Minto, John Elliot acted as his father's Private Secretary during the latter's term as Governor-General of India in 1807-13 (see colour illustration p.288). A sketchbook of Elliot's in the India Office Library, covering the years 1812-13, includes some fifteen drawings by Chinnery (see Archer 1969, vol.I, p.48); at this time Chinnery was on terms of friendship with several members of the Elliot family (see p. ), including John Elliot's wife, who also painted in watercolour (India Office Library). In Macau Chinnery must also have known John's cousin, Captain (later Admiral Sir) Charles Elliot, who was British Plenipotentiary to China in 1836-41, and had a group of Chinnery's works at his residence.[20]

### Mary Fendall (b.1794)
In 1816-17 Mary Fendall made a series of detailed drawings (India Office Library) of Java, where her father John Fendall had succeeded Raffles as Lieutenant-Governor. Returning to Calcutta, where John Fendall became a Member of the Supreme Council, Mary contributed designs to Sir Charles D'Oyly's lithographic press. In January 1830 she was married to his brother John Hadley D'Oyly, after the dissolution of his first marriage.

### Theodore-Auguste Fisquet (1813-1890)
As a young man Fisquet (who later became an Admiral in the French navy) accompanied the expedition of Auguste Nicolas Vaillant around the world; a number of his drawings were reproduced in lithograph in the published account of the voyage. This book also records the French travellers' meeting with Chinnery in Macau in January 1837, and their accompanying him to sketch a Chinese temple at a shaded promontory, with a passing junk.[21] The illustration on p.284, dated April 1838, is clearly a result of this sketching party.

### James Baillie Fraser (1783-1856)
The eldest of five brothers who worked in India, James Fraser arrived in Calcutta in January 1814 after spending several years managing the family's sugar plantations in Guiana (Guyana). He remained in India until 1821, pursuing a generally unsuccessful mercantile career but gaining in skill as an artist. He

*Theodore-Auguste Fisquet, The A-Ma Temple, Macau. Watercolours with scratching-out, signed and inscribed 'Pagode à Macao - D'ap. nature', and dated 'Avril 1838' on the reverse.* Hongkong and Shanghai Banking Corporation

travelled in the southern Himalayas with his impulsive brother William (1785-1835), who had been wounded during General Gillespie's attack on Kalanga (see p.133), and was eventually assassinated in Delhi. The resulting watercolours were engraved and published as *Views in the Himala Mountains* (1820).

In 1818 and 1819 James took frequent lessons from Chinnery in Calcutta, studying also under William Havell in 1818. In a letter of 24 July 1819 he referred to Chinnery as 'my friend, and one of my masters'.[22] Drawings by James Fraser in Chinnery's style survive, but Fraser's detailed, clear-cut scenes of the city —

published in aquatint as *Views of Calcutta and its Environs* (1824-6) — bear little trace of Chinnery's influence, following rather in the tradition of the Daniells' *Oriental Scenery*. James and William Fraser also commissioned a quantity of fine 'Company drawings' from Indian artists.

### Charlotte Fullarton (b.1810)
Charlotte Fullarton was born in Calcutta to John Fullarton, who was then an Assistant Surgeon; later he became known as a traveller and a defender of Tory economic policies. In 1834 he visited China, presumably with his daughter, who was responsible for a carefully-drawn 'Macao' title page derived from a composition of Chinnery (illus. Bonsall 1985, no. 40).

### George Hutchinson (1793-1852)
Hutchinson, of the Bengal Corps of Engineers, was commissioned Lieutenant in 1818 and retired in 1841 at the rank of Lieutenant-Colonel. During Chinnery's latter years in India Hutchinson was Superintendent and Director of the Foundry at Fort William. An album containing ninety-five pen-and-ink drawings of Bengal subjects, in the manner of Chinnery, was sold Christie's (South Kensington) 25 May 1989 (no. 131).

### John Willes Johnson, R.N. (b.1793)
After serving as Flag Lieutenant to Admiral Pellew in

*Captain John Willes Johnson, R.N., A junk off the China coast. Pen and ink and watercolours.* Private collection

*Marciano Baptista, The Western settlement, Fuzhou. Pencil and watercolours, signed with initials on original mount.* Mr. and Mrs. R.J.F. Brothers

*Lieutenant Walford Thomas Bellairs, R.N., The English church at Pulo Penang (St. George's). Pen and ink and watercolours, inscribed as title and dated 1846.* Datuk Lim Chong Keat

the Mediterranean, Willes Johnson was posted to China on board the *Wolverine,* at the rank of Commander and (from 1846) Captain. He painted watercolours of the China coast in a sketchy manner, but he also owned watercolours by Chinnery and attempted to copy them; occasionally he worked in oils.[23]

### William Wynne Lodder
Commissioned in 1834, Lodder served on the China coast with the 59th Regiment of Foot; he retired from the army in 1865 as an honorary Major-General. An album of his sketches in the Hong Kong Museum of Art includes a number of drawings inspired by Chinnery, and one explicitly copied from him (see Bonsall 1985, nos. 47-8).

### Harriet Low (1809-1877)
In 1829 Harriet Low sailed to China from her native Salem, Massachusetts, together with her aunt and her uncle, the merchant William Henry Low. The Lows returned in 1834; Harriet married John Hillard of Boston in 1836, and lived subsequently in England and in North America.

Harriet Low's vivid journal (see pp. 194 and 305) is a rich source of information concerning Chinnery and his contemporaries on the China coast. It also describes her own attempts to draw, under Chinnery's tutelage, and her copying of Chinnery's work; at one point (6 July 1830) she agreed to make 'twelve copies fit to send to America and to say they were copied from Mr. Chinnery', but if the project materialised, the results appear to have been lost.

### William Melrose (1817-1863)
Melrose lived on the China coast from 1842 to 1847 (initially as tea taster and buyer for Jamieson How & Co.), and from 1848 to 1853. He received some tuition from Chinnery in the last stages of the latter's life: 'I got a picture or two from him to copy and painted a head (my own) and sent them to him for instructions and he was very kind.'[24]

### Robert Morrison, Junior (1825/6-after 1862)
The second son of the missionary Dr. Robert Morrison (see p.230-3) and the eldest son of Dr. Morrison's second wife was educated in England and at the Anglo-Chinese College in Malacca. His copies after Chinnery, and drawings in Chinnery's manner, appear to have been made after the artist's death: of the dated examples, the earliest is inscribed 1 August 1852. In 1857-9 he served as 4th Attaché to the Earl of Elgin's mission to China, and made a pictorial record of his journeys.[25]

*Robert Morrison, Junior, Study of a sleeping pig, Macau. Oils on prepared paper.* Private collection

### Edouard Paris (1806-1893)
In 1826-9 Paris accompanied Dumont D'Urville as a Sub-Lieutenant on the *Astrolabe,* on his voyage around the world; later he became Curator of the Musée de Marine at the Louvre. Drawings by Paris of the China coast survive in private hands, and Gideon Nye's sale of 1858 included a picture of 'The Wayside temple at Mongha, near Macao, by Admiral Paris of the French Navy — as an interchanged Gift to Mr. Chinnery, in 1834'.

### Trevor Chicheley Plowden (1783-1836)
The Chicheley Plowden family was strongly represented in the East India Company's service: both Trevor's father (Richard) and his younger brother (William Henry) became Directors of the Company,[26] and the latter commissioned a portrait of Howqua from Chinnery in Canton (Colour Plate 53). Trevor's mother (Elizabeth) was honoured in 1788 by the Emperor Shah Alam, and was depicted in 1797 by John Russell with three of her children in Indian dress.[27] Trevor Plowden entered the Bengal service in 1801, becoming Secretary to the Board of Trade in 1816, and Collector of the 24 Parganas in 1823. He died in 1836 on board the *Hibernian,* bound for the Cape. Both he and his wife, Frances Lena Erskine, were painted by Chinnery (Plate 69 and Colour Plate 36).

Trevor Plowden was a member of Calcutta's artistic circle. On the occasion of the Waterloo celebrations of 8 December 1815, in which Chinnery and D'Oyly were also involved, the decorative illuminations at his house in Garden Reach were highly praised: 'It is said that he

had himself painted, with great taste, a transparency of the meeting of the two Marshals, WELLINGTON and BLUCHER.'[28] A group of small watercolours of Indian scenes by Trevor Plowden were passed down to the artist Duncan Grant, his descendant, and these are now at Charleston Farmhouse, East Sussex. In recent years a number of unsigned watercolours in the manner of Chinnery have been attributed, often speculatively, to Plowden.[29]

### John Prendergast

Prendergast lived on the China coast in the 1840s, serving as 'Draftsman' in the Land Officer's Department of the initial colonial government of Hong Kong. In 1848 he travelled to Manila, Honolulu and San Francisco. A few of his drawings and aquatints of Chinese subjects survive, as does a drawing by Chinnery of a young man sketching, who is identified by the shorthand inscription (cut off at the margin) as 'Mr. Prend...' (illus. Bonsall 1985, no. 25, and see no. 53). Two aquatints of Hong Kong after Prendergast are illus. in Orange 1924, pp. 385-4.

### James Prinsep (1799-1840)

Seven Prinsep brothers, sons of the indigo planter John Prinsep, followed their father to India. At least three of them were familiar with Chinnery (see also Thomas and William below). James, the seventh, arrived in India in 1819, and resided briefly at Calcutta before taking up the post of Assay Master at the Mint, Benares (Varanasi). In 1830 he returned to Calcutta, where he was Assay Master of the Mint until 1838, and also Secretary of the Asiatic Society of Bengal. A gifted and versatile scholar, he distinguished himself as a numismatist, an engineer, a chemist, a mineralogist, and above all as a decipherer of ancient inscriptions. His obsessive dedication to philology led to 'an affectation of the brain' from which he died shortly after his return to England.[30]

On his first visit to Calcutta, James and William Prinsep served on the 'Decorative committee' for the ball held in honour of Lady Hastings's return from England.[31] James also gave 'chemical lectures' at the house of his elder brother Henry Thoby (1792-1878), sometimes electrifying the servants through a string passed from hand to hand. William related that 'our artist George Chinnery made a most happy chalk sketch of him [James] in the act of exemplifying to us the powers of oxygen gas'; a copy of this drawing can be seen in the illustration above, between the bookcases.[32]

James's graphic work included measured drawings

*Auguste Borget, The A-Ma Temple, Macau. Oils.* Mr. and Mrs. P.J. Thompson

*Hon. John Edmund Elliot, The* Dasher *on the Hooghly River, with William Burke's house in Garden Reach, Calcutta. Pencil and watercolours, signed with initials; signed and dated December 1813 on the reverse.* Martyn Gregory Gallery

*Thomas Boswall Watson (colouring) and George Chinnery (outline), The Franciscan Fort, Macau. Pencil, pen and ink, and watercolours, dated in Chinnery's shorthand April 27 [18]35.* Mr. and Mrs. P.J. Thompson

(he redesigned the sewers of Benares), topographical scenes, interiors and caricatures.[33] The illustration on p.287 is his drawing of the studio at William and Mary Prinsep's house in Calcutta. He was also the author of *Benares Illustrated, in a Series of Drawings*, 1831.

### Thomas Prinsep (1800-1830)

Perhaps the most artistically talented of the Prinsep brothers, Thomas Prinsep was instructed by Theodore Fielding at the East India Company's college at Addiscombe. His elder brother William acknowledged that he had 'gained very much myself from working at his side, for in water colours, although Chinnery was famous for light and shade and for individualities, his open landscape was always inferior...'[34] Thomas made copies of Chinnery's drawings, often adding his own effects of shadow.

Thomas Prinsep came out to Calcutta in 1821, and shortly afterwards was posted Surveyor of the Sunderbans. As a Captain in the Bengal Engineers he travelled to Penang in 1824, before moving to Chittagong as Surveyor of Canals. His views of Calcutta (below) and the Ganges show him to have been a subtle and precise watercolourist.[35] He died in Calcutta of a riding accident at the age of twenty-nine.

*Thomas Prinsep, The Garden Road, Calcutta. Pencil, pen and ink, and watercolours, inscribed by William Prinsep 'An unfinished sketch by Tom of the Circular road' [with other inscriptions]. Private collection*

### William Prinsep (1794-1874)

As an artist the long-lived William was the most prolific of the Prinsep brothers, and numerous drawings from his hand survive in public and private collections. He arrived in India in 1817, and two years later became a partner in the leading banking house of Palmer & Co., which proved highly profitable until its bankruptcy in 1830. William Prinsep re-established himself in business with his brother George, and returned to Britain via the Red Sea in 1842.

In Calcutta he was involved in the activities of the Chowringhee theatre, and was a member of the artistic circle which met at the house of Sir Charles D'Oyly. At Serampore Chinnery painted the portrait of William Prinsep with his wife Mary (Frontispiece); Prinsep lent Chinnery money, and facilitated the artist's return to Calcutta (see pp.160-1). Chinnery left India with his debts unpaid, but the two men were finally reconciled when Prinsep visited Macau in 1838 (see pp.244-5). William Prinsep's 'Memoir', written in 1870 but based

*William Prinsep, Looking from the Barrier Joss House. Pen and ink over pencil, inscribed in ink as title, and dated in pencil '12 / Nov. 1838'. Private collection*

on diaries which he kept from the 1820s, is a valuable source of information concerning Chinnery and his contemporaries.

Prinsep's own drawings of Bengali village life are often based upon Chinnery's, and he took 'talc prints' or 'talc pressings' from sketches by Chinnery of both Indian and Chinese subjects. His watercolours of Calcutta, however, are closer in style to those of his brother Thomas. His artistic enthusiasms are illustrated in James Prinsep's drawing of William's Calcutta studio (see p.287), a room filled with canvases and portfolios, busts and statues, and plaster casts of hands and a leg; even the punkah is decorated with an Indian coastal landscape. Subsequently he developed a broader manner, and his vivid watercolour views of the China coast and the 'overland route' to Europe betray the influence of Chinnery to an ever-decreasing degree.[36]

### Dr. John Scarth

The Scottish doctor John Scarth lived in China from 1847 until 1859, travelling along the coast and in the interior of Guangdong province. Certain of his drawings, in the Peabody Museum at Salem, Massachusetts, are evidently inspired by Chinnery; others were used to illustrate his book *Twelve Years in China*, 1860.

### Robert Smith (1787-1873)

Shortly after arriving in India in 1805 Smith transferred from the infantry to the Bengal Engineers. In 1812 he became Engineer Aide-de-Camp to General Sir George Nugent, Commander-in-Chief in India; Lady Nugent, who engaged Chinnery to paint her husband's portrait in the same year, also obtained a number of drawings from Smith, expressing admiration for his work.

Between 1814 and 1819 Robert Smith paid two extended visits to Penang (as Consulting Engineer), where he was responsible for the completion of St. George's Church. His drawings of the vicinity of Penang were engraved in London by William Daniell, and published in 1821 as *Views of Prince of Wales Island*.[37]

Several of Smith's paintings of Malayan subjects suggest the influence of Chinnery. The engraving of one of his Penang compositions is dedicated to Chinnery, and another to Sir Charles D'Oyly, indicating that Robert Smith was a member of their circle during his Calcutta posting. After furlough in England he returned in 1822 to India, which he finally left in 1833, at the rank of Lieutenant-Colonel. He retired to Paignton in Devon, where he built himself a mansion in an Indo-European style.

### Warner Varnham

A British tea inspector, Varnham made a number of drawings and watercolours of Macau, Canton, Chusan Island and the Philippines, in the eventful years 1837-41. He returned to England via Singapore in 1842. His subject matter appears sometimes to be derived from Chinnery, but his drawing is characterised by scratchy outlines and a lack of chiaroscuro. Certain of his sketches were redrawn by Thomas Allom for publication in G.N. Wright's four-volume publication, *China...In a Series of Views*.[38]

### Dr. Thomas Boswall Watson (1815-1860)

In 1845 Dr. Watson left his native Scotland to establish a practice in Macau, in succession to Dr. Alexander Anderson; he and his family lodged at 2 Praya Grande. Here he became Chinnery's doctor, patron and pupil during the latter years of the artist's life (see pp.258-60). In 1856 he moved his practice to Hong Kong, returning to Britain in 1859.

Already an enthusiastic sketcher, Watson developed his talent under Chinnery's tutelage, sometimes adding colour to Chinnery's outline drawings (see colour illustration p.288). His wife Elizabeth, who came out to the China coast in 1846 and returned home in 1858, also executed drawings and copies after Chinnery.[39]

*Thomas Boswall Watson, Our Terrace at Macau. Pencil, pen and ink and watercolours, on blue paper; inscribed as title on original mount, and on the reverse 'Our house with Papa's love to Sophia and Janet.'* Museu Luis de Camões, Macau

### William Wightman Wood (b.1805)

The son of a Philadelphia actor, Wood came to the China coast to work for Russell & Co., and became a close friend of Chinnery in the early 1830s. He was known as a wit, a controversial journalist, and a skilful amateur artist and caricaturist. In the spring of 1832 he was giving lessons in sketching to Harriet Low. After a brief engagement to her, he moved in 1834 to Manila, where he spent most of the remainder of his life.[40] A group of his drawings with accompanying text was published as *Sketches in China* (Philadelphia, 1830). He has been mistakenly supposed to have drawn a frontispiece (in fact by Chinnery) in the Cooper-Hewitt Museum, New York.[41] A portrait said to represent Wood, by a Chinese artist, was sold at Sotheby Parke Bernet (Hong Kong), 25 May 1981 (lot 109).

# Notes and References

Where only author's name and/or date given, refer to Bibliography for full details

## Introduction

1. The principal source of these misguided assertions is R.R.M. Sée, 'George Chinnery 1748-1847', *Revue de l'art ancien et moderne* XXX, 1911, pp.255-68. Other sources are: Nye 1873; Hickey; *Dictionary of National Biography*, 1885 &c; *Grande Enciclopedia Portuguesa e Brasiliera*, Lisbon, 1935-60; Berry-Hill 1963; Hutcheon 1975.
2. Nye 1873, pp.30-1

## Chapter 1: Scribes and Embezzlers: the Chinnery Family

1. *The Compendious Emblematist, or, Writing and Drawing, made Easy, Amusing and Instructive*, n.d., preface (unpaginated).
2. For the genealogy of the early generations of the Chinnery family see Welply 1932, pp.11-31, and 1933, pp.1-15. Supplementary information is derived from a Chinnery family tree kindly supplied by Mrs. R.Teague, a descendant: its early stages were compiled by Mrs. Anne Catherine Macpherson (née Duncan, d.1904), granddaughter of Frances Chinnery, the artist's sister.
3. Massey, part 2, pp.43-5.
4. MS of forty-one unpaginated folio pages in leather binding; collection Mrs. R. Teague.
5. Rate books in the Guildhall Library and Records, London.
6. In each case the reference is primarily to William Bassett Chinnery (brother of George), whose father is said to have been a writing master; see Farington, entry for 27 March 1812, and Glenbervie, p.143, entry for 13 September 1811. It remains possible that both Farington and Glenbervie confused the two generations of William Chinnerys.
7. Gurney, 6th ed., p.47; an extract from the Book of Revelations appears on p.35, in the name of 'William Chinnery Junr. / At the Globe and Sun, Chancery Lane'; see also Geoffrey Bonsall, 'George Chinnery's Shorthand', in Hutcheon 1975, pp.149, 171

n.20. I am grateful to Geoffrey Bonsall for access to this edition of *Brachygraphy...*
8. According to Welply 1932, p.17, the 1764 exhibit was a portrait of the artist's father, but his evidence for this suggestion is not clear; the two exhibited pictures of 1764 and 1766 were misattributed to George Chinnery in Graves 1907, p.57, and this has misled others into supposing that George Chinnery lived to an extraordinary age.
9. A note accompanying the portrait of William Chinnery Junior (Plate 4), signed by Anne Macpherson (see n.2 above), reads: 'Said by my father to be his grandfather Wm. Chinnery East India Company's Service Madras. Residence and factory at Cudalore. Said also to be painted by his son George...', Arts Council of Great Britain, no. 1, the story is repeated in Cotton, J.J., p.113, in which George Chinnery is described as '...the son of William Chinnery of Fort St. David who owned the Chinnery Factory at Cuddalore, and there are some pencil and sepia sketches by the son with his titles "Our Factory in Cuddalore" and "the Chinnery Factory", the buildings being the same in each'. Cotton goes on to link William Chinnery with the Madras agency house Chase, Chinnery & Macdowell.
10. Rate books for St. Bride's, Fleet Street, in the Guildhall Library and Records, London
11. Dodwell and Miles (Madras), pp.52, 180; the agency of Chase, Chinnery & Sewell, to which Cotton refers in n.9 above as the successor to Chase, Chinnery & Macdowell, does not appear in the lists of agencies contained in the *East India Registers* or the *Madras Almanacs*. There was, however, a firm of Chase, Sewell & Chase active in the 1790s, the partners being Thomas Chase, the free merchant Richard Chase, and Henry Sewell, who in 1790 had married Rebecca Chase. Henry Sewell died at Madras in 1800: see Love, vol.4, pp.420 n.4, 476 n.1. Another Henry Sewell is first noted as a Company servant in Madras in 1806. Cotton writes of 'Henry Sewell' as his grand-maternal ancestor; it is possible that an imperfect account of Sewell's

association with the Chinnerys was passed down in Cotton's family.

One other Chinnery is recorded in India in the eighteenth century: Richard Chinnery, Ensign, was at Fort Marlborough in 1770, and at Bencoolen in 1773, but no connection can be traced between him and the family of William Chinnery.
12. Glenbervie, pp.143-4.
13. Ibid., p.144; Glenbervie was well aware that William Bassett Chinnery was no more than 'the son (legitimate I believe) of a writing master who taught half the fathers and mothers of the lords and ladies who frequent his house', p.143. Elsewhere he refers to him as 'little Chinnery', p.147. Perhaps Glenbervie's snobbery sprang from a consciousness of his own modest beginnings as a student of medicine, which were recalled in Sheridan's rhyme: 'Glenbervie, Glenbervie, what's good for the scurvy? For ne'er be your old trade be forgot', see Moore, p.442.
14. Van der Straeten, p.153.
15. Farington, entries for 27 March 1797, 4 April 1798, 21 May 1806; the British Library holds several letters written by William Chinnery at the Treasury in the years 1797-1804, which are largely concerned with the 'privilege' allowance of wine and brandy permissible to a foreign minister, Add. MSS 46836, ff. 85, 87, 103-5, 117, 122; and 46837, ff. 100, 102.
16. Strickland, vol.1, pp.174-5.
17. Lebrun, vol.2, p.148; the author mistakenly gives the age of Caroline Chinnery as fourteen.
18. Helm, p.192.
19. Royal Academy, 1802; Strickland, vol.1, p.125, states that a portrait of Mrs. William Chinnery by George Chinnery was engraved in stipple by J.Heath, as a 'private plate'.
20. Graves 1905, lists 'J. Trossarelli' as having exhibited forty pictures between 1793 and 1825, although surviving examples are signed 'G. Trossarelli'; this might be explained simply as an anglicising of Giovanni to John, but a certain Gaspare Trossarelli, who studied at Turin in the 1780s, is also supposed to have exhibited at

the R.A. in exactly the same years, see Foskett, p.665. It seems likely that, in England at least, only one Trossarelli was active.

21. For the enrolment of 'Troparelli' on 18 February 1791 see Hutchinson, p.152.

22. Van der Straeten, p.160, see also pp.158-9 for Trossarelli's portraits of the Chinnerys.

23. Lebrun, vol.2, p.148.

24. The poem was published in the *Gentleman's Magazine* of July 1810, pp.61-2. Its opening verse runs:

Will then no pitying sword its succour lend

The Gladiator's mortal throes to end

To free th' unconquered mind, whose gen'rous pow'r

Triumphs oe'r Nature in her saddest hour?

25. Rose, vol.2, pp.486-90.

26. Ibid., p.492, letter from Perceval to Rose, 16 March 1812.

27. *Gentleman's Magazine,* March 1812, p.286; May 1812, p.469; June 1812, p.657. The extent of William Chinnery's misappropriation is indicated by Christie's sale catalogue of 3-4 June 1812, offering antique marbles, bronzes, ormolu and porcelain: three of the classical statues were bought by the British Museum; other items went to Samuel Rogers and Joseph Nollekens, and the *pièce de résistance* — a figured vase representing the combat of Greeks and Trojans for the body of Patroclus — was acquired by the wealthy connoisseur Henry Hope.

28. Farington, entry for 27 March 1812.

29. Ibid., entry for 18 July 1812.

30. George Robert Chinnery's will was proved in London on 22 March 1826. Three letters written by him to Sir Robert Peel survive in the British Library; one of them, dated 11 December 1815, begins: 'Dear Peel. The Bavarian minister with whom I happen to be intimately acquainted ... ', Add. MS 40250, f.71. The British Library also holds a travel diary, Add. MS 64093, almost certainly by George Robert Chinnery, describing the author's travels on the Continent with Canning in 1819-20.

31. Farington, entry for 18 July 1812

32. Glenbervie, pp.174-5.

33. Van der Straeten, p.155-60.

34. Douglas, vol. 2, p.319.

35. Letter from George Chinnery to the Earl of Minto, 12 July 1814, National Library of Scotland, MS 11325, p.149; Minto had possibly met William Chinnery through the Glenbervies, whom Minto knew well, see Minto, vol. 3, pp.373, 381.

36. Elers, p.47.

37. Ibid., pp.272-4; Elers also offered Wellesley his Newfoundland dog — but this too was declined.

## Chapter 2: 'A new style of painting': London and The Royal Academy Schools

1. See registers for St. Bride's, and rate books for Gough Square, Guildhall Library and Records, London.

2. Strickland, vol.1, pp.170-5; being a miniature, this exhibit cannot have been the 'kitcat' portrait of William Chinnery which was illus. in Arts Council of Great Britain, no. 1, and sold at Christie's on 24 November 1972.

3. The identifications were made by Graves 1905, p.58; the locations of the exhibits are given in the R.A. catalogues themselves.

4. See Hutchinson, p.129.

5. St. Bride's Church burial registers MS 6543/1, entry for 22 March 1803, Guildhall Library and Records, London.

6. British Museum Add. MS 49355, ff.49-51, transcribed in Ormond 1974, p.137; Chinnery's letters to Mrs. Browne, and his 'Treatise' which are printed in the same issue of the *Journal of the Walpole Society,* are henceforth referred to as Ormond 1974.

7. D'Oyly, 1828, canto XXX, see Appendix iii.

8. See Gideon Nye, 'Foreign Art in China', *Journal of the North China Branch of the Royal Asiatic Society,* XX, 1878, p.180.

9. 'Anthony Pasquin' [John Williams], *A Critical Guide to the exhibition of the Royal Academy for 1796,* p.125.

10. 'Anthony Pasquin', *A Liberal Critique...,* 1794, p.36.

11. Graves 1905, p.58.

## Chapter 3: Ireland

1. Edwards, pp.124-5.

2. Mary Webster, *Francis Wheatley,* 1790, pp.29-30, and Farington, entry for 21 May 1797.

3. A shorthand note in Chinnery's sketchbook 1, f.34, in the collection of the Hongkong and Shanghai Banking Corporation, reads 'December 22 1838. Arrived in India at Madras 36 years ago this day. Arrived in Dublin 42 years ago'. Welply 1932, p.17, gives the date of Chinnery's arrival in Ireland as 1795; Strickland, vol.1, p.175, gives the date as 1797.

4. Strickland, ibid.

5. 'Chinnery', in *Burke's Peerage and Baronetage.*

6. See Welply 1932, p.19, and Foskett, pp.191-2.

7. Strickland, vol.1, p.172.

8. Berry, pp.117-18.

9. Strickland, vol.1, p.177; see also Berry, ibid., and White, p.70. At the exhibition of 1800, pictures by Ashford and Cuming were also purchased.

10. The list was compiled by Strickland (a former Director of the National Gallery of Ireland), vol.1, pp.170-7.

11. Strickland, vol.1, p.175, identifies the portrait of the 2nd Earl of Charlemont engraved in the *Hibernian Magazine* for March 1800 as being a miniature by Chinnery.

12. See p.19. In India in 1816 Chinnery related a story about the Earl or one of his ancestors; see Ormond 1974, p.153.

13. Strickland, vol.1, pp.171, 177. Strickland records that these two portraits were later to be seen in the Victoria Hall, Douglas, Isle of Man; they were removed at the turn of the century 'with a travelling company's scenery and taken to Liverpool, where they were subsequently sold, and all trace of them has been lost'.

14. *Dictionary of National Biography.* A miniature which has been attributed to Chinnery (private collection) bears a label in an early hand which identifies the sitter as Thomas, 2nd Earl of Clonmel; however, the sitter is an elderly man, whereas Thomas was aged twenty when Chinnery left Ireland. The background to the miniature is a plain orange-brown, which is unusual for Chinnery, but appropriate to the 1st Earl's sobriquet.

15. *Critical Review of the First Annual Exhibition of Paintings, Drawings & Sculptures, the works of the Irish Artists, at No. 32, Dame-Street, Dublin, June 1800,* Dublin, p.5.

16. See Strickland, vol.1, p.171.

17. *Critical Review...,* pp.9-13. Strickland, vol.1, p.175, seems to confuse this portrait of the Countess of Clare with a portrait of her seated at a spinning-wheel, which was engraved by H.Brocas for the *Hibernian Magazine,* March 1794, opp. p.193.

18. *Critical Review...,* pp.18-19.

19. White, p.49; Chinnery's portrait of Vallancey received a generally disapproving notice in *Critical Review...,* pp.11-12.

20. Royal Irish Academy, MS 24.K.14, p.251, entry for 6 July 1801: '...that portrait of Miss Vigne exhibited last year...'. The fly illustrated on the sleeve in the portrait of Mrs. Eustace (Plate 20) was not painted by Chinnery, but seems to have intervened in the course of photography.

21. See Barra Boydell, 'Music and Paintings in the National Gallery of Ireland', National Gallery of Ireland, Dublin, 1985, pp.73-4.

22. Hickey, vol.2, p.297.

23. Ibid., pp.190, 216-17, and see vol.3. p.377. Larkins, 'a worthy man and admirable seaman', was an old schoolfellow of Hickey's. William Greer's behaviour on the *Nassau* did not prevent him from becoming Captain of the *Belvedere* in 1788-91. A portrait of William Greer painted by Romney, together with Chinnery's portrait of Charlotte Conyngham and other family portraits, was sold at Christie's on 16 December 1921, by order of Sir Hastings Hadley D'Oyly, 11th Baronet.

24. [John Pester], *War and Sport in India, 1802-1806. An Officer's Diary* [1913], pp.26-7, 121-3, 128, 130, 315-16.

25. Royal Irish Academy, MS 24K.14, pp.207, 230.

26. Ibid., entry for 6 July 1801, p.250, and see p.244. Hugh Douglas Hamilton, who is referred to in this passage, is described on p.246 as 'decidedly the best exhibitor of this year'.

27. Ibid., pp.252 3.

28. Strickland, vol.1, pp.176-7.

29. The *Freeman's Journal*, quoted in Strickland, vol.1, p.176. This is probably the portrait which was acquired by the Royal Hibernian Academy, and reproduced in Walter G. Strickland, 'Hugh Douglas Hamilton, Portrait Painter', *Journal of the Walpole Society* vol.II, 1913, pl.LII(a). Possibly this was also the 'portrait of an artist' which Chinnery sent from Dublin to the Royal Academy in 1798. However, this exhibit is also said to have been a miniature portrait of Hamilton, seen full-face in indigo coat and waistcoat, signed and dated 1796, see G.C. Williamson, *Catalogue of the Miniatures...of F. and M. Wellesley*, n.d. (c.1918).

30. 'One may say of Fuseli, as of every mannerist of genius, that he parodies himself': entry in Goethe's diary for 2 May 1800, quoted in Tate Gallery catalogue, 'Henry Fuseli 1741-1825', 1975, p.43.

31. Royal Irish Academy, MS 24K.14, pp.251-2.

32. Ibid., entry for 15 October 1801, pp.19-20.

33. Nye 1873, pp.30-1.

34. See P. Somerville-Large, *Dublin*, 1969, p.209.

35. The palette was exhibited in Arts Council of Great Britain, no.109; the catalogue records that, as the hallmarks indicate, it was made in Dublin in 1801 by Richard Whitford. The palette is illus. in Berry-Hill 1963, pl.1.

36. A portrait of the artist Vincent Waldré; see Crookshank and Knight of Glin, pp.174-6.

37. Strickland, vol.1, p.195.

38. This group of pictures is described and illus. in Sée 1911, p.291, and Sée 1919, pp.141-51.

39. Rooker's watercolours for the 1783 editon of Fielding's *Works*, are in the Victoria and Albert Museum, London; see Patrick Conner, *Michael Angelo Rooker 1746-1801*, 1984, pp.117-18, 166-70.

40. Since Chinnery's name is not recorded in the rate books for Lower Brook Street, he was presumably renting premises there. Tresham, a Dublin-born history painter, used the premises as a picture gallery for the sale of 'old master' paintings. Chinnery drew Tresham's portrait, which was engraved by Mrs. Dawson Turner in the same year, Strickland, vol.2, p.457. It is possible that some of William Chinnery's antique vases had been supplied by Tresham, who had acquired a collection in Italy in the 1780s, and who combined the professions of artist and dealer.

41. Transcript MS letter, collection of K. Stubbings. I am grateful both to the owner of this letter and to Mr. Randolph Vigne for bringing it to my attention.

42. Strickland, vol.1, p.171; the subjects of the pictures exhibited in Dublin are not specified.

43. *Madras Courier*, 22 December 1802, p.2.

**Chapter 4: Madras**

1. The seventh of the Thackeray brothers remained in England as a curate in Hertfordshire, and lived to the age of forty-nine. Of the brothers in India the longest lived was Charles, the youngest, who 'fell victim to the demon drink, then so fashionable in India', Prynne and Bayne, p.501.

2. MS letter to Emily Prinsep, p.66, 5 June 1828.

3. See Pavière, p.105; in June 1800 Devis was declared bankrupt, and although he was rescued by a generous patron his finances remained precarious until his death.

4. Williamson 1810, vol.1, p.162.

5. Archer 1979, pp.270-2.

6. Ibid., p.270.

7. Ibid., p.177.

8. Minutes of the Court of Directors of the East India Company, India Office Library and Records, vol.111, p.79.

9. Ibid., vol.111, p.106.

10. Farington was assured that 'the Directors have no objection to an artist going [to India], but have to guard against persons going with other views but under the name of Artists', entry for 26 June 1811.

11. Archer 1979, p.218; nothing is known of Hickey's wife.

12. Williamson 1810, vol.1, p.453.

13. Ibid., pp.451-3; at dinner parties in Benares in 1820, the ladies were so outnumbered that gentlemen would book their dances a month in advance, MS letter from James Prinsep to Emily Prinsep, p.43, 10 December 1820.

14. Hickey, vol.3, p.159.

15. Graham, p.139.

16. Arnold, vol.1, pp.93-4; see also Percival Spear, *The Nabobs*, revised ed., 1963, p.57.

17. MS letters to Emily Prinsep, p.43, 18 December 1820; and p. 83, 28 August 1832.

18. Ormond 1974, letter to Mrs. Browne, 17 May 1816.

19. Lloyd's 'Red' Register for 1802, Supplement.

20. *Madras Courier*, 18 December 1802, p.2.

21. *Proceedings Relating to Ships Tendered for the Service of the United East-India Company, from the 2nd July 1806 to the 27th September 1809*, 1809, quoted Macgregor, p.206, and see p.26.

22. *Madras Courier*, 22 December 1802, p.2.

23. Text to 'Masoolah Boats' in the *Indian Magazine and European Miscellany*, 1807.

24. Ibid., and Williamson 1810, vol.1, p.127.

25. Williamson 1810, vol.1, p.137.

26. For this appointment and those given below (except the Collectorship of Colombo) see Dodwell and Miles (Madras), pp.52-3.

27. [Roberdeau], p.141.

28. Like John Chinnery, Macdowell (also spelt McDouall, M'douall, etc.) returned to the Company's service after his years 'out of employ', becoming Civil Auditor in 1809 and Dutch translator to Government in 1810; he died in Madras in 1814. Thomas Chase had served in the 1780s as Clerk to the Justices and French translator; one of his projects was to set up in 1788 a new printing works with 'Persian and other Oriental Characters', with whose aid he proposed to publish 'the hidden Treasures of Indian Learning': see Love, vol.4, pp.361-2. His brother, Richard Chase, acquired several of Thomas Daniell's paintings. On 19 January 1797 Thomas Chase was a witness, together with Henry Sewell and Henry Brown, to John Chinnery's marriage; he died in 1808.

29. *Madras Almanac*, 1806, 1807; this information does not appear in the *East India Registers* of the time.

30. See Perry, vol.2, p.112.

31. Hodgson, p.39.

32. The children were Elizabeth and Mary Chinnery, and William and Frances Duncan. The mother of the Duncan

children, Frances (Chinnery) Duncan, stayed behind in India; she had a four-month-old baby, and was three months pregnant with the next. Mary (Payton) Chinnery, who accompanied the children on the voyage, must also have been pregnant when the ship sailed, since the child, William Charles, was born in England. For the family trees of these families see Welply 1932, p.15.

33. Jardine, Matheson Archive, India Letter Books, 25 December 1804.

34. India Office MS EUR 0/5/30, vol.4, f.109v. Two other artists appear in the Madras lists during Chinnery's residence there. W.P.Rothmeyer, 'Miniature Painter', had arrived from Hanover in 1782, and lived in Black Town: 'He has taken the oath of allegiance on the 5th December 1808 and is a Man of family' (0/5/30, vol.4, pt.2, ff.207v, 221); J.P.Huber (also known as George Huber), 'Portrait Painter', last appears in the lists in December 1807.

35. *East-India Registers,* 1805 and 1806, p.246. In 1808 Robert Sherson was prosecuted, by order of an over-zealous Governor, on a charge of fraud while superintendent of the public stores of rice; he was acquitted and handsomely compensated. One of his judges was Sir Francis Macnaghten (see p.114). See Mill and Wilson, vol.1, pp.236-7.

36. To judge from another miniature portrait of the same person, painted in Madras by Charles Shirreff, illus. in John Murdoch and others, *The English Miniature,* p.192.

37. See Appendix iii, stanza III.

38. Illus. Christie's sale catalogue, 11 April 1980 (lot 167).

39. See Kenneth Garlick, *Sir Thomas Lawrence,* 1989, pls. 8-30, *passim.* The portrait of Mrs. Lord was perhaps painted to mark the occasion of the Lords' marriage in Madras on 10 March 1806.

40. Reproduced in Foskett, col. pl.18A, as by John Comerford; the miniature was subsequently found to have been signed and dated on the reverse by Chinnery.

41. A portrait drawing supposed to represent Edward Pellew was sold at Christie's 5 May 1974 (lot 78), but it may depict his eldest son. See Walker, vol.1, p.178.

42. Perry, vol.1, p.346.

43. *Madras Almanac,* 1803, p.136.

44. Ibid., p.684.

45. Ibid., pp.431-52, 541, 681-5; *East-India Registers.*

46. Mountstuart Elphinstone's journal, quoted in Colebrooke, vol.1, pp.34-6. A portrait which has been said to represent Kirkpatrick, and attributed to Chinnery, is

illus. (for example) in Archer 1979, p.361; it shows the sitter without 'mustachios' or close-cropped hair.

47. Elers, pp.179-80.

48. Ibid., p.188.

49. Thomas Carlyle, *Reminiscences,* ed. C.E.Norton, 1932, vol.2, pp.117-18.

50. Thomas Carlyle, *Sartor Resartus,* 1834, in *The Works of Thomas Carlyle,* ed. H.D.Traill, 30 vols., 1896-8, pp.113, 116; for Kitty as 'Blumine' see George Strachey, 'Carlyle and the "Rose-Goddess" ', *Nineteenth Century,* 32, July-December 1892, pp.470ff.

51. Thomas Carlyle, *Reminiscences,* ed. C.E. Norton, 1932, vol.2, p.175.

52. See Lady Constance Russell, *The Rose Goddess,* 1910, pp.1ff.

53. Ibid.

54. Hodges, p.xx.

55. See Davies, pp.25-7.

56. See Yule and Burnell, 1903, p.313.

57. Ibid., pp.660, 661.

58. D'Oyly 1828, p.256.

59. Prynne and Bayne, p.318.

60. [Roberdeau], p.126.

61. Ibid., p.113.

62. *Calcutta Government Gazette,* 24 December 1807.

63. [Roberdeau], p.117.

64. Williamson 1810, vol.1, pp.195ff. When even junior members of the judicial service went out in their palanquins, eight or ten chuprasses (servants wearing the official badge) would run after them: see [Roberdeau], p.138. The more ostentatiously-dressed soontahburdar presented in Williamson 1813, pl.VI and text, wears a breastplate of silver or brass, and carries a baton made of rosin encased in solid silver, 'ornamented with a tiger's face, or some such device'.

65. Yule and Burnell, p.659.

66. Williamson 1810, vol.2, pp.34-8; see also King, A.D., to whose excellent discussion of the origins of the bungalow I am indebted.

67. [Roberdeau], pp.134-5.

68. Graham, p.127; The *Imperial Gazetteer* of 1885, p.354, states that Ennore contained 'until lately, the oldest club house in Bengal'; this volume also includes a photograph of the lake and promontory at Ennore, showing what may be the same bungalow as that drawn by Chinnery.

69. Hunter, W.C., 1885, p.265.

70. Quoted in King, A.D., p.2; King also relates that in Lucknow a 'bungalow' haircut meant 'in the style of a British officer'.

71. See Mildred Archer, *Early Views of India. The Picturesque Journeys of Thomas and William Daniell 1786-1794,* 1980, p.224.

72. See Sutton, p.92.

73. *Madras Courier,* 26 November 1807.

74. Sketches for the Madras etchings are in the Peabody Museum, Salem, Massachusetts, and in the India Office Library, London.

75. Graham, p.130, entry for 18 August 1810. A Masonic Hall existed in Madras before the building of the Pantheon, see Love, vol. 3, pp.404n, 452.

76. *Madras Almanac,* 1803, p.138.

77. See Love, vol. 3, pp. 419-21.

78. Illus. in Robin McLachlan, 'An Admirable Arrangement', *Hemisphere* vol.22, no.3, March 1978, p.5.

79. For the relations between Dundas and the Directors see Philips, *passim.*

80. *Madras Courier,* 28 January 1807.

81. Hodgson, pp.180ff. Chinnery's portrait drawing of Parry, dated 1805, is catalogued in Arts Council of Great Britain, no.71.

82. Hodgson, pp.38, 112ff, 219-38.

83. See Archer 1979, pp. 219-21.

84. Illus. Sutton, p.84 and pl. facing p.56.

85. See Archer 1979, pp. 417-18.

86. *Madras Government Gazette,* 21 February 1805, p.2.

## Chapter 5: The Russell Commission

1. See the *Madras Gazette,* 23 July 1807.

2. Hickey, vol.4, p.384; a list of the Indian subscribers to the portrait is given in Cotton, H.E.A., 1925, p.182.

3. Hickey, vol.4, p.386.

4. Ibid.; see also *Bengal Past and Present* XXV, 1922, p.93.

5. *Calcutta Government Gazette,* 5 November 1807, p.1; advertisement dated 26 October 1807.

6. Hickey, vol.4, p.387.

7. Ibid., pp.360-1, 385.

8. The original painting in the High Court, Calcutta, is illustrated in Hutcheon 1975, p.12.

9. Zoffany's portrait of Impey is illus. in Archer 1979, pl.86.

10. Ibid., p.227 and col. pl. IX; Thomas Hickey's use of symbolism drawn from European mythology perhaps indicates not only a sense of impartiality — for which Purniya was indeed respected — but also Purniya's acceptance of British hegemony after the death of Tipu, whose minister Purniya had been.

11. *Dictionary of National Biography.*

12. Hickey, vol.4, pp.388-91.

13. Ibid., p.385.

14. Ibid., p.387.

15. Madras Public Proceedings, India Office Library and Records, MS vol. P/244/53, ff.2181-9.

16. Hickey, vol.4, pp.387-8; this letter is here reproduced from the typescript of

Hickey's *Memoirs,* which, together with the manuscript, is held by the India Office Library and Records. Spencer's edition, listed in the Bibliography, often departs from the original text.

### Chapter 6: Dacca and the D'Oylys

1. Prospectus bound into the British Library's copy of D'Oyly, 1814-27.
2. See Archer 1979, pp.288, 318.
3. Stocquelier, p.488; Stocquelier reported that the principal manufactures of Dacca were small bracelets, idols, and (remarkably) violins, which were for sale at two rupees each.
4. Heber, vol.1, p.90.
5. Ibid., vol.2, p.207; letter to Charles Watkins Williams Wynn, 13 July 1824.
6. MS lists of non-official European inhabitants in Bengal, India Office Records 0/5/27, 1808 (no.643).
7. Ibid., 1809 (no.381) and 1811 (no.194); the former entry gives Chinnery's date of arrival in Dacca as 11 July, the latter as 14 July. In the list for 1808 (no.643) it is stated that in June 1808 'George Chinarry' [*sic*] was given authority for residing in the district; his name is listed under 'Dacca' for the four years 1808-9-10-11.
8. Warren Hastings correspondence, letter from Charles D'Oyly to Warren Hastings, 15 November 1808, in the British Library Add. MS 29184, f.52.
9. Hickey, vol.4, p.354.
10. Ibid, pp.476-8; it is possible that the children listed as 'Robert Conyngham' and 'C.D.Conyngham' in Hickey's list of casualties on the *Calcutta* were the children of the late Charlotte Conyngham, who were travelling back to England with their aunt.
11. Warren Hastings correspondence, letter of 15 November 1808, British Library Add. MS 29184, f.52.
12. Ibid., ff.51-2.
13. A group of Chinnery's drawings of Dacca (including those illustrated here), with dates from 25 October 1808 to 4 March 1809, was sold at Sotheby Parke Bernet, Hong Kong, 23 November 1976. Two others, dated 27 and 29 October 1808, are in the Orange bequest at the Victoria and Albert Museum.
14. John Aikin, *Letters from a Father to his Son...*, 1793, p.266.
15. D'Oyly 1814-27, second series, p.1 and (text) p.8; third series, pp.8-9; fourth series, p.15.
16. A number of small portraits and miniatures of members of the D'Oyly family, from the collection of Mrs. C.L.V.D'Oyly, were sold at Sotheby's 15 July

1974 (lots 41-51); these included two miniatures of Sir John Hadley D'Oyly, 6th Baronet, by Chinnery; four costume portraits by Eliza (Ross) D'Oyly, second wife of Sir Charles, who is mistakenly described in the catalogue as Charlotte Thompson; three miniatures by Chinnery's pupil, Maria Browne, representing Sir Charles, his first wife Marian, and his second wife Eliza; also a group of small informal watercolour portraits by Chinnery of Sir Charles, Marian, Eliza, and other individuals not reliably identified.
17. See *Calcutta Government Gazette,* 3 July 1822, Supplement p.2. Cruttenden was portrayed in the uniform of a Major of the Bengal army. He was the cousin-in-law of William Hickey's close friend Bob Pott; Pott bequeathed several pictures to him. See Hickey, vol.4, p.491. The portrait (on which the engraving, by Charles Pote, was based) was in the possession of Nathaniel Wallich, Superintendent of the Calcutta Botanic Gardens, see *Calcutta Government Gazette,* 12 December 1822, p.3.
18. Miniature portraits of both Shearman Bird and his wife were also executed by Chinnery's pupil Maria Browne. An association between the Bird and D'Oyly families is indicated by an elaborate frame containing miniatures of both couples, which was sold at Christie's November 1988 (lot 92); one of the other miniatures in this frame was a portrait of the Birds' young daughter, named Marian D'Oyly Bird.
19. Minutes of the Court of Directors of the East India Company, 8 January 1818, India Office Library and Records. The Hon. Hugh Lindsay had been Captain of the *Rockingham,* which in 1796 had brought Chinnery's sister Frances, and his future sister-in-law Mary Payton, to India; it was his son, Hugh Hamilton Lindsay, who in 1838 arranged the reconciliation between Chinnery and William Prinsep in Macau, see p.245.
20. Warren Hastings correspondence, letter of 1 August 1809, British Library Add. MS 29188, f.281v.
21. Heber, vol.1, p.96.
22. Illus. Ormond 1974, pl.6.
23. See Appendix iii, note 10.
24. Memoir of William Prinsep, India Office Library and Records, vol.1, p.283. A sketch of a female head-and-shoulders sculpture (formerly in the possession of Stanhope Shelton Pictures Ltd.) is inscribed by Chinnery 'from a Bust [in] the possession [of Charles] D'Oyly Esq.'
25. See Ormond 1974, p.139, letter of 1 August 1814, and p.160, letter of 15 November 1817.

26. Three albums of work by the Behar [Amateur] Lithographic Press, formerly in the family of Alexander Lind, were sent for sale at Sotheby's, 21-22 June 1990 (lots 22-24). Another lithographic project, *The Amateur's Repository of Indian Sketches,* 1827-8, contains views after Chinnery and several amateur artists, including D'Oyly, William Prinsep and James Prinsep.
27. Memoir of William Prinsep, India Office Library and Records, vol.2, p.85.
28. MS descriptions and commentary by Catherine Snow attached to the pictures.
29. Warren Hastings correspondence, British Library Add. MS 29188, f.291.

### Chapter 7: Calcutta Portraits

1. In about 1820 Chinnery painted a portrait of Raja Protap Chand, perhaps the portrait illus. in Berry-Hill 1963, pl.13, left. In 1838, at the Hooghly Court House, an individual was put on trial for impersonation, having claimed to be the Raja; the portrait was brought to the Court from the palace at Burdwan, so that the matter might be settled. See Cotton, J.J., p.122; also stanza XXI of *Tom Raw, the Griffin* (see Appendix iii), which refers to an appointment made by Chinnery with an Indian sitter.
2. Illustrated in Archer 1979, p.282.
3. India Office Records, Bengal wills 1828, L/AG/34/29/43, pp.261-84, quoted in Archer 1979, p.377.
4. Illus. in Archer 1979, p.153; see also Thomas Hickey, 'Charles Brooke playing with the Nawab of Murshidabad', c.1790, in which the Indian figure is depicted in a kneeling position, illus. Archer 1979, p.217.
5. India Office Records, MS EUR O/5/27, 1812 (no.436); and see *The Original Calcutta Annual Directory and Calendar for A.D.1813,* Appendix, p.71.
6. Nugent, p.361; the present location of the picture is not known.
7. Chinnery to the 2nd Earl of Minto, 12 July 1814, National Library of Scotland MS 11325, p.150, Chinnery mentions George (a naval captain) and John Elliot, sons of Lord Minto, and their wives.
8. William Hotham, *Pages and Portraits from the Past,* 1919, vol.1, p.165, quoted in H.E.A.Cotton, 'The Story of a Lost Picture', *Bengal Past and Present,* XXIX, January-June 1925, p.109.
9. Chinnery to the 2nd Earl of Minto, 12 July 1814, National Library of Scotland MS 11325, p.149.
10. Marianne Chinnery to the 2nd Earl of Minto, sent from Dublin to London 31 May 1814, National Library of Scotland MS

11154, pp.95-6.

11. See H.E.A. Cotton, 'The Story of a Lost Picture', *Bengal Past and Present* XXIX, January-June 1925, p.105.

12. Col. Drinkwater to the 2nd Earl of Minto, 8 July 1815, National Library of Scotland MS 11803, p.56; on 27 October 1815 Charles Turner wrote to Drinkwater that he had sent the engraving to [the 2nd] Lord Minto but had received no acknowledgement , p.60.

13. See Archer 1979, p.369.

14. See Wurtzburg, p.143; the Malacca portrait, which was subsequently moved to the Colonial Secretary's residence in Singapore, is illus. facing p.96.

15. Chinnery to J.A. van Braam, 27 December 1813, National Library of Scotland MS 11334, p.70, and copy letter, p.117.

16. Copy letter from Chinnery to van Braam in Batavia, n.d. (early January 1814), National Library of Scotland MS 11334, pp.118-19.

17. See letter from Chinnery to the 1st Earl of Minto, 12 July 1814, National Library of Scotland MS 11325, p.148; the portrait is illus. in Archer 1979, p.370.

18. Ormond, p.143, undated letter to Maria Browne, c.1814.

19. Quoted by Cotton, H.E.A. 1925, p.183.

20. *The Times* obituary, 3 May 1892, p.10.

21. The small full-length portrait of Metcalfe illus. in Christie's sale catalogue of 20 July 1990 (lot 330) must be denied to Chinnery, both on stylistic grounds and because the subject is depicted in Governor-General's uniform, which Metcalfe was not entitled to wear until ten years after had Chinnery left India.

22. Illus. Archer 1979, pl.285.

23. See Kaye, *passim;* also Mark Bence-Jones, *Palaces of the Raj*, 1973, pp.99-100.

24. 'Journal of Lieutenant John Pester', vol.V, p.130, entry for 27 June 1815, India Office Records MSS Eur. D.438.

25. See Arts Council of Great Britain, no.78 and illus; another Chinnery drawing, dated 1803 and questionably claimed to represent 'Mrs. Siddons and Child', is illustrated in Berry-Hill 1963, pl.8.

26. This portrait was engraved by G.B.Black, and published by Thomas Collins.

27. The portraits of Fergusson, Macnaghten and Dr Joshua Marshman were considered by the *Friend of China*, 8 July 1852, to have been Chinnery's most successful portraits of his later years in Calcutta. A pencil portrait by Chinnery of Mrs. Fergusson, with a picture of (presumably) their Calcutta house visible

on the wall, is reproduced in Martyn Gregory catalogue 43, 1986, no.47.

28. Letter from Victor Jacquemont to Victor de Tracy, 1 September 1829, in *Correspondance de Victor Jacquemont*, 1869 ed., vol. 1, p.87.

29. See Cotton, H.E.A. 1925, XXX, pp.181-6; Chinnery's portrait of Hogg is illus. in Christie's sale catalogue of 23 February 1989 (no.141).

30. India Office Records N/1/9, p.264; other signatories were James Atkinson, Surgeon and Assay Master of the Calcutta Mint, whose wife was a pupil of Chinnery's and 'G.Abbott', perhaps the man to whom Chinnery refers in writing to Mrs. Browne in March 1817, 'Saturday I am at Abbotts or would come with pleasure...', Ormond 1974, p.156.

31. Ormond 1974, letter to Maria Browne of 2 December 1816, p.153.

32. Quoted in Archer and Falk, p.49.

33. Hickey, vol.4, pp.110-11.

34. *Calcutta Government Gazette*, 28 November 1822, 1st Supplement, p.3; the portrait in oils of Macnaghten, in damaged state, is reproduced in Hutcheon 1975, p.48. A stipple engraving of this portrait, engraved by Charles Pote, was published in 1825; see *Calcutta Government Gazette*, 1 September 1825.

35. See Ralph E. Turner, *James Silk Buckingham 1786-1855, A Social Biography*, 1934, p.193.

36. The engraving by Savignhac was judged to be a judicious combination of mezzotint and aquatint, and superior to that of Chinnery's seated portrait of Lord Hastings, which had been published ten months previously; see *Calcutta Government Gazette*, 26 January 1824, Supplement, p.3, and 26 February 1824, p.3.

37. *Parliamentary History*, XXIX, quoted in *Dictionary of National Biography*.

38. Illus. Penny, p.327.

39. *Calcutta Government Gazette*, 4 October 1822 and 31 July 1823; see also Cotton, H.E.A., 1936, p.4., the seated portrait is illus. in Archer 1979, p.371.

40. *Calcutta Government Gazette*, 27 June 1816, and see *Gould* 1951, vol.4, pp.60-2. Another portrait of Lord Hastings in masonic regalia, clearly based on Chinnery's seated portrait, is reproduced in *Bengal Past and Present* , I, p.67.

41. This drawing is contained in one of William Prinsep's albums. The album page is inscribed 'Chinnery's first ideal sketch for the public picture voted at Calcutta of Lord Hastings on quitting India.' The same album includes a sepia sketch for a more static equestrian portrait or statue,

inscribed 'Geo. Chinnery', which may also be related to the Hastings project.

42. *Calcutta Monthly Journal*, 27 July 1827, p.67. It appears that Chinnery did complete a portrait of the Marchioness of Hastings for the Calcutta Agricultural and Horticultural Society, of which she was patroness; Chinnery announced on 4 December 1823 that this portrait would be finished 'towards the close of the year', *Madras Government Gazette*, 18 December 1823, Appendix; it was exhibited nine years later in a loan exhibition of the Calcutta Brush Club, *Calcutta Government Gazette*, 30 January 1832.

43. Chinnery to Lord Minto, 12 July 1814, National Library of Scotland MS 11325, f.148v. One commission from an individual associated with Hastings was Chinnery's portrait (in a private collection) of James Munro Macnabb (1790-1860), who was Private Secretary to the Governor-General in 1822. Macnabb also owned a number of paintings by Sir Charles D'Oyly.

44. India Office Records MS B/174, p.537, 24 October 1821, and p.550, 31 October 1821.

45. *Calcutta Government Gazette*, 14 August 1823 and 22 January 1824, 1st supplement, p.1.

46. Ibid., 16 June 1828. Lawrence's portrait of Adam was engraved by Charles Turner and published in 1829; for many years it hung in Government House, Calcutta.

47. Roberts, vol.1, p.56.

48. Ormond 1974, p.129, letter of 29 May 1813; the word 'drawn' is unclear in the MS; Ormond proposes 'sham'.

49. Ibid., p.162, letter of 26 November 1820.

50. Ibid., p.140, letter of 1 August 1814.

51. Ibid., p.162, letter of 26 November 1820.

52. Ibid., p.133, undated letter c. June 1813.

53. The *English Chronicle*, quoted in Whitley 1928, Artists..., vol.2, p.131.

54. Memoir of William Prinsep, vol.1, India Office Library and Records, p.354.

55. See Crawford, p.76.

56. Of the six Thackeray brothers who came to India in Chinnery's time, the artist would certainly have known William (1778-1823), a Madras civil servant. Their sister Emily (1790-1824) married another civil servant, John Talbot Shakespear (d.1825), whose portrait was painted by Chinnery, see Prynne and Bayne, p.310); John and Emily Shakespear were close friends of the Moiras, with whom they travelled up-country in the State Barge.

57. Hunter, W.W., p.171.

58. See Ray, p.52.

59. Prynne and Bayne, p.320.

60. Ibid.
61. See Ray, pp.61-5.
62. *The Works of W.M.Thackeray*, ed. George Saintsbury, 1908, vol. XIV, pp.130-4.
63. Prynne and Bayne, p.320.
64. Hunter, W.W., p.176.
65. *The Works of W.M. Thackeray*, op. cit., vol. XIV, p.302.
66. *The Works of W.M. Thackeray*, op. cit., vol. XI, pp.761-2.
67. Arts Council of Great Britain, nos. 73 illus., 74, 76.
68. *Oriental Herald and Colonial Review* I, no.2, February 1824, p.355, referring to a meeting held on 11 August 1823. The members of the committee were Mr. Hogg, Mr. Atkinson, Mr. Palmer, and Mr. Henry Shakespear. Chinnery's portrait of the latter, who succeeded his brother John (see n.56 above) as Superintendent of Police and Chief Magistrate in Calcutta, is referred to in the *Calcutta Government Gazette*, 8 October 1839.
69. Ormond 1970, p.136, undated letter, c.1813.
70. Jane Comyn died at Cawnpore on 30 January 1831, aged forty.
71. Rider Haggard, *Allan Quartermain*, 1887, p.277; although African-born, Nyleptha, 'the White Queen', is conspicuously fairer than her olive-complexioned twin sister, p.139.
72. Paget, p.30.
73. Ibid., pp.143-4, 144, 146-7, 149, 150.
74. Ibid., p.176, letter of 17 May 1825.
75. Yale Center for British Art catalogue, 'English Portrait Drawings and Miniatures', no. 94.
76. India Office Records, WD.3385, ff.1-50.
77. See Penny, pp.259-60; the portrait was engraved (as 'Cornelia'), with some alterations, in 1791.

## Chapter 8: Freemasonry and the Theatre

1. James Prinsep MS letters, letter of 20 April 1824, private collection.
2. Memoir of William Prinsep, India Office Records, MSS Eur. D.1160, vol.1, pp.307, 344; vol.2. pp.225-8.
3. *India Gazette*, 12 September 1807.
4. The portrait of Lewis was engraved for the *Monthly Mirror* of November 1798, opp. p.260; that of Kemble was engraved by James Heath for the same periodical in 1799.
5. See Carey, vol.1, pp.131-3. Robert Home is reported to have presented to the Chowringhee Theatre in 1814 'an exquisite drop scene', *Calcutta Government Gazette*, 2 June 1814; William Prinsep in 1818 was 'painting scenes and devising costumes' at

the same theatre, Memoir of William Prinsep, India Office Records, vol.1, p.287.
6. *Calcutta Government Gazette*, 30 November 1815, p.5.
7. *Selections from the Calcutta Gazettes*, ed. H.D. Sandeman, vol.IV, p.408.
8. Hickey finally quarrelled with a rival lodge, was accused of unmasonic behaviour, and resigned; see Hickey, vol.3, pp.313-4, 348, and vol.4, p.23.
9. Gould 1899, pp. 165-7. Umdat-ul-umara, the last reigning Nabob of the Carnatic, was also installed as a mason in 1775, although later he 'seems to have fallen from masonic grace'. He was initiated into freemasonry by the Provincial Grand Master, Dr. Terence Gahagan, whose daughter Lucy (Lord) was later painted by Chinnery (Colour Plate 9). See Gould 1951, vol.4, pp.67-8, and Julius James Cotton, *List of Inscriptions on Tombs or Monuments in Madras*, Madras, 1905, p.129, no.680.
10. *India Gazette*, 13 December 1813; reprinted in *Selections from the Calcutta Gazettes*, ed. H. D. Sandeman, vol. IV, p.340.
11. *Calcutta Government Gazette*, 27 June 1816, and see Gould 1951, vol.4, pp.60-2.
12. See Firminger 1911, p.3.
13. See Firminger 1906, pp.143, 148, 138-9. In Calcutta Compton became Master of 'the Moira Lodge, Freedom and Fidelity'.
14. *Madras Almanac*, 1803, p.138.
15. Firminger 1906, p.148; *Bengal Past and Present* XXX, 1925, p.132 n.4.
16. This portrait was engraved as the frontispiece of *A Memoir of Major-General Sir R.R.Gillespie*, 1816; here the picture is said to have been 'painted by Mr. Chinnery, at Calcutta, in 1814'; see also Henry Beveridge, *A Comprehensive History of India*, 1856, vol.3, p.12.
17. Firminger 1906, p.167.
18. Gould 1906, pp. 187-9.
19. *India Gazette*, quoted in *Selections from the Calcutta Gazette*, ed. H.D. Sandeman, vol.V, p.517.
20. Ibid., vol.V, p.518-9. Other decorations included 'shields adorned with drapery and garlands' and a large landscape at the end of the room, which were possibly also devised by Chinnery.
21. Memoir of William Prinsep, India Office Records, vol.2, pp.225-8, 29 Feb. 1836.

## Chapter 9: Village Life in Bengal

1. Ormond 1974, letter of 5 December 1814, p.142.
2. Drawing dated 15 May 1816: Martyn Gregory Gallery catalogue 28, 1982, no.44 (not illus.).

3. Drawings in the Peabody Museum, Salem, Massachusetts, dated 30 September 1824, and the India Office Library and Records, WD 3385.
4. Ormond 1974, p.182: 'General shadow' is distinguished from 'Natural shadow', which is 'occasioned solely by the Shape of Objects'; 'Artificial shadow', which is cast 'from an object *in* the Picture'; and 'Cavity shadow', which is 'occasioned by any hollow space wh. is open at one end only — Such as a Trumpet...' In the case of 'General shadow', Chinnery adds, 'the great rule must be observed, that the Centre of it is the darkest & the Edges the Lightest — even when it falls on a flat object', pp.181-2.
5. Examples taken from drawings in the sources given in nn. 2 and 3 above.
6. Ormond 1974, p.183.
7. See respectively Martyn Gregory Gallery catalogue 38, 1984, no.59, and Victoria and Albert Museum, illus. in Hutcheon 1975, p.24.
8. India Office Library and Records, WD 3385.
9. See Martyn Gregory Gallery catalogue 18, 1977, no.81.
10. See Grant, p.7; descriptions and illustrations of other craft are given on pp.4-11. Grant came to Bengal in 1832, and followed the professions of painting and writing there for nearly fifty years; as a long-term resident artist he was one of Chinnery's few successors in India. For Chinnery's studies of boats see India Office Library, WD 3385.

## Chapter 10: Sons and Rivals

1. 'When one of these Burra Civilians gives a dinner, it is not a moderate performance either: for a table loaded with plate about from 30 to 65 sit down and quaff claret @ 40 Rs per dozen and champagne at 80 rupees. It is necessary to give the guests a 70 rupees English *Ham*, 20 rupee cheeses; ice-cooled water in this hot climate & Enlish raspberry jam...Fortunately Bachelors are not obliged to entertain, but after two years I shall be called upon for a Ball & Supper', MS letter from James Prinsep to G.Haldimand, 29 March 1821, p.14.
2. Letter of 25 February 1808, quoted in Reading Museum & Art Gallery, p.10.
3. Letter of 10 April 1815, p.302; facsimile in Reading Museum & Art Gallery, p.43.
4. Redgrave, vol. 1, p.520.
5. Quoted in Archer and Falk, p.48, letter of 29 April 1818.
6. Ormond 1974, p.157, letter to Mrs. Browne dated both 'March 1817' and '1

April 1817'.

7. Redgrave, vol.1, p.520.

8. See Foster, p.34; also Redgrave, vol.1, p.520, and Reading Museum & Art Gallery, pp.15, 33.

9. Minutes of the Court of Directors of the East India Company B/164, p.860, 7 January 1817; *Calcutta Government Gazette*, 'Extraordinary', 28 July 1817.

10. Drawing in the Peabody Museum, Salem, Massachusetts. Chinnery added further inscriptions at subsequent dates: 'October 22nd 1835. She is now 36 years old', and 'Jany. 21 1848. She is now 48.'

11. D'Oyly 1828, canto V, stanza XIX, see Appendix iii.

12. Quoted in Archer and Falk, p.48, diary entry for 7 July 1819.

13. India Office Records, MS N/1/11, f.38, Matilda Chinnery's marriage; and MS N/1/10,f.508, marriage of John Hadley D'Oyly to Charlotte Thompson, 26 December 1818.

14. See Buckingham; also Ralph E. Turner, *The Relations of James Silk Buckingham with the East India Company 1818-1836*, Pittsburgh, 1930.

15. Minutes of the Court of Directors of the East India Company, B/166, p.1124, 3 March; and p.1176, 13 March 1818.

16. Quoted in Ormond 1974, p.157.

17. Quoted in Hodgson, p.180, letter of 22 October 1807.

18. Ibid., pp. 233-5. By this time Parry had no surviving children; his other grandchild died on the same day as himself, p.246. The will also provided 1000 rupees each for 'Miss Elizabeth Chinnery, Miss Mary Chinnery, and Mrs Charles Chinnery [*sic*]' — the three unmarried children of George Chinnery's brother John. Charles did not marry, so that 'Mrs' is probably a mistake for 'Mr'.

19. Ormond 1974, p.161.

20. *Calcutta Government Gazette*, 20 June 1822, 2nd Supplement, p.2.

21. Wilson, p.182, no.698.

22. 'Edward Charles Chennery' was buried in Calcutta in January 1841, 'aged 27 yrs. 3 months 4 days'; in September 1841 he was followed by 'Henry Collins Chinnery aged 28 yrs.', India Office Records, MS N/1/62, ff.8, 104.

23. India Office Records, MS N/1/11, f.352.

24. *Calcutta Annual Directory* for 1835; list p.5.

25. Quoted in Kenneth Ballhatchet, *Race, Sex and class under the Raj*, 1980, p.100.

26. Quoted in the *Calcutta Courier*, 12 March 1836, p.4.

27. *East India Magazine*, July 1837, p.376;

see also 1835, p.563.

28. See Sir Harry Evan A. Cotton, 'The Editor's Note Book', *Bengal Past and Present* XXXV, January-June 1928, pp.101-2.

29. *Calcutta Government Gazette*, 12 June 1839, p.2; for Henry Chinnery's application for discharge see *Calcutta Government Gazette*, 10 April 1839, p.2.

30. See n.22 above.

31. *Calcutta Annual Directory* for 1835, list, p.5.

32. India Office Records, MS N/1/44, f.69. In the absence of his parents, the register was signed on Edward Chinnery's behalf by a certain J.H. Boileau. After Edward's death, his widow married John Richard Yeoward, Writer, aged twenty, on 26 September 1844, India Office Records, MS N/1/66, f.71.

33. *Calcutta Monthly Journal*, August 1837, pp.569-70.

34. India Office Records, MS N/1/62, f.8.

35. Marianne Chinnery's death is noticed in the *Brighton Herald*, 30 December 1865, p.2, and see the Brighton Directory for 1865. For the death of Matilda see Welply 1932, p.18, who also records the death of her husband James Cowley Brown in Calcutta on 15 January 1852.

**Chapter 11: Escape from Debt**

1. See Archer 1979, pp.242, 271, 312, 323, and *passim;* also Penny, p.58.

2. Illus. in Ormond 1970, p.250.

3. Letter from George Parkyns to William Jardine, 17 December 1830, Jardine, Matheson Archive, Macao Letters, incoming.

4. Letter from George Chinnery to R.J. Gilman, 25 February 1848, Hongkong and Shanghai Bank; in the same letter Chinnery refers to his fee of $50 for 'the Picture of the little Tanka'.

5. See Archer 1979, pp.260, 152.

6. Carey, vol.2, p.200; Carey adds that 'his [Chinnery's] prodigality was so great that he largely exceeded his income'; *Friend of India*, 8 July 1852.

7. Letter from George Chinnery to Lord Minto, 12 July 1814, National Library of Scotland MS 11325, f.149.

8. D'Oyly 1828, canto V, stanza XXVII, see Appendix iii.

9. Williamson 1813, preface, p.4; Williamson 1810, p.175, gives a minimum cost of £150 for house rent and the same again for servants' wages; and letter from 'Claudio', 1 May 1823, in *Selections from the Calcutta Gazettes*, ed. Hugh D. Sandeman, vol.V, 1869, p.535.

10. Ormond 1974, pp.151-2, letter of 25 November 1816.

11. Ormond 1974, p.158, letter of 15 November 1817.

12. Ormond 1974, p.164, undated letter, c.1821.

13. Hunter, W.C. 1885, p.273.

14. Read, vol.2, p.215.

15. Whitley, Art..., pp.155-6.

16. Farington, entry for 6 September 1809.

17. Ormond 1974, p.139, letter of 1 August 1814.

18. Warren Hastings correspondence, British Library Add. MS 29,184, f.280v, letter from Charles D'Oyly to Warren Hastings of 1 August 1809.

19. Warren Hastings correspondence, British Library Add. MS 29,183, f.242, letter from Sir John Hadley D'Oyly to Warren Hastings, 16 April 1808; Sir John also ran into debt, partly, as his son wrote, 'owing to his assistance in my difficulties', Add. MS 29,184, f.280v, 13 January 1810.

20. See Mannoni, pp.97ff.

21. [Roberdeau], p.146.

22. Jacquemont, p.30, letter of October 1829. See also [Roberdeau], p.120: 'To this place fly all those whose circumstances are involved in Ruin, as they are completely safe from their Creditors. Among this class of Men were many Sporting Characters who used on Sundays (when the law is dead) to repair to Calcutta and its vicinity and enter into the mania of Horse-racing.' There is no suggestion, however, that Chinnery was a 'Sporting Character'.

23. See Auber, pp.107ff.

24. Carey, vol.2, p.200.

25. Memoir of William Prinsep, vol.1, India Office Records, p.350.

26. Heber, vol.I, p.44.

27. Memoir of William Prinsep, vol.1, India Office Records.

28. Prinsep album in the collection of Sven Gahlin; beneath the drawing William Prinsep inscribed on the album page 'Original design by Chinnery for the portrait he painted of WP, MP.'

29. In 1817 James Young (1782-1848) was Secretary to the Government in the Military Department, and Hon. aide-de-camp to the Governor-General. In the following year he resigned his commission, and joined the banking firm of Alexander & Co. in Calcutta. In 1832 he became editor of the *Bengal Hurkaru*, the leading liberal newspaper in Calcutta. Certain of the lithographs produced on Sir Charles D'Oyly's press are based on drawings by Young.

30. Memoir of William Prinsep, vol.1, India Office Records, p.352.

31. Ibid., p.353.

## Chapter 12: Canton and the Chinese

1. *Calcutta Monthly Journal,* August 1826.
2. The portrait is illus. in Sotheby's sale catalogue of 8 March 1989 (lot 63); here Lindsay (1798-1853) is stated to have worked in the Bengal Civil Service with Chinnery's son-in-law, James Cowley Brown. The painting depicts Lindsay as a young man, and is in the style of Chinnery's Bengal portraits.
3. Log of the *Hythe's* voyage 1825-6, India Office Library and Records, final page.
4. Hunter, W.C., 1885, p.268, states that Chinnery spent two years at Canton, which is probably an overestimate; Hunter was back in America for most of the time in question.
5. Latimer papers, Library of Congress, Box 12, folder 104, MS invoice of 12 December 1827.
6. Ibid., MS letter of 12 December 1827 to Latimer.
7. MS letter in the Peabody Museum, Salem, Massachusetts; partly quoted in Hutcheon, 1975, pp.105-6. The portrait by Lamqua may coincide with a portrait ($9^1/_2$ x 8 ins) of Robert Bennet Forbes executed by a Chinese artist working in the manner of Chinnery, which has descended in the Forbes family, and is illus. in Peabody Museum, pl.XXII.
8. Hunter, W.C., 1882, p.104.
9. Museu Luis de Camões, 1985, Toyo Bunko nos.146-52.
10. Nye 1886, p.180.
11. A previous Howqua served as a Hong merchant from 1784 until 1788, when he absconded after four troubled years. It has been assumed, by H.B. Morse and the many others who have followed him, that this Howqua was the father, or at least the close relative, of Wu Bingjian, and the latter has therefore been described as Howqua II, and Wu Bingjian's two Hong merchant sons as Howqua III and IV. But recent research into the Chinese documents has shown that the Howqua of the 1780s had the Chinese surname Lin, and so was probably unrelated to the Wu family which formed the nineteenth-century dynasty of the Howquas: see Kuo-Tung Anthony Ch'en, pp.115-7. Ch'en prefers to designate Wu Bingjian as Howqua I, and his sons as Howqua II and III. A further source of confusion is the fact that Wu Bingjian was also known as Puiqua in the earlier part of his career.
12. Annotation of Captain Thomas B. Ward, published in Whitehill, p.307.
13. See Downs, pp.426, 441.
14. Forbes, S.H., vol.1, pp.62-3.
15. Hunter, W.C., 1882, pp.48, 43-4, and see Downs, pp.434-5n.
16. Greenberg, p.199.
17. See Kuo-Tung Anthony Ch'en, pp.113-16.
18. Ibid., pp.252ff., and Hunter, W.C., 1882, p.45.
19. Ibid., p.118; and *United Service Journal,* 1841, part 2, p.245: 'Old Howqua is a very fine old man, now nearly seventy-five years old, with hair and moustache as white as snow. The others are fat, jolly fellows who appear to know what good eating is, particularly old Mowqua.' Harriet Low described Mowqua as 'a great character...He was very gallant, I assure you', Loines, p.115: entry for 1 November 1829; however 'he speaks [English] very badly, it is almost impossible to understand him', MS diary, 4 Feb. 1830. Later Mowqua sent Harriet's aunt 'a splendid Japan lacquered work box' as a present, MS diary, 22 April 1831. This Mowqua was often described as 'old Mowqua' to distinguish him from the other members of his family who were known by the same commercial name.
20. Greenberg, p.86.
21. Ellis, p.417: Ellis and other members of Lord Amherst's embassy visited Howqua's house on 12 January 1817.
22. For Dunn see Lee, p.15; Madame Tussaud's catalogue quoted in Gardner, p.311.
23. See Orange 1920, p.91; and Orange 1924, pp.233, 265.
24. Plowden returned to the China Coast in 1832, and left finally in January 1834: see Morse 1926-9, vol. IV, pp.219, 368.
25. William Alexander, *Picturesque Representations...of the Chinese,* 1814, text to pl.22.
26. Daniell, text to 'Chinese Barber'.

## Chapter 13: Macau

1. Victoria and Albert Museum nos. E1633-1928.
2. Monroe, R.K., vol.86, 1950, p.24.
3. See Gregory, no.32; a drawing by Watson of this building is inscribed by the artist 'Macao — Mr. Forbes's house — Praya Grande'.
4. John Francis Davis, *Sketches of China,* 1841, vol.2, p.18.
5. *The Anglo-Chinese Kalendar for 1841,* pp.58-60.
6. Quoted in Teixeira, p.29. In March 1827 Chinnery's name first appears in the annual census taken of non-Portuguese residents: see Morse, 1826, vol. IV, p.148.
7. *Directory for Macau in 1830,* 4pp., British Library PP 2571.d.
8. See Fr. Manuel Teixeira, 'The House of Chinnery', *Hong Kong Sunday Post-Herald,* 21 March 1974. The author observes that Chinnery's supposed occupation of *Travessa* de Ignacio Baptista is based on a misunderstanding; he also states that, according to modern numbering, Chinnery's residence in *Rua* de Ignacio Baptista was no.12. It has been claimed that Chinnery lived, at least during his early years in Macau, at the house of the merchant Christopher Fearon and his wife Elizabeth: see Hong Kong City Hall Art Gallery catalogue by J.R. Jones, 'George Chinnery 1774-1852', 1965, p.18, no.35, but it is not clear on what evidence this proposal is made. The Fearons lived until 1836 in the Rua do Hopital — the modern Rua de Pedro Nolasco da Silva — and subsequently in Rua de Largo da Sé: see Fr. Manuel Teixeira, 'Housing Problems in old Macau', *Hong Kong Sunday Post-Herald,* 21 April 1974.
9. Loines, p.125, extract from a letter, and p.126: 5 April 1830. (For a note on Harriet Low's journals in MS and printed versions see Bibliography.)
10. Ibid., p.118: 25 December 1829. No entry for this date appears in the MS journals; the text located at this point in the printed version is presumably an excerpt from one of Harriet Low's letters home.
11. Ibid., p.160: 28 August 1832.
12. Ibid., p.183: 26 April 1833.
13. Nye 1873, p.32.
14. Loines, p.118: 23 November 1829.
15. Ibid., p.118: 8 December 1829.
16. Ibid., p.181: 2 April 1833; MS journal entries for 11 February 1830, 20 June 1831, 1 August 1831, 16 May 1832.
17. Latimer papers, Library of Congress, letter from George Chinnery to Latimer, 12 December 1827.
18. Loines, p.181: 2 April 1833; MS journal entry for 16 May 1833, and from December 1829 to September 1830 *passim.*
19. Ibid., p.152: 6 May 1832.
20. Wood's proposal is recorded in the Harriet Low's MS journal entry for 11 December 1832.
21. Loines, p.170: 8 January 1833.
22. Ibid., p.129: 18 August 1830.
23. Ibid., pp.181-2: the MS journal entries for 9 and 10 April 1833 are conflated under 9 April in the printed version.
24. Ibid., pp.182-5: 15 April, 4 May, 10 May and 15 May 1833, and MS journal entry for 25 April 1833 (addition of book to portrait, see p.198 and Colour Plate 69).
25. Ibid., p.182: 15 April 1833.
26. Ibid., pp.184: 10 May 1833, and 185: 15 May 1833.

27. MS journal entry for 9 May 1833.
28. The portraits of William and Abigail Low are reproduced in Loines, following p.10.
29. Hunter, W.C., 1885, p.272.
30. Loines, p. 127: 22 June 1830; Harriet Low's definition of a lady was no doubt highly exclusive.
31. Letter from George Chinnery to Gilman, 23 February 1848, Hongkong and Shanghai Bank; see Chapter 11, n.4.
32. See Fay, p.322.
33. Read, vol.2, p.196.
34. Ljungstedt, p.212.
35. Downing, vol.2, p.246.
36. Peabody Museum, Salem, M3810-61A; see also M9765-23 in the same collection, a pencil drawing of a boatwoman dated 1839, in which a fragmentary line of shorthand reads '...the second sitting of Alloy in which the system has succeeded...'
37. See Berry-Hill 1963, and (for a greatly elaborated version) James Clavell, *Taipan,* 1966.
38. Downing, vol.1, pp.28-9.
39. Wood, p.290.
40. Shorthand on Lisbon no.100, dated 14 July '33, in Museu Luis de Camões, 1985.
41. Wood, pp.289-90; see also Downing, vol.1, p.28.
42. Nye 1886, pp.179-80.
43. George Henry Mason, *The Costume of China, Illustrated by sixty engravings,* 1800, text to pl.XXXVII, 'A Tinker'; see also pl.XIX, 'A Blacksmith'.
44. Daniell, text to 'Chinese Husbandman'.
45. Loines, p.191.
46. See *The Travels of Peter Mundy in Europe and Asia, 1608-1667,* vol.3, pt.1, Hakluyt Society, 1919.
47. Monroe, R.K., vol.86, 1950, p.268.
48. Ibid., vol. 87, 1951, pp.127-8.
49. Sketches in the Peabody Museum, Salem, M9760-15; the shorthand accompanying one sketch reads 'Peacock / Mr Beale's Aviary'. Harriet Low, who visited Beale's aviary on 26 October 1829, noted the Bird of Paradise ('by far the most beautiful') and the gold and silver pheasants: see Loines, p.114.
50. George Culley, *Observations on Live Stock,* 1794, p.174; see also John Claudius Loudon, *An Encyclopaedia of Agriculture,* 5th ed., 1844, pp.106-8.
51. Loines, p.129: 6 August 1830.

**Chapter 14: China Traders**

1. See Morse 1910-18, vol.1, p.72.
2. Letter from Canton 26 April 1832, in James Matheson's Private Letter Books, C5/1 p.95, Jardine, Matheson Archive.
3. Letter from George Parkyns of 17 December, 1830, Macau Letters, incoming, Jardine, Matheson Archive.
4. Letter from Macau to William Lyall in Calcutta, 19 June 1839, in James Matheson's Private Letter Books, Jardine, Matheson Archive.
5. Offered for sale at Christie's, London, 19 November 1990 (lot 66, illus.).
6. Memoir of William Prinsep, vol.3, India Office Library and Records, p.117.
7. Copy letter of 1 December 1838; see Ormond 1970, p.245.
8. Letter from William Jardine in Macau, no. 257; Jardine, Matheson Archive.
9. Letter from Macau, 14 August 1841, in James Matheson's Private Letter Books, vol. VII, Jardine, Matheson Archive.
10. Jardine, Matheson Archive, letter from Macau, 17 August 1841; India Letter Books. Presumably these debts were separate from the money owed by Chinnery to William Prinsep and his associates, which were said by Prinsep to have been discharged by 1838, see p.245.
11. Accounts Current A4/19, pp.88-9, and A4/20, p.180. Other payments to Lamqua are $34 on 31 July 1840; $60 on 31 October 1841, for an order placed by Henry Wright, James Matheson's partner; and $138 on 29 August 1843, for an order placed by his nephew Alexander Matheson.
12. The portrait of Henry Gribble by Chinnery is in the Hong Kong Museum of Art; a portrait of Captain Hine (clearly not Chinnery's original) is illus. in Keswick, p.136; and a portrait sketch by Chinnery, sold by Sotheby Parke Bernet (Hong Kong) on 23 November 1976 (lot 126), is inscribed in shorthand 'Mr. Grant and family February 1st 1837'.
13. Illus. in Keswick, 1982, p.136.
14. See Lubbock, pp.71-2.
15. See Nazir; and R.P. Massani, 'Sir Jamsetjee Jeejeebhoy', *The Indian Review* vol.XXX, September 1929, pp.600-6. For Jamsetjee's trading with Jardine, Matheson see Greenberg, *passim.*
16. See Martyn Gregory Gallery catalogue no.43, 1986, no.101. The other portrait of Jamsetjee by John Smart is illustrated in Conner 1986, p.58.
17. Monroe, R.K., vol.86, pp.22-3, 259.
18. Hunter, W.C., 1885, p.273.
19. The shorthand also identifies the sitter as H-R-J S-K-J.
20. In Christie's, London, sale of 18 March 1977 this picture was catalogued as 'Portrait of a Lady said to be Mrs Baynes' (lot 129).
21. See Morse 1926-9, vol.4, pp.234ff. Harriet and Abigail Low followed Mrs. Baynes to Canton, but were obliged to return after eighteen days.
22. Loines, p.134: 8 January 1834.
23. 'Register of baptisms, marriages and deaths at Macao and Whampoa 1820-1833', India Office Library and Records.
24. MS journal of Harriet Low, entry for 29 March 1831; on 8 January 1831 she decribed Charles Marjoribanks as 'a shrewd Scotchman', Loines, p.134. An oil painting by Chinnery of a small girl standing on a sofa, illus. Bonsall 1985, no.12, is identified by a typed label as 'Miss Marchbanks of Bushey'; the sofa in this picture is similar to that depicted in the 'Marjoribanks' group portrait (Colour Plate 93).
25. Peabody Museum M3810-21, illus. Peabody Museum, pl.XXI; the translation of the shorthand given in this catalogue (no.55) has subsequently been corrected by Geoffrey Bonsall.
26. Monroe, R.K., vol.86, p.391.
27. Ibid., pp.317-18.
28. Loines, p.113: 18 October 1829; an exclamation mark is added after 'bachelor' in the printed version.
29. Ibid., p.170: 6 January 1833.
30. Ibid., p.171: 1 February 1833.
31. Ibid., pp.172-181 *passim.* For Chinnery's portrait of Harriet Low see pp.198-90.
32. [Ljungstedt] 1834, pp.24-5. This account was also printed in the *Chinese Repository* III, December 1834.
33. Ibid., pp.40-6.
34. Ibid., pp.25-6.
35. Museu Luis de Camões, 1985, Lisbon no.33 (verso); the drawing in question is of a column, which was not adopted in the final composition.
36. Loines, p.180: 31 March 1833.
37. [Ljungstedt] 1834, p.26.
38. Loines, p.181: 2 April 1833; the MS journal continues: 'He (Afun) considers it no.1 good luck to be put in the picture.'
39. Ibid., p.225: 19 July 1834.
40. [Ljungstedt] 1834, pp.42-6; letters from Dr. Watson to Dr. Barnett in 1856, quoted in Gregory, p.43.
41. See Simon S. Brook, 'Chinese curiosi: 19th century examples of the east-west titration', *Journal of the Royal Society of Medicine,* vol.78, November 1985, pp.945-8.
42. See [Colledge], pp.14, 40-41.
43. The portrait of Ljungstedt not illustrated here is in the Swenska Portrattarkwet, Nationalmuseum, Stockholm.
44. See Simon S. Brook, 'The Contribution of Guy's and St. Thomas's Hospitals to the Introduction of Western Medicine in China', pt.1, *Guy's Hospital Gazette,* 7 December 1985, pp.424-5.
45. See Morse 1926-9, vol.4, p.187; in 1829 John Russell Reeves earned £500 as Deputy

Inspector, but in 1833 he received £2,000, having superseded his father as Inspector, ibid., p.346.

46. MS journal of Harriet Low, entry for 1 June 1830.

47. Mui, p.21.

48. See Whitehead, pp.193-233.

49. [Morrison] 1839, vol.2, p.424.

50. See Cheong, pp.244-5. A drawing of John Russell Reeves by Chinnery, dated 1838, is in the Natural History Museum, London.

51. See Downs, pp. 425, 434; and Morse 1926-9, vol.3, p.327.

52. This portrait is reproduced in colour in Lee, p.37; a watercolour version of the portrait, which carries the signature of Tingqua, is in the Metropolitan Museum of Art, New York; see also Clunas, pp.54-5, 62. The most impressive of the Chinese oil portraits of Howqua have generally been attributed to Tingqua's brother Lamqua.

53. Hunter, W.C., 1882, p.269.

54. Ibid., p.267.

55. Loines, p.135: 25 January 1831, and see Arthur W. Hummel, 'Nathan Dunn', Quaker History vol.59, Spring 1970, p.36; Harriet Low also described Dunn as 'an old bear', and 'too fat to walk with', MS journal entries for 2 and 4 July 1830.

56. Dunn, pp.118-19, and see Lee, p.15.

57. See Downs, pp.432-3.

58. Peabody Museum, nos.8 (illus.) and 10.

59. Read, vol.2, p.213; and Downs, p.436. A Chinnery pencil study for a portrait, offered for sale at Christie's 19 November 1990 (lot 65), is inscribed in shorthand 'Mr. Sturgis December 3rd '35'.

60. Samuel Wells Williams, quoted in Frederick Wells Williams, The Life and Letters of Samuel Wells Williams, New York, 1889.

61. [Morrison] 1839, vol.2, p.406, letter of 2 September 1828.

62. Ibid., vol.2, p.383.

63. Ibid., vol.2, pp.424-5, letter of 24 February 1829.

64. Ibid., vol.2, p.427, letter of 10 February 1829.

65. Ibid., vol.2, p.390.

66. Ormond 1974, p.136, letter of 1813 to Maria Browne.

67. [Morrison] 1839, vol.2, p.524.

68. A version of this drawing, in which Robert Morrison's tomb appears alone, is illus. in [Morrison] 1839, frontispiece to vol.2.

69. Ljungstedt 1836, p.27.

70. See Dictionary of National Biography; Gentleman's Magazine, 1844, part I, p.210; Morse 1926-9, vol.4, p.342.

71. Loines, p.48, letter from Harriet Low to her brother Abbot Low, 18 December 1831.

72. Medhurst, p.364.

73. Gutzlaff 1834, p.413; and Gutzlaff 1838, vol.1, pp.508-9. Gutzlaff's colleague Walter Medhurst was similarly ambivalent about the opium trade, Medhurst, pp.25, 56-7, but declined to travel in an opium ship, instead hiring his own vessel to distribute tracts up the coast.

74. See Berry-Hill 1963, pl.31, and Martyn Gregory Gallery catalogue, 1977, no.127.

75. Chinnery entry in Graves, 1905.

76. Peabody Museum, illus. pl.XVIII.

**Chapter 15: Images of the Artist**

1. Read, vol.2, p.213.

2. China Mail, 3 June 1852, and see also 10 June 1852.

3. Hunter, W.C., 1885, p.264.

4. Ibid., pp.265-6.

5. Ibid., p.267.

6. Ibid., p.269.

7. Ibid., p.268: 'After two years' residence in the Imperial Hong [in Canton], during which Mr Chinnery made remittances to his wife ("there goes another thousand rupees," he would say), and having arranged for a yearly sum "to keep her quiet", he took up his quarters in Macao...'

8. Ibid., pp.269-70.

9. Peabody Museum, Salem, no. M13693; a further note on the same drawing reads 'This sketch was made about the year 1840.'

10. Loines, p.181: entry for 2 April 1833.

11. Read, vol. 2, p.214.

12. Hunter 1885, p.273.

13. Nye 1886, p.180.

14. See Penny, no.149.

15. R.A. no.2240, presented in 1948 by Percy Moore Turner.

16. This drawing was acquired by Nicholas Bernard Allen from the estate of Mrs. C.M.V. D'Oyly; it was sold at Sotheby's, London, on 18 July 1974 (lot 50). Harriet Low's journal entry of 2 April 1833 is quoted in Loines, p.181. The only hookah mentioned by Harriet Low is that of Captain Clifton, '...smoking a splendid hookah, which custom is brought from Calcutta', ibid., p.128, entry for 2 August 1830. Clifton would have been able to replenish his expensive equipment on his regular visits to India. If Chinnery had maintained his hookah-smoking in Macau, Harriet Low would surely have mentioned it.

17. Illus. in Ormond 1968, p.90.

18. This painting was bought by the Metropolitan Museum in 1943 from Dr. Woodhouse, who had acquired it from Mrs. Percy Madeira of Philadelphia, grand-daughter of Benjamin Wilcocks. The portrait is discussed briefly in Margaret Jeffery, 'A Memento of the China Trade', Metropolitan Museum of Art Bulletin vol.IV, no.2, October 1945, pp.55-7.

19. Ormond 1974, p.179.

20. Nye 1886, p.179.

21. In addition to those illustrated or mentioned in the text, a number of Chinnery's pencil studies for self-portraits survive, including the following dated examples: a sketch in the National Portrait Gallery, inscribed and dated Canton 1832, with further shorthand on the sheet which does not refer to the portrait, illus. Ormond 1968, p.91; and a small sketch in the Victoria and Albert Museum, E1324-1928, dated 22 December 1847; another small sketch, sold at Christie's, London, on 13 November 1990 (lot 58), came from a group of drawings dated 1834-7.

22. Letter of 29 August 1845, f.3, to Lancelot Dent, in the National Portrait Gallery archive.

23. Art-Union Monthly Journal, 1846, p.180.

24. Loines, 1953, p.181: 2 April 1833.

25. The Memoir is MS Eur. D.1160 in the India Office Library and Records, by whose kind permission excerpts are reproduced here. For a fuller account of William Prinsep's journey to the China coast see Conner 1990, pp.312-16.

26. Memoir of William Prinsep, vol.1, p.282.

27. Ibid., pp.282-7, 350-4.

28. Ibid., vol.3, pp.111-13.

29. Ibid., pp.115-18.

**Chapter 16: The Opium War, and After**

1. Berry-Hill 1963, p.28, and Hutcheon 1975, p.22; even less plausible is the proposal that D'Oyly's reference to Chinnery's 'smoky meditation' (see Appendix iii, stanza XXVI) is an allusion to opium.

2. Hillard, p.197, entry for 15 April 1833.

3. Holman, vol.3, p.93.

4. Mcpherson 1842, p.245.

5. R.B.Forbes, 'History of a portrait', 1838, MS in Forbes family collection, lodged in the Peabody Museum of Salem, Massachusetts.

6. See Morse, 1910-18, vol.1, p.258.

7. Jardine, Matheson Archive, Macao Letters, incoming.

8. Keswick family scrapbook, vol.1, p.63; at the top of the first page is added 'Only pray do call'. This letter has been partially quoted in Maurice Collis, Foreign Mud, 1946, pp.244-5, but mistakenly placed in the context of 1839; in Ormond 1970, p.247, the letter is more accurately quoted but dated 1841. The version printed in

Collis is copied by Berry-Hill 1963, p.52, and Hutcheon 1975, p.118; the latter however gives the correct date of 1840.

'Dr. Anderson', with whom Chinnery took refuge, was Alexander Anderson, whose medical practice in Macau was taken over by Dr. T.B. Watson in 1845. Strickland, p.174, lists portraits by Chinnery of both Dr. Anderson and his wife; and a Chinnery drawing in the Peabody Museum of Salem, M9760-9, is inscribed in shorthand 'Mrs. Anderson's harp November 21st 1832'.

9. Museu Luis de Camões 1985, Lisbon no. 159.

10. Cunynghame, vol.2, p.238.

11. A drawing of Fort Monte, in the Peabody Museum, Salem, is inscribed 'The Citadel for Dent', see this museum's exhibition catalogue 'George Chinnery', 1967, no.48; drawing no. M13695 in the same collection (not catalogued) is inscribed 'Draw on Messrs. Dent & Co. for 30 Dollars'. A portrait of Lancelot Dent painted in the manner of Chinnery is illus. in Lubbock, opp. p.158.

12. Letter of 29 August 1845, f.3, to Lancelot Dent, National Portrait Gallery archive.

13. 'The want of a *moorah*, or some other substitute, for raising the legs and feet to a horizontal position, is always felt most severely by every old inhabitant of India', Williamson 1813, pl.X, f.3; the 'horizontal position', adopted also inside the palanquin, represented not merely comfort but leisure, status and seniority.

14. Morse 1926-9, vol.4, p.337.

15. See Teixeira, p.115.

16. Vaillant, tome 3, p.181; Durran also escorted the French party from Macau to Canton — a journey enlivened, it seems, by his good humour — and entertained them also at Macau, see pp.206, 212.

17. Chinnery's painting was exhibited at the Loan Exhibition, Hong Kong, in 1876, the owner being William Keswick; in his notes to the exhibition Gideon Nye (who had lived on the China coast since 1834, and known all the participants) described this picture as representing 'the front verandah of the late Mr Durand's residence, Praya Grande'; he adds that the Hunter was the owner of the performing dog sitting up on its hind legs., see Nye 1886, p.179.

18. Lubbock, appendix and p.227.

19. Monroe, R.K., vol.87, 1951, p.140, letter of 10 July 1845, and vol.88, 1952, p.52, letter of 28 September 1846.

20. Hunter, W.C., 1885, p.276; Hunter 1882, p.143, the author criticises the actions of the merchants in provoking the war: 'We were all equally implicated'.

21. These include a half-length study in oils on oval canvas, in the Yale Center for British Art; a seated three-quarter length in oils, with distant view of Macau, in the Hongkong and Shanghai Bank collection, illus. Tillotson, pl.14; and a seated three-quarter length in watercolours, signed and dated 1838, in the Peabody Museum, Salem.

22. Hunter, W.C., 1882, p.154.

23. Bernard, vol.2, pp.446, 483.

24. Museu Luis de Camões 1985, Lisbon no.73.

25. Illus. in Peabody Museum, pl.XIV.

26. Album in Watson family collection.; in a diary, in the same collection, jointly written by Thomas Watson and his wife Elizabeth, Durran is mentioned as one of a party of gentlemen setting off at 4 a.m. to visit the hot springs, entry for 31 October 1848.

Durran was also acquainted with other artists; when William Prinsep had come to the China coast in 1838, it was Durran who had escorted him, and introduced him to Auguste Borget: see Memoir of William Prinsep, India Office Library and Records, vol.3, pp.67, 20 October 1838, and p.114, 6 November 1838. Prinsep describes Durran as 'a pleasant Frenchman in some way connected with Dent's house'.

27. Letters to Captain D'Aguilar and R.J.Gilman respectively, reprinted in Hutcheon 1975, pp.161-2.

28. Hunter, W.C., 1885, p.273; and MS mandate (in Portuguese) over Chinnery's goods, in favour of T.B.Watson: Watson family papers.

29. Jardine, Matheson Archive, Private Letter Books, vol.6, 22 January 1841.

30. *Friend of China*, vol.1 no.1, 17 March 1842, p.1, 'Address'; from the second issue, the newspaper was published as the *Friend of China and Hongkong Gazette*.

31. Letter from Lord Palmerston to Captain Elliot, 21 April 1841, in Morse 1910, vol.I, p.642.

32. Robert Fortune, *Three Years' Wanderings in the Northern Provinces of China*, 1847, pp.12-13.

33. Smith, p.58.

34. Illus. in Christie's (London) sale catalogue 13 November 1990 (lot 57).

35. Loines, p.163: 29 October 1832; opium is not mentioned by Harriet Low during her visit to Lintin, although on 9 November she notes that 'many things happen that I do not put in my journal, partly from laziness and partly from prudence', p.164.

36. Levien, p.178; the Dents' 'Pagoda House' illus. p.141.

37. Letter from Chinnery in Macau to Captain D'Aguilar, 20 February 1848, in the collection of the Hongkong and Shanghai Bank; the letter, which is given in full in Hutcheon, p.162, includes a reference to a previous commission: 'I have removed the figures you wished and have added others in their stead.'

38. Tiffany, p.249.

39. Smith, p.452; the building of St. John's Cathedral was begun in 1847.

40. 'Memoir of the family of Watson', typescript in the family's possession; the author was Thomas Boswall Watson (1850-1941), the son of Chinnery's doctor.

41. Letter of 5 August 1847 from William Ash, then aged fifteen, in the Sword Family Papers, Historical Society of Pennsylvania, Philadelphia.

42. Paul Durran was presumably a relation of J.A. Durran, perhaps the son: Rebecca Kinsman refers to the presence of the Durrans 'father and son' in Macau in July 1845, Monroe, R.K., vol.87, 1951, p.140; however, the *Anglo-Chinese Kalendar* lists J.A Durran together with 'A.' or 'Adhemar' Durran in the years 1844-5-6.

43. Watson family collection, unpaginated MS journal, *passim*.

44. Ibid., entries for 11 September 1848, 28 October 1848, 17 October 1849 and 6 November 1847.

45. The drawings are in the Victoria and Albert Museum, nos. E.1765-1928 and 1767-1928; for another version of the painting see Tillotson, pl.117.

46. Letter published posthumously in the *Friend of China and Hongkong Gazette*, 2 June 1852.

47. Hunter, W.C., 1885, pp.273-4.

48. Nye 1873, p.32.

49. Hunter, W.C., 1885, pp.273-4; the same picture, or perhaps a drawing for it, is described in Nye 1886, pp.178-9; Chinnery had referred to his departure from Calcutta 'by sketching himself standing, hat in hand, in the stern of the ship's boat, bidding adieu to the "City of Palaces" by the expressive words "too hot!".'

50. The sale was announced in the *Hong Kong Register*, 13 July 1852, and the *Friend of China and Hong Kong Gazette*, 24 July 1852; claims on the estate were notified in the *Hongkong Register*, 31 August 1852.

51. *Hongkong Register*, 27 July 1852.

52. *Bengal Hurkaru*, 3 July 1852, reprinted in the *Hongkong Register*, 17 August 1852.

53. *Friend of China*, 8 July 1852; *Friend of China and Hongkong Gazette*, 2 June 1852; for another obituary see the *China Mail*, 3 and 10 June 1852.

54. An obituary notice in the *Brighton Herald*, 30 December 1865, p.2, records the

death on 23 December of Mrs. George Chinnery, at 13 Charlotte Street, Brighton, in her eighty-ninth year; if this is correct, Marianne was twenty-one or twenty-two at the time of her marriage on 19 April 1799.

55. *Calcutta Monthly Journal* no. 382, August 1826, pp.30-1. Samuel Prout died three months before Chinnery; born in 1783, he was perhaps too young to have known Chinnery in London.

56. Letter from Kane to Watson, 16 July 1858, in the Watson family papers, quoted in Gregory, p.70; the visitor was 'Mr Johnston...an American gentleman and a cousin of Mrs Rowley.'

57. Letter from Middleton to Watson, 24 April 1857, quoted in Gregory, p.10.

58. Letter to T.B.Watson from his nephew Alexander Watson in Hong Kong, 19 January 1859, indicating that Alexander did not have time to send his uncle's 'case of Chinnerys' by the *Carthage*, but would send it 'by next mail'; Watson family papers, p.71.

59. *Hong Kong Daily Press,* 19 July 1876.

**Chapter 17: Chinnery and Lamqua**

1. Downing, vol.2, pp.90-1.

2. See Nye 1886, p.179; the *Canton Register*, 8 December 1835; Read 1840, vol.2, p.215; and Memoir of William Prinsep, India Office Library and Records, vol.3, p.72.

3. Cunynghame, p.237.

4. Downing, vol.2, pp.90-112.

5. William Fane de Salis, *Reminiscences of Travel in China and India in 1848,* p.12.

6. Downing, vol.2, p.112.

7. Ibid., p.114.

8. For the relationship between Spoilum and Lamqua see Conner 1986, pp.50-1, and Crossman 1991, p.55.

9. Memo Book 3, September 1819-January 1820, Robert Waln papers, Historical Society of Pennsylvania, Philadelphia; the list is quoted in Crossman 1991, p.54.

10. For examples see Conner 1986, no.65; Crossman 1991, col. pl.14 and pl.16; and Lee, no.169 — the latter, a portrait of Henry Mandeville, is dated 1822.

11. Crossman 1991 takes the view that there was indeed another 'Lamqua' who preceded 'Chinnery Lamqua'; he proposes that this first 'Lamqua' was responsible for a series of portraits which appear too early in date to have been painted by 'Chinnery Lamqua'. On the other hand it may be observed that in the many references by western visitors to (Chinnery) Lamqua, there is no mention of any previous artist of that name; whereas in the 1850s and 1860s there are a number of allusions to the

'Elder' and 'Younger' Lamquas, referring to 'Chinnery Lamqua' and his son.

12. See Crossman 1972, p.26, and 1991, p.72.

13. Latimer papers Library of Congress, cash book 12, box 13, entry of 4 June 1832; ledger 6, box 15, entry of 28 September 1833.

14. *Canton Register,* 8 December 1835.

15. Jardine, Matheson Archive, Accounts Current A4/19, p.88: entry for 31 July 1840, and A4/20, p.180: 31 March 1842, and cash book A3/33: 29 August 1843 (all Lamqua); A4/19, p.88: 31 Oct. 1840, and p.89: 31 Jan. 1841 (both Chinnery).

16. Downing, vol.1, p.38, and vol.2, p.114.

17. Ibid., vol.2, p.114.

18. M. La Vollée, first published in *L'Artiste: Revue de Paris,* 1849, translated in the *Bulletin of the American Art Union,* 1850, the translation reprinted in Gardner, pp.316-18.

19. Eighty-six paintings are in the Yale Medical Library, twenty-three are in the Gordon Museum of Guy's Hospital, London, and one is in the Countway Library, Boston. See Gulick, pp.72-3, 114, 153, 244-5; for Lamqua and Guan A-to see George B. Stevens, *The Life, Letters...of Peter Parker, M.D.,* 1896, p.133.

20. See Crossman 1991, p.82 and pls.25, 26; and the *New Chinese Repository,* vol.III, no.2, December 1989, p.2.

21. Undated Madame Tussaud's poster reproduced in Pat Barr, *Foreign Devils,* 1970, p.49.

22. Public Record Office, Kew: Foreign Office Records 233/185 of 1844, no.27; I am indebted for this reference to Joseph Ting of the Hong Kong Museum of History. See Conner 1986, pp.56-7, for two portraits dated 1864 whose inscriptions (on the stretchers) identify the artist as 'Guan Shicun (alias) Lamqua'.

23. Monroe, R.K., vol.86, 1950, letters of 16 December 1843 and 16 May 1844.

24. *Chinese Repository,* 1 September 1845.

**Appendix i: Technique and Theory**

1. Ormond 1974, p.141.

2. The manuscript was sold at Sotheby's, London, on 3-4 March 1969 (lot 363) by Miss Esmé Browne, a descendant of Maria Browne. It was bought by Paul Mellon, who also bought a group of Chinnery's letters to Mrs. Browne, but generously allowed these to go to the British Museum (whose books and manuscripts are now designated as the British Library), since the British Museum already held another section of the correspondence.

3. See Ormond 1974, p.124.

4. Ibid.,pp.209-13. James Munro Macnabb was portrayed by Chinnery (private collection) and was a member of the D'Oyly circle. He spent the years 1812-23 in Calcutta and its environs (apart from furlough 1816-19). In 1820 he married Jane Mary Campbell, a cousin of Lady Hastings, and in 1822 he became Lord Hastings's Private Secretary.

5. Ibid., pp.174, 179, 175.

6. Ibid., p.193.

7. Ibid., p.195.

8. Farington, entry for 31 December 1795.

9. Ormond 1974, p.196.

10. Ibid., pp.130-2.

11. Reynolds, p.143 (8th Discourse).

12. Ormond 1974, pp.174-5.

13. See M.Kirby Talley Jr. in Penny, p.65.

14. Ormond 1974, p.139.

15. Ibid., p.173.

16. Ibid., pp.178-9.

17. Ibid., pp. 135, 151.

18. Ibid., p.162.

19. Ibid., pp.184-5.

20. Reynolds, pp.27, 42 (3rd and 4th Discourses).

21. Ormond 1974, p.168, and see p.150.

22. Reynolds, pp.60, 14 (5th and 2nd Discourses).

23. Ormond 1974, p.137, and see p.182.

24. Ibid., p.130.

25. Ibid., pp.135, 145, 162, 164.

26. Quoted in Archer and Falk, p.49, entry for 17 January 1819.

27. Ormond 1974, pp.197-209.

28. Shorthand on the same page reads: 'If I have one sitting or 29 I paint over the head at each sitting. Romney 1798.'

**Appendix ii: Chinnery's Shorthand**

1. The reference in *Don Juan,* canto I, 189, is to William Brodie Gurney, grandson of Thomas.

2. See Matthias Levy, *The History of Short-Hand Writing,* 1862; Thomas Anderson, *History of Shorthand,* 1882; and W.H. Gurney Salter, *A History of the Gurney System of Shorthand,* 1924.

3. Gurney.

4. Ibid., pp.47, 48.

**Appendix iii: Chinnery's Studio (notes as published with the poem in 1828)**

1. A celebrated portrait painter, who, in Europe, would rank high among the best alive of the present day.

2. Two ranges of buildings erected to the north of the church by the late chief engineer, in each of which there are six

houses adjoining each other.

3. A gentleman of considerable weight in Calcutta.

4. We must beg our readers to excuse the string of bad puns which we have been obliged to introduce in this canto, as there would be no chance of portraying the character of the eminent painter without them; and the worse they are, the more faithful will be the likeness.

5. The red brick dust from the Calcutta roads, being the only material used in their repair.

6. All these expressions will be recollected by those who have the pleasure of knowing Mr C.

7. By a few touches of charcoal we have seen ably represented a key hanging on a nail, shadow and all.

8. The artist is very fond of the prismatic system.

9. Five dots being indiscriminately put down on paper (by any one), it behoves the artist to represent a human figure — the five points forming the head, legs, and arms.

10. Mr C. originally practised in miniature; but nature, alarmed at his prototypic progress, and fearing he would come up to her, robbed him of one of his visual organs, and rendered the other too weak to admit of his following this branch of the art.

## Appendix iv: Artists and Amateurs Associated with Chinnery

1. With the Martyn Gregory Gallery in 1992.

2. Alexander Michie, *The Englishman in China...the career of Sir Rutherford Alcock*, 2 vols., 1900.

3. See Walker, nos. 25, 203, 586, 824, 826, 930; a series of Atkinson's drawings of Afghanistan is catalogued in Archer 1969, vol.I, pp.96-9.

4. Walker, no.836, p.39 and pl.820.

5. Ormond 1974, p.210 and pl.23c.

6. India Office Records N/1/10, f.508.

7. See César Guillen-Nuñez, (ed.), *Marciano Baptista e A Sua Arte*, Macau, 1990; and Patrick Conner, *Marciano Baptista 1826-1896*, Martyn Gregory Gallery, 1990.

8. See Martyn Gregory Gallery catalogue, 'Lieutenant Walford Thomas Bellairs R.N.', 1982, p.6.

9. Memoir of William Prinsep, India Office Records, vol.3, pp.67, 111.

10. Illus. in Bonsall 1985, no.24.

11. Draper's, New York, auction catalogue 28 April 1858, no.15.

12. The list of Mrs. Browne's 'Originals', 'Profiles' and 'Copies of Miniatures' is reproduced in Ormond 1974, pp.209-13.

13. Both the letters and the 'Treatise' are published in Ormond 1974, pp.123-209, together with illustrations of several of Mrs. Browne's miniatures and a portrait drawing of herself by Chinnery.

14. Cree Journals, National Maritime Museum, vol.X, 1846, opp. pp.22 and 23; for a published selection from Cree's illustrated journals see Levien.

15. Warren Hastings correspondence, British Library, Add. MS 29188, f.237.

16. For D'Oyly's oils see Col. M.H. Grant, *The Old English Landscape Painters*, 1960, vol.6, p.439. Several collections of D'Oyly's lithographs exist, some of them entitled 'Amateur's Repository of Indian Sketches'.

17. Warren Hastings correspondence, British Library, Add. MS 29188, f.238v.

18. See Archer 1969, vol.I, p.163, and 1970, pp.173-181.

19. *Journal of Mrs. Fenton*, 1901, pp. 63, 174.

20. See Vaillant, pp.157-8.

21. Ibid., pp.159-65.

22. Quoted in Archer and Falk, p.47; the aquatints after James Fraser are reproduced in this book, together with many of their collection of Company drawings.

23. See Martyn Gregory catalogues 18 (1977), 38 (1984) and 56 (1990); and Bonsall 1985, no.41.

24. Letter from Melrose of 20 May 1852, quoted in Mui, p.209.

25. See Martyn Gregory cat. 41, 1985, nos. 96-104.

26. See Walter F.C. Chicheley Plowden, *Records of the Chicheley Plowdens A.D. 1590-1913*, 1914, pp.163-5.

27. Illus. in Archer 1979, pl.328.

28. *Calcutta Government Gazette*, 14 December 1815.

29. However, a watercolour of a Bengali figure, no.23 in Hartnoll & Eyre, 'British Artists in India', 1970, is recorded as signed by Plowden on the reverse.

30. For James Prinsep's work on Indian scripts see John Keay, *India Discovered*, 1988 ed., pp.46-63.

31. Memoir of William Prinsep, India Office Library and Records, vol.1, pp.307-8.

32. Ibid., p.306; William Prinsep adds that this sketch became the property of Mrs. Wilson, the daughter of James Prinsep,

while William retained 'a bad copy in oils' — perhaps the picture visible on p.287. A copy in pencil and watercolour of (presumably) the same sketch, depicting James Prinsep beside his chemical apparatus, survives in an album compiled by William Prinsep (coll. Sven Gahlin), with the inscription 'James Prinsep from Chinnery'. The sketch illustrated on p.287 is contained in this album, inscribed by William Prinsep on the album page 'My studio in Calcutta — House behind the Bank of Bengal. 1827'. The inscription on the drawing itself indicates that it was given by James to William and Mary's young son William Haldimand (b.1824).

33. For examples of James Prinsep's work see Archer 1969, vol.1, p.288, and Eyre & Hobhouse Ltd., 'The Other Side of the Verandah', 1981, nos. 8-10.

34. Memoir of William Prinsep, India Office Library and Records, vol.2, pp.23-4.

35. See 'Thomas Prinsep (1800-1830): Drawings received from India', Colnaghi/Martyn Gregory catalogue, 1988.

36. The India Office Library holds an album of William Prinsep's drawings carried out in the 1820s, which also includes works by Chinnery, D'Oyly and others. A fine series of watercolour views of India, by William and Thomas Prinsep, was exhibited by Spink & Son Ltd. in April 1982. William's watercolours of Aden and Egypt, which he visited in 1842, are illustrated in Conner 1984. A group of his watercolours of Canton and the China coast was sold at Sotheby Parke Bernet (Hong Kong) on 28 November 1977 (lots 57-90).

37. It has been proposed that Robert Smith was also the artist of a group of fine oils of Penang scenes, which correspond with Daniell's aquatints; alternatively they may have been executed by Daniell himself, on the basis of preliminary drawings supplied by Smith, see Lim Chong Keat, pp.103-10.

38. See Conner 1986, pp.36-7, and the Museum of the American China Trade, Milton, Massachusetts, catalogue, 'Warner Varnham. A visual diary of China and the Philippines', 1973.

39. For examples of the work of both Thomas and Elizabeth Watson see Gregory.

40. Hunter, W.C., 1885, pp.270-72.

41. Edna O'Donnell, 'An Album of Chinnery Drawings', *Cooper Union Museum Chronicle*, New York, October 1949, pp.14-23.

# Bibliography

## Manuscript Sources
More specific references are cited in the footnotes

British Library: Correspondence between George Chinnery and Mrs. Maria Browne; draft 'Treatise' by George Chinnery and Mrs. Browne; letters from W.B. Chinnery; letters from G.R. Chinnery (Robert Peel Correspondence); letters from Sir Charles D'Oyly (Warren Hastings correspondence).

Cambridge University Library: Jardine, Matheson Archive.

Forbes family collection, Peabody Museum, Salem, Massachusetts: R.B. Forbes, 'History of a Portrait'.

Historical Society of Pennsylvania, Philadelphia: Sword and Waln papers.

Hongkong and Shanghai Bank, Hong Kong: Letters from George Chinnery to Captain D'Aguilar, and to R.J. Gilman.

India Office Library and Records: Lists of residents in Madras and Calcutta; log of the *Hythe*, 1825; Madras Public Proceedings; Memoir of William Prinsep; minutes of the Court of Directors of the East India Company; MS and typescript of William Hickey's journals.

Keswick family collection.

Library of Congress, Washington D.C.: Latimer papers, and Low-Mills correspondence, including the journal of Harriet Low (see right).

Matheson & Co., London: Letter from George Chinnery to James Matheson.

National Library of Scotland: Minto papers.

National Maritime Museum, Greenwich: Journals of Edward Cree.

National Portrait Gallery, London: George Chinnery's letter accompanying his self-portrait.

Private collection, London: Journals of James Prinsep.

Royal Irish Academy, Dublin: Anonymous journal of 1801.

Watson family collection.

## A Note on the Journal of Harriet Low

The journal kept by Harriet Low in 1829-33 is the principal source of evidence of Chinnery's activities in Macau at this time. It was sent home in instalments from Macau to her sister in Salem. The manuscript journal was donated to the Library of Congress in 1943 by the author's granddaughter, Miss Elma Loines, with the exception of the volume covering the period from 2 September 1830 to 1 March 1831, which is missing. An abridgement was published in Boston in 1900, edited by Katherine Hillard, one of Harriet Low's daughters. A more substantial (but still partial) edition appeared in 1953, edited by Elma Loines, see under Printed Works.

Both editors adopted a policy of altering some of Harriet Low's phrasing and punctuation, with a view to producing a more readable and smoothly-flowing narrative. This resulted in some accidental changes of meaning. For example, Harriet Low objected to 'a very ugly person' in Chinnery's portrait of her; in the printed versions this becomes 'a very ugly face' (15 May 1833). In an assessment of Chinnery's character (2 April 1833), Harriet wrote that the artist 'buckles to' — meaning, presumably, that he worked hard; in the printed books she is made to say that he 'buckles to me' — a very different proposition. Moreover, the printed versions contain a series of interesting references (19 March-4 May 1832) to 'Hunter', who has naturally been identified as William Hunter, the American China trader and author. But the manuscript clearly reads 'Huddleston' in each case, and thus refers to Chinnery's neighbour Robert Hudleston of the East India Company.

For the most part, however, the alterations do not significantly affect the sense, and wherever possible, references in the notes of the present work are made to the Loines edition of 1953. The manuscript journal is cited only when the sense is markedly different and, of course, when the entry does not appear in the printed versions.

**Printed Works**

Place of publication is London, unless otherwise specified

Abeel, David, *Journal of a Residence in China*, New York, 1836.

Anon., *A Critical Review of the First Annual Exhibition of Paintings, Drawings & Sculptures, the works of the Irish Artists, at No. 32, Dame-Street, Dublin, June 1800*, Dublin.

Archer, Mildred, *British Drawings in the India Office Library*, 2 vols., 1969.

Archer, Mildred, '" The talented baronet": Sir Charles D'Oyly and his drawings of India', *Connoisseur* vol.175, no.705, November 1970, pp.173-81.

Archer, Mildred, *India and British Portraiture 1770-1825*, 1979.

Archer, Mildred, and Toby Falk, *India Revealed: the art and adventures of James and William Fraser 1801-35*, 1989.

Arnold, William Delafield, *Oakfield*, 2nd ed., 2 vols., 1854.

Arts Council of Great Britain, 'George Chinnery 1774-1852', introd. Allan Carr, London and Edinburgh, 1957.

Auber, Peter, *Supplement to an Analysis of the Constitution of the East India Company*, 1828.

Bernard, W.D. (ed.), *Narrative of the Voyages and Services of the Nemesis, from 1840 to 1843...*, 2nd (enlarged) ed., 2 vols., 1844.

Berry, Henry F., *A History of the Royal Dublin Society*, 1915.

Berry-Hill, Henry and Sidney, *George Chinnery 1774-1852, Artist of the China Coast*, Leigh-on-Sea, 1963.

Berry-Hill, Henry and Sidney, *Chinnery and China Coast Paintings*, Leigh-on-Sea, 1970.

Bonsall, Geoffrey, 'George Chinnery's Views of Macau', *Arts of Asia* vol.16, no.1, January-February 1986, pp.78-92.

Bonsall, Geoffrey (ed.), *George Chinnery: His Pupils and Influence*, Hong Kong Museum of Art, 1985.

Borget, Auguste, *Le Chine et les Chinois*, Paris, 1842, published in London in 1842 as *Sketches of China and the Chinese;* see also Forgues, and Hutcheon, 1979.

Bovill, E.W., 'George Chinnery (1774-1852)', *Notes and Queries* n.s. vol.1, May 1956, pp.212-16, and June 1956, pp. 266-9.

Bradford, Alan, 'The Chinnery Restoration', *The Hongkong Bank Group Magazine* no.14, 1979, pp.2-8.

Buckingham, James Silk, Autobiography, 2 vols., 1855.

Buckland, C.E., *Dictionary of Indian Biography*, 1926.

Cameron, Nigel, *Barbarians and Mandarins. Thirteen Centuries of Western Travellers in China*, New York, 1970.

Cameron, Nigel, *An Illustrated History of Hong Kong*, Hong Kong, 1991.

*Canton Press and Price Current*, Canton and Macau, 1835-44.

*Canton Register*, Canton, 1827-43.

Carey, W.H., *The Good Old Days of Honorable John Company*, 2nd ed., 2 vols., Calcutta, 1906.

Chan Hsin-pao, *Commissioner Lin and the Opium War*, Cambridge, Massachusetts, 1964.

Cheong Weng Eang, *Mandarins and Merchants: Jardine Matheson and Co.*, Scandinavian Institute of Asian Studies Monograph no.26, 1979.

*China Mail*, Hong Kong, 1845-1911.

*Chinese Repository*, Canton and Hong Kong, 1832-51.

Chinnery, William [Snr.], *The Compendious Emblematist, or, Writing and Drawing, made Easy, Amusing and Instructive*, n.d. [c.1760].

Christman, Margaret, 'Adventurous Pursuits: Americans and the China Trade 1784-1844', National Portrait Gallery, Washington, D.C., 1984.

Clunas, Craig, *Chinese Export Watercolours*, 1984.

Coates, Austin, *A Macao Narrative*, Hong Kong, 1978.

Colebrooke, Sir T.E., *Life of Mountstuart Elphinstone*, 2 vols., 1884.

[Colledge, Thomas R., et al.], *The Medical Missionary Society in China*, n.d.

Conner, Patrick, 'The Overland Route of William Prinsep (1794-1874)', Martyn Gregory catalogue 37, 1984.

Conner, Patrick (ed.), 'The China Trade 1600-1860', Brighton Museums, 1986.

Conner, Patrick, 'In pursuit of Chinnery', *Apollo*, November 1990, pp.312-16.

Cotton, Sir Harry Evan A., 'Memoirs of the Supreme Court 1774-1862', *Bengal Past and Present*, vol.XXX, 1925.

Cotton, Sir Harry Evan A., *A Descriptive List of the pictures in the Viceroy's residences at New Delhi, Simla and Calcutta*, Calcutta, revised ed., 1936.

Cotton, Julian James, 'George Chinnery, Artist (1774-1852)', *Bengal Past and Present* vol.XXVIII, January-June 1924, pp.113-26.

Crawford, D.G., *Roll of the Indian Medical Service 1615-1930*, 1930.

Crookshank, Anne, and the Knight of Glin, *The Painters of Ireland*, 1978.

Crossman, Carl, *The China Trade*, Princeton, 1972; enlarged ed., *The Decorative Arts of the China Trade*, Woodbridge, 1991.

Cunynghame, Capt. Arthur, *An Aide-de-Camp's Recollections of Service in China*, 2 vols., 1844.

Daniell, Thomas and William, *A Picturesque Voyage to India by the Way of China*, 1810.

Davies, Philip, *Splendours of the Raj. British Architecture in India, 1660 to 1947*, 1985.

Dodwell, Henry H. and W. Miles, *An Alphabetical List of the Hon. East India Company's Bengal Civil Servants 1780-1839*, 1839.

Dodwell, Henry H. and W. Miles, *An Alphabetical List of the Hon. East India Company's Madras Civil Servants 1780-1839*, 1839.

Douglas, Sylvester, *The Diaries of Sylvester Douglas (Lord Glenbervie)*, ed. Francis Bickley, 2 vols., 1928; see also Glenbervie.

Downing, C. Toogood, *The Fan-Qui in China in 1836-7*, 3 vols., 1838.

Downs, Jacques M., 'American Merchants and the China Opium Trade, 1800-1840', *Business History Review* XLII, no.1, winter 1968, pp.418-42.

D'Oyly, Sir Charles, *Antiquities of Dacca*, 1814-27.

D'Oyly, Sir Charles, *Tom Raw, the Griffin. A Burlesque Poem in Twelve Cantos*, 1828, see Appendix iii.

Dunn, Nathan, 'Ten Thousand Chinese Things': A Descriptive Catalogue of the Chinese Collection, Philadelphia, 1839.

Edwards, Edward, *Anecdotes of Painters*, 1808.

Elers, George, *Memoirs of George Elers*, ed. Lord Monson and G.L. Gower, 1903.

Ellis, Henry, *Journal of the Proceedings of the late Embassy to China*, 1817.

Elphinstone, Mountstuart, see Colebrooke, Sir T.E.

Farington, Joseph, *The Diary of Joseph Farington*, ed. K. Garlick and A. Macintyre, Yale, 1978, &c.

Fay, Peter Ward, *The Opium War 1840-1842*, 1976.

Firminger, Walter F., *The Early History of Freemasonry in Bengal and the Punjab*, Calcutta, 1906.

Firminger, Walter K., *The Second Lodge of Bengal in Olden Times*, Calcutta, 1911.

Forbes, Robert Bennet, *Personal Reminiscences*, Boston, 1876.

Forbes, Sarah Hughes (ed.), *Letters and Recollections of John Murray Forbes*, 2 vols., Boston, 1899.

[Forgues, Emile], 'Old Nick', *La Chine Ouverte*, Paris, 1845.

Foskett, Daphne, *Miniatures: Dictionary and Guide*, Woodbridge, 1987.

Foster, Sir William, 'British Artists in India, 1760-1820', *Journal of the Walpole Society* vol.XIX, 1930-31.

*Friend of China and Hongkong Gazette*, Hong Kong, 1842-59.

Gardner, Albert Ten Eyck, 'Cantonese Chinnerys: Portraits of Howqua and other China Trade paintings', *Arts Quarterly*, Detroit Institute of Arts vol.16, winter 1953, pp.304-23.

Glenbervie, Lord, *The Glenbervie Journals*, ed. Walter Sichel, 1910; see also Douglas, Sylvester.

Gomes, Luis G., 'No Bicentenario de George Chinnery', *Noticias de Macau*, 5 January 1973.

Gould, Robert F., *Military Lodges. The Apron and the Sword, or, Freemasonry under Arms*, 1899.

Gould, Robert F., *Gould's History of Freemasonry*, ed. H. Poole, 4 vols., 1951.

Graham, Maria, *Journal of a Residence in India, 1809-1811*, 1812.

Grant, Colesworthy, *Rural Life in Bengal*, 1860.

Graves, Algernon, *The Royal Academy of Arts: A Complete Dictionary of Contributors*, 1905.

Graves, Algernon, *The Society of Great Britain. The Free Society of Artists 1761-1783: A Complete Dictionary of Contributors...*, 1907, reprinted Bath 1969.

Greenberg, Michael, *British Trade and the Opening of China 1800-1842*, Cambridge, 1951.

Gregory, Martyn, 'Dr. Thomas Boswall Watson (1815-1860): physician and amateur artist in China', catalogue 40, 1985.

Guillen-Nuñez, César, *Macau*, Hong Kong, 1984.

Guillen-Nuñez, César, 'Buildings from Macau's past', *Arts of Asia* vol.16, no.1, January-February 1986, pp.66-71.

Gulick, Edward V., *Peter Parker and the Opening of China*, Cambridge, Massachusetts, 1973.

Gurney, Thomas, *Brachygraphy: or Short Writing, made Easy to the Meanest Capacity*, first published 1753, 6th ed., 1767.

Gutzlaff, Charles, *Journal of Three Voyages along the coast of China in 1831, 1832 and 1833*, 1834.

Gutzlaff, Charles, *China Opened*, revised by Andrew Reed, 2 vols., 1838.

Heber, Reginald, *Narrative of a Journey through the Upper Provinces of India*, 2nd ed., 2 vols., 1844.

Helm, W.H., *Vigée-Lebrun 1755-1842. Her Life, Works and Friendships*, n.d.

Hickey, William, *Memoirs of William Hickey, 1745-1809,* ed. Alfred Spencer, 4 vols., 1913-25.

Hillard, Katherine (ed.), *My Mother's Journal 1829-1834,* Boston, 1900.

Hobson-Jobson, see Yule, Col. Henry.

Hodges, William, *Travels in India during the years 1780, 1781, 1782 and 1783,* 1793.

Hodgson, G.H., *Thomas Parry, Free Merchant, 1768-1824,* Madras, 1938.

Hoe, Susanna, *The Private Life of Old Hong Kong: Western Women in the British Colony, 1841-1941,* Hong Kong, 1991.

Holman, James, *Memoirs of the Blind Traveller,* 3 vols., 1834.

*Hongkong Daily Press* [known as *Daily Press* 1857-60], Hong Kong, 1857-1911.

*Hongkong Register,* Hong Kong, 1843-63.

Hummel, Arthur W., *Eminent Chinese of the Ch'ing Period,* Washington, D.C., 1943-4.

Hunter, William C., *The 'Fan Kwae' at Canton before Treaty Days, 1825-1849,* 1882, reprinted Taipei 1970.

Hunter, William C., *Bits of Old China,* 1885.

Hunter, Sir William W., *The Thackerays in India,* 1897.

Hutcheon, Robin, *Chinnery: the man and the legend,* Hong Kong, 1975.

Hutcheon, Robin, *Souvenirs of Auguste Borget,* Hong Kong, 1979.

Hutchinson, Sidney, 'The R.A. Schools...', *Walpole Society* vol.XXXVIII, 1960-2.

Itier, Jules, *Journal d'un Voyage en Chine en 1843, 1844, 1845, 1846,* 3 vols., 1848-53.

Jacquemont, Victor, *Letters from India 1829-1832,* tr. Catherine Phillips, 1936.

Jones, Mark Bence-, *Palaces of the Raj,* 1973.

Kaye, John W., *The Life and Correspondence of Charles, Lord Metcalfe,* 2nd ed., 1858.

Kee Il Choi (ed.), *The China Trade: Romance and Reality,* De Cordova Museum, Lincoln, Massachusetts, 1979.

Keswick, Maggie (ed.), *The Thistle and the Jade: a celebration of 150 years of Jardine, Matheson & Co.,* 1982.

King, Anthony D., *The Bungalow: the production of a global culture,* 1984.

King, Frank H.H. and Prescott Clarke, *A Research Guide to China-Coast Newspapers 1822-1911,* East Asian Research Center, Harvard University, 1965.

Kinsman, see Monroe.

Kuo-Tung Anthony Ch'en, *The Insolvency of the Chinese Hong Merchants 1760-1843,* Academia Sinica Institute of Economics Monograph Series no.45, Taipei, 1990.

Lebrun, Vigée, *Souvenirs de Madame Vigée Le Brun,* n.d., 2 vols.

Lee, Jean Gordon, *Philadelphians and the China Trade 1784-1844,* Philadelphia Museum of Art, 1984.

Levien, Michael (ed.), *The Cree Journals,* Exeter, 1981.

Lim Chong Keat, *Penang Views 1770-1860,* Singapore, 1986.

[Ljungstedt, Sir Anders (Andrew)], *A Brief Account of an Ophthalmic Institution, during the years 1827, 1828, 1829, 1830, 1831, and 1832, by a Philanthropist,* Canton, 1834.

Ljungstedt, Sir Anders (Andrew), *An Historical Sketch of the Portuguese Settlements in China,* Boston, 1836.

Loines, Elma (ed.), *The China Trade Post-Bag of the Seth Low Family,* Manchester, Maine, 1953.

Love, Henry D., *Vestiges of Old Madras 1640-1800,* 4 vols., 1913.

Lubbock, Basil, *The Opium Clippers,* 1933.

Macgregor, David, *Merchant Sailing Ships 1776-1815,* 1985.

Mcpherson, Duncan, *Two Years in China. Narrative of the Chinese Expedition,* 1842.

Mannoni. D.O., *Prospero and Caliban,* tr. Pamela Powersland, 1956.

Massey, William (of Wandsworth), *The Origin and Progress of Letters,* 1763.

Medhurst, Walter H., *China: Its State and Prospects,* 1838.

Metcalfe, Lord, see Kaye.

Metropolitan Museum of Art, *The China Trade and its Influences,* New York, 1941.

Mill, James, and Horace H. Wilson, *History of British India from 1805 to 1835,* 9 vols., 1840 &c.

Minto, 1st Earl, *The Life and Letters of Sir Gilbert Elliot, First Earl of Minto,* ed. Emma E.E.M. Kynynmound (Countess of Minto), 3 vols., 1874.

Monroe, Mary Kinsman, 'Nathaniel Kinsman, Merchant of Salem, in the China Trade', *Essex Institute Historical Collections* vol.85, Salem, Massachusetts, April 1949, pp.101-42.

Monroe, Rebecca Kinsman, 'Letters of Rebecca Chase Kinsman to her Family in Salem', *Essex Institute Historical Collections* vols. 86-8, Salem, Massachusetts, 1950-1.

Montalto de Jesus, C.A., 'George Chinnery', *China*

Journal vol.8, no.6, June 1928, pp.294-7.

Moore, Thomas, *Memoirs of the Life of the Rt. Hon. R.B. Sheridan*, 1825.

[Morrison, Mrs. Eliza (ed.)], *Memoirs of the Life and Labours of Robert Morrison*, D.D., compiled by his widow, 2 vols., 1839.

Morrison, John Robert, *A Chinese Commercial Guide*, Canton, 1848.

Morse, Hosea B., *The International Relations of the Chinese Empire*, 3 vols., Oxford, 1910-18.

Morse, Hosea B., *The Chronicles of the East India Company trading to China 1635-1834*, 5 vols., Oxford, 1926-9.

Mui, H. and L.H. (eds.), *William Melrose in China 1845-1855*, Edinburgh, 1973.

Museu Luis de Camões, *George Chinnery*, introd. Luis G. Gomes, 1974.

Museu Luis de Camões, *George Chinnery: Macau*, introd. César Guillen-Nuñez, Macau, 1985.

Nazir, Kuvarji Sohrabji, *The First Parsee Baronet*, Bombay, 1866.

Nugent, Maria, *Lady Nugent's Journal,* ed. Frank Cundall, 1934.

Nye, Gideon, *The Morning of my life in China,* Canton, 1873.

Nye, Gideon, 'Notes and Queries', *Journal of the China Branch of the Royal Asiatic Society for the year 1885,* vol.20, 1886.

'Old Nick', see [Forgues].

Orange, James, 'The Life and Works of George Chinnery in China', *Studio* vol.80, 1920.

Orange, James, *The Chater Collection: pictures relating to China, Hongkong, Macao 1655-1860,* 1924.

Orange, James, 'George Chinnery, Pictures of Macao and Canton', *Studio* vol.94, 1927.

Ormond, Richard, 'George Chinnery's Image of Himself', *Connoisseur* vol.167, February and March 1968, pp.89-93 and 160-64.

Ormond, Richard, 'George Chinnery and the Keswick family', *Connoisseur* vol.175, December 1970, pp.245-55.

Ormond, Richard, 'Chinnery and his pupil, Mrs Browne', *Journal of the Walpole Society* vol.XLIV, 1974, pp.123-214.

Paget, Edward, *Letters and Memorials of General the Hon. Sir Edward Paget, G.C.B.,* ed. Eden Paget, 1898.

Pavière, Sidney H., *The Devis family of painters,* 1950.

Peabody Museum, Salem, Massachusetts, 'George Chinnery 1774-1852 and other artists of the Chinese scene', text by Francis Lothrop, Salem, 1967.

Penny, Nicholas (ed.), *Reynolds,* Royal Academy, 1986.

Perry, Rev. Frank, *The Church in Madras,* 3 vols., 1904.

Philips, C.H., *The East India Company 1784-1834,* 1940.

Prynne, Jane Townley, and Alicia Bayne, *Memorials of the Thackeray Family,* 1879.

Qu Zhi-ren, 'George Chinnery, Painter', *Arts of Asia* vol.4, no.2, March-April 1971.

Ray, Gordon, *Thackeray: the Uses of Adversity,* 1955.

Read, George C., *Around the World: A narrative of a voyage in the East India Squadron under Commander George C. Read,* 2 vols., New York, 1840.

Reading Museum and Art Gallery, 'William Havell 1782-1857', 1981.

Redgrave, Richard and Samuel, *A Century of Painters in England,* 2 vols., 1866.

Reynolds, Sir Joshua, *Fifteen Discourses delivered to the Royal Academy,* Everyman ed., n.d.

[Roberdeau, Henry], 'A Young Civilian in Bengal in 1805', *Bengal Past and Present* vol.XXIX, January-June 1925.

Roberts, Emma, *Scenes and Characteristics of Hindostan,* 2 vols., 1837.

Rose, George, *Diaries and Correspondence of the Rt. Hon. George Rose,* ed. Rev. L.V. Harcourt, 2 vols., 1860.

Scarth, John, *Twelve Years in China,* Edinburgh, 1860.

Sée, Robert R.M., *English Pastels 1750-1830,* 1911.

Sée, Robert R.M., 'Gouaches by George Chinnery', *Connoisseur* vol.54, 1919, pp.141-51.

Smith, Rev. George, *A Narrative of an Exploratory Visit to each of the Consular Cities of China and to the Islands of Hong Kong and Chusan,* New York, 1847.

Stocquelier, J.H., *The Hand-Book of India,* 1844.

Strickland, Walter G., *A Dictionary of Irish Artists,* 2 vols., Dublin, 1913.

Sullivan, Michael, 'Chinnery the Portrait Painter', *Orientations* vol.11 no.4, April 1980, pp.27-35.

Sutton, Thomas, *The Daniells. Artists and Travellers,* 1954.

Tate Gallery, London, 'Loan Exhibition of Works by George Chinnery, R.H.A. 1774-1852', 1932.

Teixeira, Fr. Manuel, *A History of the old Protestant Cemetery in Macau,* Macau, n.d.

Tiffany, Osmond jun., *The Canton Chinese, or the American's sojourn in the Celestial Empire,* Boston, 1849.

Tillotson, Giles, *Fan Kwae Pictures,* 1987.

Vaillant, *Voyage autour du monde exécuté pendant les années 1836 et 1837 sur la corvette LA BONITE, commandée par M. Vaillant,* Paris, 1852, tome 3.

Van der Straeten, 'Viottiana', *Connoisseur* vol.XXXI, 1911.

Vigne, Randolph, 'The Eustaces and Hardys: a Carlow background to two Chinnery Portraits', *Carloviana. The Journal of the Old Carlow Society* n.s. vol.2 no.25, 1976, pp.32-3.

Waley, Arthur, *The Opium War through Chinese Eyes,* 1958.

Walker, Richard, *Regency Portraits,* 2 vols., 1985.

Welply, W.H., 'George Chinnery, 1774-1852, with some account of his family and genealogy', *Notes and Queries* vol.152, nos.2-5, January 1927, pp.21-4, 39-43, 58-61, 75-8; a revised version of the above was published in the *Journal of the Cork Historical and Archaeological Society* vol. 37, 1932, pp.11-31, and vol.38, 1933, pp.1-15.

White, Terence de Vere, *The Story of the Royal Dublin Society,* Tralee, 1955.

Whitehead, Peter J.P., 'The Reeves Collection of Chinese Fish Drawings', *Bulletin of the British Museum (Natural History),* Historical Series vol.3, no.7, 1970.

Whitehill, Walter Muir (ed.), 'Remarks on the China Trade and the Manner of Transacting Business', Essex Institute Historical Collections 73, no.4.

Whitley, W.T., *Artists and their Friends in England 1700-1799,* 2 vols., 1928.

Whitley, W.T., *Art in England 1800-1820,* Cambridge, 1928.

Williamson, Captain Thomas, *The East India Vade Mecum,* 2 vols., 1810.

Williamson, Captain Thomas, *The European in India,* 1813.

Wilson, C.R. (ed.), *List of Inscriptions on Tombs or Monuments in Bengal,* Calcutta, 1896.

Wood, William Maxwell, *Fankwei; or the San Jacinto in the Seas of India, China and Japan,* New York, 1859.

Wurtzburg, Charles E., *Raffles of the Eastern Isles,* 1954.

Yule, Col. Henry, and A.C.Burnell (eds.), *Hobson-Jobson. A Glossary of Colloquial Anglo-Indian Words and Phrases...,* 2nd ed., 1903, reissued 1985.

# Chinnery Family Tree

George Chinnery's immediate predecessors and descendants, based on the genealogy compiled by W.H. Welpy (see Bibliography), supplemented by information generously supplied by Mrs. Teague, a descendant of the artist, and other sources

William Chinnery Senior
1708-1791

William Chinnery Junior = Elizabeth Bassett
1740/1-1803                          d.1812

Thomas Welch
b.1772

Frances Hughes
1777-1829
= John Duncan, M.D.
d.1819

Elizabeth Harriett
b.1768

William Terry
1764-5

William Bassett = Margaret Tresilian
(of the Treasury)      d.1840
1766-1834

John Terry =    Mary Payton
(Madras merchant)   1776/1-1847
1770-1817

George = Marianne Vigne
(artist)        1777-1865
1774-1852

Caroline
1791-1812
(d. unmarried)

George Robert
1791-1826
(d. unmarried)

Walter Grenfell
d.1802
(d. young)

Charles b.1800
(d. in infancy)

Elizabeth Marianne
1801-1871

daughter b.1803
(d. young)

2 illegitimate sons
Edward Charles
1813-1841
Henry Colin 1813-1841

James Cowley Brown = Matilda
d.1852                        1800-79

John Eustace
1801-22
(d. unmarried)

Matilda Margretta b.1797
= Capt. Samuel Hodgson

Mary Henrietta
1802-1885

William Charles
1805-39
(d. unmarried)

2 sons and
2 daughters

2 sons and
5 daughters
(all married)

William      Frances      Mary      John      Charles Stewart      Isabella

# Glossary

Terms used by westerners in India and on the China coast.

Amah, ayah: Native nursemaid or other domestic female servant.

Anglo-Indian: Relating to the British in India (also used at a later date in preference to 'Eurasian', i.e. of mixed descent).

Bangla: Bengali dwelling of mud and thatch; probably the origin of bungalow.

Bibi, beebee: Indian mistress or common-law wife of a western expatriate, formerly used as the title of certain Indian princesses.

Catamaran: Craft made of two or more logs lashed together, in use in the coastal surf of southern India.

Charpoy: Light bedstead.

Chattar: Umbrella.

Chobdar: Mace-bearer, often preceding a palanquin.

Choppar: Thatched roof; on a boat, forming an upper deck.

Chowkidar: Village watchman.

Diwan: Royal court or council, or a minister of state.

Durbar, darbar: Royal assembly or audience.

Factory: Trading establishment, especially the headquarters in the East of a western company.

Godown: Warehouse.

Gopuram: In southern India, a pyramidal gateway at the entrance to a temple.

Guldasta: Ornamental pinnacle usually surmounted by a floral motif.

Hong: A business, or the building in which business is transacted; often synonymous with Factory (q.v.).

Hong merchants: Chinese wholesale merchants, collectively known as the Co-Hong, responsible for conducting trade with westerners at Canton.

Hookah, huqqa: Water pipe, hubble-bubble, maintained by a *hookahburdar*.

Jhaump, jhanp: Hurdle used as a door or shutter.

Masula, mussoola: Light craft made of planks sewn together, in use on the Coromandel coast.

Moorah: Hassock for supporting the feet of a reclining individual.

Munshi, moonshee: Teacher of Indian language; also secretary, interpreter.

Musnud: Ceremonial cushion occupied by an Indian ruler, or the power which it symbolised.

Nargila: Simple hookah, with a bowl often made from a coconut shell.

Nautch: Stage entertainment, especially one performed by dancing girls.

Palanquin, palankeen, palkee, palki: Covered litter.

Praya: Sea-wall or embankment supporting a coastal road.

Pukka: Substantial, permanent, reliable; of houses, brick-built.

Pulwar: River boat, sometimes used in a convoy as a kitchen boat.

Punkah: Large rectangular fan of cloth hung from the ceiling and operated by rope.

Putelee: Baggage craft.

Sepoy: Native Indian soldier in the service of the British.

Snow: European two-masted merchant vessel.

Soontahburdar: Palanquin attendant who carries a ceremonial *soontah* or baton.

Syce: Groom.

Tanka boat: 'Egg-boat', covered sampan operated by boatwomen on the China coast.

Tatty: Mat of woven grass, hung at doors and windows and frequently watered, as a means of cooling the air.

Thannah, tana: Police station; hut used by a *chowkidar*.

# Photographic Acknowledgements

Photographs have kindly been provided by the owners except in the following instances where they have been supplied by:

Thomas Agnew & Sons Ltd., Plates 27, 114.
The Asian Collector Ltd., Colour Plate 87.
Bill Thomson, Albany Gallery, Colour Plate 32; Plate 38.
Alan Bradford, Colour Plates 1, 69.
Christie's, Colour Plates 41, 55, 80; Plates 14, 40, 103, 119, 120, 130, 154, 162; page 282 (D'Oyly Bengal).
Courtauld Institute of Art, Plates 41, 151.
Giles Eyre and Charles Greig, Plate 65.
Richard Green, Colour Plates 35, 92.
Martyn Gregory Gallery, Colour Plates 6, 20, 21, 37, 39, 40, 42, 43, 45, 49, 50, 60, 72, 74, 81, 85, 90, 100; page 288 (Watson); Plates 16, 39, 43, 53, 70, 75, 82, 84, 86, 91, 92, 94, 99, 110, 111, 126, 129, 132, 134, 137, 138, 139, 141, 142, 153, 166; pages 281, 282 (Dalrymple and D'Oyly Cattle), 284 (Johnson).
Benno Gross Associates Ltd., Colour Plates 4, 14, 15.
Angelo Hornak, Colour Plate 88.
Malcom and Ursula Horsman, Colour Plates 10, 16, 67; Plate 37.
Leger Galleries, Plates 63, 76, 117, 127, 144, 159, 167, 169.
Maas Gallery, Plates 79, 106, 164.
John Mitchell & Son, Colour Plates 76, 94.
National Portrait Gallery, London, Plate 32.
National Portrait Gallery, Washington D.C., Colour Plate 107.
Phillips, London, Plate 98.
Mark Sexton, Plates 147, 160, 172, 173.
Sotheby's, Colour Plate 26; Plates 35, 46, 47, 48, 49, 50, 52, 54, 61, 109, 168.
Spink & Son Ltd., Colour Plates 62, 77, 104; Plates 11, 12, 13, 23, 71, 90, 131, 152.

Figures in italics indicate an illustration

Abbott, G., 296 n.30
Adam, Sir John, 93, 119-20, 126, 133, 155
Afun, 222-4, 300 n.38 (ch.14), *232*
*Alceste* (ship), 148
Alcock, Henrietta, 280, *280*
Alcock, Sir John Rutherford, 280
Alefounder, John, 50
Alexander, William, 177-80
Allom, Thomas, 290
Alloy, 202
Allport, Mrs., 196
amahs (ayahs), 105, 220-1, *225, 228*
Amaral, Governor, 259
Amboyna, 59
*Amelia,* 44, 45, *47*
Amherst, William Pitt, 1st Earl, 110, 119, 148
Amoy (Xiamen), 215, *280*
Anderson, Dr. Alexander, 250, 290, 301-2 n.8
Angerstein, John Julius, 21
Anstruther, Sir John, 85-6
Arcot, 56
*Ariel* (ship), 245
Armstrong, 'Colonel', 60, *68*
Arnott, Frederick, 90
Ashburton, Lord, 30
Ashford, William, 33-4, 292 n.9
*Asiatic Journal,* 53
Assor, 202
Astley, John, 31-2
*Astrolabe* (ship), 286
Atkinson, George Franklin, 280
Atkinson, James, 106, 271, 280, 296 n.30
Atkinson, Jane, 280
Ayok, 224
Azim-ud-Daula, Nawab, 83, *80*

Baccelli, Giannetta, 20
Baden-Powell, Baron, 22
Baird, General Sir David, 132
Ball, Charles, 61
Balzac, Honoré de, 281
*banglas,* 75, 91-2, 136-9, 201, *138, 139, 158, 159*
Bankipur, 95-6, *97*
Baptista, Marciano, 280-1, *285*
Baring Brothers, 229
Barrackpore, 160

mutiny, 127
  theatre, 130
Barry, James, 26-7, 31, 41
Batavia (Jakarta), 61, 108-9
Baynes, Mrs. Julia, 218, 220, *222*
Baynes, William, 218-20
Beale, Thomas, 196, 199, 209, 300 n.49
Beaumont, Sir George, 148
Becher family, 122
Behar (Amateur) Lithographic Press, 95-6, 295 n.26
Bellairs, Lt. Walford Thomas, 281, *285*
Benares (Varanasi), 53, 150, 287, 293 n.13
Bencoolen, Sumatra, 112, 291 n.11
*Bengal Hurkaru,* 261, 298 n.29 (ch.11)
Bentinck, Lady, 215
Bentinck, Lord William, 60, 83, 216, *80*
Berhampore, 152-3
billiards, 96, 111, *97*
Bird, Judge Shearman, 93, 95, *94*
Blacker, Valentine, 79-80
Blake, William, 24, 41
Blight, James, 196
Blücher, Marshal Gebhard von, 131, 287
Bombay, 51, 149, 150, 212, 216, 217, 227, 252
  Supreme Court, 78
*Bonité* (ship), 252
Borget, Auguste, 281, 302 n.26, *281, 288*
Boston, Massachusetts, 226, 229, 267, 286
Bremer, Sir Gordon, 250
Brighton, 21, 154, 261, 298 n.35
British Museum, 20, *20*
Brown, 'Blow-hard', 239
Brown, James Cowley, 150, 298 n.35, 299 n.2 (ch.12)
Brown, Matilda (née Chinnery), see Chinnery, Matilda
Browne, Mrs. Maria (née Roberts), 25, 53, 95, 109, 121, 126, 137, 152, 156, 232, 271-4, 281
Browne, Marmaduke, 53, 271, 281
Buckingham, James Silk, 115, 150-1, 161, 229
bungalow, 75-8, 160, 230, *77*
Burke, Edmund, 106
Burke, William, *288*
Byron, Lord, 161, 237, 275

Calcutta, 23, 38, 50-2, 61, 66, 74, 75,

84-7, 92, 96, 102-34, *passim,* 148-61 *passim,* 164, 198, 214, 218, 229, 240, 244-5, 248, 252, 260, 261, 280-90 *passim*
  'Black Hole', 60
  Bund, 260
  Chinnery's house and studio, 84, 96-8, 261, 276, *99*
  Chowringhee, 122, 130, 289, 297 n.5 (ch.8)
  Court House, 115
  Custom House, 133
  Garden Reach, 78, 114, 131, 286-7, *115, 288*
  Government House, 112, 131
  Mint, 280
  Park Street Cemetery, 123
  St. John's Cathedral, 133, 150
  Town Hall, 84-7, 118, 130-1, 133-4, 276
  Writers' Buildings, 130
*Calcutta* (ship), 90
*Calcutta (Government) Gazette,* 84, 115, 131, 152-3, 280
*Calcutta (Monthly) Journal,* 150-1, 261
Caldwell, James T., 281
Camden, 2nd Earl of, 19-20
Camões, Luis Vaz de, 188
Canning, George, 21
Canton (Guangzhou), 164-82, 194, 196, 202-3, 212, 216-37 *passim,* 245, 248-67 *passim*
  China Street, 169, 263
  Chung Qua's Hong, 167, *167*
  exclusion of women, 165, 218, 238, 245
  Fa-ti gardens, 165
  Folly forts, 165, *166*
  Hongs (Factories), 165-7, 220, 231, 259, 262, *164-7*
  Lamqua's studio, 263-7, *263*
  New China Street, 264
  Red Fort, 165-7, *166*
  Respondentia Square, 167, 177, *167*
  trading regulations, 165
  *see also* Honam
*Canton Register,* 196, 231, 239, 265
Cape Town, 106, 283
Carlyle, Thomas, 63
Caroline, Queen, 19, 275
Carvalho, Judge, 260
*Castle Huntly* (ship), 216
catamarans, 55, *54, 57*

Caulfield, James, see Charlemont
Cavanagh, Anne, 151
Ceylon (Sri Lanka), 149
Chand, Raja Protap, 295 n.1
Chantrey, Sir Francis, 280
Charlemont, Anne, later Countess, 19, 34
Charlemont, 1st Earl of, 34
Charlotte, Queen, 121
Chase, Chinnery & Macdowell, 18, 56-8, 291 n.9, 291 n.11
Chase & Sewell, 81-2, 291 n.11
Chase, Richard, 293 n.28
Chase, Thomas, 18, 56-7, 293 n.28
Cherubini, Luigi, 20
*China Mail*, 194, 238
*Chinese Courier*, 196
Chinnery, ancestors in Ireland, 11, 32
Chinnery, Sir Brodrick, 32-3
Chinnery, Caroline, niece of the artist, 20, 21, 45-6
Chinnery, Edward, illegitimate son of the artist, 123, 153-4, 298 nn.22, 32 (ch.10)
Chinnery, Elizabeth (née Bassett), mother of the artist, 17
Chinnery, Frances, sister of the artist, see Duncan, Frances
Chinnery, George

**Career**
early years in London, 24-30
portraits of his family, 20, 24, 32, 35, 37, 40-2, *18, 31, 33, 36, 37, 40*
attends R.A. Schools, 24-7
assisted by brother William, 19-20
intercedes for William, 22
critical reviews, 27, 35-7, 38-42
in Ireland, 30, 31-46, 292 n.3
marriage, 33, 151-2, 238-9
reasons for leaving Ireland, 42-3

travels to Madras, 46, 50-5, 292 n.3
assisted by brother John, 56-9
social status in India, 52-3, 104
travels to Dacca, 89, 295 n.7
depicts Indian village scenes, 75, 93, 135-45, 289
moves to Calcutta, 84, 95, 105
receives official commissions, 84-7, 104-9, 114-20, 132, 155, 161, *86, 113, 115*
fails to complete commissions, 118-20, 161
earnings and expenses, 52, 155-6, 161, 261, 298 n.6 (ch.11)
debts, 32, 106, 149, 152, 155-61, 199, 212-14, 244-5, 261, 289
Treatise, 271-4, 281
rejoined by wife and children, 149-52
takes refuge at Serampore, 154, 157-60
sails to China coast, 118, 161, 164-5
visits to Canton, 165-70

settles in Macau, 165, 193-4
travels to Hong Kong, 256
death and post-mortem, 260

**Personality,** 10-12, 148-50, 156, 161, 238-9, 244-5, 266, 276-9
appearance, 98, 239-44, 277-8
temper, 150, 277-8
lunacy (supposed), 87-8
illness and hypochondria, 87-8, 95, 156, 240, 260
misogyny (supposed), 238-9
philandering (supposed), 11
as raconteur, 76-7, 196, 198, 238-9
as teacher, 91, 263, 271-4, 280, 282, 284
as actor, 134, 195, 239, 244
smokes cigars, 196, 240
takes snuff, 240
smokes hookah, 156, 240, 248, 279, 301 n.16, *99, 239*
eating and drinking habits, 11, 156, 196, 278

**Art**
development of drawing technique, 44-5, 67-70, 144, 245
book illustrations, 44-5, *47*
history-painting, 27, 82-3
topographical draughtsman, 55, 65-7, 70, 75-9, 91-3
prefers landscape to portraiture, 129, 135
stage-design, 130, 195, 244
transparencies, 131, 133-4
studio practice, 271-2
varnishing, 274
colour theory, 40-1, 272
use of vermilion, 37, 38, 61, 63, 121-2, 134, 137, 227, 231-2, 241, 264, 272
effects of shadow, 138, 211, 245, 272-4, 289, 297 n.4 (ch.9)
self-portraits, 27, 98, 227, 230, 238-44, 252, *238-44*
shorthand, 8, 138-44, 275
Chinnery, George Robert, nephew of the artist, 20, 21, 22, 23
poem, 292 n.24
will, 292 n.30
Chinnery, Henry, illegitimate son of the artist, 123, 153-4, 298 n.22 (ch.10)
Chinnery, John Eustace, son of the artist, 33, 42, 119, 152-3
Chinnery, John Terry, brother of the artist, 18, 23, 24, 51, 56-9, 61, 82, 87
children, 298 n.18 (ch.10)
Chinnery, Margaret (née Tresilian), sister-in-law of the artist, 19-22, *21*
Chinnery, Maria (née Murray), 154
Chinnery, Marianne (née Vigne), wife of the artist, 33, 37, 41, 42, 51-2, 81, 82, 152-4, 238-9, 248, 261, 298 n.35, *31, 33, 36*

travels to India, 151-2
described by George Chinnery, 238-9
Chinnery, Mary (née Payton), sister-in-law of the artist, 23, 56, 57, 87, 294 n.32, 295 n.19
Chinnery, Matilda, daughter of the artist, 33, 42, 93, 149, 154, 298 n.35
Chinnery, Matilda, niece of the artist, 56, 57
Chinnery, Richard, Ensign, 291 n.11
Chinnery, Walter, nephew of the artist, 20, 23, 45-6
Chinnery, William (senior), grandfather of the artist, 15, 17-18, 23, 24, *15, 16, 18*
Chinnery, William (junior), father of the artist, 15, 17-18, 23, 24, 25, 275, *18*
Chinnery, William Bassett, brother of the artist, 11, 18-23, 34, 45-6, 56, 57, 157
Chinnery, William Charles, nephew of the artist, 23, 45-6, 294 n.32
Chittagong, 289
Chow Kwa, 266
*chowkidar*, 136, 144, *136, 137*
Chowringhee, see Calcutta
Chuenpi Convention, 255
Chung Qua, 167
Chuprah, 152
*City of London* (ship), 84
Clare, Countess of, 35, 292 n.17
Clare, Lord Chancellor of Ireland, 35
Clifton, Captain, 196, 216, *218*
Clive, 1st Lord, 82
Clive, 2nd Lord, 65, 79, 82
Clonmel, 1st Earl of, 35, 292 n.14
Cochrane, Rear-Admiral, 281
Cole, Stephen Thomas, 29
Coleridge, Samuel Taylor, 261
Colledge, Caroline (née Shillaber), 221, 222, 224, *229*
Colledge, Dr. Thomas, 217, 221-6, *229*
hospitals, 221, 224-6, *224*
portrayed with his patients, 221-4, 266-7, *232*
Colman, George (the younger), 195
Colombo, 56
*Colonel Young* (ship), 235
Comerford, John, 44, 294 n.40
Comilla, 94
Compton, Sir Herbert, 78, 79, 114, 132, 271
house in Garden Reach, 114, *115*
Comyn, Capt. Thomas Powell and Mary (née de Courcy), 126
children, 126, *125*
Confucius, 159
Conyngham, Charlotte (née Greer), 37-8, 89, 293 n.23, *39*
children, 295 n.10
Conyngham, Robert, 38
Cooke, Thomas, 39-40

Cooper, Sir Astley, 221
Coote, Sir Eyre, 65
Cornwallis, Charles, 1st Marquess, 65, 82, 155
Corsica, 106
Cosway, Richard, 27, 29, 58
Cowper, William, 41
Cradock, General Sir John, 83, *80*
Cree, Edward, 257
Cruttenden, George, 93, 132, 295 n.17
Cuddalore, 17, 18, 291 n.9
Cuming, William, 34, 44, 292 n.9
Cushing company, 171

Dacca (Dhaka), 87, 89-94, 105, 138, 157, 282, 295 n.7, *92*
 *Antiquities of Dacca,* 89, 91
D'Aguilar, General George, 257, 258, 267
D'Aguilar, Captain, 257
Dalrymple, Mary, 282, *282*
Daniell, Anthony and family, 218-19
Daniell, Harriet (later Mrs. Masterman Williams), 219, *223*
Daniell, James F.N. and family, 218-19
Daniell, Thomas, 24, 78, 82, 89, 135, 170, 203-6, 284, 293 n.28
Daniell, William, 78, 89, 135, 170, 206, 224, 284, 290
Darwin, Erasmus, 275
Da Silva, Mrs., *116*
Das, Jairam, 95
Davis, Mrs. Emily, 220, 239
Davis, John Francis, 220, 253
de Carvalho, Manuel and Rita, 193-4
Delhi, Viceroy's Residence, 118, 284
Dent & Co., 212, 221, 227, 251
Dent, John, 244, 253, 257, 260
Dent, Lancelot, 243-4, 252, 256
Dent, Wilkinson, 257
'Dent's Veranda', 250-5, *250, 251*
Derby, Earls of, 29
Devis, Arthur William, 50, 51, 53, 155, 293 n.3
Dinapore, 94, 132, 148
Douglas, Sylvester, see Glenbervie
Downing, Toogood, 263, 266
D'Oyly family, 38, 89, 281, 295 nn.16, 18
D'Oyly, Sir Charles (7th Bart.), 26, 53, 89-98, 106, 112, 125, 128, 132, 133, 150, 155-7, 244, 271, 282-3, 286, 289, 290, 296 n.43, *92, 93, 96, 97, 98, 282*
 lithographs 95-6, 295 n.26, 304 n.16
 *Tom Raw, the Griffin,* 26, 74, 96, 98, 126, 134, 276-80, 283, *99*
D'Oyly, Sir Charles Walters (9th Bart.), 283
D'Oyly, Lady Elizabeth (née Ross), 95-6, 125, 128, 155, 283, *96, 97, 98*
D'Oyly, Sir John Hadley (6th Bart.), 38, 89, 93, 150, *89*
D'Oyly, Sir John Hadley (8th Bart.), 96, 280, 283, *97*

D'Oyly, Lady Marian (née Greer), 89, 90, 93, 95, *93*
Dublin, 31-46, 50, 130, 149, 244
 Allen's Rooms, 35
 Bank of Ireland, 42
 Daly's Club, 32, 34
 Dublin Theatre Orchestra, 40
 Parliament House, 32, 34, 38, 41, 42, 43
 Royal Dublin Society, 33-4, 36, 43, 44
 Royal Irish Academy, 32, 34, 38
 *see also* Society of Artists of Ireland
Dum Dum, 118
Dumont D'Urville, 286
Duncan family, 293-4 n.32
Duncan, Frances, sister of George Chinnery, 17, 23, 295 n.19
Duncan, John, 23
Duncombe, Lady Louisa (née Stuart) and William, 129
Dundas, Henry, see Melville
Dunn, Nathan, 175, 199, 227-9, 301 n.55, *229*
 Chinese Museum, 229
Durran (Durant), Euphemia, 252
Durran (Duran, Durant), J.A., 196, 243, 251-2, 254, 283, 302 nn.16, 17, 26, 42, *246, 250, 251, 254*
Durran, Paul, 259, 262

*Earl of Balcarres* (ship), 215
East, Sir Edward Hyde, 114
East India Company, 50-2, 56-61, 70, 80, 82, 106, 150-1, 170, 183, 216, 218-20, 221, *70*
 chaplains, 61, 219
 charter, 188, 212
 Directors, 51, 65, 74, 114, 149, 151-2, 289, 293 n.10
 officers, 17, 52, 56-61, 78, 85, 104, 122, 156, 164, 188, 194-5, 218-20, 238, 281, 289
 regulations, 50-2, 56-7, 74, 150
 surgeons, 122, 221
 tea inspectors, 226-7
*East India Registers,* 18, 56-8
Edmonstone, Neil Benjamin, 119, 126, 132, 271
 children, 126, *127*
Edridge, Henry, 59
Elers, George, 23, 62-3
Elgin, 8th Earl, 286
Elliot family, 281, 295 n.7 (ch.7)
Elliot, Capt. Charles, 249-50, 255, 283
Elliot, John, 123, 271, 283, *288*
Elphinstone, James Ruthven, 93, 105
Ennore, 76, 294 n.68, *77*
Erskine, Margaret, 121, *117*
Eton College, 110, 112
Eurasians, 61, 123, 126, 153-4, 202
Eustace, Mrs., 37, 292 n.20, *37*
Exmouth, 1st Viscount, 61, 284

Fairlie Fergusson & Co., 105
Farington, Joseph, 19, 21
Farnborough, 1st Baron, 20
Fearon family, 196, 299 n.8 (ch.13)
Fendall, John, 283
Fendall, Mary, 283
Fergusson, Robert Cutlar, 114, 119, 132
Fergusson, Mrs., 296 n.27
Fielding, Henry, 44-5, *47*
Fielding, Theodore, 289
Fisquet, Theodore-Auguste, 283, *284*
Fitzgerald, Lord Edward, 42
Flaxman, John, 41
Forbes family, 221, 229, 259
Forbes, John Murray, 171-2
Forbes, Robert Bennet, 170, 192, 230, 248, 259, 299 n.7 (ch.12)
Ford, Richard, 15
Fort St. George, Madras, 55-6, 58, 66, 70, 80
Fortune, Robert, 255
Fox, Charles James, 30, *27*
Fraser, James Baillie, 114, 148, 150, 273, 283-4
Fraser, William, 284
Free Society of Artists, 17
freemasonry, 79, 118, 131-3, 294 n.75
*Friend of China (and Hongkong Gazette),* 255, 261, 296 n.27
*Friend of India,* 261
*Friendship's Offering,* 213
Fullarton, Charlotte and John, 284
Fuseli, Henry, 41, 59, 293 n.30
Fuzhou, 280, *285*

Gahagan, Dr. Terence, 297 n.9 (ch.8)
Gainsborough, Thomas, 102, 136
George III, 10, 38, 83, 132
George IV, formerly Prince of Wales and Prince Regent, 105, 132, 262
Gibson, Emma Louise, 152
Gillespie, General Robert Rollo, 132, 284
Gilwell Hall, Essex, 19-22, 46, 57
*Gilwell* (ship), 46, 53-5, 57
Gladstone, William Ewart, 126
Glenbervie, Lord, 19, 22, 23, 291 n.13, 292 n.35
Goa, 74
Gordon, George James, 214
Gough Square, London, 17, 24
Graham, Maria, 53, 76
Grant, Capt. Alexander, 192, 216, and family, 219-20
Grant, Colesworthy, 297 n.10 (ch.9)
Grant, Duncan, 287
Grant, John, 85
Grant, Maria Teresa, 219
Grattan, Henry, 32
Greer family, 38, 90
Greer, Charlotte, see Conyngham
Greer, Harriet, 90
Greer, William, 38, 293 n.23

Grey, Lord, 134
Gribble, Capt. Henry, 215, 249
Guan A-to (Kwan A-to), 266-7, *268*
Gudin, Jean-Antoine, 281
Gurkhas, 118, 126, 133
Gurney, Joseph, 275
Gurney, Thomas, 17, 275
Gutzlaff, Charles, 235-7, *236*
*Gypsy* (ship), 253

Haggard, Rider, *Allan Quartermain*, 126, 297 n.71
Hall, Capt. William H., 55, 251, 253-4, 267, *250*
Hamilton, Hugh Douglas, 39, 40, 293 n.26, 293 n.29
Harington, William, 57
*Harington* (ship), 57
Hastings, Francis Rawdon, 2nd Earl of Moira, 1st Marquess of Hastings, 94, 105, 111, 112, 118-20, 131-4, 271, 303 n.1 (Appendix i)
  early career, 118
  transparency in his honour, 133-4, *131*
  portraits, 96, 98, 105, 118, 120, 132, 161, 296 nn.40-1, *97, 99, 113, 119*
Hastings, Marchioness of (Countess of Loudun), 98, 119, 133, 287, 296 n.42, 303 n.4 (Appendix i)
Hastings, Warren, 38, 90, 106, 125, 155, 275
  correspondence with Sir Charles D'Oyly, 90-1, 93, 98, 282
Havell, John, 148
Havell, William, 148-9, 284, *150, 151*
*Hawkesbury* (ship), 62-3
Heard, Augustine, 267
Heber, Bishop Reginald, 89-90, 94, 160
Henderson, Captain and Mrs., 154
*Henry Porcher* (ship), 151
Herbert, Major, 122
*Hercules* (ship), 216
*Hibernian* (ship), 286
Hickey, Thomas, 31, 50, 51, 52, 53, 66, 81, 82, 85, 104, 295 n.4 (ch.7)
Hickey, William, 38, 52, 74, 84-8, 114, 294-5 n.16, 295 n.17
  freemason, 131
Hillard, John, 286
Hine, Capt. John, 215, 300 n.12
Hodges, William, 19, 65
Hogarth, William, 144
Hogg, James, 114
Holman, James, 248, *248*
Home, Robert, 51, 81, 82, 87, 89, 104, 130, 155, 297 n.5 (ch.8)
Honam (suburb of Canton), 165-7, 259, *259*
Hone, Nathaniel, 31
Hong Kong, 61, 194, 201, 236, 243, 249, 255-8, 260, 267, 280-1, 290
  East Point, 257

Lamqua's studio, 267
loan exhibition (1876), 26, 262
Murray Barracks, 258, *246, 257*
old church, 257, *246, 257*
Spring Gardens, *258*
*Hongkong Daily Press*, 262
*Hongkong Gazette*, see *Friend of China*
Hoo Loo, 224
Hooghly River, 144, 147, 160, 164, *140, 158*
  river craft, 147, *146*
hookah, nargila, 96, 112, 137, 144, 156, 196, 240, 248, 301 n.16, *97, 106, 107, 140, 239*
Hope, Henry, 292 n.27
Hoppner, John, 46
Horne, Brigadier Matthew, 131
Hoseason, Thomas, 79
Houses of Parliament, London, 21, 32, 42-3, 275
Howqua (Wu Bingjian), 171-7, 221, 227, 229, 266, 267, 286, 299 n.19 (ch.12), *172*
Howqua family, 299 n.11 (ch.12)
Huber, J.P. or George, 294 n.34
Hudleston, Robert, 194, 195, 305, *194*
Humayun Jah, Nizam, 153
Hume, David, 106
Humphry, Ozias, 50, 51
Hunter, William, 169, 227, 238, 239, 251-4, 260, 299 n.4 (ch.12), 305, *250*
Hurjeebhoy Rustomjee, 217
Hutchinson, Mr. (artist), 153
Hutchinson, George, 284
Hyderabad, 62, 63, 65, 111, 149
  Nizam of, 62, 111, 119
*Hythe* (ship), 161, 164-5
Hyder Ali, 67

Impey, Sir Elijah, 85, 106
*India Gazette*, 132, 133-4
*India Magazine*, 78-9, *57, 64*
India Office Library and Records, 129
Inglis, Robert, 195, 244, 245, 252
Ingres, J.-A.-D., 266, *265*
Ireland, 11, 20-1, 26, 30, 31-46, 89, 105, 152, 242
Irish Volunteer Movement, 32, 34

Jackson, John, 194, 195, 231
Jahangir, Emperor, 89
Japan, 183, 187, 280
Jardine, Andrew, 249
Jardine, Matheson, 57, 212-16, 221, 229, 257, 265
Jardine, William, 172, 212-16, 225, 235, 236, 245, 248, 251, 255, *214, 215*
Java, 94, 106, 108, 283
Jeejeebhoy, Sir Jamsetjee, 216-17, *219*
Johnson, John Willes, 284-6
Johnson, Samuel, 24

Johnstone family, 19
junks, 170-1, *168, 169, 171*

Kane, Dr. William, 262
Kemble, John Philip, 112, 130
Kerr, Rev. Richard Hall, 61, 79, 132, *60*
Keswick, William, 302 n.17
Kettle, Tilly, 50
Keying, Commissioner, 267
Killarney, 40, 44
Kinsman, Rebecca, 207, 217, 220-1, 267
Kirchoffer, Henry, 38
Kirkpatrick, Col. James and Khairunnissa, 62-3, 104
Kirkpatrick, Katherine (Kitty), 61-5, 84, 104, *73*
Kirkpatrick, William, 61-5, 84, 104, *73*

*Lady Mary Wood* (steamer), 281
Lamqua (Guan Qiaochang), 169-70, 214, 217, 263-7, 301 n.52, *263-6, 268*
  family, 264-5, 267, 303 n.11 (ch.17)
  rivalry with Chinnery, 169-70, 263-6
  self-portrait, 264, *264*
Larkins family, 125-6, *124*
Larkins, John Pascal (senior), 38, 125, 293 n.23
Larkins, John Pascal (junior), 38, 119, 125-6, 132, 133
Larkins, Mary (née Robertson), 126
Latimer, John, 169-70, 196, 265
Law & Co., 53
Lawrence, Sir Thomas, 24, 41, 59, 102, 120, 121, 156
Lear, Edward, 140
Leite, Fr. Joaquim, 194
L'Emerque, Monsieur, 160, 245
Leslie, Mr., 250
Lewis, Josiah, 275
Lewis, William Thomas, 130
Lin Tse-Lsu (Zexu) or Lin Wen-chung, Commissioner, 248-9, 267
Lindsay, Charles Robert, 93, 120, 132
Lindsay, Hon. Hugh, 295 n.19
Lindsay, Hugh Hamilton, 93, 237, 245, 295 n.19
Lindsay, Robert, 164, 298-9 n.2
Lintin, 216, 230, 248, 256
Lintot, Bernard, 15
Ljungstedt, Sir Anders, 221, 224, *226*
Locker, Captain William, 115, *110*
Lodder, William Wynne, 286
Long, Charles, see Farnborough
Lord, Hugh, 59
Lord, Lucy (née Gahagan), 59, 294 n.39, *69*
*Louisa* (ship), 216
Loutherbourg, Philippe de, 130
Low, Abigail (née Knapp), 194-5, 198, 299 n.19 (ch.12), 300 n.21, *195*

Low, Harriet, 11, 194-9, 206, 209, 218, 220-40 *passim*, 248, 256, 273, 286, 300 n.21
portrait, 221, *193*
Low, William, 194-6, 198, 199, *195*
Lucknow, 53
Lushington, Charles May, 59-60, 119, *59*
Lyall, Harriet and family, 213
Lyall, Matheson & Co., 214
*Lyra* (ship), 252

Macartney, 1st Earl of, 11
Macau, 147, 149, 156, 161, 165, 167, 183-237 *passim*, 242-5, 248-67 *passim*, 280-90 *passim*
A-Ma (or Ma-Kok) temple, 188, 286, *189, 190, 191, 284, 288*
Casa, 188, *187*
Chinnery's house and studio, 156, 193-4, 195-9, 230, 238, 249, 299 n.8 (ch.13)
churches and seminaries, 184-7, 190, 193-4, 281, *184, 185, 186, 188, 205, 208, 209*
clinics and hospitals, 221-6, *224*
forts, 183, 184, 210, 218, *185, 288*
Grotto of Camões, 188, *186*
Inner harbour, 188, 193, *187, 192*
Praya Grande, 183, 190-1, 211, 217, 241, 249, 251, 252, 290, *182, 183, 190-2, 203*
Protestant cemetery, 188, 226, 233, 252, 260, *233*
regatta, 260-1
Macdowell, John, 18, 56, 293 n.28
Macnabb, James Munro, 271, 296 n.43, 303 n.4 (Appendix i)
Macnaghten, Sir Francis Workman, 114-15, 294 n.35, 296 nn.27, 34, *115*
Macpherson, Duncan, 248
MacQueen, Mrs. and David, 220
*Madagascar* (steamer), 250
Madeira, 55
Madras, 17, 23, 30, 45, 51-83, 91, 111, 114, 130, 138, 144, 149, 152, 155, 232, 282, *54, 57, 64, 66, 67, 71*
Asylums, 56-7, 61
Banqueting Hall, 65-6, 79, *64*
Crow's Tope, 78, *77*
freemasons, 131, 132
Government House, 79, *64*
Lunatic Hospital, 87
*Madras Almanac,* 57
Madras Bank, 56
Madras Native Infantry, 248
Pantheon, 79-81, 130
St. Mary's Church, 66-7, *64*
'Town Temple', *67*
Magee, John, 35
Magniac & Co., 212, 216
Mah Chih Ping, 177, *176*
Mahabalipuram, 70, *72*

Maharajpore, battle of, 110
Malacca, 108, 183, 193, 230
Anglo-Chinese College, 230, 231, 253, 286
Manila, 183, 287, 290
Marathas, 82, 118
Marjoribanks, Charles and family, 220, 300 n.24, *225*
Marlborough, Duke of, 19
*Marquess of Wellesley* (ship), 57, 82
Marshman, John Clark, 159-60
Marshman, Dr. Joshua, 159, 296 n.27, *161*
Mason, William, 275
masula boats, 55, *54, 57*
Masulipatam, 63
Matheson, Alexander, 213, 231, 265
Matheson, Hugh, 214
Matheson, James, 212-15, 249-50, 255
*Matilda* (ship), 57
Mauritius, 108, 118, 132
Medhurst, Walter, 301 n.73
Melrose, William, 286
Melville, 1st Viscount, 80-1, 134, *81*
Mengs, Anton, 20
Metcalfe, Sir Charles Theophilus (later Baron), 52, 111-12, 153, *112*
*Midas* (ship), 253
Middleton, John and family, 258, 262
Milne, William, 230
Milton, John, 41
*Minerva* (ship), 149
Minto, Gilbert Elliot, 1st Earl of, 22, 93, 104, 105-9, 110, 111, 119, 283
early career, 106
portraits, 108-9, 280, *108*
Minto, 4th Earl of, 108
Mir Alam, 62
Mirabeau, André Boniface Rignetti, Comte de, 106
Mohammed Ali, Pasha of Egypt, 150
Moira, 2nd Earl, see Hastings, 1st Marquess
Moore, Rev. J., 24
Moore, Sir John, 127
Moore, M. Scott, 55
Mordaunt ('Col. Mordaunt's Cock Match'), 105
Morland, George, 11, 136
Morrison, Mrs. Eliza (née Armstrong), 196, 231-2, 240, 286, *236*
Morrison, John Robert, 234-6, *235*
Morrison, Robert (missionary), 11, 177, 180, 194, 226, 230-5, 253, 286, *231, 237*
translations into Chinese, 224, 230-1, *231*
Morrison, Robert (junior), 286, *286*
Mowqua (Lu Yuankin), 172-5, 221, 299 n.19 (ch.12), *173, 176*
Mundy, Peter, 206
Mylapore, *67*
Mysore Wars, 82-3

Nagasaki, 187
Nanking, Treaty of, 253, 255, 267, 280
Napier, 9th Baron, 232-4
Napoleon Bonaparte, 80, 267
Nash, Edward, 51
*Nassau* (ship), 38, 293 n.23
*Nemesis* (steamer), 253, 267
New York, 229, 230, 267
Newman, James, colourman, 156, 272
Nollekens, Joseph, 292 n.27
Northcote, James, 25
Nugent, General Sir George and Lady, 105, 290
Nye, Gideon, 12, 171, 190, 203, 241, 281, 286

Oliver, Mrs., 27
Oliver, Archer James, 24, 25
Opie, John, 276
opium, 125, 160, 171-2, 212, 216, 227, 229-31, 239, 247-56 *passim*, 267, 283
opium clippers, 216, 235-7, 244, 247, 252, 256, 301 n.73
Opium Wars, 165, 174, 177, 215, 229, 235-6, 247-55, 281
George Chinnery as opium smoker, 247-8, 301 n.16 (ch.16)
Ormsby, Lt.-Col. William, 60, *68*
Oudh, Nawab of, 104, 122
Oxford University, 20

P. & O., 281
Paget, General Sir Edward, 126-9, 145
Paget, Harriet (née Legge) and her children, 126-9, *128*
Paiva, Mrs., 259
palanquin, 70-5, 111, 193, 294 n.64, *71, 76, 183*
Palmer & Co., 244, 289
Palmer, John, 161
Palmer, General William, 105
Palmer, William (banker) of Palmer & Co., 111, 119, 124, 156
Palmerston, Viscount, 216, 232, 249, 255
Paris, Edouard, 286
Parker, Admiral, 267
Parker, Dr. Peter, 225, 266-7, *268*
Parkyns, George, 213
Parry, Mary, 152
Parry, Thomas, 80, 81-2, 152
Parsees, 192, 202, 212, 216-17, 221, 227, 264, *216, 217, 219*
'Pasquin, Anthony', see Williams, John
Patna, 94, 95-6, 283, *97*
Patuck family, 217
Pearson, Mrs. Jane, *117*
Pearson, John, 114, *114*
Pearson, Thomas Hooke, 110, *109*
Peel, Sir Robert, 292 n.30
Peking, 11, 134, 148
Pellegrini, Domenico, 27
Pellew, Edward, see Exmouth

Pellew, Fleetwood, 61, *60*
Penang, 148, 164-5, 290, *285*
Perceval, Spencer, 20-1
Pereira, Manuel, 188, 194, 196
Perkins & Co., 171, 230, 252
Perkins family, 171, 229
Pery family, 109, *103*
Pester, John, 38
Peter, Rous, *150*
Philadelphia, 169, 199, 227
  'Chinese Museum', 175
Phillips, Capt. James Winsloe, 63
Pindaris, 118
Pitman, Isaac, 275
Pitt, William (the younger), 18, 42, 80
Plassey, 65
Plowden, Chicheley, family, 286
Plowden, Frances (née Erskine), 120, 134
Plowden, Trevor C., 119, 131, 286-7, *130*
Plowden, Parker, 134
Plowden, William H.C., 177, 190, 195,
  218, 286, 299 n.24 (ch.12)
  Catherine, 220
Plunket, 1st Baron, 34, 40
Pope, Alexander, 273
Porter, Jane, 27
Porter, Sir Robert Ker, 27
Portugal and the Portuguese, 74, 153,
  183-94 *passim*, 226, 232, 249, 259
Pottinger, Sir Henry, 267
Pratt, John Jeffreys, see Camden
Price, Miss, 35
Prendergast, John, 287
Prinsep family, 50, 53, 134, 304 nn.32, 33
Prinsep, Emily, 130, 160
Prinsep, George, 289
Prinsep, James, 50, 53, 120, 130, 134,
  287-9, 304 nn.32, 33, *287*
Prinsep, Mary, 160, 281, 289
Prinsep, Thomas, 120, 287, 289,
  304 n.36, *289*
Prinsep, William, 120, 122, 130, 134,
  160-1, 213, 244-5, 287-90, 295 n.19,
  297 n.5 (ch.8), 304 nn.32, 36, *289*
  portrait of William and Mary Prinsep,
  160, 289, *Frontispiece, 160*
Prinsep, William Haldimand, *287*
Prout, Samuel, 261, 302 n.55
Purniya, 85, 294 n.10

Raffles, Thomas Stamford, 94, 108-9
Rainier, Admiral Peter, 83, *80*
Ranjeet Singh, 110
'Raw, Tom' see D'Oyly, Sir Charles
*Red Rover* (ship), 216, 235, 256
Redgrave, Richard and Samuel, 149
Reeves, John, 226-7, 300 n.45, *227*
Reeves, John Russell, 227, 300 n.45
Renaldi, Francesco, 89, 105
Reynolds, Sir Joshua, 25-6, 37, 91, 102,
  118, 129, 155, 159, 272-3, 279

*Discourses on Art*, 25-6, 272-3
  influence on George Chinnery, 11,
  25-6, 91, 239, 272-3
  resemblance to George Chinnery,
  238-40
Reynolds, Samuel, 85
Rigaud, John Francis, 27
Ritchie, Mrs., 207
*Robarts* (ship), 153
Robertson, Dr., 109
Rogers, Samuel, 292 n.27
Romney, George, 40, 41, 59, 279
Rooker, Michael 'Angelo', 45
Rose, George, 18, 20, 21
Rossi, John, 19
Rothmeyer, W.P., 294 n.34
Rousseau, Jean-Jacques, 41
Rowlandson, Thomas, 24, 44
Royal Academy, 11, 17, 19, 20, 24-5, 27,
  30, 33, 45-6, 66, 82, 83, 134, 177,
  202, 215-16, 224, 237, 240-1, 243,
  261, 267
Royal Academy Schools, 20, 24-7, 33
  261, 272
Rumbold, Sir William, 111-2, 119, 132,
  271, *109*
Ruskin, John, 10
Russell & Co., 171, 194, 230, 239,
  252-3, 290
Russell, Sir Henry, 63-4, 84-8, 89, 114,
  115, *86*
Russell, John, 286
Russell, Samuel, 252
Russell Sturgis, 230
Rustomjee, Hurjeebhoy, 259, 260

St. Botolph's, Bishopgate, 15, 18
St. Bride's, Fleet Street, 16-17, 24
Salem, Massachusetts, 171, 194
Salt, Henry, 46
Savage, Lt.-Col. Patrick, 118, *111*
Savignhac, 115, 296 n.36
Scarth, Dr. John, 290
Scott, John, see Clonmel
Serampore, 95, 154, 157-60, 244, *158, 159*
  College, 159
Seringapatam, 65, 82, 132
Shah Alam, Emperor, 82, 286
Shakespear, John and Emily, 296 n.56
Shams-ud-Daulah, Nawab of Dacca, 94
Shanghai, 280
Shee, Martin Archer, 31, 44
Sheen, Captain, 55, 58
Sheridan, Richard B., 10, 291 n.13
Sherson, Robert, 58, 294 n.35
Sherson, Mrs., 58, *58*
Shillaber, Caroline, see Colledge
Shirreff, 294 n.36
Siddons, George, 112, *106, 107*
Siddons, Sarah, 112, 296 n.25
Singapore, 245, 249, 290
Smart, John (miniature painter), 51

Smart, John, 217
Smith, the Misses, 23
Smith, George, 258
Smith, John Raphael, 11
Smith, Robert, 290
Smith, Robert 'Bobus', 110
Smyth, Capt. Henry Carmichael, 122-3
Snow, Mrs., 96
Society of Artists of Ireland, 34, 35, 38,
  43, 46
Society of Painters in Watercolours, 148
Spain, 184
Spencer, William, 19
Spoilum, 264
Squib, the artist's dog, 147, *144*
Standford, Mr., 35
Stanley, Lady Elizabeth, 29, *26*
Stewart, James and Charlotte, 122,
  *123,* 125
Stewart, Patrick and family, 258-9, 260
Stuart, Gilbert, 32
Sturgis family, 229
Sturgis, James Perkins, 230
Sully, Thomas, 169-70
Sunqua, 266
Swallowfield, 63-4
Swedish East India Company, 226
*Sylph* (ship), 235-6, 252

Tanka boatwomen, 199-202, 274, *197,
  199, 200*
Taylor, Samuel, 275
tea trade, 171, 212, 266-7
Thackeray family, 50, 122-4, 126,
  293 n.1, 296 n.56, *123*
Thackeray, Anne (née Becher), 122-3
Thackeray, Richmond, 74, 112, 122-4
  daughters, 123
Thackeray, William Makepeace, 123-4
  *The Newcomes*, 10, 123-4
  *Vanity Fair,* 124
Thirlestane House, 234, *234*
Thurlow, Lord, 18
Tingqua, 301 n.52
Tipu, Sultan of Mysore, 55, 80, 132
  freemason, 132
Tiruvarur, 70
Trant, William and family, 112
Tresham, Henry, 293 n.40
Trincomalee, 131
Trossarelli, Giovanni (or Gaspare), 20,
  290-1 nn.20-2, *21*
Trott, Benjamin, 169-70
Turner, Charles, 108
Turner, J.M.W., 24, 78
Twist, Charles, 254

Umdat-ul-Umara, Nawab, 82,
  297 n.9 (ch.8)
Ure, Dr. and Mrs., 62-3

Vaillant, Auguste Nicolas, 283
Valentia, Lord, 46
Vallancey, General, 36-7, *35*
van Braam, Jacob Andries, 108-9, 132
Varnham, Warner, 290
Vellore, 60, 79
Victoria, Queen, 262
Vigée-Lebrun, Marie, 20
Vigne, Elizabeth (née Eustace), 33
Vigne, Henry George, 33
Vigne, James, 33, 35-6, 42, 43, 44
Vigne, Maria, 33, 40-2, *40*
Viotti, Giambattista, 19, 20, 22

Waldré, Vincent, 293 n.36
Wales, James, 51, 82
Washington, George, 175
*Water Witch* (ship), 244
*Waterloo* (ship), 199
Watson, Maj.-General Samuel, 94

Watson family, 258, 259, 283, 290,
    303 n.58
Watson, Dr. Thomas Boswall, 254,
    258-60, 262, 283, 290, *290*
Watson, Thomas Colclough, 94-5, 224, *98*
Wedgwood, Dublin, 32
Wellesley, Sir Arthur, see Wellington
Wellesley, Richard Colley, Marquess, 57,
    65, 80, 94, 104
Wellington, 1st Duke (Arthur Wellesley),
    23, 79, 83, 94, 131, 175, 277
  transparency representing, 131, 287
Welsh, Jane, 63
West, Benjamin, 11, 82, 83, 272
Whaley, Hon. Anne, 35
Whaley, Thomas, 34, 35
Whampoa, 169, 170-1, 201, *171*
Wheatley, Francis, 32
Wilcocks, Benjamin Chew, 169, 172,
    227, 240, *233*
Wilkinson, Robert, 196

William IV, 153
Williams, John, 27, 29
Williams, Mrs. Harriet Masterman, see
    Daniell, Harriet
Winterhalter, Franz, 262
*Wolverine* (ship), 286
Willison, George, 50
Wilson, Capt. Peter, 164-5
Wood, William W., 196, 198, 239, 290
Wordsworth, William, 148
Wright, Henry ('Old Wright'), 216, *218*
Wright, Henry the younger (Harry), 216

Young, Col. James, 134, 161,
    298 n.29 (ch.11)
  *see also* Colonel Young
*York* (ship), 220

Zebunissa, 105
Zhao Changling, General, 267
Zoffany, Johann, 50, 51, 85, 155